Competition among Financial Centres in Asia-Pacific

The **Pacific Economic Cooperation Council (PECC)** is one of the Asia-Pacific's most influential organizations. Since its foundation in 1980 it has been a policy innovator in trade, finance, information technology and capacity-building, among others. PECC brings together leading thinkers and decision-makers from government and business in an informal setting to discuss and formulate ideas on the most significant issues facing the Asia-Pacific. PECC is the only non-government official observer in APEC. For more details visit http://www.pecc.org.

The **Korea National Committee for Pacific Economic Cooperation (KOPEC)** is a non-profit organization formally created in 1981 to represent Korea in the Pacific Economic Cooperation Council (PECC). KOPEC draws its members mainly from the academia, the business community, and the government. Since its founding, KOPEC has been an active contributor to the work of PECC. On behalf of KOPEC, Dr Soogil Young coordinated the work of PECC on trade issues during 1983–1986, founding the PECC Trade Policy Forum in 1986. Also, on behalf of KOPEC, Dr Soogil Young coordinated the work of PECC on financial issues during 2001–2005, founding and running the PECC Finance Forum. In recent years, KOPEC has been strengthening its domestic work program on regional economic integration in order to build support at home for community-building in the Asia-Pacific. For more details visit http://www.kopec.or.kr.

The **Institute of Southeast Asian Studies (ISEAS)** was established as an autonomous organization in 1968. It is a regional centre dedicated to the study of socio-political, security and economic trends and developments in Southeast Asia and its wider geostrategic and economic environment.

The Institute's research programmes are the Regional Economic Studies (RES, including ASEAN and APEC), Regional Strategic and Political Studies (RSPS), and Regional Social and Cultural Studies (RSCS).

ISEAS Publications, an established academic press, has issued more than 1,000 books and journals. It is the largest scholarly publisher of research about Southeast Asia from within the region. ISEAS Publications works with many other academic and trade publishers and distributors to disseminate important research and analyses from and about Southeast Asia to the rest of the world.

Competition among Financial Centres in Asia-Pacific

Prospects, Benefits, Risks and Policy Challenges

EDITED BY
Soogil Young, Dosoung Choi, Jesús Seade and **Sayuri Shirai**

Korea National Committee for Pacific Economic Cooperation
Pacific Economic Cooperation Council

KOPEC

INSTITUTE OF SOUTHEAST ASIAN STUDIES
SINGAPORE

First published in Singapore in 2009 by
ISEAS Publishing
Institute of Southeast Asian Studies
30 Heng Mui Keng Terrace
Pasir Panjang
Singapore 119614

E-mail: publish@iseas.edu.sg
Website: <http://bookshop.iseas.edu.sg>

ISEAS Library Cataloguing-in-Publication Data

Competition among financial centres in Asia-Pacific : prospects, benefits, risks and policy challenges / edited by Soogil Young ... [et al.]
Papers presented at the PECC International Conference "Competition among Financial Centers in the Asia-Pacific : Prospects, Benefits, and Costs — Stumbling Blocks or Building Blocks towards a Regional Financial Community?", organized by the Korea National Committee for Pacific Economic Cooperation (KOPEC) in collaboration with the Korea Securities Research Institute (KSRI), on 15–16 October 2007 in Seoul, Korea.
1. Competition—Asia—Congresses.
2. Competition—Pacific Area—Congresses.
3. Financial institutions—Asia—Congresses.
4. Financial institutions—Pacific Area—Congresses.
5. Asia—Economic integration—Congresses.
6. Pacific Area—Economic integration—Congresses.
I. Young, Soogil.
II. Han'guk T'aep'yŏngyang Kyŏngje Hyŏmnyŏk Wiwŏnhoe.
III. Han'guk Chmngkwŏn Yŏn'guwŏn
IV. Pacific Economic Cooperation Council.
V. PECC International Conference "Competition among Financial Centers in the Asia-Pacific : Prospects, Benefits, and Costs — Stumbling Blocks or Building Blocks towards a Regional Financial Community?" (2007 : Seoul, Korea)
HG3881 C731 2009

ISBN 978-981-230-855-9 (soft cover)
ISBN 978-981-230-930-3 (hard cover)
ISBN 978-981-230-931-0 (PDF)

Typeset by Superskill Graphics Pte Ltd
Printed in Singapore by Utopia Press Pte Ltd

Contents

List of Tables viii

List of Figures xi

Preface xv

Contributors xvii

Executive Summary xxix

Keynote Address
International Financial Centres: The Terms of Competition and Prospects for the Asia-Pacific Region xxxvii
Dominic Barton

Part I: Overview and Policy Recommendations

1. Competition among Financial Centres in Asia Pacific: Prospects, Benefits, Risks and Policy Challenges 3
Dosoung Choi, Jesús Seade, Sayuri Shirai and *Soogil Young*

Part II: Case Studies

2. Hong Kong and East Asia's Financial Centres and Global Competition 61
Jesús Seade

3. Singapore as a Leading International Financial Centre: Vision, Strategies, Roadmap and Progress 99
Tan Khee Giap

4. Promoting Tokyo as an International Financial Centre 130
Sayuri Shirai

5. Can Tokyo Become a Global Financial Centre? 179
Masahiro Kawai

6. Making Australia a Supplier of Fund Management to the World 193
Nicholas Gruen

7. Building the Shanghai International Financial Centre: Strategic Target, Challenges and Opportunities 231
Xu Mingqi

8. The Kiwi that Had to Fly: Path Dependence and Evolutionary Niches among International Financial Centres 245
Roger J. Bowden

9. Seoul as an International Financial Centre: Roadmap, Progress and Challenges 277
Hansoo Kim

10. Comments on Case Studies by Discussants
Session I: Hong Kong and Singapore 296
(1) *Sang Kee Min* and (2) *David Hong*

Session II: Tokyo and Sydney 302
(1) *Simon Cooper*, (2) *Hugh Patrick* and (3) *Tan Teck Meng*

Session III: Shanghai, Wellington and Seoul 324
(1) *James Rooney* and (2) *Sang Yong Park*

Part III: International Perspectives

11. Financial Centres in the Asia-Pacific Region: Recent Trends and Developments 333
David Cowen

12. Competition and Integration: Financial Centres and Financial Market Integration in Asia 344
Jong-Wha Lee

13. Financial Centres in the Asia-Pacific Region 353
John Walker

Part IV: Observations

14. Issues and Findings 365
(1) *Kihwan Kim,* (2) *Yung-Chul Park* and (3) *John Burton*

Appendices

I. Korea's Financial Globalization and Challenges Ahead 375
Dinner Speech by Yong-Ro Yun
Vice-Chairman, Korean Financial Supervisory Commission

II. Programme of the Conference 379

Index 385

List of Tables

1.1	SWOTs of Hong Kong as an IFC	7
1.2	SWOTs of Singapore as an IFC	9
1.3	SWOTs of Tokyo as an IFC	12
1.4	SWOTs of Sydney as an IFC	13
1.5	SWOTs of Shanghai as an IFC	15
1.6	SWOTs of Wellington as an IFC	17
1.7	SWOTs of Seoul as an IFC	19
1.8	Top Ten International Financial Centres	36
2.1	Leading East Asian Stock Exchanges: Domestic Market Capitalization	64
2.2	Locational Statistics: External Positions of Banks — Liabilities	66
2.3	Locational Statistics: External Positions of Banks — Assets	66
2.4	Consolidated Statistics: Claims of Reporting Banks	69
2.5	Number of Banks in Major Banking Centres	70
2.6	Number of Banks and Branches in Largest Banking Centres, 2004	71
2.7	Number of Foreign Banking Institutions	71
2.8	Cumulative Distribution of Asset Holdings among the World's 1,000 Largest Banks Measured by Assets	72
2.9	The Fifteen Largest Banks in the World	73
2.10	Banks with Most Assets Abroad	74
2.11	Share of Domestic Assets and Deposits Held by the Five Largest Banks	76
2.12	Share of the Three Largest Banks in all Commercial Bank Assets 1990–2005	77
2.13	Selective Regulatory Indicators, 2006	79

2.14	Number of Online Banking Users by Region	81
2.15	Global Foreign Exchange Market Turnover	84
2.16	Geographical Distribution of Foreign Exchange Market Turnover	84
2.17	Currency Distribution of Foreign Exchange Market Turnover	86
2.18	Bonds Outstanding as a Share of GDP	88
2.19	Relative Composition of Finance: Bank Lending, Equities and Bonds	89
2.20	Bond Finance 1995–2005: Shares in GDP	90
3.1	2007 Update of ISEAS-NTU Overall Progress Ranking on Financial Reforms and Liberalization of ASEAN 10+5 Economies	102
3.2	Central Provident Fund (CPF) Board Holdings of Singapore Government Securities (SGS), CPF Members' Balance and Fund Management Industry	124
4.1	Japanese Assets Held by Non-Residents	147
4.2	Ratio of Foreign Investors to Market Capitalization	147
4.3	Asset Composition of Major Institutional Investors in Japan	149
4.4	Outstanding Securitized Securities Issued in Japan	156
4.5	Foreign Assets Held by Japanese	158
4.6	Geographic Distribution of Reported Foreign Exchange Market Turnover	162
4.7	Currency Distribution of Reported Foreign Exchange Market Turnover	163
4.8	Reported Foreign Exchange Market Turnover by Currency Pair	165
4.9	Geographic Distribution of Reported OTC Derivatives Turnover	166
6.1	Australia and Ireland Compared	198
6.2	Tax Snapshot — Then and Now	203
6.3	Recent Developments in the Regulation of Finance since 2000	206
6.4	Mercer Cost of Living Survey 2004 Top Cities	211

7.1	Strategic Evolution of the Shanghai International Financial Centre	233
7.2	Financial Market Element Concentration in Shanghai since 1990	234
7.3	Main Targets in the Eleventh Five-Year Plan for Building the Shanghai Financial Centre	241
8.1a	NZD Uridashi Issues	263
8.1b	Eurokiwi Issues	266
11.1	Sovereign Wealth Funds in the Asia-Pacific Region	336
11.2	Panel Least-Squares Estimate of Determinants of Capital Inflows, 1998–2006	339
11.3	Panel GMM Estimation of the Determinants of the Volatility of Capital Inflows, 1998–2006	340
12.1	Bond and Equity Markets	350
12.2	Cross-border Financial Activity, 2003	351
12.3	Global Financial Centres Index (GFCI): Ranks and Ratings of Selected Financial Centres	351

List of Figures

1.1	Financial Services Clustering in Financial Centres: Index Rating	29
1.2	Comparison of Selected Financial Centres by Infrastructure Index, 2007	31
2.1	Cross-border Liabilities	67
2.2	Cross-border Claims	68
2.3	Average Cost/Income Ratio by Region, 2006	81
2.4	Benchmark Yield Curves — LCY Bonds, 2006	91
3.1	Investment of Funds by Instruments	125
4.1	Share of Market Capitalization of the Top Three Stock Exchanges	145
4.2	Total Value of Share Trading on Major Stock Exchanges	146
4.3	Growth Rates of Share Trading Value on Major Stock Exchanges	146
4.4	Composition of Japanese Household's Financial Assets	148
4.5	Composition of Households' Financial Assets in Japan and the United States	149
4.6	Number of Foreign Firms Listed in Major Stock Exchanges, 2006	152
4.7	Size of Outstanding Bond Issued	153
4.8	Composition of Outstanding Issuance of JGBs by Investors, June 2006	154
4.9	Major Sources of Liabilities by Non-Financial Firms	155

4.10 Composition of Japan's Foreign Assets and Liabilities 158
4.11 Yen-denominated Foreign Bond and Euro-Yen Bond Markets 160
4.12 Yen- and Foreign Currency-denominated Offshore Market 163

6.1 Australia's Funds Management Cluster 200
6.2 Pages of Australian Government Primary Legislation 204
6.3 The Virtuous Circle of Tax and Regulation in a Financial Centre 210
6.4 The Competitiveness of Melbourne as a Financial Centre 212
6.5 Comparison of Total Production Costs for Equity Funds by Member State Based on Current Average Fund Sizes 213
6.6 Per Capita Income per Year in Selected European Countries 226

8.1a Monthly Spot FX Trading Volume with NZD as Terms or Commodity 254
8.1b Monthly Spot FX Trading Volume with USD as Terms or Commodity 254
8.2 Comparative Personal Savings Rates 255
8.3 NZ Current Account Balances 258
8.4 Comparative Short-term Interest Rates 258
8.5 Household Indebtedness 261
8.6 Eurokiwi and Uridashi: Volume and Redemption Shadow 269
8.7 The Press in Worry Mode 269
8.8 Flows on a Typical Eurokiwi or Uridashi CIRS 270
8.9 Generalized Currency Swaps with NZD as One Leg 271
8.10 Third-Party Generalized Currency Swaps 272

9.1 Contribution of Financial Sector to GDP 279
9.2 Increase in Foreign Shares in Korea's Stock Market, 1997–2004 280
9.3 Market Capitalization of Regional Stock Markets, 2006 281
9.4 Trade Volume 282
9.5 International and Domestic Bonds, 2006 282
9.6 Stock Index Derivatives 284
9.7 Assets under Management, 2006 285
9.8 Policy Paradigm Shifts 286

9.9 Three-stage "Northeast Asian Financial Hub Promotion Strategy" 287
9.10 Proportion of Equity Investment of Major Pension Funds 288
9.11 Changes in Financial Regulation with the Capital Market Consolidation Act 289

11.1 Emerging Asia Capital Flows — Recent Surge 335
11.2 Asia-Pacific Intra-Regional Portfolio Investment 335
11.3 Asia-focused Hedge Funds 337

12.1 Financial Assets 349
12.2 Bond and Equity Market Size 350

13.1 What Are the Key Financial Regions? 354
13.2 Top Twenty World Economies, 2040 355
13.3 Share of World GDP, 2002–2040 356
13.4 Partnerships Create Value: Macquaire Korea's Assets in Korea and Abroad 357
13.5a Korea as an Example of Competition 359
13.5b The New World of Competition 359
13.6 Competition-spurred Growth 360
13.7 Macquarie's Organizational Culture 360

Preface

The Korea National Committee for Pacific Economic Cooperation (KOPEC) convened, in collaboration with the Korea Securities Research Institute (KSRI), an International Conference on *Competition among Financial Centres in Asia-Pacific: Prospects, Benefits and Costs — Stumbling Blocks or Building Blocks towards a Regional Financial Community* in Seoul, Korea, on 15–16 October 2007 as part of its contribution to the work of the Pacific Economic Cooperation Council (PECC). Noting that several or more financial centres in Asia-Pacific were respectively engaged in efforts to become premier international financial centres in competition with one another, KOPEC organized this conference to examine the prospects for success for the respective financial centres, weigh the costs and benefits of such competition for local economies as well as the region as a whole, and derive implications of the ongoing competition for cooperation among the regional governments.

The conference examined the cases of seven financial centres in the region — Tokyo, Seoul, Shanghai, Hong Kong, Singapore, Sydney, and Wellington. The conference drew the participation of authoritative finance experts from the economies where these cities were located as case study authors and of a number of distinguished experts and practitioners from in and out of Korea as discussants. The conference was also attended by Mr Dominic Barton, Chairman, Asia McKinsey & Co., who gave the keynote address, as well as Messrs David Cowen, Jong-Wha Lee, and Masahiro Kawai, three senior officials respectively representing the International Monetary Fund (IMF), Asian Development Bank (ADB), and ADB Institute, who provided their insights on the subject matter. The conference drew an attentive audience of about 150 finance professionals and academics, both Korean and international.

The present book consists of papers and commentaries presented at the conference as well as a synthesis paper on the findings. The synthesis paper was jointly authored by Professor Sayuri Shirai of Japan, Professor Dosoung Choi of Korea, Professor Jesús Seade of Hong Kong, and myself, whose respective principal contributions constitute the report in the order listed here. The synthesis paper was publicly released in its preliminary version at the conference on *Global Financial Crisis and the International Financial Centre Competition in Asia-Pacific: Implications and Challenges for Asia and Korea* held in Seoul, Korea, on 4 November 2008, co-organized by KOPEC and the Seoul Financial Forum.

On behalf of KOPEC, I would like to thank all those experts who participated in the 2007 conference as presenters and discussants for their contributions. I also express my gratitude to Asia McKinsey & Co., the IMF, ADB, ADB Institute, the Singapore Committee for Pacific Economic Cooperation (SINCPEC), the Chinese Taipei Pacific Economic Cooperation Committee (CTPECC), Kookmin Bank, and UBS Hana Asset Management Korea for their generous support of the 2007 conference. I am also grateful to the *Financial Times* for its generous Media Partner support for the conference and to Mr John Burton, Singapore Bureau Chief of the *Financial Times*, for his participation in the conference as a panelist. I would like to thank Professors Dosoung Choi, Jesús Seade, and Sayuri Shirai for the honour and pleasure of collaborating with them in organizing the conference, writing the synthesis paper, and editing the conference volume. Finally, I would like to thank the staff of the KOPEC Secretariat for their dedication to the success of the present project.

Soogil Young
Chair
Korea National Committee for Pacific Economic Cooperation
(KOPEC)

Contributors

(In order of the contents)

Soogil Young, President of the National Strategy Institute, an independent think-tank in Seoul, has been serving as Chair of the Korea National Committee for Pacific Economic Cooperation (KOPEC) since November 2006. He served as a Senior Economist at four governmental economic research institutes during 1978–98, including the Korea Development Institute (KDI) as a Senior Fellow, Korea Transport Institute as President, and the Korea Institute for International Economic Policy (KIEP) as President. He served as Korea's Ambassador to the OECD in Paris during 1998-2001 where he concurrently served as Chairman of the Advisory Board on the Development Centre. He has been active on many blue-ribbon committees for the Korean government on economic policy matters since the early 1980s, including three Presidential Commissions. He was the founding Coordinator of the PECC Trade Policy Forum during 1983–86 and also of the PECC Finance Forum during 2001–05. He obtained his Ph.D. in Economics from the Johns Hopkins University in the United States. He was decorated with the Medal of National Service Merit of the Dongbaik Order for his contribution to Korea's epochal *Real-name Transactions Reform* in 1993. He has written extensively on trade, development, and international cooperation from Korea's perspective.

Dosoung Choi has been a member of the Monetary Policy Committee at the Bank of Korea since April 2008. He was a Professor of Finance at Seoul National University (SNU) during 1994–2008. He also served as President of Korea Securities Research Institute (KSRI) from 2005 to 2008 including at the time of his participation in the present project. Before joining SNU in 1994, he taught at the State University of New York at Buffalo and the University of Tennessee. He was a commissioner of the Securities and Futures Commission of Korea during 2001–04. He served as President of two academic societies, Korea Finance Association and Korea Securities Association. He received his B.A. in Business Administration (1974) and M.B.A. degree (1976) both from SNU. He earned his Ph.D. in Finance from the Pennsylvania State University (1980). Over the past three decades, he has published numerous articles in such fields as corporate finance, the market for corporate control, and capital markets in a number of prestigious journals including the *Journal of Finance* and *JFQA*. He has also authored a number of books on M&As, corporate bankruptcies and reorganizations, financial derivatives and risk management, and corporate finance.

Jesús Seade is the Vice-President of Lingnan University since September 2008. He joined Lingnan in January 2007 initially as Chair Professor of Economics. He has been a leading contributor to economic theory, policy and practice from a range of senior positions in academia, government, and international economic organizations. He was Chair of Public Economics at Warwick University in the United Kingdom whose Development Economics Research Centre he co-founded and headed, and was Director-founder of Mexico's leading Economics Department, El Colegio de Mexico's. He has been Mexico's GATT Ambassador and Chief Uruguay Round Negotiator; Deputy Director-General of the World Trade Organization (WTO); and Senior Adviser at the International Monetary Fund (IMF) where he led the internal review work on financial mega-crises cases Brazil, Turkey, and Argentina. Professor Seade's main research interests are in financial markets, fiscal analysis, and trade. At Lingnan, he teaches and leads a research programme on International Financial Centres and heads the Hong Kong APEC Study Centre, which is conducting research and preparing upcoming conferences on finance and trade integration in the region. He is an Honorary Professor at Warwick and Leicester Universities in the United Kingdom and senior advisory board member at Georgetown Law School in the United States.

Sayuri Shirai is a Professor of Economics at the Faculty of Policy Management, Keio University. She gave lectures on International Finance and Japanese Economy at the graduate and undergraduate schools of Sciences-Po, France as a Visiting Professor from 2007 to 2008. She graduated from Keio University and holds a Ph.D. in Economics from Columbia University. She was formerly an Economist at the International Monetary Fund (1993–98) and a Visiting Scholar at the ADBI Institute (2000–03). She also worked as a consultant for UN ESCAP and OECD and as a Visiting Scholar for JICA and Tokyo Foundation. She also participated in a number of committees and commissions organized by the Ministry of Finance (MOF), Cabinet Office, Ministry of Economy, Trade and Industry (METI) and other government institutions. Her research interests cover a wide range of areas, including international financial system, macroeconomic policy, economics of development, as well as global and Japanese economies. She is the author of numerous articles in professional journals. She has also published seven books in Japanese (all single authored) on China's exchange rate regime, Hong Kong's currency board system, IMF policy, economic crises, Japan's macroeconomic policy, and ODA policy. She also co-edited *How to Strengthen Banks and Develop Capital Markets in Post-crisis Asia* (Keio University Press, 2004).

Dominic Barton, McKinsey's Chairman of Asia, is a leading thinker on financial sector reform, sustainability, and corporate governance in both the public and private sector. His advisory in such areas as consumer finance, banking and securities, private equity, and insurance has helped to transform clients from local and regional players into global leaders and top performers. In the area of financial sector reform, his experience has been sought by such diverse audiences as the top government planning body in China, the National Development and Reform Commission, the Korean Financial Supervisory Commission, and the Monetary Authority of Singapore. He also serves on McKinsey's shareholder committee, the firm's senior governance body, and has been with the firm for twenty-one years. He is the author of *Dangerous Markets: Managing in Financial Crises* (2002) and *China Vignettes: An Inside Look at China* (2007). McKinsey & Company is a leading strategic management consultancy with more than 13,000 employees in its 83 offices across 45 countries.

Tan Khee Giap graduated with a Ph.D. from the University of East Anglia, England, U.K. in 1987. He has consulted extensively with the various government ministries, statutory boards and government-linked companies of the Singapore government, including the Ministry of Finance; Ministry of Trade and Industry; Ministry of Manpower; Housing and Development Board; Civil Aviation Authority of Singapore; Singapore Tourism Board; Trade Development Board; Maritime Port Authority; Ministry of Information, Communications and the Arts; Media Development Authority; Singapore Press Holdings; Mendaki; StarHub; and Capital Land, on policies concerning financial, fiscal, trade, tourism, public housing, labour, telecommunication, tourism, creative industry, media, airport and seaport activities. He has also served as a consultant to such international agencies as the Asian Development Bank; Asian Development Bank Institute; United Nations Industrial Development Group; World Gold Council; ASEAN Secretariat, Central Policy Unit, Hong Kong; Kerzner International; Las Vegas Sands; and other international financial institutions and multinational corporations. He has published in international refereed journals, including *Applied Economics, Asian Economic Papers, Review of Pacific Basin Financial Markets and Policies,* and *Competitiveness Review* in the areas of capital flows, economic forecasting, financial sector liberalization and macroeconomic competitiveness.

Masahiro Kawai joined the Asian Development Bank Institute (ADBI) in 2007 after serving as Head of the Asian Development Bank's Office of Regional Economic Integration (OREI) and Special Adviser to the ADB President in charge of regional economic cooperation and integration. Prior to his assumption as Head of OREI, ADB in October 2005, he was a Professor of Economics at the University of Tokyo's Institute of Social Science. He also served as Chief Economist for the World Bank's East Asia and the Pacific Region from 1998 to 2001, and as Deputy Vice-Minister of Finance for International Affairs at Japan's Ministry of Finance from 2001 to 2003. Kawai began his professional career as a Research Fellow at Brookings Institution (Washington, D.C.) from 1977 to 1978 and then as an Assistant and Associate Professor in the Department of Economics at Johns Hopkins University (Baltimore) from 1978 to 1986. Afterwards, he served as an Associate and Full Professor at the Institute of Social Science, University of Tokyo. He served as a consultant for the Board of Governors of the Federal Reserve System and the International Monetary Fund, both in Washington, D.C. He was also Special Research Adviser at the Institute of Fiscal and Monetary Policy (currently Policy Research Institute) in Japan's Ministry of Finance and a visiting researcher at the Bank of Japan's Institute for Monetary and Economic Studies and at the Economic Planning Agency's Economic Research Institute (currently the Cabinet Office's Economic and Social Research Institute). He has written books and numerous academic articles on international economics; economic globalization and regionalization; regional financial integration and cooperation in East Asia, including lessons from the Asian financial crisis; and the international currency system. He earned his B.A. and M.A. degrees in Economics from the University of Tokyo's Economics Department, and his M.S. in Statistics and Ph.D. in Economics from Stanford University.

Nicholas Gruen is trained in History, Statistics, Law and Economics and has published internationally on various issues including economic liberalization and fiscal policy architecture. He has qualifications in Law (Hons.), History (Hons. — First Class), and Education (Dip. Ed.), all from the University of Melbourne, and Economics and Public Policy (Ph.D.) from the Australian National University. He was adviser to Senator John Button on industry policy and to John Dawkins, both when he was Minister for Employment Education and Training and as Treasurer.

He was appointed to the Productivity Commission in 1994 and again in 1995 where he was Associate Commissioner on five inquiries and Presiding Commissioner on one inquiry and an industry study.

He joined the Business Council of Australia in 1997 where he directed the BCA's "New Directions" programme. In 2000, he founded <www.lateraleconomics.com.au> and <www.peaches.com.au>, a discount finance broker. He is Chairman of <www.onlineopinion.com.au>, Australia's eighteenth most popular Internet site — and a substantial contributor to Australia's thriving policy blog scene. He was a weekly columnist for the *Courier Mail* in 2005 and 2006 and still writes columns frequently for both *The Age* and the *Australian Financial Review*. Lateral Economics' report on making Australia an exporter of fund management services received a good deal of attention when it was published earlier this year. Lateral Economics has consulted to a wide variety of firms and governments both large and small in its seven-year existence. It has recently completed or is in the process of consultancies for the Victorian, South Australian, and New South Wales governments, all focusing on regulating more efficiently.

Xu Mingqi currently holds a full Professorship of International Economics at Shanghai Academy of Social Sciences and serves as the Deputy Director of the Institute of World Economy. He is an Executive Council Member and the Deputy Secretary-General of the Chinese Society for World Economy Studies and the Secretary-General of the Shanghai Society for World Economy Studies. He is also the Executive Director of the Shanghai Research Center for International Finance and a member of the Advisory Board to the Shanghai Municipal Government. He received his university education at Xiamen University and obtained his M.A. and Ph.D. degrees in Economics at Shanghai Academy of Social Sciences. He furthered his studies at the University of Western Ontario in Canada from 1987–88 and did postdoctoral research at Harvard University in the United States during 1995–96. He has frequently been invited to international conferences and has given public lectures both in China and abroad. He has published extensively in professional journals in the fields of international finance, trade, and open macroeconomics mainly in Chinese as well as in English. His most recent book is *Competition and Corporation: Foreign Capital in Yangtze Delta Region* (Shanghai University of Finance and Economics Press, 2008).

Roger Bowden is a Professor of Economics and Finance at the Victoria University of Wellington and director of Kiwicap Research Ltd. Prior to returning to his native New Zealand, he worked or researched at a number of offshore institutions, including the Universities of Manchester, Western Australia, and New South Wales as Professor of Finance and Foundation Director of the Asia-Pacific Centre for Banking and Capital Markets. In addition, he has been Visiting Professor of Economics at the Universities of California at Berkeley and British Columbia; held a Humboldt Foundation Senior Research Award (Forschungspreis) at Bonn University; and visiting fellowships or appointments at the Institute of Advanced Study in Vienna, CEPREMAP in Paris, and the IBRD Development Research Department in Washington D.C. He holds the degrees of B.A., B.Sc., M.A. (Auckland), and Ph.D. (Manchester). Bowden has published many research papers in international journals of finance, economics, econometrics, statistics, management science, and law. He has also been proactive in the development of instrumental or "learning by doing" financial education. He is co-originator of the Victoria International Applied Finance programme at Victoria University of Wellington and more recently has been a contributing author to the risk management and financial risk mathematics modules for the AMCT qualification of the London Association of Corporate Treasurers.

Hansoo Kim is a research fellow at Korea Securities Research Institute (KSRI). Prior to joining KSRI, he was a research fellow at Samsung Economic Research Institute. He holds a doctorate degree in Economics from Indiana University. His primary research interests are international finance and macroeconomics. He is particularly interested in bridging rigorous analysis and practical policy-making. Since joining KSRI in 2006, he has worked in many research projects, including "Importance of KORUS FTA: Financial Services Sector" (with Dr Pil Kyu Kim of KSRI), "Financial Reform in Australia and its Implications to Sydney's Competitiveness as an International Financial Centre" (with Dr Pil-Kyu

Kim), "Strategy to Develop Asset Management Sector in order to Build Financial Hub in Korea" (with Dr Jaechil Kim of KSRI).

Sang Kee Min has been a Professor of International Finance at Seoul National University since 1977. He is currently the Chairman of the Seoul Investment Banking Forum. He was previously the Executive Vice-Chancellor and Dean of the Graduate School at Seoul National University from 2000 to 2001. As Chairman of the Committee for Financial Development in the Ministry of Finance and Economy from 2001 to 2004, he was in charge of financial development and progress in Korea. He also assumed the role of Commissioner of the Korea Stock Exchange Commission in 1997. He was Chairman of the Korea Money and Finance Association from 2002 to 2003 and President of the Korean Academy of International Business from 1994 to 1995. He received his Ph.D. in International Business from the University of Michigan.

David Hong is the President and Senior Research Fellow of the Taiwan Institute of Economic Research, the first private economic think-tank in Chinese Taipei. Before taking the post, he had been Vice-President of the institute from 1997 to 2005. He was also the Director leading the institute's Energy and Environment Division before 1997. In 1993, Hong was named Director of the Bureau of Finance by the Taipei City government. He was the Financial Forecasting Manager of Northern States Power Company in Minneapolis, MN, U.S.A. (1984–93). He was an Adjunct Professor of St Thomas College in Minneapolis (1989–90). He also served as Economic Service Manager, Minnesota Department of Public Service, St Paul, MN, U.S.A. (1975–84). He holds a Ph.D. in Economics from the University of Minnesota.

Hong's research interests include industrial development, economic forecasting, and energy and environmental economic analysis. His recent studies comprise Promotion of New Industries and Technologies, Globalization, BOT, Environmental, Cross-strait Economics, Knowledge-based Economy, Financial Competitiveness, Fiscal Reform, Sustainable Development, Age Concerns, Unemployment, Privatization in general and Taiwan in particular. After being named the Director General of both the Chinese Taipei APEC Study Centre and CTPECC, he has further extended his research interests to APEC and PECC related issues.

Simon Cooper assumed the position of President and Chief Executive Officer of HSBC in Korea effective from 17 March 2006. HSBC employs some 1,250 staff and a further 800 contract workers in Korea and manages its business through eleven branches. Before moving to Korea, he was the Managing Director and Head of Corporate and Investment Banking in Singapore. As Head of Corporate and Investment Banking, he was responsible for the business activities of the Investment Banking Advisory, Investment Banking Financing (Debt Capital Markets, Project Finance, Structured Capital Markets), Transaction Banking, Securities Services (including Bank of Bermuda), and Corporate and Institutional Banking divisions of HSBC in Singapore.

Cooper was previously the Deputy Chief Executive and Head of Corporate and Investment Banking in HSBC Thailand from 2001 to 2003. Prior to his role in Thailand, he had twelve years of experience as a Director in corporate finance with the HSBC Group in London, Hong Kong, and Singapore. He is a graduate of the University of Cambridge and holds an M.A. in Law. He is an alumnus of Columbia Business School.

Hugh Patrick is Director of the Center on Japanese Economy and Business at Columbia Business School, a co-director of Columbia's APEC Study Center, and R.D. Calkins Professor of International Business Emeritus. He joined the Columbia faculty in 1984 after some years as Professor of Economics and Director of the Economic Growth Center at Yale University. He has been a Visiting Professor at Hitotsubashi University, University of Tokyo, and University of Bombay. He has been awarded the Guggenheim and Fulbright fellowships and the Ohira Prize. His professional publications include sixteen books and some sixty articles and essays. He is on the Board of Directors of the U.S. Asia-Pacific Council and is a member of the Council of Foreign Relations. In November 1994, the Government of Japan awarded him the Order of the Sacred Treasure, Gold and Silver Star (Kunnito Zuihosho). He completed his B.A. at Yale University in 1951, earned M.A. degrees in Japanese Studies (1955) and Economics (1957) and a Ph.D. in Economics at the University of Michigan in 1960.

Tan Teck Meng is an accountancy graduate of the University of Singapore and the University of New South Wales. He holds Fellowships in the Institute of Certified Public Accountants of Singapore, Australian Society of CPAs, Institute of Chartered Secretaries and Administrators, Chartered Management Institute, U.K. and The Association of Chartered Certified Accountants, U.K. In 1997, he became the first Singaporean to garner the U.S.-based Wilford L. White Award. He is currently a Professor of Accounting at Singapore Management University where he was the

Founding Deputy President and Provost from 1998 to 2001. Prior to joining SMU, he was Dean of the School of Accountancy and Business (SAB) at Nanyang Technological University (July 1990 to March 1998). Currently he chairs the Singapore National Council for Pacific Economic Cooperation (SINCPEC); the College Advisory Committee of the Meridian Junior College; Hospital Medifund, KK Women's & Children's Hospital; the Entrepreneurship Advisory Committee, National Youth Council; and the GST Board of Review. He serves on the Board of Directors of k1 Ventures Ltd, Kim Eng Holdings Limited, Oriental Century Limited, Raffles Education Corporation, Singapore Reinsurance Corporation Limited, Singapore Shipping Corporation Ltd, Hyflux Ltd, and China Auto Corporation Ltd.

James Rooney was born in Scotland, and he lived in the United States. He has been based in Seoul since 1996. He holds an M.B.A. from Harvard Business School, 1983, Boston. He is a well-known and respected investor, adviser, analyst, consultant and commentator on Korea's economy and financial sector, living in Northeast Asia since 1996, and published the One Million Jobs Report in 1998 focusing on critical policy measures for Korea's economic recovery. He has been participating in the healthy long-term development of the Northeast Asian economy as a market participant, investor, adviser, consultant, and catalyst for change. He also has been internationalizing the Northeast Asian economy to build its future strength by attracting FDI, foreign partners, and companies; by building strategic links to other economies and companies around the world; and by focusing on national and regional development opportunities and strategies. He is currently Chairman and CEO of Market Force Company. He serves as the Vice Chairman of Seoul Financial Forum, and is an outside director for Macquarie Korea Oportunities Management Company.

Sang Yong Park is a Professor of Finance and Dean of the School of Business at Yonsei University in Seoul, Korea. Dr Park received his M.B.A. and Ph.D. in Financial Economics from Stern School of Business at New York University and joined the faculty of Yonsei University in 1984 after an appointment at the University of Southern California. His major areas of research include corporate finance and capital markets. Dr Park has published articles widely in academic journals, including *Journal of Financial Economics*, *Journal of Business*, and other local journals in Korea. He has also participated in the numerous public research projects for reformation of the financial industry and corporate governance in Korea. For the past decade, he held various positions of public nature, including a non-standing Commissioner of the Financial Supervisory Commission, a member of the National Economic Advisory Council for the President of Korea, Treasurer of Yonsei University, the President of Korea Securities Research Institute, a member of the Public Funds Oversight Committee (PFOC) and the Chairman of Asset Disposal Sub-committee of PFOC, the President of Korea Money and Finance Association, and the President of Korea Institute of Directors (KIOD). Dr Park's current positions include a member of the Presidential Committee on Green Growth, an independent Director of POSCO and Shinhan Card, and the Chairman of the Asian Financial Regulatory Committee.

David Cowen is currently a Deputy Division Chief in the IMF's Asia and Pacific Department in Washington. Previously, he was in the IMF's Regional Office for Asia and the Pacific in Tokyo, where he covered regional capital market developments, including for the Fund's *Asia-Pacific Regional Economic Outlook*. He has also worked at IMF headquarters on the India desk. During this assignment, he co-edited a book on India's and China's experience with reform and growth (published in 2005), including comparative experiences with financial sector and capital account liberalization. He has also worked extensively on Vietnam, focusing on public finance and banking sector issues. A U.S. national, he holds a Ph.D. in Economics from the University of Texas at Austin.

Jong-Wha Lee is Head of the Asian Development Bank's (ADB) Office of Regional Economic Integration. He is also the Acting Chief Economist. He has over twenty years of professional experience as an economist and an academic. He worked as Economist at the International Monetary Fund and taught at Harvard University as a Visiting Professor. He had served as a consultant to the Asian Development Bank, the Harvard Institute for International Development, the Inter-American Development, the International Monetary Fund, and the United Nations Development Programme, and the World Bank. He also served as a member of the National Economic Advisory Council in the Republic of Korea. Prior to joining ADB, he was the Director of the International Center for Korean Studies and a Professor of Economics at Korea University. He has published numerous books and reviewed journal articles in English and Korean, especially on topics relating to human capital, growth, financial crisis, and economic integration. A national of the Republic of Korea, he obtained his

Ph.D. and Master's degrees in Economics from Harvard University, and his Master's and Bachelor's degrees in Economics from Korea University in Seoul.

John Walker is Executive Director of Macquarie Bank Limited and Chairman of Macquarie Group of Companies, Korea. He established Macquarie's Korean business in 2000 and it now comprises thirteen businesses. He has been responsible for leading major infrastructure projects and privatizations globally. John has also raised significant private equity and established Macquarie's first overseas-raised and -based investment funds in both infrastructure and general private equity. Prior to joining Macquarie, he was Executive Vice-President of Bankers Trust, Australia and earlier in his career was a very senior Australian Government Official holding a number of CEO posts. He was awarded the Honour of the Order of Australia in 1999. In Korea, he has received the President's citation as "Excellent Contributor in Foreign Direct Investment Inflow in 2005" encouraging Macquarie's contribution to Korea's financial sector. John was the first foreigner to be appointed as a director of the Korea Securities Dealers Association which recently changed into Korea Financial Investment Association. He is also a member of International Financial City Advisory Committee in Seoul Metropolitan Government and a member of Invest Korea Advisory Council which is part of Korea Trade-Investment Promotion Agency (KOTRA).

Kihwan Kim currently serves as Chair of the Seoul Financial Forum and an International Adviser to Goldman Sachs, Asia. His distinguished career bridges academia, public service, and the business world. Following his graduation from Grinnell College in 1957 with a B.A. in History, Kim earned an M.A., also in History, from Yale, and a Ph.D. in Economics from the University of California, Berkeley. Before his return to the Republic of Korea in 1976, Kim taught Economics at a number of universities in the United States, including the University of California, Berkeley.

Since his return to Korea, he has held many important positions in government, including Vice-Minister of Trade and Industry, Chief Trade Policy Coordinator and Negotiator, and Chief Delegate to the South-North Inter-Korean Economic Talks. During the 1997–98 Asian financial crisis, he served as Korea's Ambassador-at-Large for Economic Affairs, playing a key role in the resolution of the crisis. Other important positions he has held in the public sector include President of Korea Development

Institute (KDI) and a Member of the Monetary Policy Board. For most of the 1990s, he was a Senior Adviser at Kim and Chang, the largest and most prestigious law firm in Korea. From 1999 to 2002, Kim served as Chairman and CEO of Media Valley, Inc., a private-public sector initiative to accelerate the development of information-technology industries in Korea.

He served as Chair of the Korea National Committee for the Pacific Economic Cooperation Council (PECC) from 1992 to 2006, and International Chair of PECC from 2003 to 2005. He frequently contributes articles and columns to both domestic and international publications.

Yung-Chul Park is a Research Professor and Director of the Centre for International Commerce and Finance at the Graduate School of International Studies, Seoul National University. He was a member of the National Economic Advisory Council (2003–04), Ambassador for International Economy and Trade, Ministry of Foreign Affairs and Trade (2001–02), and Chairman of the Board at the Korea Exchange Bank (1999–2001). He previously served as the Chief Economic Adviser to the President (1987–88), President of the Korea Development Institute (1986–87), President of the Korea Institute of Finance (1992–98), and as a member of the Central Bank's Monetary Board (1984–86). He also worked for the International Monetary Fund (1968–74). He has written and edited several books, including Economic Liberalization and Integration in East Asia (Oxford, 2006), A New Financial Structure for East Asia (Edward Elgar, 2006) and Financial Development of Japan, Korea, and Taiwan: Growth, Repression, and Liberalization (Oxford, 1994).

John Burton has been the *Financial Times* correspondent in Singapore since 2001 and was previously the newspaper's correspondent in South Korea (1992–2001) and Sweden (1989–92). He also worked in Tokyo and Washington D.C. for several newspapers and business publications before joining the *Financial Times*. He attended George Washington University in Washington, D.C., with a B.A. major in East Asian Studies and a minor in journalism.

Executive Summary

1. THE LANDSCAPE — *POLICY COMPETITION WILL HELP SHAPE COMPARATIVE ADVANTAGES*

Competition among financial centres is intense globally but, in particular, in Asia-Pacific. There are many cities in the Asia-Pacific region that serve as financial centres in their respective jurisdictions or local areas. They do not just compete with one another. They also compete with many financial centres outside the region, especially with such global centres as London and New York.

Our examination of several representative financial centres in the region demonstrates that each of those centres has its unique set of SWOTs (strengths, weaknesses, opportunities, and threats). This means that while a financial centre may not excel in terms of the overall finance business performance, it may do so in specific lines of finance business in which it possesses a comparative advantage. Together with the dynamic nature of competition, it also means that the performance overall, or in specific lines of business, of a finance centre, five or ten years from now, may differ from what is today. The future shape and fortune of the individual financial centres will very much be the result of their policy efforts today. Policy competition matters and is thus quite intense.

2. PROSPECTS — *STRONG POTENTIAL FOR THE GROWTH OF FINANCIAL CENTRES IN THE REGION*

Asia-Pacific's strong macroeconomic fundamentals create a strong potential for the growth of its financial centres as a whole. The region continues to generate huge savings and accumulate wealth. Economic growth in the region will continue to remain high and account for increasing shares in the growth of the global economy. The region also has strengths in its financial industry that augur well for growth in the years ahead. With market economies and globalizing strategies firmly in place for several decades throughout the region, policies and frameworks are wholly supportive of efficiency and expansion. In addition, the Asian financial crisis a decade ago left in its wake a raft of improvements in financial policies and institutions that place these policies and institutions on a solid footing as the region moves on.

Specific policy and structural developments supportive of further growth of the region's financial centres include:

- — deeper domestic financial markets;
- — improvements in market infrastructure;
- — continuing liberalization of trade in services, the capital account, and exchange restrictions;
- — increased securitization of domestic assets; and
- — rapid growth in Islamic finance.

3. INTERNATIONAL FINANCIAL CENTRE (IFC) COMPETITION — *BREEDS EFFICIENCY IN FINANCING AND INCREASES RETURNS ON INVESTMENT*

Not all financial centres may become internationally competitive, but efforts to compete will be beneficial to them all, enhancing efficiency and economic performance.

Competition breeds efficiency through a number of channels: It rewards excellence among firms; it changes the role and behaviour of regulators and supervisors from a culture of permits and enforcement to focus on quality and results. Competition requires and fosters fairer, more transparent, and, therefore, more reliable financial and capital markets in each jurisdiction. It leads to greater opportunities for profit from and confidence in using cross-border providers, thus expanding international financial business in the region as a whole. It will also promote financial integration among the regional economies with all the attendant benefits as argued below, including increased returns to savers and investors in the region. All this will lower the cost of financing and enhance the efficiency of operators and their ability to compete outside the region.

4. IFC COMPETITION — *MAY BRING INCREASED RISKS, ESPECIALLY INCREASED VOLATILITY, THUS POSING POLICY CHALLENGES*

4.1. Regional Market Fragmentation or Integration?

It is often argued that financial centre competition will lead to greater market fragmentation, and so it will if based on market closure or subsidies to secure the local champion. But IFC competition in the region is not of that persuasion: it consists of a relentless reduction of barriers to trade, to investment, and to movement of capital; and improvements in infrastructure and in legal and regulatory frameworks. All these expand trade, including in financial capital and services, without distorting it and increasingly allow the best player in any particular niche or sub-market to excel and grow. Integration should, if anything, increase.

Greater financial integration will bring many benefits to the regional economies, such as

— lower capital costs for investment;
— less scope for currency and maturity mismatches that underlay the Asian financial crisis in late 1990s and thereby enhance confidence in the system; and
— improve financial resource allocation in the region.

4.2. Increased Volatility from Market Integration?

The development of a financial centre tends to reduce volatility by developing the market and its diversity and liquidity, all of which are stabilizing buffers. But financial competition and integration may also increase exposure to volatility through greater transmission of risks across countries and regions of the world — a point that the U.S. subprime mortgage debacle illustrates. The question is: How best to protect my jurisdiction from potential shocks from abroad. The solution is not isolation, which makes you stable but poor, but a proper and constantly adapting regulatory framework and practice in the face of the constant flow of new financial products and problems. This requires cooperation across constituencies to exchange best practices and jointly address common problems.

4.3. Regulatory Laxity and Forbearance?

Could financial centre competition encourage regulatory laxity and forbearance, again contributing to increased financial risk contagion? The U.S. subprime mortgage crisis alerts us to the serious threat to financial and economic stability from lax oversight. Regulatory laxity and even failure to constantly improve and adapt to the cutting edge of new financial products and problems can pose serious financial risk. This is only a cautionary note for the region as there is no evidence that the problem is significant in Asia-Pacific, and, in fact, major financial markets in the region do have strong regulatory systems in place. Still, the regulatory authorities in the region need to be on a high level of alert to these risks as they try to update as well as internationalize their financial industries.

This task calls for a delicate balancing act on the part of the regulators. On the one hand, regulators need to allow market participants as much flexibility as possible in the provision and innovation of services, enhancing competitiveness of their financial industries. At the same time, they should seek to improve the transparency of the markets, strengthen financial and non-financial corporate governance, and ensure an effective management of systemic risks to the financial industry as a whole, especially as new financial techniques and products emerge over time.

With markets increasingly interdependent and problems intertwined, this again calls for coordinated international efforts to develop an effective yet flexible regulatory system — in short, a "good" regulatory system in each jurisdiction, with appropriate mechanisms for consultation and cooperation, at the regional level but also coordination of policies both in the Pacific region and at the global level.

4.4. Harmful Competition with Tax Incentives or Subsidized Facilities?

Competitive pressures may also make it attractive to use fiscal instruments to attract business or give domestic suppliers an edge in the competitive area through tax incentives or subsidized facilities or even broader reductions in tax levels. The issues are complex. The reality is that there are no best practices on the level of taxation. Still disparities can give rise to friction, particularly if they take the form of targeted tax or subsidy concessions, and create possibilities for investors to evade or avoid tax obligations utilizing those differences across jurisdictions. In the present WTO-compliant policy environment, there is less room for competition through targeted tax concessions or subsidies *per se*. But even those disciplines are less developed for service sectors than they are for goods. If deemed necessary by a number of regional governments, consultative dialogues should be held among the tax policy authorities of the regional governments on tax issues in the manner of the Organization for Economic Cooperation and Development (OECD) dialogue to avoid harmful tax competition.

4.5. Regional Integration — Too Low in Finance and Calls for Facilitation through Regional Cooperation

Integration of regional financial markets has been increasing but so slowly that the level of intra-regional financial flows has stayed very low. Less than 9 per cent of total foreign portfolio investment made by East Asia in 2003 was done within Asia. Why is regional integration so weak in Asia-Pacific? Why do users of financial services in the region choose to place only a markedly small proportion of their financial business in the region while taking most of it to the global financial centres outside the region? The following issues may be raised here:

First, Asian financial systems may have been carrying sustained perceptions of higher risk than those of Europe and North America, perhaps accentuated by the Asian financial crisis of the late 1990s.

Second, market participants seem to prefer established names across financial centres as much as among institutions. Breaking through is a major challenge. Distance in finance matters much less. Global players can be dominant in regional financial markets through branches and subsidiaries and also service customers from afar. The importance of incumbency and relative absence of transport costs create enormous economies of scale both among institutions and among supply centres. These economies of scale result in levels of concentration of world financial business that are ever increasing, creating a causal cycle where being large lowers costs, attracts business, renders it larger, and so on that make London and New York very difficult to contain let alone beat in the search for business, including Asia-Pacific related business.

Third, markets in Asia-Pacific remain segregated, divided into several separate smaller local markets; separate capital markets; separate trading markets in each sub-sector of finance; and separate legal systems, regulatory frameworks, and institutions. Most critically, there is no common, integrated regional payments system.

Fourth, financial centres in Asia have not been able to provide Asian investors and governments with ample, diverse financial products, like those present in London and New York.

Fifth, Asian countries continue to depend heavily on the U.S. dollar as an invoice currency, a foreign reserve currency, as well as an intermediary currency in the foreign exchange markets. As a result, demand for U.S. financial products tends to be greater than financial products denominated in regional currencies.

Lastly, the disclosure system (particularly, accounting and auditing of the financial statements of listed firms) is regarded more reliable in the United Kingdom and United States, as compared with Asian countries.

6. CONCLUSION — *COOPERATE TOWARDS AN INTEGRATED ASIA-PACIFIC IFC NETWORK*

Competition should be pursued alongside cooperation among the regional governments to manage the risks identified above as well as to foster and accelerate financial integration in Asia-Pacific. The ultimate aim in this cooperation should be to create a seamless, unified business area for finance in the region, linking the individual financial centres with one another in a regionwide network of integrated markets with financial institutions operating in those markets in competition and cooperation with one another as internationalized operators, thus forming an "Asia-Pacific IFC Network". This would enable regional financial centres to realize scale economies and compete with global financial centres effectively with consequent gains shared among them through the market competition process.

In a range of respects, having appropriate mechanisms for cooperation and consultation is much needed. To cope with the problem of the risk of volatility, which may be made worse by market integration or possible regulatory laxity attendant on the IFC competition in the region, the national governments should seek regional cooperation to:

- make coordinated efforts to make, and maintain, the national regulatory systems effective, flexible, and mutually consistent, through consultation and cooperation; and
- enhance the existing macroeconomic and financial policy dialogues for early warning signals of possible monetary and financial

instabilities, promoting close collaboration among the national early warning centres.

The mandate and agenda for ASEAN+3 (APT) Finance Ministers' Meeting and the EMEAP (Emerging Market Economies of Asia-Pacific Central Bankers) Meeting should be broadened and strengthened to meet those needs for cooperation.

In order to facilitate regional financial integration, the governments are also advised to pursue regional cooperation in the following four key areas:

— Move towards a seamless space for financial business in the region, starting with the payments system;
— Launch further initiatives towards the creation and expansion of regional bond markets in the Asia-Pacific along the lines of the Asian Bond Market Initiative, which seeks to develop local currency denominated bonds through promoting securitization, credit enhancement, bond settlement systems, and credit rating functions in the region; the Asian Bond Fund (ABF) initiatives, that is, ABF 1 (denominated in the U.S. dollar) and ABF 2 (denominated in local currencies) invested in by EMEAP; and expanding the scope of double listings and cross-listings in stock exchanges in the region;
— Launch ambitious in-region, WTO-consistent free-trade negotiations in financial services among the members of the ASEAN+3 or the ASEAN+6 as a first step towards a regionwide FTA;
— Create arbitration procedures at the regional level to greatly enhance legal comfort for cross-border co-investments and partnerships;
— Promote regulatory convergence in the disclosure systems of financial statements, for example, rule-based *versus* principle-based regulation, U.K.-based single *versus* U.S.-based multiple supervisory system, and regulations over mergers and acquisitions; and
— Further deepen the Chiang Mai Initiative as a mechanism to meet regional short-term liquidity shortages in the event of internationally systemic financial crises, such as the one currently unfolding globally.

In the wake of the Asian financial crisis, the East Asian countries launched a range of financial and monetary cooperation efforts in the context of the

APT Finance Ministers' Meeting Process in the form of the Chiang Mai Initiative, the Asian Bond Market Initiatives, and various policy dialogues. Such efforts should be further enhanced and accelerated, deepening their level of ambition as well as enlarging their scope and addressing the specific suggestions listed above and surely going beyond.

The present time is most opportune for rising to the challenge of regional cooperation for the initiatives listed here. In the wake of the current global financial crisis, there is an urgent need to critically reassess and reform the global financial regulatory system, as well as restructure the financial industry worldwide. Asia-Pacific can and should play a leading role in these processes. The global leadership for financial development coming from the existing global centres in New York and London has been impaired significantly by the crisis. The leadership now has to be repaired and enhanced with cooperation from the rest of the world. The financial centres in Asia-Pacific, and the national governments that regulate and promote them, are well prepared, with the reform and strengthening of their financial markets and industries since the Asian financial crisis of 1997–98 and with the parallel efforts to modernize them under the IFC drives, to contribute to this process collectively as new major participants.

They should contribute not so much with rhetoric but with actions — actions to strengthen themselves as a regional network of IFC and create the regional infrastructure to support this network. Specifically, they should continue their efforts to enhance and internationalize their national regulatory systems and financial industries, cooperating to strengthen both of these at the level of the region and to facilitate businesses across the region, thus progressing toward an integrated Asia-Pacific IFC network. These efforts will hopefully herald the emergence of an Asia-Pacific financial community as well as the ascendancy of a new global financial system with the Asia-Pacific financial centres as an IFC network joining the ranks of market leaders, such as London and New York, in a richer and more balanced array of international financial centres.

Keynote Address

International Financial Centres: The Terms of Competition and Prospects for the Asia-Pacific Region

Dominic Barton

The changing patterns in the global flow of capital are reshaping the world's economic system, and Asia's major financial centres are now poised to gain even greater prominence as hubs of commerce and creativity. As talent, technology and the drive for innovation speed the global mobility of capital, Asia's aspiring financial centres would be wise to examine the processes that have helped the world's leading financial centres to establish their track records of success. By applying those strategies for success, and understanding and anticipating the financial market deepening and shifts in Asia, the Asia-Pacific region's leading cities can seize the coming opportunity to be leading global financial centres.

In this paper, I would like to cover four topics:

1. Context: Changes underway in the global financial system;
2. Overview of the financial centre strategic map;
3. Key criteria for success as an international finance centre;
4. Implications for cities in Asia-Pacific.

GLOBAL CONTEXT

The fall of the Berlin Wall in 1989 signalled the start of tremendous shifts in the world's financial flows and investment patterns. Since the historic moment when the Wall came down and a half-century of economic barriers dissolved, four forces have ultimately helped determine which cities and which countries would prosper as financial centres. First, liberalization — synonymous with each market's degree of deregulation — allowed capital to move more freely. Second, standardization — the gradual international convergence of the rules that apply to factors like corporate governance, accounting standards and regulatory oversight — clarified the relative merits of competing financial centres. Third, mobility — the easier flow of capital among financial venues — promoted the search for the best return on capital among an ever-wider array of global markets, beyond the traditional hubs of London and New York. Fourth, digitization — the improvement in the amount of information and the speed of its transfer around the world enabled capital to move very quickly (at the touch of a computer button) and allowed investors to

GLOBAL FINANCIAL STOCK HAS GROWN TO $140 TRILLION

$ Trillions

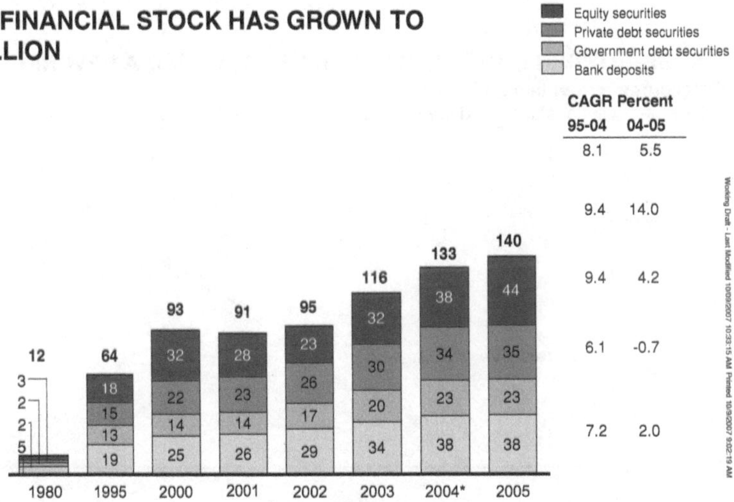

	1980	1995	2000	2001	2002	2003	2004*	2005	CAGR 95-04	CAGR 04-05
Nominal GDP $ Trillions	10.1	29.4	31.7	31.6	32.8	36.9	41.4	44.5	4.2	7.5
Depth (FS/GDP), %	109	218	292	289	290	315	322	316		

* 2004 figure dropped from $136 trillion to $133 trillion due to estatement of data by individual countries.

** Extrapolation off of 2005 base, with components grown at 2000-05 CAGRs

Source: McKinsey Global Institute Global Financial Stock Database

speed the movement of capital toward the places where it would find its most productive uses and achieve the highest return. (Of course, as many investors have also come to learn, the increasing speed of capital mobility has a downside as well as an upside.)

These trends have converged to both increase the amount of stock and mobility of that financial capital. Financial stock has grown from roughly US$12 trillion in 1980 to about US$140 trillion in 2005. Leverage levels however, which have underpinned this growth, will not likely continue at the same rate.

Cross-border financial flows have seen a similarly dramatic increase since 1989: While those flows had been growing at 4.3 per cent per year in the 1980s, they are now growing at almost 11 per cent per year. With money able to move quickly across borders in search of higher returns, the world's stock exchanges have enjoyed unprecedented flows of funds — particularly those in Asia, where a significant proportion of investors now come from outside the region.

The map of the financial world has thus begun to change. The primary sources of capital remain the North America and the Eurozone of Europe (New York and London in particular), which are home to most of the

CROSS-BORDER CAPITAL FLOWS HAVE REACHED A NEW HIGH
Total cross-border capital inflows
$ Billions, 2005 constant $ and constant foreign exchange

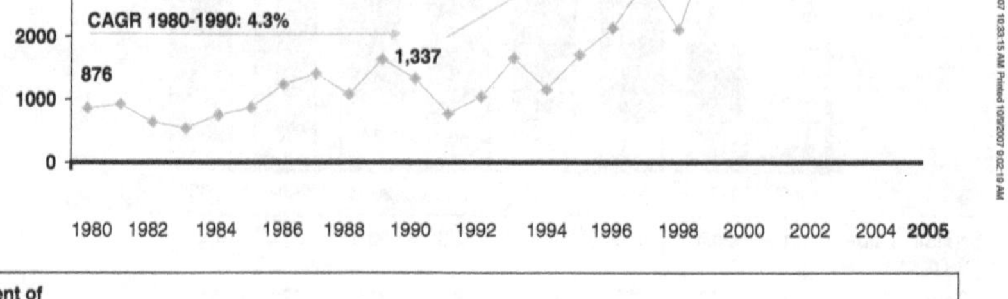

Percent of global GDP	4.6	3.4	3.6	5.5	4.4	5.0	3.7	3.8	6.5	6.0	14.2	7.2	12.1	**13.9**

Source: McKinsey Global Institute Capital Flows Database

world's financial stock. Yet as cross-border flows accelerate, other international financial centres are coming to the fore. Until recently, for example, Asia has been a relatively small part of the overall global financial system, and it has been a relatively modest source of funds. Analysis at McKinsey & Company, however, suggests that that old pattern is destined to change dramatically. The trends in Asia strongly suggest that there will be an astonishing increase in financial activity within this region — which leads us to argue that the time is now to establish a place in participating in this market.

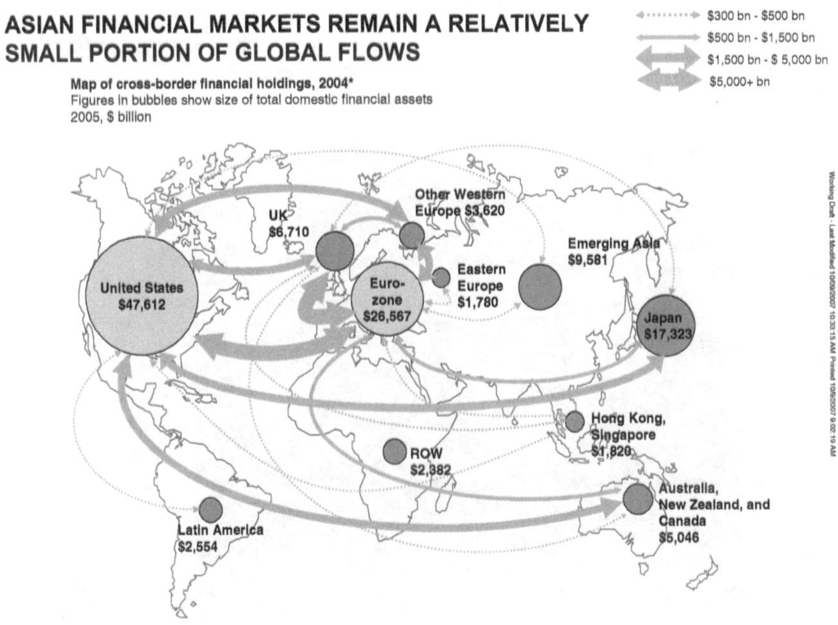

Asia's promise as an ever-stronger financial region becomes clear as we discern the six over-arching trends driving the rise of Asia. Those trends are:

1. The emergence of Asia as a global economic power — Asia has crossed a critical economic size threshold over the last five years;
2. The rise of a massive new Asian consumer class;
3. The increase of intra-Asian trade and integration;

4. The re-emergence of the historic Silk Road that once linked the great trading centres of Asia and the Middle East;
5. The evolution of Asia's financing and business ownership structures;
6. The prospect of an Asian merger-and-acquisition boom, in most sectors, accompanied by industry consolidation.

First, consider the emergence of Asia as a global economic power. As measured by its proportional share of the world's GDP, Asia (including Japan) will be more significant than Europe by 2018.

① ASIA IS EMERGING AS A GROWTH ENGINE FOR THE NEXT TWENTY YEARS, GROWING FASTER THAN ANY OTHER REGION

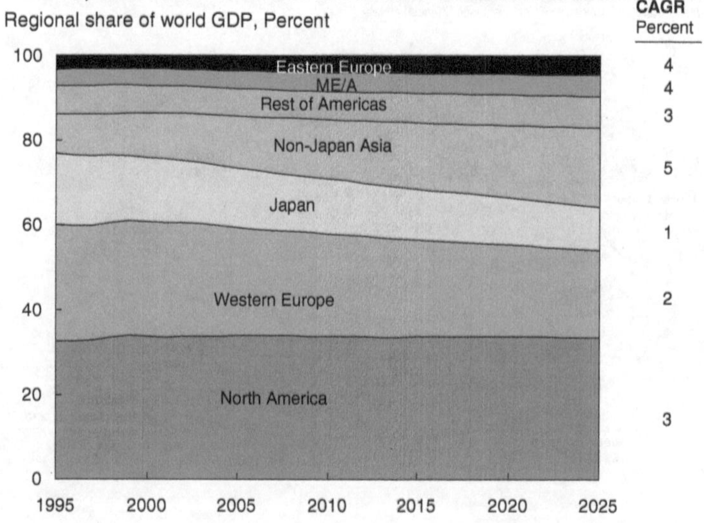

Source: Global insight

One example of this rapid growth is the city of Shenzhen — the site of the initial Chinese policy experiment of the economically liberalizing leader Deng Xiaoping, who famously said, "I don't care if the cat is black or white, so long as it catches mice." A photo taken in the same place in 1987 and 2004 illustrates this dramatic change in Shenzhen (See appendix). Shenzhen epitomizes the speed and scale of the change that is underway throughout the Asia region, where just the infrastructure expenditure may reach about US$2 trillion per year. The capital needs of the booming region — as nation after nation seeks investments in transportation, energy, and other infrastructure priorities — will bring opportunities on a vast scale for the region's financial players.

Second, consider the rise of a massive new consumer class in Asia. In China and India alone, roughly 800 million people will enter the middle class over the next ten years — historically, the world's largest single event in terms of economic upward mobility. (By "middle class" we mean US$5,000 GDP per capita, which may seen low but is the threshold at which major increases in consumption are realized.) Any financial-services company will benefit from this rising tide.

2 RAPID EMERGENCE OF A NEW CLASS OF CONSUMERS

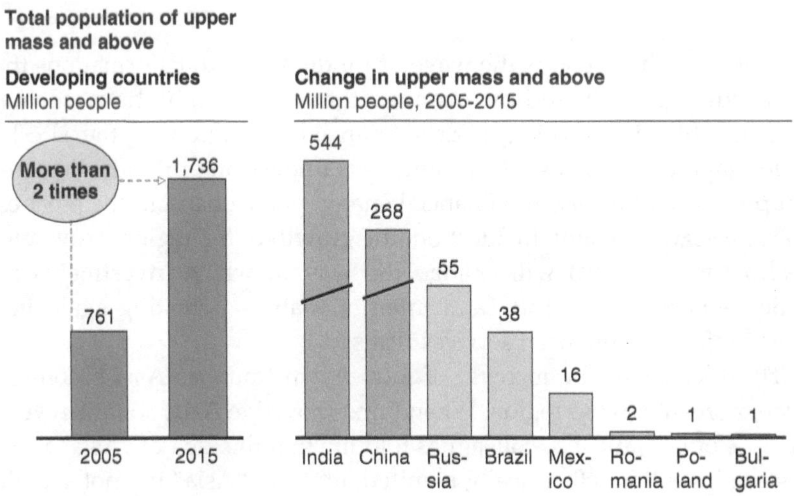

The proportion of *Fortune Global 1000* corporations located in Asia will increase from about 18 per cent in 2004 to about 30 per cent 2010. Most of those leading companies had, in the past, been based in Japan — but now Chinese, Indian and Korean champions are entering the scene.

RISE OF ASIAN GLOBAL CHAMPIONS
US$ Billions

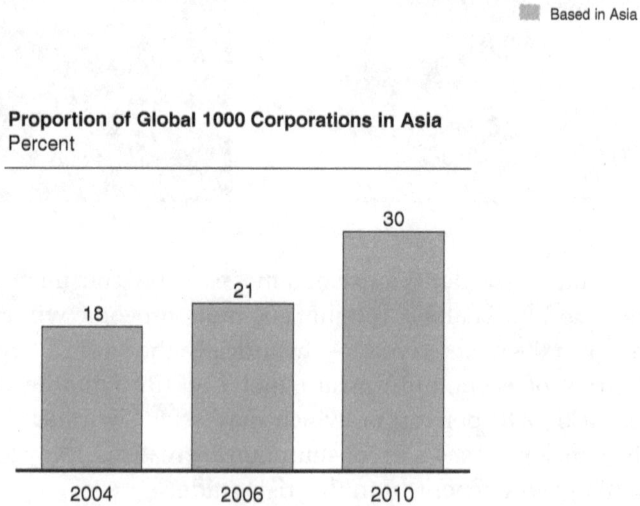

Source: Datastream, Bloomberg

Linked to that trend is the wave of fundamental transformations that are occurring — including changes that once might have seemed inconceivable. The world's largest financial institution — the US$2.7-trillion Japanese postal savings bank — is undergoing privatization, and that process will release the financial energy of a tsunami in the Japanese financial services sector. In addition, the growth of the region's sovereign wealth funds (SWFs) will change the way in which investments are made — both domestically and internationally — creating again new opportunities for financial services firms.

Third, consider the increase of intra-Asian trade, as Asia becomes a much more integrated region. When I first moved to Asia, about ten years ago, one of my Japanese colleagues told me that the idea of "Asia" was a Western invention. Historically, a united, uniform "Asia" has not actually existed, in terms of geography or culture or governance. Yet today Asia is indeed becoming much more closely integrated.

For example, the amount of trade within Asia dwarfs the amount of trade that Asia conducts beyond the region — and intra-Asia trade is increasing at a far faster rate than the region's trade beyond Asia (though much of that is destined for trade outside the region). In terms of financial service centres, intra-Asian linkages are becoming ever more important: It's not merely ensuring the centres' links to the traditional global hubs of New York and London, but creating and strengthening their relationships to other cities within Asia. There will surely be room, I believe, for a number of international financial centres in Asia, with each centre playing a different set of specialized roles.

3 INCREASING INTRA-ASIA TRADE
USD billions

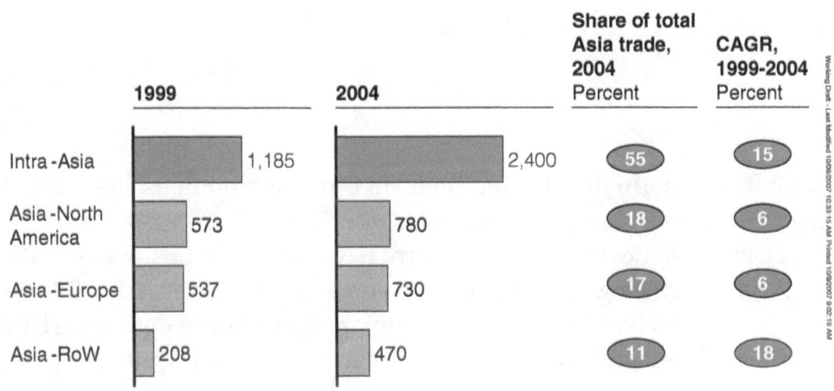

Fourth, consider how these forces have led to the re-emergence of the historic Silk Road — the trade route that, as far back as the twelfth century, linked the great trading centres of Asia, the Middle East and Europe. We believe that a New Silk Road has emerged. It was once the world's most significant trade route, and it is destined to be just as prominent again. The sources of so-called "petrodollars" in the Middle East, and the central banks of East Asia that have vast accumulations of

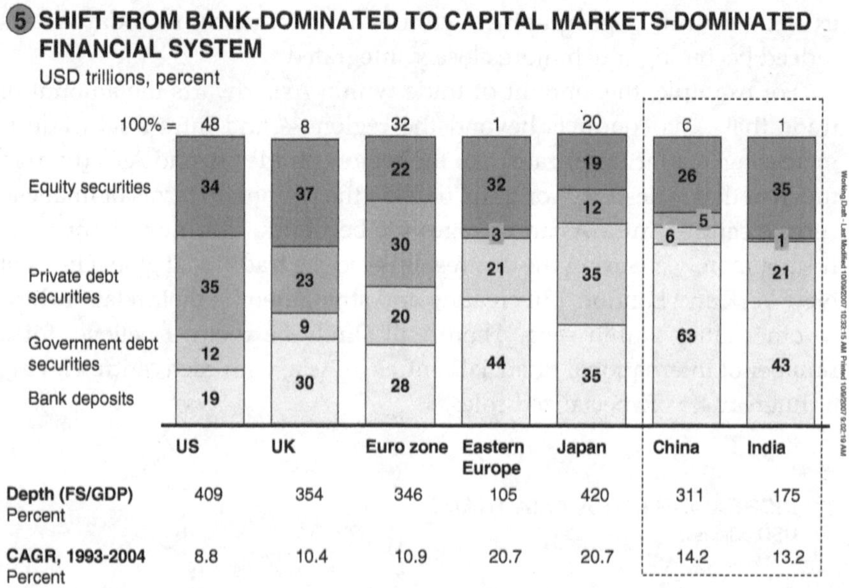

Note: Some numbers do not add to 100% due to rounding error
Source: MGI Global Financial Stock Database; Global Insight

capital, are gradually shifting their investment ambitions from Europe and the United States towards Asia.

Fifth, these developments, in turn, have spurred a positive evolution of Asia's financing and business ownership structures. The financial markets themselves have been undergoing significant change, from bank-dominated systems to more capital-markets-oriented systems. That is creating a much more fluid, more dynamic Asian market, with the opportunity for flows of capital not just on a nation-by-nation basis but on a more regionwide scale.

Coupled with this is a shift in corporate ownership structures. Compare Asia to the United States, for example. About 60 per cent of publicly traded companies in Asia are controlled by a single shareholder — typically a family group — and many of those families are going through a demographic shift.

As the older generation ages, an inter-family demographic transition is destined to occur, and the new generation of leaders will rely more on the

ASIAN FAMILY-OWNED BUSINESSES WILL FACE IMPORTANT TRANSITIONS AND CHALLENGES

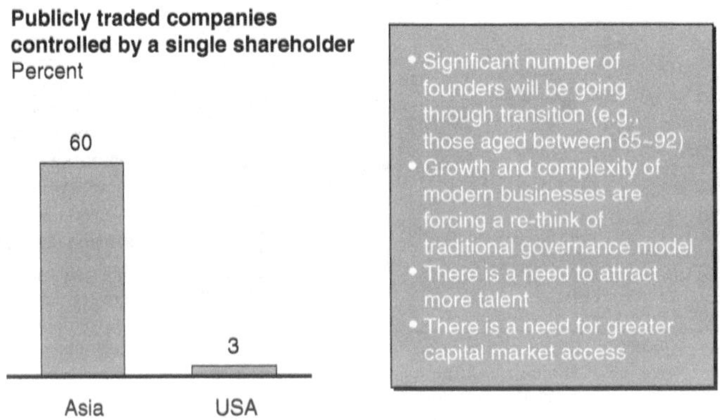

Source: Far Eastern Economic Review 8/14/03; World Bank;McKinsey analysis

capital markets than on the old banking system — particularly as those companies have grown dramatically in size and complexity, and with the global education of the new generation of leaders.

Sixth and finally, consider how these trends, taken together, have reinforced the mergers and acquisition (M&As) boom and industry consolidation. This is happening and will accelerate in every sector in Asia. This will be a huge opportunity for financial service firms — which, themselves, will experience much more consolidation. After Asia's last period of financial crisis and consolidation a decade ago, about 50 per cent of the top 500 regional financial service players dropped out of existence (merged or went bankrupt), and another 50 per cent of this list will likely drop out over the coming five to seven years.

Taken together, these trends portend changes of historic proportions for the Asian financial sector. As the huge, rapidly moving financial market has truly become global in scope, there will be a dramatically changed role for Asia. Although Asia's financial centres have, in the

6 DISCONTINUITIES FROM CONSOLIDATION ACROSS INDUSTRIES, AS WAS THE CASE IN ASIAN BANKING

Increased consolidation and market exit in Asia

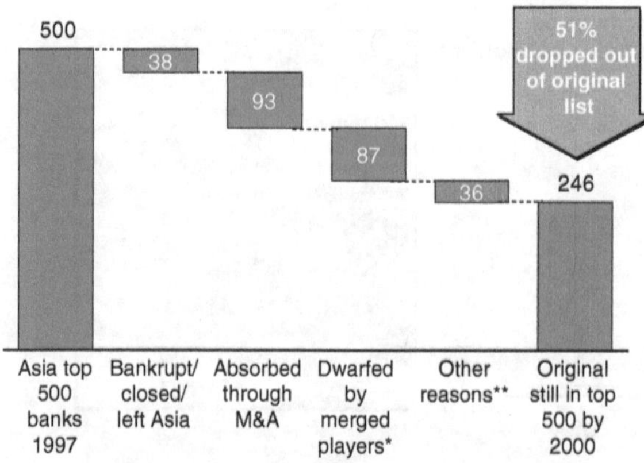

Key competitive trends

- Trends toward government bank deregulation expected to drive increased privatization and consolidation
- Foreign banks actively seeking M&A opportunities
- Privately owned market movers actively attacking assets of large state owned institutions

* Minimum asset value of USD2,235mn in 2000 compared to USD402mn in 1997
** Reclassification of entity by Bankscope to non-bank etc
Source: Bankscope

past, been a relatively small player on the global stage, the transformation of the international system means that Asia will over time see vast inflows of financial assets, as well as outflows — particularly with the sovereign wealth funds. Asia's contribution (including Japan) to the growth in financial services' profits can be conservatively expected to grow from about 15 per cent of the global total to about 25 per cent — and perhaps as much as 30 per cent, depending on the projections one makes about the economic activity among the upcoming 800 million new, middle-class, upwardly mobile consumers.

Today, three Asian banks now rank among the world's top ten, when measured by market capitalization, with Industrial and Commercial Bank of China (ICBC) now rated as the world's most valuable bank. In addition to today's powerful Chinese institutions, several Indian banks seem likely to join the list of top-ranking global financial institutions over the next five years, given their ambition and underlying growth.

These shifts in Asian banks' positions in the global rankings should give Korean institutions pause for serious reflection: Although Korean

IMPORTANCE OF ASIA IN FINANCIAL SERVICES PROFIT GROWTH WILL INCREASE DRAMATICALLY

Regional share of total banking profit growth; 2006–15; percent

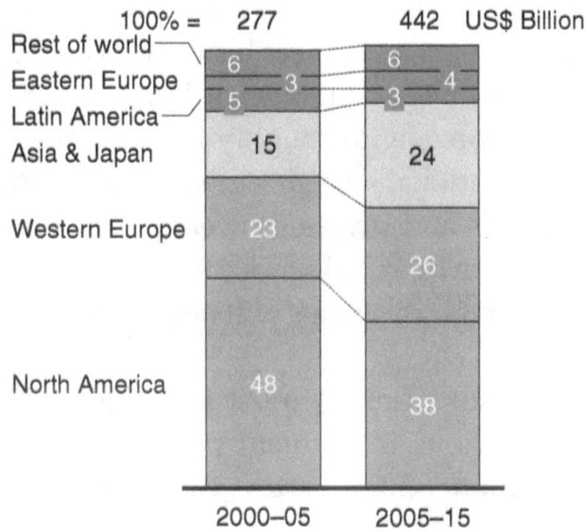

Source: McKinsey analysis

ASIAN BANKS ARE RISING AS GLOBAL PLAYERS

US$ Billions

Based in Asia

2004 Market value	
1. Citigroup	259
2. HSBC	163
3. Bank of America	118
4. Wells Fargo	97
5. RBS	89
6. UBS	86
7. JP Morgan Chase	85
8. Mitsubishi Tokyo	63
9. Wachovia	61
10. Bank One	60

3rd September, 2007 Market value	
1. Ind & Com Bank of China	283
2. Citigroup	233
3. Bank of America	225
4. HSBC	213
5. China Construction Bank	186
6. Bank of China	183
7. JP Morgan Chase	151
8. Wells Fargo	122
9. Banco Santander	114
10.Royal Bank of Scotland	110

Source: Datastream, Bloomberg

banks are fairly large on a relative basis today in Asia, they are likely to be overshadowed within the next decade unless they think carefully about their growth and acquisition strategies, particularly on a regional basis.

Underscoring the changes underway throughout the financial system, McKinsey & Company recently released a report looking at some of the system's major new players or "power brokers". The Asian central banks and the utilization and investment of their large forex reserves are going to be much more of a force, with roughly US$3.1 trillion in accumulated assets, one of the international system's greatest shifts. And these players, including pension funds and sovereign wealth funds will need guidance and strategic counsel from financial service firms, representing a substantial opportunity. Their strategic decisions will help define the financial service landscape in the region.

For example: A major decision must soon be made in China about where to locate the various investment professionals within the China Investment Corporation (CIC) — the fund that will deal with the

ASIAN CENTRAL BANKS ARE AMONG THE MOST SIGNIFICANT NEW PLAYERS IN THE GLOBAL FINANCIAL SYSTEM

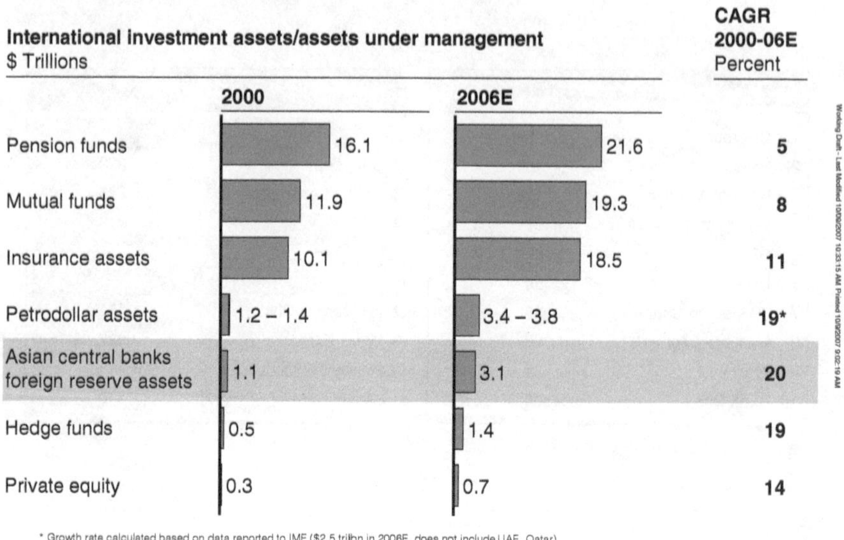

* Growth rate calculated based on data reported to IMF ($2.5 trilbn in 2006E, does not include UAE, Qatar)
Source: IMF, Ministry of Economic Affairs Taiwan, Global Insight, UBS Asian Economic Monitor, Hedge Fund Research, Venture Economics, PE Analyst, AVCJ, EMPEA, IFSL estimates based on Watson Wyatt, Bridgewell, Merrill Lynch, ICI, SwissRe, Hennessee Group data, Press, McKinsey, MGI Cross-Border Claims Database 26

foreign exchange reserves that China has amassed — perhaps as much as US$1.2 trillion eventually. The extent to which CIC bases its investment decisions in Beijing, Shanghai or Hong Kong makes a huge difference in terms of the future of each city as a financial centre.

Korea faces similar decisions. It must decide how best to leverage the many players handling significant pension fund assets.

Many issues arise from this discussion about the new Asian financial centres, and their role among the shifting global financial service landscape. Financial service leaders would be wise to consider the overarching trends that are destined to affect their entire sector. There will be more consolidation and convergence, so the size needed to rank among the top thirty players will continue to go up. There will be more dis-aggregation of the financial system, with more specialists coming in to deal with specific parts of the system. Leading firms will need ever-larger scale to do that, which means that they will need a regional footprint. Wholesale and personal financial service offerings are globalizing. Consumer needs in each market are becoming more similar, and the need for differentiation from nation to nation is no longer vital: Middle-class Koreans will increasingly seek the same products and services as their counterparts in, say, Singapore or China.

These trends have serious implications for financial centres. The rise of new global hubs is significant, because firms and individuals want to operate in one place, where they can get all of the critical mass of assets together. Dubai, for example, has literally come out of the desert and built itself as a financial centre with very strong ambitions. Mumbai, similarly, is driving forward. All aspiring financial centres must have a substantial number of foreign players in the market. Consider the experience of the United Kingdom, where "the Big Bang" of 1976 opened up the system and launched a new era of creativity in financial services. The Big Bang set an example, and other aspiring financial centres should draw a lesson from it: It does not really matter who owns the assets; the fundamental factor is that the people managing those assets must live in that centre. Governments and private sector participants must focus on overcoming that stumbling block.

Moreover, an aspiring global centre must adopt the common standards that prevail in the rest of the world's leading centres. If a nation has a different set of standards from the rest of the world, financial players simply will not do business there: They will not put up with multiple, differing regulatory regimes that impose starkly higher compliance costs and managerial burdens. That is one of the points of tension now between New York and London. To reiterate: financial centres need to move to global standards, away from local standards — and the longer that process is delayed, the further behind an aspiring centre will fall. Korea is among the players in the region that need to continue making progress in this area.

FINANCIAL CENTRE STRATEGIC MAP

International competition among would-be global financial centres has been intensifying over the past ten years. A number of cities in both Europe and Asia have launched major initiatives, supported by their governments and private sector institutions, to build their stature as financial centres. In Europe, many would-be financial service centres are trying to figure out what their relative position is by comparison with London, gauging what role they might play and what niche they might fill. Since none of them can realistically overcome London's leading role — at least in the near-term — although Frankfurt in particular tried very hard, they must seek a role that is complementary to that of London.

Some cities have "punched well above their weight" in terms of significance. For example, in Central America, Panama has great ambition to become one of the pre-eminent financial centres of South America. For every would-be financial centre worldwide, it's well worth looking at what aspiring nations are doing to position themselves as future financial-services success stories.

Aspiring financial centres can gauge their chances of success by measuring along two dimensions. First, they should consider the breadth of "the offer" they make to investors, with London and New York at one end of the spectrum. Second, they should weigh how domestic, or how global, they can be.

In the Asian context, Singapore has made dramatic strides over the past seven years. Seoul is moving as well, although the scale of its future success remains uncertain. Shanghai is also developing very fast. Five years ago, when I was speaking at a financial services conference here, I was very bullish on Shanghai taking on the role immediately. Realistically, Shanghai has not moved quite as far or as fast as I said it would: I thought it might quickly overtake Hong Kong — but Hong Kong has retained its

FINANCIAL CENTRE POSITIONING NEEDS TO BE EVALUATED

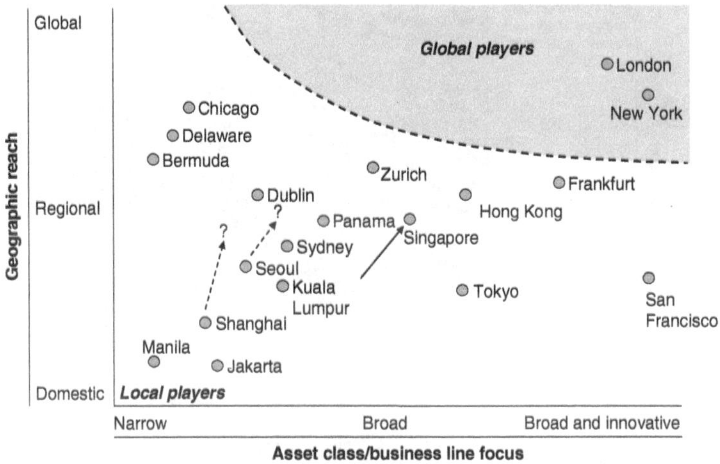

Source: McKinsey analysis

leading position. Nonetheless, I believe that Shanghai is poised to move forward again, with the right type of private–public leadership cooperation and with a critical mass of local players now located there.

In short, perhaps the essential factor working in Shanghai's favour, suggesting its success for the long term, is the size of the domestic market it serves and its rapidly concentrating group of asset managers. The banking market in China will be the second-largest in the world, in absolute size, within about seven years. With the number of institutions there in Shanghai, the city's infrastructure has, wisely, been improved significantly — and the local focus on quality-of-life concerns for expatriate executives has been intensified, as well. One of the major issues that Shanghai will face is whether foreign law firms will be permitted to play a significant role. Given the city's history and heritage — Shanghai, after all, was a major financial centre about seventy years ago, when the city gave birth to such firms as HSBC and AIG — the city's ambition to remain a major financial centre seems likely to be fulfilled.

FINANCIAL CENTRES MUST CHOOSE HOW BEST TO POSITION THEMSELVES FOR SUCCESS

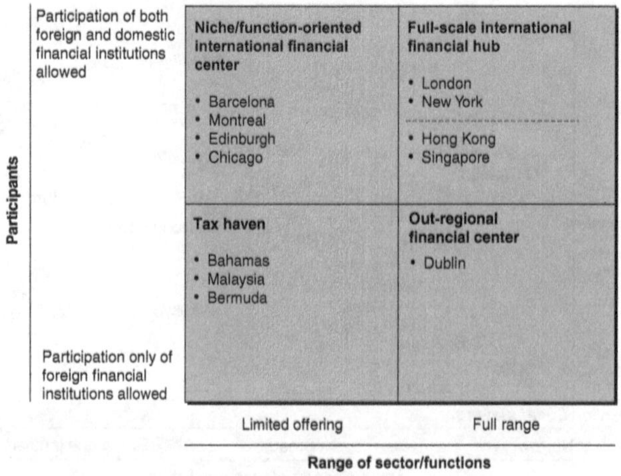

Source: "The Money Market and Its Institutions," 1955, Marcus Nadler et al., International Journal of Bank Marketing, Vol. 9; No. 5; 1991; Michael A. Goldberg,The Economist, June 27, 1992, "What Makes a Successful International Financial Center; Banking World; Vol. 11; No. 6, June 1993; McKinsey analysis

An additional question that aspiring financial centres might ask themselves is this: To what extent do you have a special zone for only foreign players, where you can open up the market to multiple players? This involves favourable tax treatment. In Dublin, for example, there are many back-office processing centres. There are, after all, many different types of financial centres. New York and London may have a wide lead over the rest of the world's financial centres, yet there are many niche players — for example, in areas such as derivatives, offshore tax havens, in asset management or in private banking. Each aspiring financial centre can seek to fill a particular role — and that is especially true for Asia, where there are many market niches still to be filled.

KEY SUCCESS CRITERIA

It is interesting to note that in the City of London financial-centres index (2007), four of the top ten institutions are in Asia. That number could increase over the next five to seven years, as Asia increases its role in the system.

There are several specific key factors to consider, as a would-be financial centre gauges its potential for success, including intrinsic factors like time zone, geography and underlying size of market. Among the most important is the cost and the ease of doing business. It is in this area that New York and London continue to manoeuvre to find an advantage over the other.

One other often overlooked but important factor is the attractiveness of the place to live. Financial professionals want to locate in a city that is environmentally livable, fun, intellectually stimulating and family-friendly. The City of London Global Financial Centres index, alongside a McKinsey survey of about 1,000 top global financial service companies, bears this out.

This factor directly affects a top criterion for success: The availability of professional workers — which is a particular challenge in many parts of Asia. The so-called "war for talent" is especially intense in financial services. Looking to the future, Chinese corporations will face a shortage of about 70,000 leaders. Ensuring the availability of highly skilled talent thus ranks alongside such factors as a fair and predictable legal environment and a responsive regulatory environment as absolutely critical.

Any city with ambitions to become a financial centre would be wise to look at New York and London — and at the healthy competition and rivalry between them. A major effort was launched last year when Mayor Bloomberg, Senator Schumer, and others realized that New York was beginning to decline relative to London. Although New York has many advantages over London — in terms of the depth and liquidity of the capital markets, as well as in its infrastructure — there were major legal and regulatory concerns that seemed to be making London relatively more business-friendly.

IMPLICATIONS FOR CITIES IN ASIA

A financial centre's strategy for success includes having a clear vision of what it wants to become and what deliberate process it will take to get there. In addition, these strategies must be simple. The United States is now trying to take action on this front: The Americans have realized that they have lost ground to their competitors in terms of such factors as the ease of doing business. The United States is thus wisely considering major initiatives to try to recapture its onetime advantages.

FOUR OF THE WORLD'S TOP TEN IFCs ARE BASED IN ASIA (1/2)

■ In Asia

Rank	Cities	Key features
1	**London**	• Most criteria are rated excellent – London is in the top quartile in over 80% of its instrumental factors. Especially strong on people, market access, and regulation. The main negative comments concern corporate tax rates, transport infrastructure, and operational costs
2	**New York**	• Most areas are very strong – New York is also in the top quartile in over 80% of its instrumental factors. People and market access are particular strengths. Respondents cited regulation (particularly Sarbanes-Oxley) as the main negative factor
3	**Hong Kong**	• Hong Kong is a thriving regional center. It performs well in all of the key competitive areas, especially in regulation. Headline costs are high but this does not detract from overall competitiveness. Hong Kong is a real contender to become a genuinely global financial center
4	**Singapore**	• Most areas are very good and banking regulation is often cited as being excellent. Has made major move on asset management and private banking. It performs well in 4 of the key competitive areas but falls to 9th place on general competitiveness factors alone. The 2nd Asian center just behind Hong Kong
5	**Zurich**	• A very strong niche center. Private banking and asset management provide a focus. Zurich performs well in 3 of the key competitiveness areas, but loses out slightly in people factors and in general competitiveness

Source: The City of London's Global Financial Centers Index

FOUR OF THE WORLD'S TOP TEN IFCs ARE BASED IN ASIA (2/2)

■ In Asia

Rank	Cities	Key features
6	**• Frankfurt**	• Despite a strong banking focus, suffers from inflexible labor laws and skilled staff shortages. Market access, infrastructure, and business environment are strong, but Frankfurt falls outside the Top 10 GFCI rankings for people and general competitiveness. Has seen gains through derivative specialization
7	**• Sydney**	• A strong national center with good regulation, offering a particularly good quality of life. Sydney is strong in 4 of the key competitive areas, but falls outside the Top 10 for people – many financial professionals leave for larger English-speaking centers
8	**• Chicago**	• Number 2 center in the U.S. Hampered by the same regulatory regime as New York. It scores highly for people, but is let down by its infrastructure and market access rankings. Unlikely to overtake New York, it remains a powerful regional and specialist center
9	**• Tokyo**	• Does not fare well in terms of regulation and business environment, but the size of the Japanese economy means Tokyo has good liquidity. It fares poorly on people but has good infrastructure and market access
10	**• Geneva**	• A strong niche center similar to Zurich. Private banking and asset management continues to thrive. Geneva is strong in business environment and general competitiveness, but is let down by infrastructure

Source: The City of London's Global Financial Centers Index

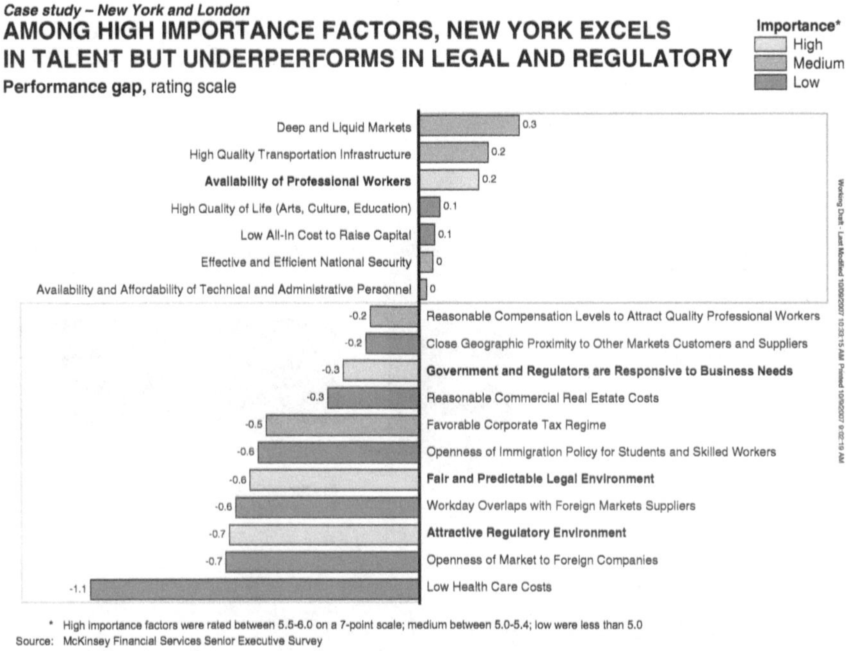

Let me highlight the case of Singapore in this regard, and its success in strengthening its position as a leading financial centre. Maintaining a business-friendly environment remains an essential factor.

Notably, Singapore achieved the needed change as a public-sector/private-sector partnership — with private-sector working groups set up in seven key areas to solicit a wide range of viewpoints. That signalled that the government wanted the private sector to come up with ideas to try to make Singapore more of a financial centre. Once those ideas were evaluated, the government moved more to the regulatory front and examined the various actors that needed to change. The government again invited private-sector market participants — it also sought input from people in other regulatory environments, such as experts from the Bank of England and from the U.S. Federal Reserve.

Many of Singapore's reform initiatives focused on adjusting its regulatory approach and on the liberalization of its financial-related services. It had been a highly controversial issue, for example, for foreign law firms to play a role in Singapore — yet this field was opened up.

Case study – New York and London

LONDON IS SEEN AS HAVING A MUCH BETTER LEGAL ENVIRONMENT, ESPECIALLY AS IT RELATES TO PROPENSITY TOWARD LEGAL ACTION

Ranking by response, percent

Which legal environment is more business-friendly?

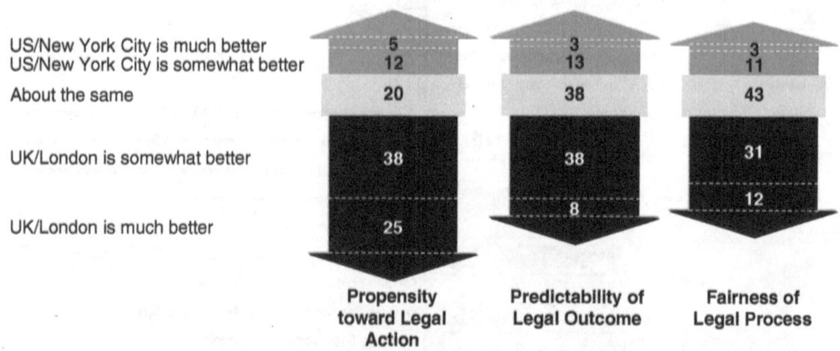

Source: McKinsey Financial Services Senior Executive Survey

Case study – New York and London

UK IS PREFERRED ACROSS MANY REGULATORY DIMENSIONS BUT IS MOST DISTINGUISHED IN COST AND SIMPLICITY OF REGULATIONS

Ranking by response, percent

Which regulatory environment is more business-friendly?

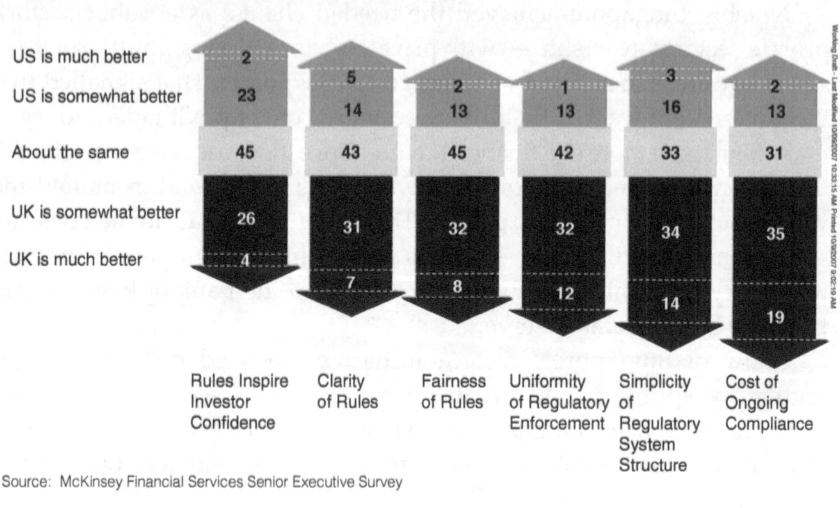

Source: McKinsey Financial Services Senior Executive Survey

Case study – Singapore

FROM 1998-1999, SINGAPORE DEVELOPED ITS FINANCIAL CENTRE STRATEGY THROUGH A JOINT PUBLIC-PRIVATE PARTNERSHIP

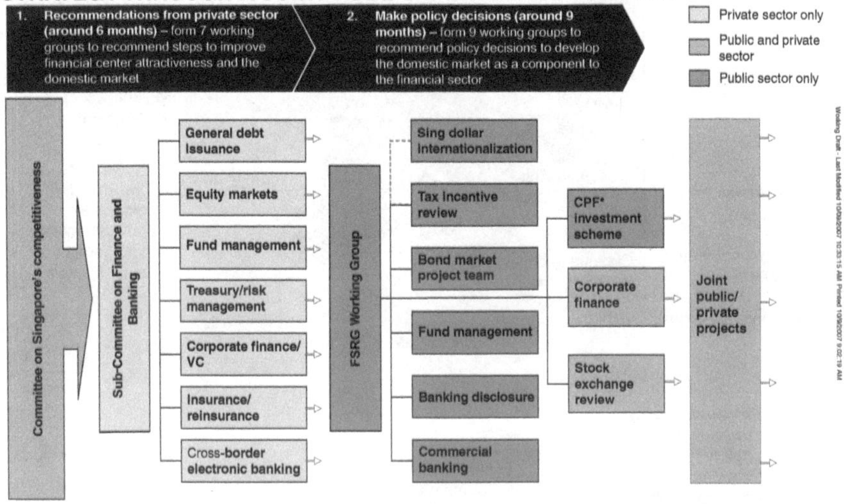

* Central Provident Fund – public, fully funded pension scheme mandatory for all Singaporeans

Securities dealers were allowed to use more foreign and expatriate talent. Local asset management companies opened up their assets to foreign advisers. At about the same time, GIC — the government investment corporation of Singapore — was opening up significantly, allowing some proportion of its assets to be managed by foreigners. By making Singapore more attractive to highly skilled asset managers, Singapore helped secure its position as a financial centre — as a player that allowed for top-quality advice. That spirit of openness to talent of all nationalities is a factor that all aspiring financial centres should reflect on.

The case of Singapore also underscores the role of financial flexibility and the role of innovation. For example, ten years ago there was no significant debt market in Singapore. Sceptics often asked: Why would you want a debt market in Singapore, when the government there habitually ran a surplus rather than a deficit? Yet Singapore needed to have a mechanism that set a long-term yield curve, to allow other financial instruments to work. In meeting the need to create a debt market, Singapore

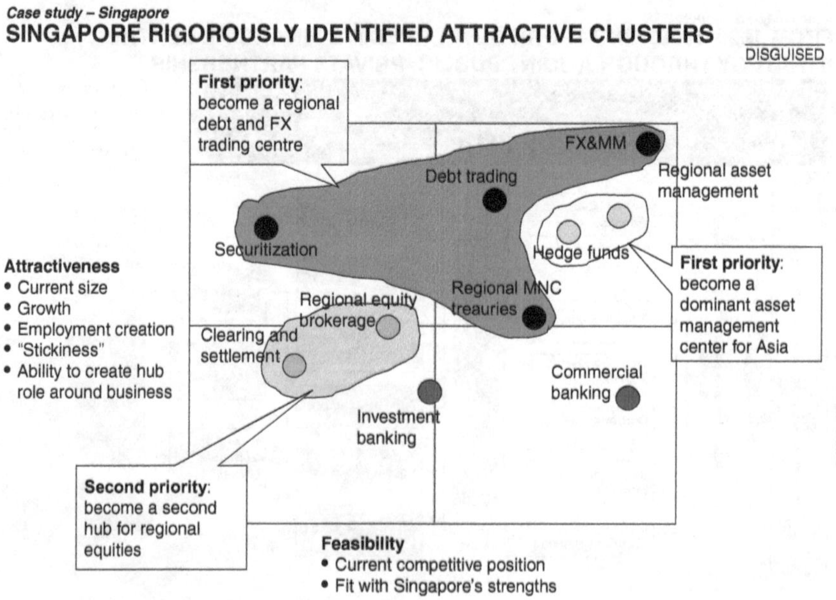

broke a lot of orthodoxies, and it was finally able to push through this innovation. It required a well-planned and coherent effort, but the initiative was, over time, successful in moving Singapore's market forward.

As we envision the future of Asian financial centres, there seems to be room for at least three, probably more, major centres in the region, given the growing size of the region's market. But to be successful, would-be financial centres need to have very specific aspirations about their role and their potential market share in such areas as debt markets, equity markets and asset management. Aspiring financial centres need to be specific about their market-share goals — much like a corporation — in order to move forward.

Looking at the factors that determine the success or failure of a would-be financial centre in Asia, I suggest that there are seven key criteria:

- First, a financial centre must have alignment with its national government, whose regulatory and compliance framework is critical. Outside of Hong Kong and Singapore, there has not been much progress here.

Case study – Singapore

SINGAPORE MOVED FAST TOWARDS INTERNATIONAL STANDARDS FOR OVERALL "MARKET INFRASTRUCTURE"

	From	To
1. **Supervisory and regulatory approach**	• Policy makers focused on regulation of individual components • Performance based regulation • Ad hoc national system	• Policy makers focused on market supervision and development in collaboration with market players • Reliant on self-regulated organizations and other market associations • Disclosure based regulation • Global standards
2. **Legal framework and support**	• Ill-defined legal framework • Lack of lawyers	• Conducive legal framework defined in close collaboration with market players and leveraging foreign country experience • Domestic and foreign law firms supporting market development
3. **Transparency and information**	• Ad hoc national accounting rules • Sketchy unreliable issuer information • Few rated issuers • Information asymmetry in the secondary market	• International GAAP • Standardized issuer information in line with international accounting standards • Majority of issuers seeking rating firm internationally recognized agency • Full transparency on price and volume information
4. **Market mechanisms**	• Ad hoc country specific mechanisms	• Market mechanisms in line with international practices and domestic characteristics
5. **Settlement and clearing**	• Lack of reliable electronic infrastructure	• Scripless markets • Settlement and clearing in line with international standards – e.g., Group of 30

Benefits of early adoption of global standards

- Implement capital markets reforms faster
- Ensure international credibility
- Avoid trial and error that could be harmful to the real economy and the financial system

Source: Interviews; McKinsey analysis

Case study – Singapore

SINGAPORE'S PUBLIC ACTIONS IN THE FIRST 18 MONTHS OF IMPLEMENTATION

Debt markets

SGS market	• Issue a 10-year instrument • Step up issuance level • Implement regular auction calendar • Appoint one more primary dealer • Appoint SGS brokers • Open Repo market to non resident investors
Corporate debt market	• Get government-linked companies to issue for funding • Organize seminar with large corporate CFOs
Securitization	• Review regulatory, legal and fiscal framework • Build information infrastructure for the primary mortgage market • Support private sector through MAS on a deal by deal basis
International S$ market	• Open S$ bond market to international issuers on a swap basis • Allow Singapore issuers to tap S$ bond market to fund projects abroad • Supranational aggressively tapping the market
"Infrastructure"	• Gradually shift to fully scripless market • Move to international standard of disclosure

Source: Lit search

- Second, a financial centre must have a smooth-functioning public-private understanding and sense of collaboration. Private-sector players must do as much as they can, and they must work in harmony with public-sector regulators. In Korea, there are questions about whether the private-sector players are doing everything they can — an issue worth debating. Without the combination, very little can happen.
- Third, there must be a clear financial sector vision and strategy.
- Fourth, having senior government leadership that is capable of driving that vision and strategy is crucial. It is not sufficient to approach this on an *ad-hoc* basis, or to delegate this function to someone in the Ministry of Finance on a part-time basis. In Singapore the person who did this, who led this, is the current prime minister: He took on the challenge personally. Similarly, in Dubai, Sheik Mohammed Bin Rashid Al Maktoum drove the programme; and in New York, Mayor Bloomberg made sure there was very clear accountability.
- Fifth, adopting global standards. An aspiring financial centre must decide how it will move toward and adopt global standards — there is no alternative.
- Sixth, the ability to adapt and move. Global markets will continue to adapt, and any financial centre must be flexible enough to adapt along with them. Even a city as financially sophisticated as New York has had to re-evaluate its structures and processes, in order to keep up with the continuing threat to its pre-eminence posed by London. Interestingly, at the same time that the two cities are competing, they are engaged in a joint effort to improve both cities' roles as financial centres. They are both competing and cooperating — offering a good model for Asia, and other regions, by signalling that each financial centre does not have to look at each of its rivals necessarily only as a competitor.
- Seventh, the living environment and infrastructure. It bears repeating: This factor, over time, can prove to be crucial.

* * *

Asia's influence in global financial markets is destined to grow, and Asia's leading financial centres now seem poised to take their place on the global stage. Over the next ten years, Asia's prominence as a source of capital and as a destination for investment will grow quickly and present huge opportunities. There is no magic to success: If the leadership of both the public and private sectors in Asia exert determined effort and take far-sighted action, they can help ensure that Asia's financial centres will capitalize on the region's strong prospects for success.

CRITICAL FACTORS TO CONSIDER (1/3)

Today
Tomorrow

1. Capital. How attractive and welcoming is the capital and financial environment, including free flows, domestic and international?

Unattractive — Highly attractive

2. Ease of doing business. How easy is it to conduct business (incorporation, licensing, market conduct, competitiveness, M&A)?

Difficult — Very easy

3. Cost efficiency. How efficient is it to conduct business and is there a cost advantage?

Inefficient — Very efficient

4. Wiring. Are we adequately wired into the global financial system (culture, trade, infrastructure, location)?

Not wired — Highly wired

CRITICAL FACTORS TO CONSIDER (2/3)

Today
Tomorrow

5. Legal. How predictable balanced, and certain is the legal environment (contracts, rights, administration, adjudication)?

Unpredictable — Very predictable

6. Regulation. How attractive, effective, and efficient is financial regulation (principles-based, transparent, fairness, cost)?

Unattractive — Very attractive

7. Supervision. How effective and prudential is financial supervision (constructive engagement, prompt corrective action, enforcement)?

Ineffective — Very effective

CRITICAL FACTORS TO CONSIDER (3/3)

	Today / Tomorrow	
8. Tax. How attractive is the corporate and individual tax environment?	Not attractive	Very attractive
9. Skills. Are the necessary professional and technical skills readily available and easily acquired (education, immigration, employment laws)	Unavailable	Very available
10. Leadership. Is the necessary leadership available (private sector, public sector, public-private partnership)?	Unavailable	Readily available

PART I

Overview and Policy Recommendations

1

COMPETITION AMONG FINANCIAL CENTRES IN ASIA-PACIFIC
Prospects, Benefits, Risks and Policy Challenges

Dosoung Choi, Jesús Seade, Sayuri Shirai and Soogil Young

1. INTRODUCTION

More than several cities and countries in Asia and the Pacific region are striving to become financial centres where financial institutions, investors, corporations, legal and accounting service providers, and many other types of financial market participants interact to help capital flows move to and from the centre. When the centre is used by international participants, it is an international financial centre (IFC henceforth). Hong Kong and Singapore have had early starts in the competition. Tokyo used to be the front-runner but, while still having the largest market capitalization in the region, as an international centre it fell behind during the past decade. Late-starter cities like Sydney, Seoul, and Shanghai are making efforts to catch up with the front-runners.

Many of the IFC aspirants in the Asia-Pacific region have been making a good deal of progress during the past few years. The national and metropolitan authorities for those cities have launched ambitious programmes to achieve this objective. Indeed, there is quite active competition among the cities to become the most competitive IFC in the region through one measure or another. The competition is real and fierce. While there are opinions that such competition may be harmful because, among other reasons, there will presumably be duplication of efforts and over-investment of resources, it is also argued that such competition will enhance the efficiency of the financial industry in the region, which will be beneficial both to the host economies concerned and to the region as a whole. It will be both interesting and meaningful to review and evaluate the efforts being made by the respective financial centres and examine the issues these efforts when considered together pose for the future of the individual centres and for the governments in Asia-Pacific.

The primary concern in this project was to see what these ambitions and policy drives being pursued by the individual financial centres in the region will add up to in the end. Which ones among the competing financial centres are likely to be the winners? If they cannot all become successful international financial centres, what would this mean for the unsuccessful ones and their economies? What are the risks posed by the competition, which can be excessive, with deregulation? For example, will the risk of financial instabilities be increased as a result? Is the competition a beneficial development for the region as a whole? Would the competition facilitate the emergence of an Asia-Pacific financial community with the individual financial centres thus serving as building blocks toward this community by helping the financial industry of the region become more efficient and the financial markets better integrated? Or would the financial centres serve as stumbling blocks toward a regional financial community by thwarting regional financial integration through beggar-thy-neighbour competition? What are the policy implications for the financial institutions and national governments in the region, including those for regional cooperation? These are the issues to be explored in this report.

The substantive analysis will begin, in Section 2, with a summary review of the case studies done on seven selected financial centres in the region — Tokyo, Seoul, Shanghai, Hong Kong, Singapore, Sydney, and Wellington, examining and comparing their visions, strategies, and roadmaps. Detailed and comprehensive case studies of those cities as would-be financial centres will be found in this volume. Each case study will be concluded with a SWOTs analysis, considering strengths, weaknesses, opportunities and threats facing the financial centre in question. This analysis will be followed, in Section 3, by a comparative assessment of the international competitiveness of the individual financial centres by each of its five determinants, establishing in the minds of the reader the probable landscape of the international financial centres in Asia-Pacific in the long term.

In Section 4, the central issue of the volume is addressed: What are the benefits, risks, and challenges from the Asia-Pacific region's perspective of the international financial centre competition. Section 5 concludes with policy recommendations for regional cooperation. The goal for such cooperation in all those recommendations will be to connect all regional financial centres and integrate them into an Asia-Pacific network of international financial centres.

2. IFCS IN ASIA-PACIFIC: STRATEGIES AND SWOTS

For a decade or more, cities and countries in the Asia-Pacific region have been making various efforts to become international financial centres. An IFC can be defined as a city or country to and from which international financial flows move so that financial resources tend to converge towards that centre. As major participants in the international financial markets, IFCs host a significant number of international banks, securities firms, and other affiliated firms. Some in Asia, such as Hong Kong and Singapore, have already made substantial progress towards becoming global IFCs, while others are pressing hard to become viable competitors.

As global IFCs, London and New York City are attracting not only financial flows but human resources with advanced knowledge and skills. These cities have evolved into IFCs over more than a century as a result of the voluntary gathering of businesses, commerce, trade, insurance, finance, and banking institutions. Geographical proximity to the centres of trade and commerce is essential to garner mutual benefits and sustain growth. Contrarily, most of the IFCs in Asia and the Pacific have been launched and are driven by the governments. This is because IFC development is expected to make the domestic financial industry more efficient, and this industry is a high value-added industry with huge growth potential, offering many high income employment opportunities.

According to the first issue of the Global Financial Centres Index (GFCI, hereafter) published in early 2007 by the City of London Corporation, among the forty-eight financial centres in the world, nine are in Asia-Pacific. Hong Kong and Singapore are the front-runners with several others following although at significant distances. By means of case studies, this section examines and evaluates their respective IFC development strategies, their strengths, weaknesses, opportunities, and threats (SWOTs). Constrained by time and research resources available, the following seven cities were selected for the case studies. They are, in order of the GFCI ranking, Hong Kong, Singapore, Tokyo, Sydney, Shanghai, Wellington, and Seoul.

2.1. Hong Kong[1]

Hong Kong, while a former British colony, always had a dual identity of trade and financial centre: Serving as a gateway to China as well as an important international entrepot in the region. With the Communist revolution in the 1940s, financial companies and human capital based in Shanghai moved to Hong Kong thereby naturally increasing the latter's role as a financial centre.

Hong Kong has experienced missed opportunities and crises over the past century, such as the failure to launch the Asian dollar market and a banking crisis in 1965. These experiences have served as a catalyst for advancement in financial regulation and infrastructure. Gradually, through the development of the financial industry and related services industries, increasing involvement of foreign banks, low finance-related taxes, and regulatory system reform, Hong Kong is continually maturing into an IFC.

It has been ten years since Hong Kong was restored to China. Invigorated by China's economic growth, Hong Kong serves to connect China and Taiwan to the international financial markets. Chinese companies make up half the aggregate value of the listed stock in the Hong Kong securities market (US$40 billion in 2006) and the number of initial public offerings (IPOs) and mergers and acquisitions (M&As) taking place therein have increased rapidly.

Second only to Tokyo in overall size as a financial centre, Hong Kong has established a leading position in Asia as an IFC. Seventy-three among the top 100 investment banks make their Asian regional headquarters in Hong Kong, intermediating between fund suppliers and users. Also, Hong Kong has some of the world's finest hard and soft infrastructure established. The City of London's GFCI, published twice annually since 2007, consistently placed Hong Kong third in its global list of leading IFCs for three times up to early 2008, behind London and New York and just ahead of Singapore.

Hong Kong's position as an IFC is largely based on its major role as a gateway to China however, lagging much behind the two global market leaders. Its aspiration is, therefore, to leap forward and join the ranks of London and New York as a global financial centre. In order to achieve this, Hong Kong is currently focusing on high value-added financial transactions, such as private banking, as well as on the development of the infrastructure necessary for further economic integration with the mainland. It is also is making efforts to address its problem of air pollution as well as to attract Islamic funds by reforming laws, taxation, and regulatory policies.

Hong Kong's strengths, weaknesses, opportunities, and threats in becoming a global/regional IFC are summarized in Table 1.1.

Table 1.1
SWOTs of Hong Kong as an IFC

Strengths
• High level of transparency of the government and its policies • Political and social stability • Equitable treatment of foreigners • Foreign exchange stability and abundant liquidity • Superb financial infrastructure • Minimal interference by financial supervisory/regulatory authority • Predictable legal environment • Workforce with good financial expertise and international experiences • English-speaking population • Regional headquarters for many global financial institutions, including investment banks
Weaknesses
• Limited local market size • Serious air pollution
Opportunities
• Physical proximity with China, which is becoming increasingly more influential in the world economy • The role of a bridge connecting foreign companies to the investors in mainland China
Threats
• Competition with Shanghai as a financial centre

2.2. Singapore[2]

After launching the Asian dollar market, Singapore has experienced a dramatic increase of international financial transactions in foreign exchange and now provides some of Asia's best intermediation for international banking. Since the 1960s, the government of Singapore has strategically cultivated its financial industry to make it internationally competitive. For this purpose, the government eased tax burdens and regulatory constraints and accelerated the open-door policies for onshore as well as offshore investors and corporations. The Monetary Authority of Singapore (MAS), the supervisory agency providing integrated regulation, was established to pursue efficient regulation and supervision in order to promote sound and competitive financial markets.

The financial centre policy of Singapore's government has been quite successful. Still, there are some dimensions that need further improvement. The opening of the financial market has been progressing in phases. This is because over 60 per cent of its financial services customers are offshore clients, thus leaving Singapore highly vulnerable to the economic shocks from abroad. As a result, Singapore still has some restrictions with respect to the use of Singapore dollars in the offshore markets.

Shaken by the Asian financial crisis and threatened by China's aggressive move to attract foreign investment, the Singapore government has launched a new plan for the development and strengthening of its financial sector.[3] Singapore is now emerging as an asset management and private banking hub in Asia, thanks to the government's IFC strategy. Singapore experienced a rapid increase in assets under management (AUM) following the government's measure that standardizes the procedure to establish a foreign asset management firm (including hedge funds). It also saw a quick increase of offshore investor funds due to tax benefits for offshore investors.

Singapore is firmly establishing itself as the leading IFC in Asia as it begins to build an international financial gateway for the quickly rising markets in India and the Middle East countries. As India does not yet have mature financial markets, global investors tend to pass through Singapore. Furthermore, countries in the Middle East with abundant oil money prefer to manage their money in Singapore because it is geographically close and politically stable. Many Muslims in the population will help Singapore be an IFC for Islamic banking as well. Recently, the Monetary Authority of Singapore (MAS) became a full member of the Islamic Financial Services Board (IFSB) and will contribute to its Supervisory Review Process.

Furthermore, free trade agreements (FTAs) with a growing number of countries in the Middle East can give Singapore another competitive advantage.

It is noteworthy that in the GFCI 4 published in September 2008, Singapore moved up in its ranking from fourth to third, overtaking Hong Kong. Singapore's strengths, weaknesses, opportunities, and threats in becoming a global IFC are summarized in Table 1.2.

Table 1.2
SWOTs of Singapore as an IFC

Strengths

- Political stability and efficient government
- Strong and effective government leadership
- Transparency and efficiency in laws, regulations, and their enforcement
- Low taxes and business friendly regulations
- Excellent living environment for foreigners in terms of education and medical services
- English-speaking population
- Workforce with financial expertise and international experience
- Simple and easy procedures in raising capital
- Abundant liquidity available in the financial markets
- Market stability maintained by efficient financial supervision
- Efforts to attract foreign human capital

Weaknesses

- Small domestic economic base
- Relatively small capital market size
- Restrictions on the use of Singapore dollar in cross-border capital movements

Opportunities

- Benefits from India's economic boom
- Due to strict EU policies against tax avoidance, large investors are moving their funds from Europe to Singapore
- 17 per cent of Singaporeans are Muslims, opening doors to Islamic banking
- FTA discussions with countries in the Middle East

Threats

- Shallow first-mover advantages while other countries (for example, Australia and Korea) mimic Singapore's strategy to gain competitiveness.
- Asset management companies may move to locations where the capital supply from pension funds is rapidly growing (for example, Korea's National Pension and Sydney's Superannuation)

2.3. Tokyo[4]

Induced by its rapid economic growth in the 1960s and 1970s with its trade balance in surplus, the development of yen denominated bonds (*samurai* bonds), and a fast growing stock market, Tokyo rapidly grew into a world-class IFC alongside New York and London. But by the 1990s, the Japan's historical eminence was lost as the Japanese stock market collapsed, the real estate bubble burst, and the competitiveness of Japanese financial firms deteriorated. In terms of economic power and the strength of the yen, Japan's domestic financial market size is comparable to that of London and New York. In terms of cross-border transactions, however, Japan falls behind significantly.

Recognizing that the nation's financial industry was deteriorating, the Japanese government in 1996 set about reforms called the Japanese Big Bang which promoted "free, fair and global" as its banner. But despite attempts to internationalize the stock and bond markets through the Big Bang, the results were rather dismal. Progress and change were only gradual. Japanese investors are conservative: Individual investors prefer to keep more than 50 per cent of their funds in banks while institutional investors prefer bonds to stocks in their asset management portfolios. The percentage of foreign investors in the Tokyo Stock Exchange peaked at 28 per cent in 2006 and declined to 27.6 per cent as of March 2008. Considering its size, the largest in Asia and once even larger than the New York Stock Exchange, the percentage of global investors seems low. The bond market is even worse with only about 5 per cent of the investors being foreign. The bond market in Japan is largely domestic, and nearly 90 per cent of issues are centred on government bonds. Corporations raise funds through banks, contributing to the mediocrity of the corporate bond market. Additionally, the size of the *samurai* bond market has also been declining lately.

Recognizing the severity of the problem, especially with a rapidly aging society, the Japanese government was compelled to try to revitalize the financial markets and industry, to regain the IFC status it was once a prime candidate for. In 2006, the government introduced the Financial Instruments and Exchange Law (passed in June 2006, taking effect in September 2007) by amending and consolidating the existing Securities and Exchange Law and other financial laws with the aim to protect investors by requiring listed firms to file quarterly information disclosure and internal control reports, covering a wide range of financial products and services under the same regulation; differentiating between professional (wholesale) and general (retail) investors with respect to user protection; and implementing strict counter measures against unfair trading. The Bill for Amendment of the Financial Instruments and Exchange Law, which would allow the establishment of new exchange markets (which would allow exemptions from current disclosure requirements, instead being subject to the rules set by exchanges) exclusively for professional investors, passed in the Diet in June 2008. The bill would also allow diversification of FTFs and revamp the firewall regulations among securities firms, commercial banks, and insurance firms. This move is a promising step toward developing more efficient, attractive, and fair financial and capital markets.

The above moves were reflected on the new initiatives announced by the Financial Supervisory Administration (FSA) in December 2007. The new deregulation effort includes plans to: (1) vitalize the capital markets (through an increase in diverse exchange traded products, the review of securities taxes, strengthening of the self-regulatory operations by exchanges, and the creation of a market for professional investors); (2) improve business environment (through the deregulation of firewalls and a better management system to cope with the conflicts of interest arising from the removal); (3) introduce a better regulatory environment (through the emphasis of principle-based regulation, improvement of staff supervisory capacities, and greater collaboration with foreign exchanges); and (4) increase financial professionals and improve urban infrastructure. These initiatives are to establish Tokyo as a global IFC that attracts more foreign investors and capital and, at the same time, can serve as the fundraising market for foreign corporations.

Tokyo's strengths, weaknesses, opportunities, and threats in becoming a global/regional IFC are summarized in Table 1.3.

2.4. Sydney[5]

Traditionally, Sydney developed its financial industry centred on the banking industry. However, with the establishment of the Australian retirement (superannuation) scheme in 1992, Australia now has the world's fourth largest asset management industry and has made the industry the main engine for the financial industry. With the growing amount of assets under management, Australia seeks to advance its asset management industry by employing dynamic investment schemes and innovative management styles.

Table 1.3
SWOTs of Tokyo as an IFC

Strengths

- Massive size of household financial assets of US$14 trillion (as of December 2007), the second largest in the world
- Large number of institutional investors
- The largest capital market in Asia
- Large number of viable high-technology firms that could constitute the demand base for capital
- Foreign exchange trading volume ranked the third in the world
- The Japanese yen is the most important hard currency in Asia

Weaknesses

- Lack of progress in globalizing the financial markets
- Lack of innovative and diverse financial products
- Local investors are overly conservative
- High corporate taxes and nontransparent regulatory environment
- Firewall (cross-entry) regulations between banking, securities, trusts, and insurance business
- Shortage of professionals with English proficiency

Opportunities

- Tokyo Stock Exchange signed MOU with Abu Dhabi Securities Exchange to seek possible cooperation over product development and dual listings (January 2008)
- Listing of KODEX 200 ETF (KOSPI200) on the Tokyo Stock Exchange (November 2007) and KODEX Japan ETF (TOPIX 100) on the Korea Exchange (February 2008)
- Listing Index Fund China A Shares (Panda) CIS 300 on the Tokyo Stock Exchange (April 2008)
- Ongoing cooperation between Tokyo Stock Exchange and LSE over establishment of a new Tokyo-based market for growing domestic and Asian companies in early 2009 based on LSE's successful AIM Market

Threats

- Declining investment volume of foreign investment banks with international funds being attracted to Hong Kong and Singapore
- Detrimental impact of the massive public debt (about 180 per cent of GDP) on the economy

Australia seeks a unique IFC model by becoming a financial exporter. More specifically, it wants to set Australian standards for international funds management and to invite global funds to Australia. To succeed as a financial exporter, the Australian government has been making efforts to bring forth changes in regulations and taxation schemes. In particular, regulation has been made flexible, customized to the demands for financial products and services. The new regulatory practices have raised investor trust in Australia and provided assurance for a pleasant business environment. Financial companies have also benefited from transparent taxation, fair tax benefits, and clear regulations in the Australian market.

Sydney, however, has a few major problems that it has to overcome to become a global IFC. They are the livability and access problems. While the educational environment has improved, the remuneration level for finance professionals in this country is not competitive. Sydney is a low-cost city. It may seem an advantage in attracting people, but the low living cost is a double-edged sword. It may reflect difficulties in attracting top talent to work in Sydney, thus making it difficult for Sydney to develop into a global financial centre. A lot of effort has been made to make the city business-friendly, but more work needs to be done to eliminate cumbersome regulations and the heavy tax burden. The tax rate, in particular, remains very high in comparison to their rivals.

Geographically, Australia is too far away from the international centres of business. It takes a long time for people to fly from Europe or the

Table 1.4
SWOTs of Sydney as an IFC

Strengths
• Large real economy • Dynamic and attractive domestic financial market • High quality of life and Western culture • Financial industry workforce with expertise and language proficiency • English-speaking population
Weaknesses
• Regulation regarding financial firms and funds are not yet flexible enough • Low tax benefits in comparison to other financial centres • Geographical distance from other major Asian cities
Opportunities
• Functional regulation/supervision schemes
Threats
• Asian financial centres trying to become an IFC focusing on asset management

Americas. Tax rates and compensation packages are not as attractive to top talent. What is needed is the attraction of human resources. Australia's promotional efforts have not managed to garner the reactions it was hoping from financial institutions. It appears that instead of pulling in front-line revenue-generating institutions, global companies such as JPMorgan, UBS, and Morgan Stanley have made Sydney a hub for their various back office functions.

Sydney's strengths, weaknesses, opportunities, and threats in becoming an IFC are summarized in Table 1.4.

2.5. Shanghai[6]

The Chinese government has proclaimed its intention to shape Shanghai into an international financial centre by the year 2020, and is currently establishing the necessary financial infrastructure and strategies in phases. Given the size of the domestic economy and the huge magnitude of foreign trade, the city will become a formidable IFC if developed properly. However, the IFC development has been very slow so far.

Shanghai is aspiring to be the centre of the Asia-Pacific region. It has launched initiatives to become an international economic centre, an international financial centre, an international trade centre, and a sea transportation centre. The central government has created and implemented a series of five-year action plans. As part of the Eleventh Five-year Plan (2006–10), Shanghai is aggressively increasing the market volume and the scale of financial institutions. It has already accomplished the feat of becoming a domestic financial centre.

Shanghai has tried to internationalize the financial markets during the past decade. The government opened the Shanghai securities market to both investors and issuers from foreign countries. Further deregulation is expected such that foreign government entities and international organizations can issue bonds and other debt securities in Shanghai. Foreign securities companies will be granted licences to do intermediation businesses, such as managing Chinese portfolio investment abroad. Moreover, efforts to enhance full convertibility of its currency, the renminbi (RMB), and opening the Shanghai foreign exchange trading centre to more financial institutions are underway.

China is a growing economic power as well as a super power. China has the potential to develop Shanghai into an onshore IFC like New York in the United States. Because of the sheer size of its domestic economy and the magnitude of its exports of manufactured goods, China has the potential to develop an onshore IFC. To do this, however, it must overcome many hurdles. First, it must deregulate and open its financial markets to foreign financial institutions. Second, it must build the market infrastructure, better governance, a better legal system, an accounting system, a prudential regulatory structure, just to name a few. All these things will take time to develop and become effective. However, the biggest obstacle to the IFC initiative for Shanghai is that the market mechanism has yet to function well. Government interventions and initiatives take precedent over market mechanisms. While Shanghai is focusing on hard infrastructure, the city is more in need of improvement of soft infrastructure, such as a transparent legal system and a credible culture of property rights protection.

China has set the target date for the IFC drive at 2020. This may be too slow an approach considering the fact that other IFCs are pushing very aggressively. China's seeming lack of aggressiveness on the IFC drive may be explained by two reasons. One, the Chinese have access to excellent international financial services supplied by the Hong Kong market, which is the leading regional financial market. They can buy and sell financial services through Hong Kong. Second, Chinese leaders

Table 1.5
SWOTs of Shanghai as an IFC

Strengths

- Very large economic power and abundant human resources
- Large domestic capital market
- Very good potential for continuation of high growth
- Possesses a large amount of domestic savings

Weaknesses

- Regulations hindering efficient functioning of the market mechanism
- Limited openness to foreign investment
- Slow internationalization of the capital markets
- Soft financial infrastructure development lagging behind hard infrastructure development
- Limited command of English among the local population

Opportunities

- Opening of the market to foreign firms and investors

Threats

- Competition with Hong Kong to become the champion IFC in China have apparently shifted the strategy of economic development to be more inward-looking. Having to consider social equity, regional balance, and the environment, China would find it very hard to deregulate their financial institutions. The Chinese leaders might have to rely on state-owned institutions to achieve these domestic economic policy objectives. China's slow speed with the IFC drive creates unique opportunities for the other IFC contenders in Asia. China is going to continue to be the major supplier of global savings, perhaps the largest supplier of global savings. Chinese savers will need to import many kinds of financial services in order to channel their savings to their users. In this respect, other regional IFCs in East Asia including Hong Kong will respectively have opportunities to acquire large or significant amounts of China-related businesses. Singapore, and to a lesser extent Tokyo and Seoul, may be well positioned to seize these opportunities.

Shanghai's strengths, weaknesses, opportunities, and threats in becoming a global/regional IFC are summarized in Table 1.5.

2.6. Wellington[7]

Wellington has become a candidate for an IFC because of the serious current account deficit of New Zealand. The deficit has been financed mostly by Japanese investors through the yen carry trade. New Zealand has been a chronic borrower. Its current account deficit amounts to 10 per cent of GDP, even higher than the U.S. current account deficit. The New Zealand dollar is one of the most fluctuating currencies in the world. The volatility in the value of the currency invited trading of cross-currency interest swaps and development of currency derivative products. Naturally, a big currency market has been formed to accommodate currency trading, and skills for the relevant risk management and portfolio management developed, thus making Wellington a unique financial centre specializing in high-yield bonds and currency derivatives. There is no government plan to make Wellington an IFC. Instead, it is the market that forces Wellington to serve as a financial centre.

However, if the financial centre is the place where various financial and legal services are produced, sold, and exported, like underwriting, trading, dealing, and brokerage of services across borders, it is not clear if Wellington is a regional IFC. While there is substantial cross-border activity in New Zealand, thus making Wellington a small but potent IFC by carving out a niche market for medium-term bonds that are taken up by

Japanese individual investors, the fact that there is an overseas bond demand does not necessarily mean that Wellington would be capable of selling these bonds to other parts of Asia. Moreover, it has yet to be demonstrated that Wellington's expertise is good enough to sell services related to marketing and underwriting these bonds in global or even regional marketplaces.

Wellington also claims that securitization of agricultural products and currency trading can be useful in attracting financial flows to New Zealand. Indeed, New Zealand has securitized its land and dairy products, among others. However, there does not appear to be substantial demand in the region for such securitized financial products. The country has also demonstrated active currency trading. It is true that New Zealand has acquired a tremendous amount of experience in managing currency trading, simply because the New Zealand currency has been flexible for a long time. But, when it comes to currency trading, location matters. We do not know if Wellington would be an ideal place for currency trading. Currency trading seems to be taking place mostly in New York, London, Tokyo, and other major financial centres. It appears that Wellington is too far away from where the action is.

Wellington's strengths, weaknesses, opportunities, and threats in becoming a regional IFC are summarized in Table 1.6.

Table 1.6
SWOTs of Wellington as an IFC

Strengths
• Active markets exist where various currency derivatives are traded • Risk management capabilities • English-speaking population
Weaknesses
• Small size of the economy • Limited cross-border markets for currency derivatives and securitized products
Opportunities
• Securitization of agricultural and dairy products
Threats
• Vulnerable to the risk of contraction of the yen carry trade

2.7. Seoul[8]

In 2003, the government of Korea headed by the then President Roh Moo-Hyun launched the so-called Northeast Asian Financial Hub project. The purpose of the project was to strengthen Korea's competitiveness with its rapidly growing financial industry. Recognizing that the financial crisis in 1997–98 was partly due to the weakness in the financial sector, the government proposed to build an international financial hub to strengthen the financial industry so that it could survive the global competition. In fact, the IFC project was intended to make the financial industry a new growth engine for the economy.

The proposed IFC initiative was to be implemented in three phases. The first phase to be completed by 2007 is to strengthen the foundation of the financial industry; the second phase for the period of 2008–10 is to establish a financial centre specializing in asset management. The third and final phase for the period, 2011–15, is to push Korea to grow into a major financial hub in Asia. During the first phase, the government pursued seven major tasks to: (1) foster asset management business as the key component of the IFC; (2) further develop the financial markets; (3) develop specialized financial services; (4) strengthen the global financial network; (5) create the Korean Investment Corporation as a sovereign fund to invest in foreign currency assets, cooperating with global asset management companies for which the regional headquarters were to be located in Korea; (6) reform the financial regulation and supervision; and (7) improve business and living conditions for global businesses and foreign nationals.

It appears that Korea has performed well during the first stage. In particular, legislation of a new financial regulatory framework known as the Capital Market Consolidation Act was a very significant achievement. The new legislation to become effective in February 2009 will create a new business type, named "financial investment companies", which will be consolidations of former securities companies, derivatives companies, asset management companies, and other capital market-related businesses. The legislation also meant a shift from industry line regulation to functional regulation of capital market businesses.

Other achievements include easing the regulations of foreign exchange trading, establishing the Korea Investment Corporation, relaxation of the portfolio investment restriction of public pension funds, enactment of a new corporate pension law, allowing the establishment of private equity funds, launching of a financial hub supporting team within the government, establishing a graduate school of finance at KAIST (Korea Advanced Institute of Science and Technology), among others.

However, there are still many tasks that remain. Fair and transparent enforcement of regulations is necessary in addition to further deregulation. Fair competition between domestic and international players should be promoted. Also essential are providing more foreigner-friendly government services and building facilities to attract foreigners.

An IFC initiative must have a clearly defined objective. Korea has been pushing to develop a financial centre that specializes in asset management services. Korea may have advantages in asset management. There is a fast growing supply of capital in Korea that will have to find investment opportunities overseas. For example, some government institutional investors, namely the National Pension Services and Korea Investment Corporation, will have accumulated a huge sum of investment funds in the near future. Korea will need high-calibre international asset

Table 1.7
SWOTs of Seoul as an IFC

Strengths
• Third largest capital market in Asia and Korean economy's strong growth potential • Very large market for exchange-listed derivatives • Large and fast growing demand for asset management services • Advanced IT infrastructure
Weaknesses
• Powerful and militant labour unions • The regulatory environment not friendly enough for foreign business English is not a business language. • Inconvenient living environment for foreigners, including children
Opportunities
• Rising regional demand for infrastructure investments • Growing demand for debt restructuring services in the region • Listing of index derivatives on the Globex and cooperation with Chicago Mercantile Exchange(CME) Group • Cooperation with Tokyo Stock Exchange
Threats
• IFC competition from other Asian cities

managers who will help make Seoul a hub of international institutional investors.

Despite such progress, Korea has to take seriously the sceptics' claim that its motives for creating an IFC are not clear and that the vision of an IFC varies among government officials and finance businessmen. Skyscrapers that house many international investment banks and commercial banks do not constitute an IFC. The city that brings in top talent for the financial services industry is not necessarily a financial centre. An IFC is a city where international financial flows pass through, leaving substantial added value and employment to the city. The sceptics would argue that the IFC initiative of Seoul does not go far enough to address its few decisive weaknesses in a persuasive and decisive manner so as to promote such international financial flows. This is in fact what Seoul's low ranking in the GFCI seems to signify.

Seoul's strengths, weaknesses, opportunities, and threats in becoming a global/regional IFC are summarized in Table 1.7.

3. ASSESSMENTS OF IFC COMPETITIVENESS

In his keynote speech[9] at the conference, Dominic Barton of McKinsey suggested that the factors that affect the competitiveness of an IFC include human resources, business environment, market accessibility, infrastructure, and quality of life. In the GFCI (2007), the following five factors were used to rate the competitiveness of financial centres: People, business environment, market access, infrastructure, and general competitiveness, such as livability. Similarly, Hong Kong Securities and Futures Commission (2006) identified several factors for evaluating IFC competitiveness, such as availability of skilled personnel and access to supplies of professional services (that is, human resources); regulatory environment and government responsiveness (that is, business environment); access to international financial markets and access to customers (that is, market accessibility); corporate and personal tax regimes; availability of business infrastructure; and a fair and just business environment; among others. In this section, the five factors identified by Barton are used in assessing competitiveness of the seven IFCs in Asia and the Pacific under consideration here to evaluate each in terms of the IFC competitiveness and its determinants.

3.1. Human Resources

The financial industry is a knowledge industry and its success critically depends on the quality of the human resources. The quality of human resources of related industries, such as legal services, accounting services, the information technology (IT) services, and the regulatory/supervisory services, are also critically pertinent. Being the frontrunners and having been recognized as regional IFCs in the global market, Hong Kong and Singapore are home to several Asia-Pacific headquarters of global banking institutions, global law firms, and global accounting firms. These two IFCs already possess the necessary human resources and their own knowledge networks around the globe. Furthermore, very fine academic institutions in Hong Kong and Singapore produce a large number of professionals each, feeding into the system of the financial industry and other related industries.

It is interesting to note that there has been no known strategy specifically in place to improve the quality of the people working in the financial industry in Japan. This is not to say that the quality of human resources in the financial industry in Japan is lagging behind other competitors in Asia-Pacific. Quite the contrary, Tokyo is the home of the regional headquarters of major global banks and investment companies. Also, Tokyo is the city where the world's second largest stock exchange is located, where millions of skilled professionals are already working in the financial sector. In 2007, Japan's Financial Supervisory Administration (FSA) announced a "Plan to Strengthen the Competitiveness of Japan's Financial and Capital Markets". This plan proposes the four pillars of reform, one of which pertains to human resource development. Japan intends to develop and accumulate internationally competitive human resources specializing in finance, law, and accounting.

Meanwhile, Sydney and Seoul have government-initiated strategies in place to develop human resources for the financial industry. In Sydney, the government established Axiss Australia, which has been absorbed by Invest Australia. Through Axiss Australia, the government has set up two very important initiatives in terms of personnel development. The government and training institutions work closely to develop personnel working in the financial industry. People working in the financial industry are also trained within that sector to develop their skills further. The government even offers scholarships to groom outstanding individuals who choose careers in finance.

Similarly in Seoul, the national government is leading efforts to put a system in place that develops finance professionals. It has launched a graduate school of finance at KAIST for the specific purpose of training finance professionals. This has kindled competition among universities and colleges to launch graduate finance programmes, which offer practical education in banking and finance and risk management, among others. Meanwhile, the banking and finance industries, having realized that they need finance professionals, have begun to invest heavily in recruiting and training.

We do not have much information about strategies for human resources development in either Shanghai or Wellington. This, however, does not imply a lack of professionals and/or skilled human resources in these cities. We just do not know whether or not the government has any strategy in place to aggressively develop finance professionals. Let us not forget that China has a vast pool of human resources that can be trained to become finance professionals. Wellington has a good number of quality educational institutions that are producing a number of highly educated professionals.

Having said that, it is perhaps interesting to raise the question as to whether national or city governments can play an effective role in human resources development for the financial industry. Apparently, the governments in Hong Kong and China do not seem to have much involvement in human resource development for the financial industry. On the other hand, Australian, Singaporean, Korean and Japanese governments are putting a lot of effort, including government subsidies, in developing finance professionals. Given that finance and banking skills are more tacit than explicit knowledge, the extent to which the government-led, in-class training can be effective as on-the-job, over-the-shoulders' training by the industry is not clear. Another important issue is the language barrier. English is the common language in the global financial and banking markets. It is not surprising that Hong Kong and Singapore are the frontrunners in the IFC competition in Asia-Pacific. These two cities, together with Sydney and Wellington, have competitive advantages because English is either the mother tongue or at least very widely used. It is obvious that English-speaking professionals would feel more comfortable in one of these four cities than living in a city like Tokyo, Seoul, or Shanghai, where English communication is not as easy.

3.2. Business Environment

Regulatory environment is very critical because the financial industry is built on the foundation of legal and regulatory frameworks. Indeed, the GFCI lists "regulatory environment" as the second-most important factor in determining IFC competitiveness, second only to the availability of skilled personnel. The most interesting case study of this dimension is the seemingly excessive financial regulation in the United States, which is signified by the Sarbanes-Oxley Act, making London a major beneficiary.[10]

Hong Kong, Singapore, Sydney and Wellington have followed the legal framework of the common law tradition similar to that of the United Kingdom and the United States. Under this legal framework, the so-called negative-list regulation rules with regulations allowing everything except the ones listed in the statutes. In such a legal environment, it is very easy to introduce new products and services so long as they are not prohibited by the law. It is not surprising that investment banking and the capital markets are deeper and more advanced in these countries than those that follow the civil law tradition, such as Japan and Korea, and to some extent, China.[11]

Under the legal framework of the civil law tradition, the so-called positive-list regulation rules, under which regulations do not allow anything unless it is specifically listed in the written statute. In this legal environment, it is not easy to benefit from financial innovation because of the uncertainty that the new product or service may not be approved by the legal authority. To overcome this impediment, both Japan and Korea have attempted to change the regulatory orientation from the positive-list regulation to the negative-list regulation. Under the Koizumi administration, Japan introduced and passed a bill called the Financial Instruments and Exchange Act (2006) that enhances disclosure by listed companies, strengthens the self-regulatory operations by exchanges, and introduces more effective investor protection regulations over a large scope of financial products. In 2007, the FSA made the announcement that it would take another step to further deregulate the financial industry. This effort also attempts to strengthen the competitiveness of Japan's financial markets and to raise their attractiveness so that they can fulfil their role in meeting the demands of domestic and foreign users. The new deregulation effort includes plans to expand the scope of exchange tradable products; to lower the barriers that have hindered synergies among banking, securities, and insurance businesses; and to enhance transparency and predictability of regulation and supervision, among many others.

In 2007, Korea successfully legislated the Capital Markets and Financial Investment Services Act. This new law which will take effect in February 2009 is also called the "Capital Market Consolidation Act" because it consolidates the fragmented sectors of securities and capital markets businesses into a single, comprehensive "financial investment industry". The primary feature of the law is to introduce the negative-list regulation for new products and services and the negative-list regulation of the business areas of financial investment companies. This law constitutes the third milestone of Korea's deregulatory reform. The first was the regulatory/supervisory agency consolidation to create Financial Supervisory Services in 1999, and the second milestone was the consolidation of exchanges to create the Korea Exchange (KRX), the consolidated, demutualized exchange in 2005. The new administration of President Lee Myung Bak launched in early 2008 is expected to continue with deregulation.

Both Seoul and Tokyo have claimed that they would move to principles-based supervision from rules-based supervision. It will be tough, as well require time, to do this although the respective governments seem determined to do so. Critiques argue that Korea's supervisory authority is not even rules-based, much less principles-based. In Korea, in particular, an IFC will be very hard to attain until the regulatory efficiency and predictability provided for by the principle-based supervision is in place.

While Seoul and Tokyo are trying hard to catch up with the frontrunners to become IFCs, such as Hong Kong and Singapore, Shanghai has not been as active as those two cities. This seems so because Shanghai serves huge domestic market needs while Hong Kong, as a regional IFC, can serve much of the international finance needs of China.

Many of the reform efforts of Seoul and Tokyo lag behind the reform efforts of Australia, Hong Kong, and Singapore. Australia made many important reforms such as the pension reform and the financial regulatory reform in 2000. Hong Kong and Singapore consolidated the exchanges and the back-office functions, such as clearing and settlement, by forming a holding company. It is interesting to note that capital market reform in Hong Kong, Singapore, and Sydney has followed the common sequence — exchange consolidation, that is, market consolidation, followed by regulatory consolidation/reform, which promotes innovative activities in the financial services industry.

3.3. Market Accessibility

IFCs play a significant role in bringing together users of capital and the providers of capital who happen to be located in different countries. International as well as domestic market accessibility is thus critically important for any city to be an IFC. Market accessibility as defined by the GFCI (2007) consists of the levels of securitization, the volume and value of trading in equities and bonds, and the clustering effect of having many firms involved in the financial services sector together in one centre.

Historically, major cities and centres of power developed into major financial centres, like Tokyo and Shanghai for example. However, today, Hong Kong and Singapore, major trading centres whose historical roots lie in their strategic locations, are the top financial centres in Asia. These smaller cities are able to cater to the needs of financial companies in terms of tax incentives and regulatory supervision in a more intentional and versatile manner than can cities serving large domestic economies like Tokyo, Shanghai, Seoul, and Sydney.

Tokyo, Hong Kong and Singapore have excellent access to international financial markets. Tokyo is a major financial centre on a scale as large as New York or London, serving both domestic and international finance needs. In terms of the international activity of banks, Japan holds 6.9 per cent and 2.5 per cent shares in total global cross-border assets and liabilities, respectively, Singapore 2.3 per cent and 2.4 per cent, and Hong Kong 2.2 per cent and 1.3 per cent. Hong Kong is a highly diversified financial centre with its strengths in banking and equities. Singapore is just behind Hong Kong overall but is very strong in foreign exchange markets and over-the-counter (OTC) derivatives. And of course, Tokyo, with the second largest economy in the world, has the largest stock exchange, foreign exchange, and derivatives turnovers in the Asia-Pacific region.

Singapore's strategy to become an IFC was highly concerted; its first priorities were in building a regional debt and foreign exchange trading centre and becoming a dominant asset management centre in Asia. Its second goal was to become a hub for regional equities. Developing a public-private partnership between the government and firms, the government handled the legal and regulatory framework with input from players who had the expertise. To build up the asset management industry, the Government Investment Corporation (GIC) of Singapore gave foreigners money to manage, which brought training and foreign talent to Singapore. They also freed up competition between intermediaries by taking ownership of brokerage limits from 40 to 70 per cent. The funds were established by revamping the pension system and developing highly active traders.

This strategy has been and is continuing to be emulated in Sydney and in Seoul with Australia's superannuation savings and Korea's KIC and pension funds. But unlike Singapore, Korea lacks a public-private partnership and the government is leading the way. The success of an IFC initiative will be difficult without strong private backing. Australia's pension fund has lost momentum because of its domestic focus. Although Australia's funds management industry is the fourth largest in the world, its ambiguous taxation policies, lackadaisical pursuit of meeting the industry's regulatory needs and its domestic focus hinder it from exporting its expertise and attaining an international scale.

Tokyo does not provide diverse or innovative financial products commensurate to its economic power. Tokyo has yet to realize its potential in terms of granting access to domestic and foreign entities and creating an active and disciplined wholesale market. By 2006, there were only eleven exchange traded funds (ETFs) on the Tokyo Stock Exchange, in comparison to Seoul's twelve and Singapore's thirteen. Resistance from banking, securities, and insurance industries hindered it from introducing comprehensive and drastic reforms to promote a more competitive international environment. Although foreign participation accounts for 30 per cent of market capitalization, the number of foreign firms listed on the Tokyo exchange is remarkably small, reaching twenty-five in 2006 while it was 127 in 1991. Additionally, the low-risk institutional and household appetite has kept the wholesale market from diversifying and creating innovative new financial products. Although Tokyo has many strengths and reasons to become a global international financial centre, it must internationalize its financial market more. To the extent that the near-zero interest rate regime hinders development of complex financial instruments, Tokyo needs to normalize its monetary policy by gradually raising the policy rate.

Similar weaknesses are found with Seoul. Very few foreign firms are listed on the Korean Stock Exchange. While Seoul excels in the derivatives market, it lacks variability in terms of financial products. The Shanghai Stock Exchange has also just begun to allow foreign companies to list on the exchange. In order for it to become competitive in terms of scale and liquidity, it will have to separate its A and B share market. China lacks a vital degree of freedom that will allow its markets to naturally mature.

Although much smaller, Wellington has a slew of equity derivatives, warrants, options, convertible notes, trust or fund units, including equity options, with the Sydney Futures Exchange. It also has large off-market crosses in the Australian stock market. Thus given the small economy, Wellington is heavily influenced by outside capital movements.

Asian exchanges must become more efficient and competitive or they will lag behind. There has been a trend toward cross-border consolidation of exchanges. Big exchanges are merging, for example, New York Securities Exchange with Euronext, London Stock Exchange with Bursars Italiana, and international securities exchanges of New York with German stock exchanges. Financial exchanges are now also increasingly demutualizing and becoming publicly traded firms.

Like these larger exchanges in April 2007, four members of the Council of Economic and Fiscal Policy recommended that the Tokyo Stock Exchange and the commodities counterpart merge. The rationale was to facilitate cross-selling and enhance global presence through exploiting various advantages arising from economies of scale (different skills and experiences, increased number of assets, etc.). In Sydney, the Australian prime minister proposed to establish the carbon trading exchange by 2012. Currently, the only European climate exchange is in London and the annual turnover is 10 billion Euro (US$12.9 million). This could be very important in attracting foreign business to the Australian Stock Exchange.

In bond markets, Japan, Korea, Australia, and Singapore have the highest bond market capitalization to GDP. In terms of pure amounts of international bonds and notes and domestic debt securities, Japan, China, Australia, and Korea have the highest volume of bond activity. However, only Australia has high international activity in the bond market; in the other Asian nations, foreign investors hold a small percentage of the bonds. The absence of an international securities depository and the withholding of taxes from interest income are major reasons for low internationalization of Korea's bond market.

In bond markets, aside from Japan, bond finance is relatively young and not very deep in Asia, due in part to short yield curves. Hong Kong has low bond activity relative to its banking and stock market because it relies more on short-term bank deals. It has a low number of public bond issues, in comparison to Singapore which made it an IFC strategy to issue sovereign bonds regularly in the late 1990s even in the presence of surplus, and had yields up to fifteen years, allowing other instruments to work.

New Zealand's debt markets have a range of instruments dating ten to twelve years, and there is a shortage of volume. The government is seeing massive budget surpluses and the pricing signals are not vitalizing the bond market although bank CDs are flourishing.

In addition to capital market information, market accessibility is also measured by the clustering effect. A true financial hub not only houses financial companies but several complementary service firms to facilitate business and information sharing. Hong Kong, Singapore, and Tokyo have a dynamic business environment as they are the regional headquarters of many multinational corporations. These three Asian cities also house global investment banks, while Tokyo also houses twelve Global 500 companies, whereas Hong Kong or Singapore houses none. However, because of preferential tax treatments by Hong Kong and Singapore, low infrastructure costs and lower regulations, many hedge funds interested in Japanese markets have located themselves in these cities instead. Thus, Japan has been losing international presence to competition from these small cities, whose financial and capital markets have been increasing in presence relative to their smaller sizes. In comparison to these cities, according to a study by the Korea Securities Research Institute (2007), Seoul, Sydney, and Shanghai each lack a highly diversified professional pool in terms of the presence of accounting firms, law firms, top banks, and global firms.

3.4. Infrastructure

Infrastructure is another key criterion financial companies consider when choosing the appeal of a financial centre. Infrastructure consists of the cost and availability of building and office space, country situation, property prices, and other variables such as connectivity, travel, utility, and other overhead costs.

Asia has demonstrated an uncanny ability to adapt rapidly to modern economic situations. The rapid growth of Japan and the Asian Tigers evidences this capability. In terms of building the infrastructure needed to house an international financial centre, many Asian nations, especially emerging ones, have the funding, government backing, mutual interest, and the technology to create attractive and pleasant environments to facilitate a financial services centre rapidly.

The Chinese are an excellent example of this. Shanghai has been developing top-level, state-of-the-art financial infrastructure in the past

Figure 1.1
Financial Services Clustering in Financial Centres: Index Rating

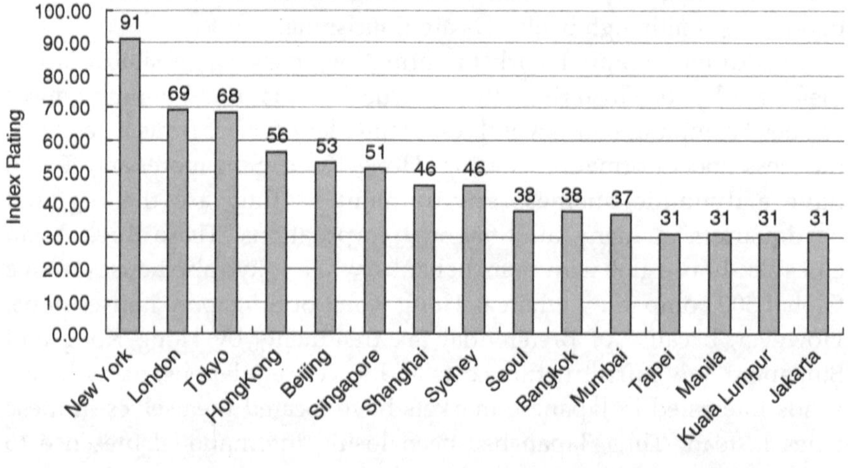

Source: Korea Securities Research Institute, Seoul's International Finance Environment: A Comparative Study, 2007.

couple of decades. Since Deng Xiaoping put forth the idea that Shanghai should be an international financial centre in 1991, Pudong, the designated financial district of Shanghai, has rocketed from a peasant and agrarian area, to a modernized, cutting-edge business district. Projected expenditure through 2010 will be over US$1 trillion on roads, airports, electrical power generation, water supply, and international events like the Beijing Olympics and the Shanghai Expo of 2010.

The difficulty, typified by the Chinese example, however, is not in building architecturally beautiful and efficient office spaces. The difficulty exists in adjusting the soft infrastructure to fit an international financial centre. Soft infrastructure, as discussed in Xu (forthcoming) in reference to Shanghai, incorporates the existence of market mechanism, a broad but fundamental understanding of property rights, and market-oriented reforms by the public and the government. Shanghai is still subject to consolidated powers and administrative layers that constrain its scale and effectiveness. When speaking of Hong Kong as a gateway to the Chinese domestic economy, its ability to stay independent of the influence of the Chinese government has been put forth as an issue that could detract from its current stature as a desirable international financial centre.

Many Western centres like Sydney, Wellington and those once patronized by the British like Hong Kong and Singapore have a history of capitalism and free market theories have been entrenched in the public consciousness. Seoul and Tokyo have rapidly adopted these ideals in the past fifty years with the development of their manufacturing centres and, especially after facing financial crises in the 1990s, are continuing to deregulate the market.

Generally speaking, Hong Kong and Singapore have excellent world class facilities and amenities, along with Tokyo and Sydney. These four Asian cities are considered the foremost cities, according to studies. Below is a chart comparing the top centres according to three differing studies, focusing only on infrastructure. The GFCI series, Korea Securities Research Institute (2007), and Mastercard's Worldwide Centres of Commerce Index measure infrastructure by focusing on different aspects.[12] These studies taken together show that Singapore has a very good network and IT infrastructure network while Hong Kong's efficiency in logistics gives the city an important competitive edge. Although headline costs in Hong Kong are high, their overall competitiveness is in general the highest in the region.

Overall, Tokyo has very good infrastructure, which is one reason why it is a thriving national metropolis. As part of its IFC initiative, the government has proposed plans to upgrade physical access to international financial markets and the business infrastructure including airport access. However, currently it appears that the Japanese institutions lag behind its regional rivals in terms of IT investment in the services sector (including business services and finance). There is a plan to bolster market functions, raise the confidence level, and improve the company disclosure system, as well as reform the tax law. Plans are also in place to develop three specialized financial districts (Marunouchi, Nihonbashi, and Roppongi) in Tokyo and possibly in Osaka. Tax incentives for developers and land owners, speedy construction permits, high-quality office buildings with amenities, English speaking schools, hospitals, and residential areas will also be provided in the zones.

For Sydney, no strategy appears to be currently in place to specifically improve the infrastructure in the financial industry. However, efforts to improve the transportation system are underway due to congestion, particularly in the central business district area. Australia has employed four primary strategies to further their cause: Promotion, attraction,

Figure 1.2
Comparison of Selected Financial Centres by Infrastructure Index, 2007

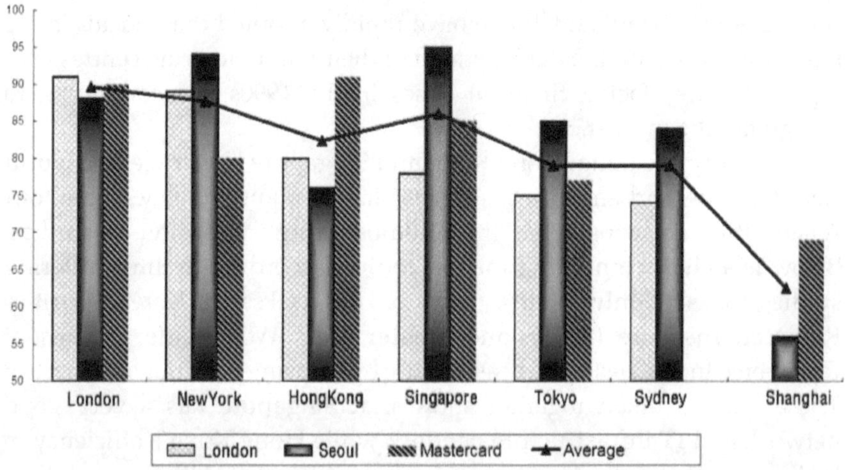

Source: See the sources cited in the present text.

facilitation, and aftercare. They promote their well-educated and skilled labour, low cost infrastructure, favourable time zone, stable regulation and political environment, advanced IT and support services, and a high quality of life. Sydney also has programmes to advise on issues like regulation, taxation, immigration, and will facilitate leaders of incoming firms to meet with the government and relevant agencies to foster better relationships and ties with all parties involved and lower overhead costs.

The Seoul metropolitan government has several construction projects underway to build a competitive international financial centre. Seoul can boast one of the world's best airports and most advanced IT infrastructure. It is revamping the subway system to connect the major business centres in Korea. Currently, the Seoul metropolitan government is building a US$1.6 billion state-of-the-art international finance centre building on Yeoido Island, one of the business districts in Seoul, attempting to reshape its skyline. Furthermore, the national government plans to develop "financial industry districts" around the country, including the special economic zone being created near the Incheon Airport where a cluster of ultra-modern business facilities is also under construction.

3.5. Quality of Life

It has been largely taken for granted that the cities that are vying for IFC status do indeed have quality living environments. One of the most important factors when determining the appeal of a financial centre is the livability, or quality of life, of the specific location. The quality of life comprises many factors like environment, culture, openness to foreigners, among other things. As an IFC strategy, many cities have made attempts to improve educational institutions and medical care facilities for foreign residents, in addition to making cities more cultural and greener.

Many cities in Asia-Pacific are already pleasant places to live. Australia and New Zealand, for instance, are rated sixth and eighth respectively on The Economist Intelligence Unit's 2008 quality of life index[13] behind France, Luxembourg, the United States and other Western nations ranking particularly high in terms of their environment, climate, and political freedom. However, these countries are located very far away from the business centres around the world, especially from those in Europe and America, to the detriment of their overall attractiveness as financial centres.

To the extent that Hong Kong and Singapore, and to some extent Sydney and Wellington, share similar cultural heritage and social systems with London, they do offer comfortable living environments to foreign residents who work for global financial institutions. For example, all four cities have the British school, which is very attractive to international executives who want their children to be educated in preparation for higher education in the United States or in Europe. Their systems of healthcare provision, sharing many aspects in common, offer very advanced medical care for both domestic and foreign residents. These cities are known for security. Law and order are well established and strictly enforced. These cities are also environmentally clean and offer many cultural activities, which can provide new experiences to foreign residents. According to the survey conducted by International Institute for Management Development (IMD) and the World Economic Forum, these cities are very highly ranked among major metropolitan cities in Asia-Pacific.

The three cities in northeast Asia, Tokyo, Shanghai and Seoul, are also very livable. Their quality of life is comparable to the cities above. However, the lack of English-speaking workers is often raised as an issue for these countries. All three are looking into building foreigner-friendly business districts.

Shanghai is no longer an old, cultural city in China. The progress in Shanghai has been breathtaking. Since 1992, the central government has backed the continued development of Shanghai to its old importance. The Lujiazui financial district has been zoned off in Shanghai to promote it as an economic, trading, shipping, and financial centre. Currently there are 306 banks and 152 securities companies located there. Already a funding centre, the large and robust community of non-local residents makes it an attractive place for foreigners to live in, although it is a long way from what Hong Kong is now. Both these Chinese cities, however, are fighting air pollution arising from China's continued development.

Seoul has made its own progress during the past five years — revitalizing the inner city river called Cheonggye Stream, creating the "Seoul Forest", modernizing the public transportation system, and enlivening a lot of cultural activities, among many others. With increased deregulation, Korea has seen the presence of foreign institutions grow and with that expatriate communities. The Seoul metropolitan government is attempting to enhance the presence of foreigner-friendly investment and living conditions by creating six "global business zones", six "global villages" and five "global cultural exchange zones". Those global zones are intended to provide one-stop, multilingual public and administrative services. The global villages will provide residential housing for foreigners. They will host international schools, hospitals, and other service facilities. The cultural zone will host cultural facilities such as theatres and museums.

In an effort to be more global, the current government of Japan has proposed the Asian Gateway Initiative. This initiative seeks to strengthen capabilities of finance professionals to a level that is internationally competitive. It also includes a plan to use Japan's resources to help develop other Asian financial and capital markets. The initiative is purported to enhance Japan's attractiveness by encouraging creative talent and by highlighting local charms, history, culture and traditions and publicizing it to the outside world. When many of the other Asian financial centres are seeking to Westernize, Japan is seeking to make its own culture attractive. It seeks to draw the rest of the world to visit, study, work and live in Japan. There will be more university programmes in English, more international cooperative programmes with foreign universities, such as joint-degree programmes. There will be more disclosure of information in English.

4. IFC COMPETITION: BENEFITS, RISKS, AND CHALLENGES

Competition among financial centres is intense globally, but, in particular, in Asia-Pacific. While the landscape in Europe and North America, in terms of the geographical distribution of financial activity, has long been fairly stable and rather concentrated at the top, Asia-Pacific has always had a far more dispersed and constantly varying structure of market leaders. Thus, several financial centres currently at the top of the region's activities according to one or another indicator were vying for the region's top positions since early last century when the regional leaders were none other than Tokyo, Hong Kong, Singapore, and Shanghai, and that in the last two decades, Shanghai as well as Mumbai, Seoul, Sydney, and others have expanded operations hugely, becoming relevant trans-regional actors and sometimes more. It is therefore, no accident that different levels of political leadership (country, city, or both) of several financial centres in the region have the stated intention of further positioning them as major international financial hubs in the medium term. The panorama is exciting and dynamic.

This section discusses the strengths and scope that the Asia-Pacific IFCs have for expansion and growth in the increasingly competitive world of global finance (sub-section 4.2); the case for competition among the regions' IFCs in terms of its effects on performance; and related to this the case for increasing regional integration in the sector (sub-section 4.3); risks that arise or that some fear may arise from IFC competition and the need to address them (sub-section 4.4); and most importantly, possible explanations for the very limited extent of financial integration that characterizes the region (sub-section 4.5). This analysis then leads to section 5 where views and recommendations are offered on priorities for the region in facing the global competitiveness challenge vis-à-vis the global leaders through market-based measures that will enhance the region's efficiency and indeed, integration in the sector. But before turning to these issues, sub-section 4.1 below shows what the state of competition is among the leading financial centres globally and the region's position in that group.

4.1. Leading Financial Centres in Asia-Pacific and Beyond: the Landscape

There are many cities in the Asia-Pacific region that serve as financial centres in their respective jurisdictions or local areas. Quite a few of them go beyond and serve as international financial centres or are engaged in efforts to become such financial centres, such as the seven such financial centres examined — Tokyo, Seoul, Shanghai, Hong Kong, Singapore, Sydney, and Wellington, which are competing with one another for larger shares of international financial business overall or in some specific lines of finance business. There are other cities in the region, such as Beijing, Melbourne, Osaka, and Kuala Lumpur that also are, or may be, considered financial centres. They, too, should be counted as regional competitors for the international finance business but were left out of detailed examination here in order to focus on more representative cases. The Asia-Pacific cities mentioned here do not just compete with one another. They also compete with many financial centres outside the region. In fact, in principle, they compete with all other financial centres around the globe. However, they may be said to compete more closely with some non-regional financial centres than others, with such financial cities as London and New York, which are the two most dominant global financial centres and do capture a large amount of financial business originating in the area, related either to investment needs or to the management of investible funds. Just outside the region, too, there are cities such as Dubai and Mumbai that are rapidly rising as financial centres in their respective regions and whose geographic proximity gives them particular relevance as competitors for financial activity in the Asia-Pacific region.

Since March 2007, the City of London has been publishing the GFCI — a ranking of the leading financial centres in the world. Updated twice yearly, the index assesses a range of objective and subjective criteria covering the legal system, talent pool, infrastructure, the environment and so on, and provides an overall ranking of the centres' relative attractiveness for business. The fourth GFCI was published in September 2008, featuring London and New York in the top two places and four Asia-Pacific centres among the global top ten (see Table 1.8). It is interesting to note in this table the significant changes that occur even between consecutive renditions of the index, but also the broad consistency in the results.

There are changes over time, despite the short span of time this table covers. Changes that do appear arise from the evolving performance and market perceptions of these centres rather than problems of measurement or analysis. Without going into the details on how the scores are computed, Singapore's dramatic rise is noticed in the recent listing (edging just past Hong Kong for the first time), reflecting survey respondents' perception of its regulatory strength and overall prospects as an IFC. Also for the first time, Hong Kong and Singapore reach the 700s in terms of score, both moving closer to the top two centres than in the past. Of course, the index is more about perception and promise than about market share. But the direction of change registered is worth

Table 1.8
Top Ten International Financial Centres

Rank	GFCI 1 (March 2007)		GFCI 2 (September 2007)		GFCI 3 (March 2008)		GFCI 4 (September 2008)	
	City	Score	City	Score	City	Score	City	Score
1	London	765	London	806	London	795	London	791
2	New York	760	New York	787	New York	786	New York	774
3	Hong Kong	684	Hong Kong	694	Hong Kong	695	Singapore	701
4	Singapore	660	Singapore	673	Singapore	675	Hong Kong	700
5	Zurich	656	Zurich	666	Zurich	665	Zurich	676
6	Frankfurt	647	Frankfurt	649	Frankfurt	642	Geneva	645
7	Sydney	639	Geneva	645	Geneva	640	Tokyo	642
8	Chicago	636	Chicago	639	Chicago	637	Chicago	641
9	Tokyo	632	Sydney	636	Tokyo	628	Frankfurt	636
10	Geneva	628	Tokyo	625	Sydney	621	Sydney	630

Source: The City of London Corporation, *The Global Financial Centres Index 1~4*.

noting as is the fact that this index was calculated in July 2008, hence missing the worst of the ongoing banking crisis which surely will affect absolute and relative strengths of leading centres. Other interesting changes in this table include Tokyo's significant relative rise in 2008 compared to 2007, and Sydney's and (more recently) Frankfurt's movements in the opposite direction. Elsewhere in the index, Dubai in particular had a major movement up, to rank twenty-two on the main list but received top ranking on the respondents' assessment of "which cities were most likely to become significant financial centres in the future" category in which Qatar and other Gulf States, as well as Shanghai and Singapore, also scored well. The general sense emerges that, outside the core of global leaders, the location of international finance is dynamic. Serious efforts at modernizing regulatory frameworks and infrastructure work, as exemplified dramatically by Dubai today or by Bahrain, Dublin, or (within the top echelons) London since the 1970s and 1980s.

As much as there is change — in fact more change the further away from the core — Table 1.8 speaks also of resilience in the results, or at least consistency. Throughout the four studies (with its own survey each), the very same ten financial centres occupy the top ten places; and the same five are the top five, or four to four — and indeed the top two appear unassailable, more so if we turn to their huge and growing advantage in market share in most major sectors of financial activity.[14] Incumbency matters and so does scale, and London and New York have a huge advantage on both as global actors. But, again, gradual change occurs, and the question is what drives such change and where do priorities lie.

We have to be cautious in accepting or interpreting the results of such competitiveness rankings. First, the ranking of financial centres can in reality be quite arbitrary: It all depends on how any one "quality" is measured and how components are then combined. The result will differ considerably depending on who undertakes the exercise or how it is done. Second, and perhaps our main concern with the approach, is the fact that the final listing (and certainly not the vast study that underlies it) amounts to a deceptively one-dimensional summary of all features of financial centres as of today. Giving a fixed weight in the final mark (say 8 per cent, or 30 per cent!) to a central variable such as "confidence in the rule of law" is misleading: It allows for other factors to compensate for it. If three variables are all essential for a viable international financial centre, each of them should in a sense have a 100 per cent weight,[15] which is to say that no single statistic can summarize those three and the remaining variables. Similarly, a one-dimensional measurement will tend to weigh down niche financial centres, whose performance may not be strong across the board but very significant in their particular areas of strength — Seoul's scale and depth in the bond industry ahead, for instance, of Singapore or indeed Hong Kong comes to mind.

Our examination of the individual financial centres has demonstrated that each financial centre has its unique set of SWOTs (strengths, weaknesses, opportunities, and threats). This means that while a financial centre may not excel in terms of overall finance business performance, it may do so in specific lines of financial business in which it possesses comparative advantages. Together with the dynamic nature of competition, it also means that the performance overall, or in specific lines of business, of a financial centre five or ten years from now, may differ from the same as of now. The future fortune of individual financial centres will very much be the result of their policy efforts today and tomorrow — the clarity, quality of implementation, and relative effectiveness of the strategies they put in place. Policy competition matters, and is quite intense.

4.2. The Case for IFC Competition: Strong Prospects for Financial Business in the Region

What is the reward participants in this IFC competition can aspire to earn? This sub-section discusses the outlook in terms of potential for market growth while sub-section 4.3 below addresses the collateral benefits through the effects of competition on efficiency. The question is will there be enough growth ahead in financial business for the region's financial centres to try to attract?

4.2.1. Macroeconomic Considerations

Asia-Pacific's strong macroeconomic fundamentals create a huge potential for the growth of its financial centres. This is an important point that was raised by several participants in the conference and was elaborated in particular by Jong-Wha Lee and David Cowen.[16] It is cautioned that some of these macroeconomic considerations refer primarily to the demand side of the equation, demand that, as some participants noted, can be and is being largely met by provision from afar, as the supply of finance (the cost and also the quality or nature of the deliverable product) is generally less affected by distance than is the case in most other industries. Nevertheless the case is compelling that financial centres in the region have plenty of room to grow in the future. Consider:

- *The region's high savings and wealth accumulation.* The holders of these resources throughout the region need to somehow place them in the market, not necessarily in the region itself, and that is the kernel of the problem. The potential customer base for industry in the region that these "local" resources represent is huge — in particular, we refer to foreign asset accumulation by sovereigns, which the IMF estimates will reach US$12 trillion by 2012;
- *The region's strong growth and increasing share in total global growth.* This continuously expanding level of activity requires an expanding financial activity, again not all of which needs to be serviced within the region, but a huge potential market for local and regional suppliers is thereby created. This refers as much to the region's large and rising foreign investment flows as to the sustained expansion of its trade with the rest of the world and increasingly within the

region, too. Historically, the growth of trade and FDI flows has consistently been followed by the development and growth of the major financial centres both in Europe and North America.

4.2.2. Microeconomic and Structural Issues

Alongside its strong macro dynamics and savings rates, hence large stocks and flows of investible funds and opportunities to use them, the region has strengths in its financial industry that augur well for its continuing growth in the years ahead. Its long history in the sector underlies a well of expertise, infrastructure, market share, and tradition, all of which are crucial factors very hard to create. With market economics and globalizing strategies firmly in place for several decades now throughout the region, policies and frameworks are wholly supportive of efficiency and expansion. Finally, the Asian financial crisis of only one decade ago left in its wake a raft of improvements in financial and financial-sector policies that place it on a solid footing as the region moves forward. The high and rising marks given to several financial centres in the region by the GFCI series are a testimony to the competitive strengths of these centres.

At a more specific level, Cowen offered at the conference six factors relating to recent microeconomic and structural developments in the region that should support further growth of its financial centres:

- Strengthened domestic financial systems;
- Deeper domestic financial markets;
- Improvements in market infrastructure;
- Continuing liberalization of the capital account, trade in services, and the progressive removal of exchange controls;
- Increased securitization of domestic assets; and
- The rapid growth in Islamic finance.

Financial centres in the region, therefore, have a favourable macroeconomic and financial environment in which to operate, where an important and growing share of world financial resources will be originating and seeking placement or will be moving internally or coming externally for investment. The servicing of these financial needs is increasingly viable from afar, and both London and New York are increasingly important players in Asian finance through subsidiaries and direct business. Nevertheless, this outlook gives the local industry an advantage to increase its share in those opportunities. At the same time, the competition for a piece of this pie is healthy for Asia not only for the financial services that may actually be attracted, but also, and perhaps more importantly, for the positive effect these efforts will have on the health of its financial industry and individual economies, effects which is discussed below.

4.3. The Case for IFC Competition: Efficiency Gains and Regional Integration

Is competition among Asia-Pacific's financial centres the best approach to follow? With a limited pie to distribute and in the face of increasingly integrated and globalized world financial markets, should these centres be competing for market share and leadership position, or should they perhaps be cooperating somehow? Is the financial sector integrating within the region, or is it primarily integrating with the rest of the world, and does competition advance or hinder one or other forms of integration? And in the end, does regional integration matter? Should it be fostered, and if so how — and how not? This conference rightly placed its focus on these questions and on trying to better understand the implications of today's keen competition for IFC status in Asia-Pacific.

The practice of protecting national champions and intervening in the financial industry, in Asia-Pacific as in all regions of the world, has in the past been as common as interventionism and protectionism in other areas of economic activity. Finance is seen as bringing riches and prestige and playing a key strategic role for the economy, and for those reasons, has often been the subject of much control by governments, in particular through frequent limitations on foreign ownership that have in turn often shielded the inefficiency of the financial industry at home.

Protectionism is a discredited guide to development policy generally that has largely been left behind, particularly so in Asia-Pacific. It is now well understood that, with appropriate regulations and safeguards, competition generally breeds efficiency and growth. This is true for finance just as for all services or manufacturing. But finance is not just any sector: It is one with a central importance to the rest of the economy. The need for competitiveness and efficiency in finance is, therefore, widely recognized as fundamental for success in today's global economy. Having a well developed, efficient and modern financial system is as essential an input to any other sectors of the economy as having a good and efficient labour force, tax system, or competitive structure. This is perhaps the backdrop for so many countries in the region wishing to pursue the creation of an international financial centre in their midst.

Although several cities in the region have been active financial centres for over a century now, IFC competition in the Asia-Pacific region was launched in earnest after the Asian financial crisis of 1997–98, driven by the desire to succeed in global markets hence the need for competitiveness generally with a shared perception that efficiency as suppliers of financial services to the world is a central element in the equation. But in this pursuit of prominence and excellence as a financial centre, whatever ranking and market share may be achieved, will be a win for the participant as the efforts to achieve that prominence lead to a host of measures that breed efficiency and quality in their financial industries to the benefit of the individual economies. Not all grow world-class IFCs, but their efforts and the competition to get there is beneficial by enhancing their efficiency and performance, and that in the end is what truly matters.

Competition breeds efficiency though a number of separate mechanisms. First and foremost of course, it rewards excellence among firms, allowing the most competitive ones to flourish and providing an incentive to them all to be the best. But apart from the incentive effect on the individual firm and on the Darwinian selection and growth among firms, competition also affects society's mentality and business practices, rewarding quality and results over the protection of privilege and turf — discrediting also the resort to unfair means to gain advantage, which is where supervision and regulation become more, rather than less, important in a competitive environment. Third, competition changes the role of regulators and supervisors and the very way they see themselves and behave, from a culture of permits and enforcement, to a focus on quality and results.

In sum, competition brings out the best in market participants. It also brings up the best market participants, and it brings out the best in regulators too, creating a culture of pursuit of quality rather than control as such.

Through all the above, competition fosters fairer, more transparent, and, therefore, more reliable financial and capital markets in each jurisdiction. This in turn leads to greater opportunities for profit from using cross-border providers and confidence in doing so, and thus to more active international financial business in the region as a whole. This all lowers the cost of financing and enhances the efficiency of individual operators, hence their ability to compete outside the region, too.

Nevertheless, competition can mean different things. Competition stands for market opening, infrastructure development, and regulatory streamlining to support the fittest. But competition can also mean regulatory laxity and cost-cutting for operators through taxes and other means. And perhaps it may lead to excess supply and fragmentation of the financial industry in Asia-Pacific, issues discussed below. But first, let us briefly discuss the related question of integration — financial market integration in Asia-Pacific, and the value of increasing financial integration in the region.

4.3.1. Greater Financial Integration

- Should lower capital costs for investment in a region with enormous investment needs due precisely to its huge rate of economic expansion — and in particular its important infrastructure agenda for the future.
- Will help further reduce future recurrences of the currency and maturity mismatches that underlay the Asian financial crisis and thereby enhance confidence in the system. Borrowing short-term in U.S. dollars for local-currency long-term investment creates the fundamental "original sin" emphasized by a number of participants in the conference.
- Would improve the allocation of the region's financial resources, as competition forces a greater focus on quality and results by private firms and policymakers alike, and on further developing financial infrastructure.

All the above refer to market-based integration, not market segmentation or distortion but on the free choice by business. Questions to answered include whether IFC competition may hinder integration by over-supplying Asia-Pacific with financial centres (and by perhaps inducing exclusionary practices) or whether, to the contrary, competition may be friendly to integration by enhancing the search for efficiency, hence more reciprocal business within the region. A key question that needs to be addressed is why integration in the region is weak, and how can it be promoted in a market friendly way, explored in sub-section 4.5 and in section 5 below.

4.4. Risks from IFC Competition and Consequent Policy Challenges

Having stressed the need for competition as the guiding principle in financial centre-policy in Asia-Pacific, it is necessary to recognize that certain risks arise or can arise where appropriate action or caution may be needed to supplement competition.

Four main areas of concern can be mentioned in some cases to identify needed actions or attention and in others to clear possible misunderstandings:

(1) *Financial volatility from integration and interdependence.* A number of important concerns arise around ways in which financial competition and integration may lead to increased volatility. At a general level, the fear is expressed that openness and competition lead to integration with global markets, which in turn creates new opportunities for risk and for the transmission of risk across countries and regions of the world — a point that the U.S. subprime debacle illustrates vividly. The question, however, is: what is the solution, to protect my jurisdiction from potential global financial shocks? The solution surely does not lie in isolation, which makes you stable but poor. It lies in a proper regulatory framework and practice; in constantly improving and adapting this regulation in the face of always new financial products and problems; and in cooperation across constituencies, both for the mutual transfer of best practice and to jointly address common problems. On the other hand the development of a financial centre also brings about opposite forces that will tend to reduce volatility through the development of the market and its increased diversification and liquidity, all of which represent stabilizing buffers.

But, will such good and well-applied regulation arise naturally alongside integration, or could competition to the contrary perhaps undermine it? This is the more important question that is raised.

(2) *Financial volatility from regulatory laxity and forbearance.* This is a major area of concern internationally and one that we must always remain attentive to in the region. A light and permissive regulatory framework reduces costs for both the regulator and the regulated, and has on occasion been an important vehicle to attract business — a vehicle whose rewards will appear to grow with the intensity of competitive pressures.

Nevertheless, the severe global financial turmoil currently underway, originating in the subprime mortgage crisis of the United States, alerts us to the serious threat to financial and economic stability that those risks can represent. The combination of financial globalization and financial innovations creates new opportunities for risk and for its transmission across countries and regions. Were regional IFC competition to lead to regulatory laxity and forbearance, or even were regulatory systems not constantly improved and adapted to the cutting edge of new financial products and problems, regional vulnerability to this risk would increase. This is only an in-principle cautionary note albeit an important one, as there is no evidence that the problem is significant in Asia-Pacific. And at least the major (and products-wise more diversified) financial markets in the region do have strong regulatory systems in place. But the regulatory authorities need to be on a high level of alert to these risks as they try to update as well as internationalize their financial industry.

The task requires a delicate balancing act. On one hand, regulators should seek to allow market participants as much flexibility as possible in the provision and innovation of services, to help enhance the competitiveness of their financial industries. The respective national authorities will be compelled to do this, driven by IFC competition. At the same time, they should seek to improve the transparency of the markets, strengthen financial and non-financial corporate governance, and ensure an effective management of systemic risks to the financial industry as a whole, especially as new financial techniques and products emerge over time.

It may be difficult or even impossible for the respective national authorities to do this effectively by themselves while the financial markets in the individual economies are highly interdependent and further continue to be integrated with one another. The task calls for a coordinated international effort, which in turn requires the national governments seeking to internationalize their own financial centres to put in place appropriate mechanisms for consultation and cooperation. Further, the region's financial stability will not only require regional-level coordination of national regulatory policies and cooperation in their application — all of which need to be tightest — but also coordination of those policies with the rest of the Pacific region and beyond.

(3) *Tax and subsidy competition.* Just as competitive pressures may make it attractive to relax standards, fiscal instruments too can be used to attract

business or to give domestic suppliers an edge in the competitive arena, for example through tax incentives or subsidized facilities to attract foreign firms or even broader reductions in tax levels generally.

The issues are complex — witness tensions that have developed in the past in Europe and elsewhere and led to — OECD — efforts to avert or discourage what some considered harmful tax competition among its member governments, a concept that was most contentious and had others retort that generally available (rather than selective) low taxes are quite unlike tax incentives available to some. The reality is that, unlike the acknowledged existence of consensus views on what constitutes best practice on matters of regulation — best practice at least for a given country situation — there is no such standard as far as the level of taxation is concerned. The region includes jurisdictions such as Hong Kong and Singapore where low taxes are extensive and reflect a social consensus rather than selective manipulation to distort competition.

Nevertheless disparities can give rise to friction, particularly if they take the form of targeted tax or subsidy concessions, and create possibilities for investors to evade or avoid tax obligations utilizing those differences across jurisdictions. Even though in the present WTO-compliant policy environment there is in some cases less room for competition through targeted tax concessions or subsidies per se, special assistance and all kinds of variations in the policies are always possible, particularly in services areas where commitments historically are much weaker than in trade in goods. If deemed necessary, consultative dialogues should be held among the tax policy authorities of the regional governments on tax issues.

On the other hand, some governments, including local governments, often invest in the creation of physical infrastructure, for example in the form of a financial district. No harm is seen in this competition to the extent that such investment would not be excessive, which in practice has been the case. On a more positive note, it may be seen that such investment does not just serve the need of the financial industry, but more broadly modern businesses in general, and in this way, it adds to the productive capacity of the national economy.

(4) *Competition: Fragmentation or integration?* A final concern often expressed is that competition risks leading to greater market fragmentation. Presumably the logic is that competition of the present variety, with several financial centres actively championed by their respective authorities, will

lead to financial centre growth and unwarranted proliferation. There should be scope for such a scenario if this sponsorship of the financial centres took the shape of competition through market closure to provide a domestic base for the local champion, or competition through subsidization of investment and activities. Then there would surely be a distorted market outcome, with more players than needed and massive duplication and waste of resources. But this is not what is happening. To the contrary, competition in Asia-Pacific consists of a relentless reduction of barriers to trade and to invest, to move capital and to exchange, supplemented by improvements in infrastructure and in the legal and regulatory frameworks. All these measures facilitate trade without distorting it and increasingly allow the best player in any particular niche or sub-market to excel in it and grow. Integration then increases.

More precisely, integration increases if and to the extent that agents want integration — that investors wish to invest, move, and raise their money within the region as happens in much larger measure within highly integrated regions such as Europe or North America. The reality, however, is that integration on the ground is fairly low in Asia and Asia-Pacific: Funds in surplus countries are not moving in very large amounts to countries in the region in need of funds; they move to the global financial centres, such as New York and London, outside the region.

4.5. Regional Integration: The Ultimate Challenge

Intra-regional flows are increasing in Asia-Pacific, but levels are very low. As Jong-Wha Lee noted in his contribution to the conference,[17] less than 9 per cent of total foreign portfolio investment made by East Asia in 2003 was done within Asia, meaning that over 90 per cent of the total was invested in other regions of the world. Correspondingly, as Seade (forthcoming) noted at the conference, the percentage share in cross-border banking liabilities held by Japan, Singapore, and Hong Kong combined (as of September 2007) add to 6.2 per cent of the world total. This is less than Germany's share alone and provides a stark comparison with the 23.5 per cent global share held by banks in the United Kingdom.[18]

These figures are in no way commensurate to the region's participation in the world economy and share in global GDP or indeed, in global growth. The question is why is regional integration weak? Why do users of financial services in the region choose to place only a markedly small proportion of their financial business in the region and take most of this business to the global financial centres outside the region? Three main sets of issues were raised in the conference:

(1) *Risk perceptions and risk preferences.* First comes what probably is the standard explanation: Business is taken to London or New York by those needing the service in (or into) Asia as a matter of preference — greater confidence in those suppliers of the service. For all their impressive growth and investors' confidence on the real side of Asian economies, Asian financial systems have suffered from sustained perceptions of higher risk compared to Europe and North America, ranging from the macro economy to the quality and strength of institutions and regulations. An important factor behind those perceptions over the last decade has been the memory, still recent, of Asia's financial meltdown of the 1990s as well as remaining perceptions of risk in exchange rates. These, some think, have affected confidence in the financial system, which may in turn reduce capital flows within and into the region. Those factors would not explain why business in U.S. dollars in the region should be affected, the currency of choice for international business in the region.

Be that as it may, such risk perceptions are probably receding as the region's leading financial centres have considerably improved the regulatory systems and their acknowledged strength. The ongoing financial turbulence affecting primarily the United States and Europe that started to unfold right after this conference may well increase East Asia's appetite to place and to source its funds in greater measure within the region. Nevertheless, the reality is that the U.S. dollar remains the currency of choice for private and sovereign investors. Particularly in finance, confidence and risk perceptions can deteriorate quickly but improve only with long-term lags.

Country risk goes well beyond the macro economy and refers also to the quality and strength of institutions and regulations. But again here it is difficult to find a persuasive explanation for the region's lack of integration — the region's lower share in the global financial business they generate. Law and order in all the major established markets in the region are strong — from Japan and Korea to Hong Kong, Singapore, and Australia — while regulatory frameworks in most of these rank with the best in the world.

Risk factors are, therefore, an unlikely major explanation for the region's weak level of financial integration. But still, investors vote with their choices and they must be judging that there are lower incentives for portfolio investment and diversification within Asia than elsewhere. In particular, investors in Japan, the largest established source of surplus funds in the region, have a marked preference for global markets over diversification in East Asia.

The explanation needs to be sought elsewhere. Two factors appear to be dominant:

(2) *Scale economies and the power of incumbency.* Strength and reputation in finance are extremely resilient: Market participants seem to prefer dealing with established names across financial centres as much as among institutions. Breaking through is a major challenge. London thus remained Europe's preferred financial centre throughout the 1950s–1970s despite having poor policies, bad politics, and Europe's weakest economy and currency of those years. Further, unlike the case of trade in goods, where cross-world distances can represent an important cost differential, distance in finance matters much less. Global players can be dominant in regional financial markets, both through branches and subsidiaries and (particularly in major and dynamic areas such as securities, derivatives and foreign exchange (forex) trading) also servicing customers from afar. This importance of incumbency and relative absence of "transport costs" create enormous economies of scale, both among institutions as well as among centres of supply. Doing business with them remains desirable and cost-effective for distant customers, such as those in Asia, making it so much more difficult to internalize within the region the region's own financial business.

These economies of scale result in levels of concentration of world financial business that are ever increasing, both among financial centres and firms, creating a causal cycle where being large lowers costs, attracts business, renders larger, and so on, that make London and New York very difficult to contain let alone beat in the search for business, including Asia-Pacific-related business.

To offer just one indicator here on the scale of concentration of financial business at the global level, consider the world distribution of market share in forex transactions — a major and perhaps a classic component of international financial activity. The sector leader is London, with a huge 2007[19] global market share of 34.1 per cent, surprisingly up from 31.3 per cent in the previous Forex data year 2004. The U.K. Forex market trades twice as many U.S. dollars as does the United States, and over twice as many Euros as all euro-zone countries combined. Its 2.8 per cent increase in global market in 2004–07 compares with Japan's and Singapore's 2007 total shares of 6 per cent and 5.8 per cent, respectively, followed by Hong Kong and Australia at 4.4 per cent and 4.2 per cent. World finance is indeed, rather concentrated, and the trend in most sectors has been towards further concentration.

(3) *A fragmented space for financial business.* Additional to the advantage that history and scale give to the leading global giants, markets in Asia-Pacific other than Japan/Tokyo are divided into several separate smaller local markets: Separate capital markets; separate trading markets in each sub-sector of finance; separate legal systems, regulatory frameworks, and institutions. But perhaps most basic of all, is their lack of a common, integrated regional payments system.

4.5.1. Payments System

It is essentially as complicated to complete a transaction across two separate jurisdictions in the region as it is between any one of them and a financial powerhouse somewhere in Europe or North America. As a result, from the perspective of an investor located in the West, completing a range of transactions with as many countries in East Asia is essentially no easier from any single base in the region than it is from a major IFC elsewhere — except if direct contact and travel are required, which increasingly is not the case particularly for larger financial business. Counting on a common financial infrastructure and common payments systems is essential for the region: The financial equivalent to building an efficient highway or railway grid among neighbouring countries.

As noted above, separateness into local financial markets arises in a range of ways. Making the payments system as a basic common ground on which to build an increasingly common financial space for Asia-Pacific has been stressed. But other barriers to seamless common business can be as important although some of them may be more difficult to address other than incrementally.

4.5.2. Capital Markets

An important limitation the region faces is the lack of common, integrated capital markets as the West has built around New York and London as dominating centres, or in Chicago, Zurich/Geneva, and elsewhere for particular sub-sectors. Asia-Pacific does not have pre-eminent giants as London and New York, nor the consolidation of particular sub-sectors in dominant niche markets that the West has. Asia-Pacific has instead a range of financial centres competing hard for position in the region and beyond. This is good for competition but denies them the benefits of scale that others have. While integrating the region's capital markets is not a feasible proposition in the medium term, more could have been done to share markets and create scale. A successful first step in this direction was the creation of the Asian Bond Fund a few years ago. Further efforts to develop the bond industry at the regional level, or to promote cross-listings or double listings across the region's exchanges, would be useful steps to address scale imbalances with the major IFCs. In fact, the ASEAN+3 (APT) Finance Ministers have been making institution-building efforts on a number of fronts for the regional capital markets under the Asian Bond Market Initiative (ABMI).

4.5.3. Law and Regulation

Yet another area to note to better appreciate the challenge Asia-Pacific faces in creating a larger seamless space for business comes from the fact that, divided as it is into several small, middle, and large economies and financial centres, their legal systems and regulatory frameworks are also separate. Regulators can consult and cooperate, and they do and increasingly will. But systems of law are more fundamentally different as well as separate. Arbitration schemes and procedures, which elsewhere have been found to be an excellent way of creating legal comfort for cross-border co-investments and partnerships, do not seem to be have been much explored in the region.

4.5.4. Policy Coordination

Finally, another inhibitor of integration in the region is the fact that the quality of the policy and business institutions in the region is quite uneven. This creates — and increases perceptions of — risks for trans-border operators and for macroeconomic and exchange-rate instabilities.

5. CONCLUSION: TOWARDS AN INTEGRATED ASIA-PACIFIC IFC NETWORK

Rhetoric apart, authorities seeking to create the biggest and the best financial centres possible and capitalize on the bright potential for growth in the sector that the region has, are inevitably engaged in a hard competition thereon, a competition for financial business. This is fundamentally a competition for quality and efficiency and this is good news for everyone. But as in all walks of economic activity, competition is not always in conflict with cooperation, or not in all respects, and the challenge is how and where to combine the two philosophies for best results. In addition, unbridled competition can and will even lead down paths that pose systemic risks, and can also extend to less meritorious ways of attracting business. In a range of respects, therefore, having appropriate mechanisms for cooperation and consultation is much needed. In particular, the foregoing discussion has identified the need for the governments in the region

- to make coordinated efforts to make and maintain the national regulatory systems effective, flexible, and mutually consistent, through consultation and cooperation; and
- to enhance the existing macroeconomic and financial policy dialogues for early warning signals of possible monetary and financial instabilities, promoting close collaboration among the national early warning centres.

The efforts of those two kinds should be made in the contexts of the ASEAN+3 (APT) Finance Ministers' Meeting and the EMEAP (Emerging Market Economies of Asia-Pacific) Central Bankers Meeting by broadening and strengthening their respective mandates and agendas.

In addition, the benefits expected to flow from greater financial integration in the region have been discussed. Financial integration would enhance the efficiency and competitiveness of the economies and also the stability of financial systems in the region. But it has also been noted that integration is not happening — investors and operators seem generally to prefer going further afield beyond Asia-Pacific, in their provision of financial services than doing it from within the region on a cross-border basis.

The question is how such integration can be fostered. That is, how can the economies in the region pursue the mutual attraction of a greater share of each other's global financial business? It has been argued earlier that the answer does not lie in restricting competition: To the contrary, let competition prevail and efficiency and growth to follow. Nor should integration be pursued through a race to the bottom on regulations or subsidies or tax concessions. But then, what remains available to policymakers?

The short answer is cooperation. Cooperation is not in conflict with competition and the region needs both. Such cooperation should be aimed at creating a seamless, unified business area for finance in the region. We also discussed earlier the importance of scale in finance. The reality is that despite the enormous qualitative and market progress by Hong Kong, Singapore, and all major financial centres in the region, in terms of size they are in a different order of magnitude compared to the two global leaders.[20]

This should include action on a number of components — with four key areas — for regional cooperation — to highlight:[21]

- Move towards a seamless integrated financial region — starting with the payments system. The last sub-section discussed the burden that having a fragmented space for financial business represents. The dialogue that exists among authorities responsible for financial infrastructure in the region should be supported, attaching the highest order of importance to the creation of an integrated infrastructure and payments system in the region. This condition, which financial centres in Europe and North America enjoy through their highly developed and seamless regional financial and payment systems, is a key means for the region's plurality of financial centres to gain scale severally and collectively and increasingly function as a single one. Only in this manner can they have the reach and size to match the global giants and accrue the large economies of scale that have consistently been driving the sector towards an unprecedented and relentless level of concentration at the global level.
- Launch further initiatives towards the creation and expansion of regional capital markets in Asia-Pacific. A significant limitation Asia-Pacific faces lies in its lack of any regional capital markets — its markets being separate institutionally, legally, regulation-wise, and operationally. The region pointed the way to what cooperation can achieve with the successful creation of the Asian Bond Fund. The bond market has room for further development in the region and merits more such collective action. The ABM Initiative should

be carried forward in full steam. Similar operational cooperation should be examined for extension to other sectors, in particular to expand the scope of double listings and cross-listings in stock exchanges in the region.

- Launch ambitious in-region, WTO-consistent free-trade negotiations in financial services. The region has suddenly espoused the WTO figure of the Free Trade Area, which until a few yeas ago it had largely rejected unlike Europe and North America which have been ardent users of the system for decades now. Many FTAs among Asia-Pacific pairs of countries have been successfully negotiated in recent years. Unfortunately, the inclusion of liberalization measures in the financial sector is highly variable, and, in addition, all regional FTAs are strictly bilateral, reducing their attraction for multi-country operators. It is recommended to adopt an ambitious stance toward the further liberalization — indeed, more easily, towards in-region liberalization — of financial services, preferably among a core group of countries to make the beneficial effects of any result much more attractive to investors. An ambitious negotiation agenda in the financial sector, expanding as much as possible the ability to do business on equal terms across the gamut of financial activities in the region, would go a long way towards endowing the region's financial houses with greater economies of scale and the ability to compete with global leaders: The negotiation of the APT FTA (or East Asia FTA) or the ASEAN+6 FTA (or CEPEA) may begin with that of a financial service FTA among willing members.
- Arbitration. The fragmentation of Asia-Pacific's financial markets that arises as a result of the separateness of legal systems as well as their differences has been noetd. Arbitration procedures have been found to be an effective means of creating legal comfort for cross-border co-investments and partnerships in previous cases of integration among partners with highly different legal systems and cultures.[22] These do not seem to have been much explored in the region.

The first two measures above — on the creation of a regional payments system and instrument-by-instrument expansion of regional capital markets — are perhaps our core recommendations at this point because they are both concrete and practicable and, most of all, because they are aimed directly at helping address the problem of asymmetries in scale vis-à-vis the leading competitor IFCs. This in our view makes them a priority.

In the wake of the Asian financial crisis, the East Asian countries launched a range of financial and monetary cooperation efforts in the context of the APT Finance Ministers' Process, in the form of the Chiang Mai Initiative, the Asian Bond Market Initiative, and various policy dialogues. That group of countries has also been discussing the need to create an appropriate regional financial architecture, which would complement the IMF-sponsored international financial architecture. Beyond the more specific suggestions listed above, we would like to argue for enhancing those efforts, to deepen their level of ambition as well as enlarge their scope.

The present time is most opportune for rising to the challenge of regional cooperation for the initiatives recommended here. In the wake of the global financial turmoil triggered by the meltdown on Wall Street, the urgent need arises to critically re-assess and to restructure the global financial regulatory system. The Asia-Pacific region can and should play a leading role in these processes. The global leadership for financial development coming from the existing global centres on both sides of the Atlantic has been significantly weakened by the crisis. It now has to be repaired and enhanced with cooperation from the rest of the world. The financial centres in Asia-Pacific, and the national governments that host and regulate them, are well prepared, with the reform and strengthening of their financial markets and industries since the Asian financial crisis of 1997–98 and with the parallel efforts to modernize and internationalize them under the IFC drives, to contribute to this process collectively as a new major participant.

They should contribute not so much with rhetoric as with actions — actions to strengthen themselves as a regional network of IFCs as well as the regional infrastructure to support this network. Specifically, they should continue their efforts to develop and internationalize their national regulatory systems and financial industries, cooperating to strengthen both of these at the level of the region and to facilitate businesses across the region, thus progressing toward an integrated Asia-Pacific IFC network. These efforts will hopefully herald the emergence of an Asia-Pacific financial community as well as the ascendancy of a new global financial system with Asia-Pacific as an IFC network joining the ranks of such global market leaders as London and New York in a richer and more balanced array of international financial centres. This is one last call for regional cooperation we make here.

Notes

1. See the chapter by Jesús Seade in the present volume for a comprehensive and informative case study on Hong Kong as an IFC, as well as Sang Kee Min and David Hong for their comments on this case study.
2. See the chapter by Tan Khee-Giap in the present volume for a comprehensive and informative case study on Singapore as an IFC, as well as Sang Kee Min and David Hong for their comments on this case study.
3. Economic Review Committee, Sub-committee on Services Industries, Financial Servicies Working Group (September 2002), "Positioning Singapore as a Pre-eminent Financial Centre in Asia", Singapore Government.
4. See the chapter by Sayuri Shirai in the present volume for a comprehensive and informative case study of Tokyo as an IFC, as well as Simon Cooper and Hugh Patrick for their comments on this chapter. Also, see the chapter on Tokyo contributed by Masahiro Kawai. It is an excellent elaboration of the author's own comments at the conference, contributed after the conference. Also, see Tan Teck Meng for his comparative assessments of Tokyo and Sydney.
5. See Nicholas Gruen in the present volume for a comprehensive and informative case study of Sydney as an IFC. Also, see Simon Cooper and Hugh Patrick for their comments on this case study, as well as Tan Teck Meng for his comparative comments on Tokyo and Sydney.
6. See Xu Mingqi in the present volume for a comprehensive and informative case study of Shanghai as an IFC. Also, see James Rooney and Sang Yong Park for their comments on this case study.
7. See Roger Bowden in the present volume for a comprehensive and informative case study of Wellington as an IFC. Also, see James Rooney and Sang Yong Park for their comments on this case study.
8. See Han Soo Kim in the present volume for a comprehensive and informative case study of Seoul as an IFC. Also, see James Rooney and Sang Yong Park for their comments on this case study, as well as the dinner speech at the conference on Seoul as an IFC by Yong-Ro Yun, then Vice-Chairman of Korea's Financial Supervisory Commission, in Appendix I of this volume.
9. See Dominic Barton in the present volume.
10. We do not claim that deregulation is good while regulation is bad. Since the subprime crisis, many have criticized the United States for not having implemented sufficient regulations, such as regulations for SIV, credit rating

agencies, and shadow banks, including investment banks and hedge funds, although the U.S. accounting for listed firms has become more stringent. It is argued here that regulation is necessary but it should be "good", and that regulation is "bad" if it is excessive.

11. See comments by Sang Yong Park in the present volume for this discussion.
12. The Global Financial Centres Index (GFCI) published by the City of London Corporation focuses on real estate assessments, occupancy costs, and other property assessments. The Korea Securities Research Institute's International Finance Environment Index combines telecommunication networking, IT infrastructure, and public transportation infrastructure like roads, airports, and rail. Finally, the Mastercard Worldwide Centres of Commerce Index divides the weighting between soft infrastructures like entering and exiting costs, efficiency in logistics, and supporting transport linkages.
13. *The Economist*, "The Economist Intelligence Unit's Quality of Life Index", 2008.
14. See Seade, op. cit.
15. Or better put, be able to disqualify the examinee all by itself, as if multiplying sub-indices by one another, instead of adding them up. This is not a game of arithmetic modelling, but the issue is what indicator accords best with the objective sought. We believe that a very bad mark in an essential criterion should weigh down the score overall, and not just fail to add to it. But, easier to be cautious in the use of indices.
16. See their respective presentations in this volume.
17. Data from IMF Coordinated Portfolio Investment Survey, 2003.
18. Data from BIS, Locational Banking Statistics, September 2007.
19. The leading source of information on Forex trade is the Bank for International Settlements (BIS), which every three years, in cooperation with national authorities, conducts a survey of all Forex transactions taking place each day during the month of April. This survey is held triennially.
20. This includes Tokyo, too, whose stock and bond markets are among the largest in the world but not so when one refers to international or cross-border business.
21. This material draws in particular from Seade and Lee, both presented in this volume.
22. For example, between the United States and Mexico in the context of NAFTA.

References

City of London Corporation. *The Global Financial Centres Index*. London: Z/Yen Limited, 2007. <http://www.zyen.com/Activities/On-line%20surveys/GFCI.htm>.

———. *The Global Financial Centres Index* 2. London: Z/Yen Limited, 2007. <http://www.zyen.com/Activities/On-line%20surveys/GFCI.htm>.

———. *The Global Financial Centres Index* 3. London: Z/Yen Limited, 2008. <http://www.zyen.com/Activities/On-line%20surveys/GFCI.htm>.

———. *The Global Financial Centres Index* 4. London: Z/Yen Limited, 2008. <http://www.zyen.com/Activities/On-line%20surveys/GFCI.htm>.

Economic Review Committee, Sub-committee on Services Industries, Financial Services Working Group. "Positioning Singapore as a Pre-eminent Financial Centre in Asia". Singapore Government, 2002.

The Economist. "The Economist Intelligence Unit's Quality of Life Index", 2008.

PART II
Case Studies

2

HONG KONG AND EAST ASIA'S FINANCIAL CENTRES AND GLOBAL COMPETITION

Jesús Seade

1. INTRODUCTION

The importance of financial activity for East Asia cannot be overstated. The enormous and fast-growing regional economy requires to be underpinned by a strong, modern and diversified financial sector. The 1990s crisis is a receding memory, but many observers agree that two important contributing factors behind it were too much dependence on bank finance and inadequate corporate accountability and regulation — both of which variables again speak of the need for a strong, reliable and well diversified financial sector. And indeed, several cities in the region have developed strong positions as national, regional or international financial centres, and many city authorities have made plain their determination to see their cities remain or become major global players in the area.

Modern banking entered the region through Hong Kong and Shanghai, both in the mid-nineteenth century. While these always remained important banking and financial centres over the next 100 years, several other centres soon developed that joined them in the region's top ranks, in particular Tokyo and Singapore, but also Beirut, Bombay (Mumbai), Seoul, Sydney. Two observations are worth drawing from the historical perspective:

First, like the major financial centres that developed early on in Europe — London, Paris, Berlin, Amsterdam — those that arose and took an early lead in Asia were also major trading centres, on major trading routes. But there is a striking contrast. The European cases were all also major cities and centres of power. In a European context it is natural to wonder which of those two factors was the key to their ascent as financial capitals: The centre of power or the centre for trade. Causality in this area is an impossible task, but Asia tells an interestingly different story. In Asia some cases were similar: For example Tokyo; perhaps Shanghai. But Hong Kong, Singapore, Beirut? As in Europe, these are all major trading centres. But most are in small countries — well connected, trade-bound, strategically located places. The historical development of financial centres in Asia seems to suggest that the trade connection is a key determinant. This is not meant to deny that other factors are crucial too, particularly when it comes to gaining a position in the global market place. We return to these issues below.

Second, all the financial centres that developed and gained importance early on in the process of European financial development remained important forever after. But one of them came clearly on top. Here we have a sharp but intriguing difference between Asia and the other major economic regions of the world — Asia never developed an early and sustained dominant player in the financial arena.

Indeed, London took the lead in Europe gradually from the early nineteenth century and decisively after 1870 — boosted by Paris having to decree a suspension of payments in the face of its war with Germany, and the latter ending up with large claims in sterling. London's lead in the European context was never to be lost, despite a weak economy and an acrimonious political climate throughout much of the twentieth century, and important challenges such as the creation of Frankfurt-based Euroland. Similarly New York City (NYC), after an initial headstart by Philadelphia as the commercial, banking and political capital of the nascent United States of America, soon took the lead as its country's prime financial centre, and retained that position ever since.

In contrast, the four lead financial centres in Asia have remained the same and have alternated in relative importance over the last 100 years, with no firm leader emerging. Tokyo was ahead in the 1910s and 1920s, but lost out through nationalism and war in the 1930s and 1940s, to Shanghai, and to Hong Kong and Singapore which were and remained important players all along. Shanghai on its part saw vigorous growth in the 1910s to 1930s, sharply increasing the number of its foreign banks and trebling its population in that period. Its international role as a financial centre went into suspense with China's shift in economic model in the late 1940s, and the following decades of strong regional economic growth saw the return of Tokyo to centre stage while Hong Kong and Singapore consolidated and consistently continued to develop their strong international positions.

This brings us to the present. Shanghai has of course made a spectacular return as a major financial centre, already boasting the second largest stock exchange in Asia-Pacific with a market capitalization of US$3,176 billion at end-February 2008, despite recent adjustments and after a meteoric four-fold increase (in U.S. dollar) in 2007 alone. On its part Hong Kong is a sophisticated and highly diversified financial centre, very strong in banking, equities and a range of areas of financial activity. The recent reports commissioned by the City of London Corporation and published six-monthly since March 2007[1] rate Hong Kong as the third strongest international financial centre, behind only global leaders London and NYC, on the basis of its strong performance across all areas of finance and all factors that make a financial centre succeed. Very similar remarks apply to Singapore, rated fourth and just behind Hong Kong by the said report, which again has a very strong presence overall and is actually ahead of Hong Kong and growing very strongly in key and dynamic sectors such as forex markets and OTC derivatives.[2] Last but by no means least, among the top tier of financial centres in the region, is of course Tokyo, which with the second largest economy in the world behind it, has the largest stock exchange and forex and derivatives turnovers in the region.

Alongside these four regional financial leaders, Taipei and particularly Seoul also are important participants in regional financial business, with large stock exchanges serving strong economies, and the latter fuelling their financial sectors more broadly. Other major centres in the broader Asia-Pacific region — particularly Sydney and Mumbai — also frequently compete for East Asian business or for bilateral financial business within it, as of course do the global giants in Europe and North America.

Table 2.1
Leading East Asian Stock Exchanges: Domestic Market Capitalization
(End-February 2008, in US$ billion)

1.	Tokyo	$4,158
2.	Shanghai	$3,176
3.	Hong Kong	$2,340
4.	Korea	$1,016
5.	Shenzhen	$784
6.	Taiwan	$692
7.	Singapore	$494

Source: World Federation of Exchanges, <www.world-exchanges.org>.

This chapter will examine the lay of the land in the region in three major areas of financial activity: Banking, foreign exchange, and debt. The choice of these is arbitrary, equities (and IPOs) are hugely important to the regions' financing and financial centres. Derivatives are an extremely dynamic component of modern financial markets, and in the performance of major financial centres in the region. But international banking and foreign exchange transactions are perhaps the epitome of international finance, and debt is an area where Asia has been widely acknowledged to lag behind other regions in the past but where the outlook has changed significantly in recent years. These three areas therefore all are highly important and interesting to examine.

Sections 2 to 6 discuss the state of competition in the three areas mentioned. For each, the focus will be on the participation of the region's major financial centres relative to the leading centres of Europe and America. Finally Section 7 briefly discusses potential scenarios for the future of locational structure in the region and offers some comments on the form cooperation in selected areas might take — against the background of continuing consolidation in financial industries globally and the region's strong economic dynamics, both of which point to the need for global players in the provision of financial service to the region.

2. CROSS-BORDER BANKING: WHERE IS THE BUSINESS?

Two different sets of data on cross-border banking activity are collected and made available by the BIS, each geared at answering different kinds of questions. These are:

- *Locational statistics*, which concentrate on the role of banks and financial centres in the intermediation of international capital flows. These therefore provide data on the gross international financial claims and liabilities of banks resident in a given country regardless of the nationality of headquarters, recording all positions including those vis-à-vis own affiliates; and
- *Consolidated statistics*, which concentrate on the global activities and risk positions of banks themselves as consolidated entities. These therefore provide data on banks' contractual lending (on-balance-sheet financial claims) by the head office and all its branches and subsidiaries worldwide, netting out inter-office accounts.

These two sets of data address different questions and may be used to complement each other in the analysis. The primary interest here — trying to measure the scope and scale of international financial activity operating from different centres — lies with locational statistics, which tell us what and how much all those (domestic and foreign) banks that are based in a given financial centre are doing. But consolidated statistics shed useful additional light, as they inform us about the global activities of financial institutions headquartered in given centres. The main purpose of consolidated statistics, however, is to provide a measure of the risk exposures of lenders' national banking systems, which is not the focus here.

The following presents summary data for East Asian countries as available, alongside selected major western markets or locations for comparison.

The overall picture for international banking as a whole is one of continuing healthy development and a steady growth. In March 2007, BIS reporting banks' cross-border claims stood at US$28,476.3 billion, having grown by 18 per cent on a year-on-year basis (December 2006 on December 2005). Cross-border liabilities stood at US$26,595.4 billion in March 2007, increasing 17 per cent (again, December 2006 on December 2005).

The locational distribution of claims is summarized in Tables 2.2 and 2.3 below. The figures are somewhat striking: Notice the disparity between Western and East Asian cross-border banking figures. Japan's, for example, are much lower both on the assets and the liabilities sides than those for the three European countries on those tables, despite its larger economy. Even Hong Kong and Singapore, whose financial systems are much more strongly focused on international activity, have cross-border bank positions roughly in proportion to the relative sizes of their economies compared to those of the European countries reported.

Table 2.2
Locational Statistics: External Positions of Banks

LIABILITIES
Selected countries, in all currencies
(Amounts: September 2007; Percentage change:
December 2006 on December 2005)

	US$ billion	% change		US$ billion	% change
Hong Kong	418.4	15.4	France	2,644.3	18.6
Japan	659.4	(–4.7)	Germany	2,012.6	17.0
Singapore	646.1	11.3	U.K.	6,943.5	24.2
			U.S.	3,553.6	27.5

Table 2.3
Locational Statistics: External Positions of Banks

ASSETS
Selected countries, in all currencies
(Amounts: September 2007; Percentage change:
December 2006 on December 2005)

Hong Kong	727.4	21.2	France	2,660.3	14.4
Japan	2,217.2	7.2	Germany	3,419.8	31.0
Singapore	736.0	11.5	U.K.	6,567.1	25.4
			U.S.	2,852.8	23.9

Source: BIS, *Locational Banking Statistics*, Sep 2007, <http://www.bis.org/statistics/bankstats.htm>.

Of course, these relatively small outstanding volumes of assets and liabilities can be explained at least partially by the Asian financial crisis that broke out only a decade ago, and by Japan's economic slump through much of the period immediately before and since. But then, one would expect that, with such catching-up still waiting to be done (recovering from those events, and catching up on the levels), and with the much faster economic growth that East Asia has consistently achieved in recent years, and on balance in recent decades compared to its Western counterparts, the recent rates of growth of their cross-border banking activities would have been correspondingly higher than the West's. It is again striking that this is not the case — on balance, the opposite is true. Local and resident banking in East Asia still has considerable room to expand to fully profit from the opportunities that the region's economic size and growth represents.

Table 2.3 contains only the latest figures available. Time paths for liabilities and for assets are shown in Figures 2.1 and 2.2 respectively.

The percentage shares in total global cross-border liabilities as of September 2007 are:

1 United Kingdom: 23.5% (6,943.5 / 29,584.6)
2 United States: 12.0% (3,553.6 / 29,584.6)
3 France: 8.9% (2,644.3 / 29,584.6)
4 Germany: 6.8% (2,012.6 / 29,584.6)
11 Japan: 2.3% (677.7 / 29,584.6)
12 Singapore: 2.5% (740.2 / 29,584.6)
17 Hong Kong: 1.4% (418.4 / 29,584.6)

Figure 2.1
Cross-border Liabilities

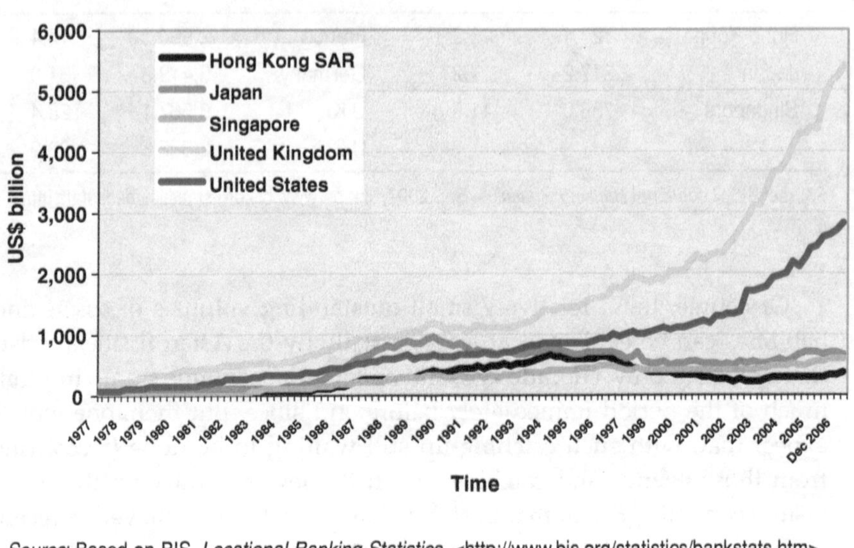

Source: Based on BIS, *Locational Banking Statistics*, <http://www.bis.org/statistics/bankstats.htm>.

Figure 2.2
Cross-border Claims

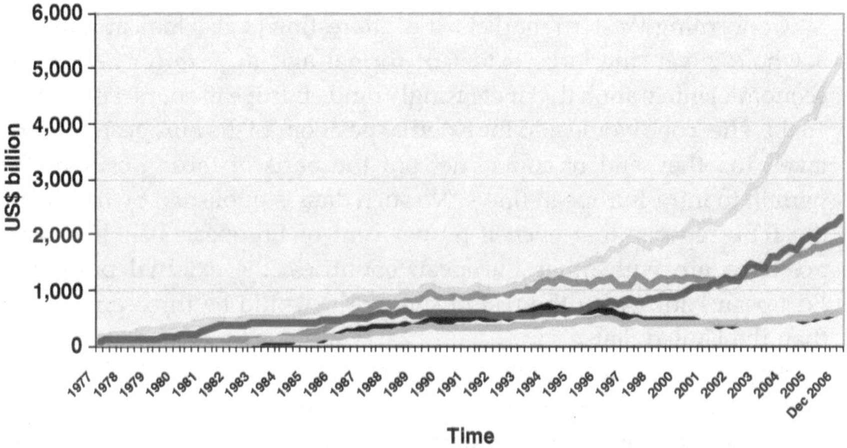

Source: Based on BIS, *Locational Banking Statistics*, <http://www.bis.org/statistics/bankstats.htm>.

where the left column provides the rank, out of the forty jurisdictions in the BIS reporting system. As for assets, time paths are given in Figure 2.2.

The percentage shares in total global cross-border assets as of September 2007 are:

1 United Kingdom: 20.6% (6,567.1 / 31,816.2)
2 Germany: 10.7% (3,419.8 / 31,816.2)
3 United States: 9.0% (2,852.8 / 31,816.2)
4 France: 8.4% (2,660.3 / 31,816.2)
5 Japan: 7.0% (2,217.2 / 31,816.2)
12 Singapore: 2.3% (736.0/ 31,816.2)
13 Hong Kong: 2.3% (727.4/ 31,816.2)

where again the listing number is rank, out of the forty reporting jurisdictions.

Figures 2.1 and 2.2 show dramatically how the decade following the mid-1990s was a rather dormant one for the industry in East Asia. In both lending and deposits, Japan fell from third rank to sixth rank globally over that period, while Singapore and Hong Kong fell several places too. Japan's withdrawal from Hong Kong was major: In 1996 it had eighty-six banks in

Hong Kong, the largest concentration outside Japan and accounting for 55.6 per cent of Hong Kong banking sector's loans. By 2003, these had withered to twenty-two, and their market share had shrunk accordingly.

Concerning Western markets, it is interesting to also look at Europe as a whole, given the large extent of formal and *de facto* (or *de jure* and economic) integration that increasingly binds European countries together. To this effect one would add the external positions of the European countries taken together, and of course net out the parts of those positions that pertain to intra-European flows. No such data is published by the BIS but the IFSL reports[3] that even if 60 per cent of European banks' external positions are with other European countries, the external position of European banks with the rest of the world would be three times larger than the United States'.

The above analysis shows the level and geographical distribution of financial activity as conducted from the respective financial centres, with numbers based on locational statistics, treating a local branch as a local bank. The picture is rather different if we look at banks' positions on a consolidated basis, that is, remitting the accounting of loans and deposits back to headquarters. For these, very briefly, the picture is as shown in Table 2.4.

Compared to the locational figures, the relative participation of U.S. banks increases hugely, which is what one would have expected given their size and importance, much of which is exercised through foreign locations — surely dwarfing cross-border lending done from the United

Table 2.4
Consolidated Statistics:
Claims of Reporting Banks
(Immediate borrower basis; in US$ billion; March 2007)

Hong Kong	363
Singapore	207
Japan	852
France	1,702
Germany	2,125
U.K.	4,244
U.S.	6,429

Source: BIS, *Locational Banking Statistics*, Sep 2007, <http://www.bis.org/statistics/bankstats.htm>.

States by non-U.S. banks. Within the East Asian region, the opposite correction is observed concerning in particular the figures for Singapore, whose participation is much more important at the locational level.

The dominant position of European and U.S. banks reflected in the above figures conforms with the more direct impression one gets by looking at numbers of banks in different jurisdictions (Table 2.5).

Total number of banks has decreased substantially in all five jurisdictions all along this period, almost without even one-year reversals in the direction of change. The changes partly reflect the progressive consolidation the industry has been undergoing. In East Asia, this has also reflected the battering the industry suffered with the crisis of the 1990s, especially of the Japanese banks, and the considerable extent of their withdrawal from regional markets in turmoil, particularly from Hong Kong.

The number of branches is not a relevant indicator among economies of very different sizes, but has some significance as among economies of broadly similar size. It is interesting to note, for instance, how many fewer

Table 2.5
Number of Banks in Major Banking Centres

	U.S.	U.K.	Japan	Hong Kong[a]	Singapore
1995	9,940	481	150	243 (179)	
1996	9,527	502	146	249 (186)	
1997	9,143	500	145	244 (182)	
1998	8,774	468	138	243 (177)	154
1999	8,580	464	137	228 (168)	142
2000	8,315	431	137	207 (154)	140
2001	8,079	428	136	203 (155)	133
2002	7,888	390	133	190 (142)	120
2003	7,770	382	134	180 (135)	117
2004	7,630	360	131	178 (136)	115
2005	7,540	347	129	172 (133)	111
2006				166 (133)	108
2007				167 (137)	

Note: a. First figure: total number of licensed and restricted license banks. In brackets: licensed alone.

Sources: Hong Kong Monetary Authority, Monetary Authority of Singapore, IFSL from Japanese Bankers Association, Federal Reserve, Bank of England, Financial Services Authority, British Bankers' Association and IFSL estimates.

branches than all other large Western countries the United Kingdom has, and Japan even fewer, while the United States, and particularly, Germany endow themselves with many branches even after accounting for their respective sizes (Table 2.6).

On the other hand, a more interesting indicator of the international engagement of financial centres is the presence of foreign banks in it, from among the totals listed in Table 2.5 above. The numbers are shown in Table 2.7.

Table 2.6
Number of Banks and Branches in Largest Banking Centres, 2004

	Number of banks	Number of branches
U.S.	7,559	72,822
Japan	129	12,539
Germany	2,171	47,581
France	897	39,825
Italy	778	30,944
UK	405	14,015
Switzerland	299	2,630

Source: IFSL, from European Banking Federation, U.S. Federal Reserve, Insurance Information Institute.

Table 2.7
Number of Foreign Banking Institutions
(March 2005; * March 2003)

London[a]	264
New York[a]	228
Paris[b]	179
Frankfurt[b]	129
Hong Kong[c]	116
Singapore[d]	103
Tokyo[a]	69

Notes: a. March 2005; b. March 2003; c. March 2007 (including thirteen restricted licences); d. March 2006.

Sources: Hong Kong Monetary Authority, Monetary Authority of Singapore, Bank of England, IFSL, *The Banker*, BIS.

London is thus the most popular centre with 264 foreign banks, followed by New York City with 228 foreign branches. The smaller number of foreign banks in New York is largely an indicator of the nature of the U.S. banking industry, which is more oriented towards serving the domestic market.

In the same vein, we note the much smaller number of foreign banks in Tokyo compared to Hong Kong and Singapore, again reflecting the Japanese banking industry's greater relative orientation towards serving the domestic economy.

3. GLOBAL BANKING AND GLOBAL CONCENTRATION

Alongside the expansion of banks' cross-border flows and establishment in other markets, discussed in the previous section, the globalization of finance has brought with it a relentless movement towards increasing concentration in the industry, both globally and in most individual markets. Consider the following figures:

Table 2.8
Cumulative Distribution of Asset Holdings among the World's 1,000 Largest Banks Measured by Assets

	Top 10	Top 20	Top 50	"Bottom" 950
1995	14	24	45	55
2005	19	32	56	44

Source: IFSL, *The Banker*.

The figures are impressive: As a result of consolidation in the banking sector:

— the share of assets of the largest ten banks worldwide has increased from 14 per cent to 19 per cent in only a decade, from 1994/95 to 2004/05;

— in terms of concentration of capital and profits (not shown), the six largest banks in the world by Tier 1 capital (core equity) account for 15 per cent of global banking capital and 17.2 per cent of aggregate profits;

— back to asset distribution, the top fifty banks have well in excess of half of all banking assets worldwide;
— the share of the remaining 950 banks consequently declined in this period from 55 per cent to 44 per cent.

With this process, the largest banks in the world have become very large:

Table 2.9
The Fifteen Largest Banks in the World by Tier 1 Capital[a]
(In US$ billion, 2007)

1.	Bank of America Corp	U.S.	91.1
2.	Citigroup	U.S.	90.9
3.	HSBC Holdings	U.K.	87.8
4.	Crédit Agricole Groupe	France	84.9
5.	JP Morgan Chase & Co.	U.S.	63.9
6.	Mitsubishi UFJ Financial Group	Japan	60.6
7.	ICBC	China	48.6
8.	Royal Bank of Scotland	U.K.	39.6
9.	Bank of China	China	38.8
10.	Santander Central Hispano	Spain	38.4
11.	PNB Paribas	France	35.6
12.	Barclays Bank	U.K.	35.6
13.	HBOS	U.K.	34.0
14.	China Construction Bank Corporation	China	32.5
15.	Mizuho Financial Group	Japan	32.3

Note: a. Core Equity Capital, as defined under Basel I and II.
Source: *The Banker*.

In 2006 Citigroup was (as in the seven previous years) the largest bank in the world, in terms of both Tier 1 capital and assets. It also had the most profits (US$29.4 billion) and is one of the most profitable banks in the world, with 37 per cent return on capital. HSBC is now a close second, with US$74.4 billion of capital and a return of 28.2 per cent.

Regions and countries with most banks among the top 1,000 were the EU (with 286 of the 1,000, accounting for 50.7 per cent of banks' aggregate assets and 37.4 per cent of aggregate profits); the United States (with 197 of the 1,000, accounting for 26.5 per cent of aggregate profits), Japan (106), Germany (94) and the United Kingdom (36).

The Asian crisis ten years ago and the bad times Japan and its banking sector had in the 1990s and earlier this decade had a substantial impact on the largest Japanese banks. Their number has declined since the mid-1990s, when Japanese banks held the top six places in the rankings of largest banks, to a still respectable three banks among the largest ten last year.

The number of U.S. and European banks at the top of the rankings has increased during this period, with a solid presence of three U.S. banks among the top four and four European among the top ten (and four more in the next five) — including one of Spain's, the latest newcomer in the top league. China's presence is beginning to be felt at the heights of this league, with its CCBC ranking just outside the top ten, and will doubtless become stronger in years to come.

Alongside the banks becoming larger, their business is becoming more global, facilitated by the reduction in barriers to international trade as well as technological developments. The world's most international banks come from a greater diversity of backgrounds than the ten or fifteen largest, as shown in Table 2.10.

Table 2.10
Banks with Most Assets Abroad
(Percentage share, 2002–03)

		Assets abroad	Staff abroad
1. American Express Bank	U.S.	86	85
2. UBS	Switzerland	84	58
3. Arab Banking Corporation	Bahrain	84	n/a
4. Credit Suisse Group	Switzerland	80	56
5. Standard Chartered	U.K.	70	n/a
6. Deutsche Bank	Germany	66	49
7. ABN Amro Bank	Netherlands	65	67
8. BNP Paribas	France	63	41
9. Investec	S. Africa	63	44
10. KBC	Belgium	58	52
11. RZB Group	Austria	58	79
12. HSBC Holdings	U.K.	57	59
13. ING Bank	Netherlands	56	61
14. Allied Irish Banks	Ireland	53	60
15. Erste Bank Group	Austria	51	74

Source: *The Banker*.

The proportion of overseas assets and income generated abroad is an indicator of the international presence of a bank. By this criterion, European banks rank high, with a solid participation of twelve among the world's fifteen banks with the most assets abroad (in 2003). The top place, however, went to American Express Bank. Interestingly, only two among the world's largest fifteen banks count among the geographically most diversified in their asset base: These are HSBC and ABN Amro.[4] This may come as somewhat of a surprise, since a major means to gain scale is through mergers and acquisitions (M&A), and these, where crossing borders, also add to the geographical diversity in question. Clearly, much as M&A have advanced internationally in the banking industry, they have done so more within national borders.

4. COMPETITIVE ENVIRONMENT: DOMESTIC MARKET CONCENTRATION AND REGULATION

Is the global concentration of banking observed in Table 2.8 above reflected in high or increasing concentration of the sector in individual countries?

Global concentration has in many cases followed from the adoption of more open regimes, which can lead to M&As among domestic banks or involving foreign entrants thus creating fewer and larger operators. But in other cases, the national processes of liberalization has arisen from highly concentrated structures, allowing for the entry of new participants thereby reducing concentration.

In turn, concentration old or new, if enjoyed behind a veil of tolerance towards monopoly practices, can be a source of inefficiency, affecting performance. But concentration can have the opposite effect if it arises out of M&A by domestic or foreign — but more efficient — market operators, who bring with them technology transfer and international best practices. Over and beyond its prime function of safeguarding the health and stability of the system, the regulatory framework is crucial in all cases to ensure efficient and competitive performance by the industry — to ensure the market is contestable by alternative domestic or foreign operators if they detect monopoly rents or the opportunity to improve results.

The careful examination of the performance of financial centres in East Asia that the above issues call for is well beyond the scope of the present chapter. Those are the central questions being addressed in the research programme underway at Lingnan University of which this chapter is a preliminary, first delivery. But it is of interest at this point to look briefly at some illustrative numbers and facts. Table 2.11 presents figures on concentration of banking activity in selected East and Southeast Asian countries as well as major developed financial centres in various regions.

No clear-cut pattern is discernible to relate concentration with scale or performance, but some broad observations may be warranted. For a given level of underlying competition and concentration, one expects larger markets to have lower measured concentration levels.[5] In this sense it is fair to say from the table that the United Kingdom's level of concentration is lower than for all other major industrial countries its size or bigger. This greater nominal competition, plus the fact that the United Kingdom's regulatory framework ensures that vicinity in the marketplace translates into actual competition, is consistent with London's extraordinary success as a financial centre in recent decades. Other low levels of concentration to note are Germany's and Luxembourg's.

From the Asian centres on the list, Hong Kong has among the lowest measured concentration levels on the list, and lower still if we again apply the above logic — which would cast it as the most fiercely competitive of the Asian banking markets, which its success in the sector seems to be consistent with.

The previous table gave us concentration defined in a certain way and from a certain source. Table 2.12 presents analogous figures but from

Table 2.11
Share of Domestic Assets and Deposits Held by the Five Largest Banks
(Selected Asia-Pacific and Western Countries, 2001)

	Deposits[a]	Assets[a]		Deposits[a]	Assets[a]
Hong Kong	58	42	Canada	87.4	80
Japan[b]	45.7	46.4	France	70	60
Korea	77.3	75.2	Germany[c]	21	20
Malaysia	57.1	55.7	Luxembourg	27.8	27.9
Philippines	45.9	43.0	Spain	43.7	53.2
Singapore	N/A	N/A	Switzerland	69	72
Thailand	70.1	64.8	U.K.	24	23
Australia	74	76	U.S.	29	30
New Zealand	85.7	85.6			

Note: a. End 2001; b. End March 2002; c. End-2002.
Source: Database from Barth, et al. (2006).

Table 2.12
Share of the Three Largest Banks in all Commercial Bank Assets, 1990–2005

	1991	1996	2001	2003	2005
East/Southeast Asia					
China	96	89	78	60	79
Hong Kong, China	94[a]	75	76	68	74
Japan	52	49	46	41	41
Korea	56[a]	48	53	52	50
Malaysia	—	49	44	39	50
Philippines	95[b]	72	64	50	60
Singapore	—	97	97	93	100
Thailand	64	54	52	52	48
Selected Industrial					
Australia	89	64	64	64	69
Canada	93	60	54	53	59
France	23	57	58	56	73
Germany	80	74	63	64	83
Luxembourg	29	26	25	28	36
New Zealand	—	81	75	70	80
Spain	99	91	82	84	70
Switzerland	37	31	87	87	37
U.K.	62	50	41	48	66
U.S.	32[b]	34	28	26	31

Note: a. 1992; b. 1993
Source: Beck et al. (2000) database, from Fitch's BankScope database.

another source, this time for the top three asset holders, and over time. In addition, this source also includes China, not available in the previous source. The period covered is interesting: Before and after the Asian crisis, Japan's problems, much of the post-Big Bang (1986) and broader reforms era for the United Kingdom. Data for the same countries as in the previous table have been selected for comparability plus China, and selected years spanning the period available. Consider then Table 2.12.

Sources and definitions differ between these two tables. We will not focus too much on comparisons except to note that both Hong Kong's and the United Kingdom's levels of concentration are less clearly lower than for countries of similar size compared to Table 2.11 — and have both gone up in recent years. Presumably, the strong competition their open banking systems face internationally and their regulatory systems, both often cited as market friendly, ensure that competitiveness is upheld with the shrinking level of competition domestically. But not too much can be read from these numbers in isolation. Two striking facts to note here are the strong movements up and down in Switzerland's reported shares, and France's sharp rise in measured concentration over the period.

The importance the regulatory framework has for competition and performance over and beyond its primary prudential function has been referred to earlier. Regulations can hinder competition in a number of ways, deterring entry directly, increasing costs for operators, or creating unnecessary forms or levels of uncertainty. Regulations are extremely diverse in their nature, form and incidence, and their proper study — let alone quantification of their effects — is an enormous task currently underway in our project. On a purely illustrative basis, a few indicators of the different forms regulations can come into play in affecting performance are presented in Table 2.13.

The second row of the table indicates the broad line of effect on competition the regulation in question might have. The first two columns, on whether more than one agency is involved in granting licences to banks, and whether more than one licence is required to engage in different banking activities, touch on the ease with which a new operator can enter the industry or an established operator can diversify into new banking business. On the first of these, most countries on the list responded "No", the exception being the United States, which has a more complicated structure of jurisdiction between the federal and state levels. The second criterion gives us a richer and more interesting division of responses among our countries. France, Luxembourg, Spain, Canada and New Zealand join the United Kingdom in having the more liberal practice here, while Germany, Switzerland and Australia share the slightly less pro-competitive approach with the United States. In our region the dichotomy is sharper, with only Hong Kong and Japan espousing universal licences, while Korea and all the ASEAN countries in the sample share the more traditional approach of Australia and the United States on this issue.

The second block of questions (columns 3 and 4) on applications received and denied is partly about regulatory response, and partly about (foreign entities') interest into entry in the sector. With the volume of applications reported being mostly in line with the size with the respective financial sectors and with virtually no denied applications reported, no further comment is offered is left.

The third block of issues is important and interesting. Column 5 asks whether there is a single supervisory agency for the financial sector, along the lines of the "one-stop shop" London created in the Financial Services

Table 2.13
Selective Regulatory Indicators, 2006

	Ease of entry		Active entry by foreigners		Burdensome supervision	Effective supervision
	1 Is there more than one agency that grants licences to banks?	2 Is more than one licence required? (e.g. For each banking activity)	3 Number of commercial banking licence applications received from foreign entities (last 5 years)	4 Of these, number denied	5 Is there a single supervisory agency for the financial sector?	6 Are supervisors legally liable for their actions? (e.g. Can they be sued for an action taken against a bank?)
Hong Kong	No	No	25	0	No	No
Japan	No	No	21	0	Yes[a]	No
Korea	No	Yes	5	0	Yes	Yes
Malaysia	No	Yes	0[b]	N.A.	No	No
Philippines	No	Yes	0	0	No	Yes
Singapore	No	Yes	N.A.	N.A.	Yes	No[c]
Thailand	No	Yes	0	0	No	Yes
Australia	No	Yes	10	0	No	No
N. Zealand	No	No	6	0	Yes	No
Canada	No	No	169	N.A.[d]	No	No
France	No	No	N.A.	N.A.	No	Yes
Germany	No	Yes	135[e]	0	Yes	No
Luxembourg	No	No	19	0	Yes	No
Spain	No	No	38	1	No	Yes
Switzerland	No	Yes	50	N.A.	No	No
U.K.	No	No	N.A.	N.A.	Yes	No
U.S.	Yes	Yes	84	0	No	No

Notes: a. Except for credit cooperatives and government banking institutions; b. Not permitted; must be locally incorporated; c. "Unless acted in bad faith"; d. Not tracked; e. Covers licences granted, and for domestic and foreign together (neither applications and denials, nor domestic and foreign, are tracked separately).

Source: Database from Barth et al. (2006).

Authority, regulator of banks, insurance companies, financial advisers and (since 2004–05) mortgage businesses and other insurance intermediaries. While this system has been criticized by some as creating a race to the bottom with its light approach to regulation, most agree that the system has worked well, and may have been the single most important factor behind London's formidable success as a financial centre over the last decade. Other countries have different arrangements and allocations of responsibilities to regulatory organs, but those on the list responding in the affirmative in column 5 have established the essentials of this streamlined approach to regulation, that considerably reduces reporting costs and uncertainties to participants in the market.

Finally, column 6 refers to the legal assurance supervisors need to have in order to discharge their duties without special consideration to power or influence. Outside the region, most countries listed do grant this protection to supervisors, the exceptions being France and Spain only, perhaps reflecting the greater weight the French civil law tradition gives to upholding institutions including the firm. It is also interesting to note the greater dispersion of answers on this question among the countries of East and Southeast Asia compared to the Western countries listed, although the three leading financial-centre countries in the region fall into the same camp on this issue.

Whatever the factors may be that determine costs of financial activity in different locations, at the end of the day efficiency does differ among centres and regions, and these differences are central to determining performance. This being a bottom-line priority in the research work underway at Lingnan University on Hong Kong and the financial centres of the region, let us only mention at this point some aggregate figures reported by *The Banker* in a recent assessment on relative bank efficiency by regions, using cost/income ratios as the measure (see Figure 2.3).

The figures suggest that Japanese banks performed relatively badly in 2006 — the weakest of the country or region groupings they report, whereas Middle Eastern banks did rather well (as they did the previous year). Although broadly in line with average performance in other regions, non-Japan Asia did fairly well at least marginally, coming second overall.

Lastly, a footnote on two novel factors beginning to intensify competition in the banking sector, with the potential to increasingly affect relative performance by different locations. These are Internet banks, and financial activity by institutions whose parent companies are not part of the

Figure 2.3
Average Cost/Income Ratio by Region, 2006

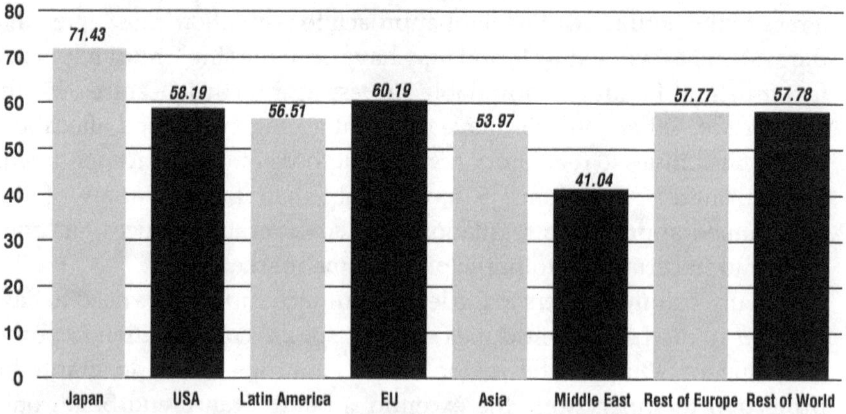

Source: *The Banker*.

traditional banking sector, including supermarket banks, insurance companies, utilities companies, transportation companies and others. While any individual bank would probably always prefer that these competitors were not there, their effect on financial markets is not necessarily negative: This competition may take market share in some cases, but this can also be market creation rather than diversion, and banks can have new opportunities in the process. Table 2.14 provides some numbers on levels of activity and rates of growth of Internet banking.

Table 2.14
Number of Online Banking Users by Region

	Europe	Asia	U.S.	Other	Europe	Asia	U.S.	Other
	Penetration (in millions)				Growth (% y-o-y)			
2000	18.6	9.9	4.9	1.0	—	—	—	—
2001	28.0	14.7	10.9	1.7	50.5	48.5	122.4	70.0
2002	37.8	17.1	18.7	3.1	35.0	16.3	71.6	82.4
2003	47.7	20.4	29.4	5.1	26.2	19.3	57.2	64.5
2004	57.9	22.8	35.6	6.1	21.4	11.8	21.1	19.6

Source: Datamonitor.

Growth of this business in different regions of the world has progressed unevenly, as IT developments have often done. The numbers speak of still quite a minority of banking customers, but are beginning to be considerable: Already in excess of 100 million worldwide back in 2004, with rates of growth of 20 per cent or so. Note also that penetration was from the beginning much greater in Europe than in the other two main market regions. Nevertheless, in the United States it is catching up, while for some reason, both the base and the growth rate are somewhat lower in Asia.

5. FOREIGN EXCHANGE

The foreign exchange market is the world's largest financial market. Global average daily turnover in foreign exchange now stands at no less than US$3.2 trillion. This is around eleven to twelve times the size of the combined daily turnover on all the world's equity markets, which in 2006 stood at around US$277 billion.[6] The volume of foreign exchange that is traded globally is around forty times what the volume of international trade would warrant. This market is also extraordinarily dynamic: the foreign exchange traded globally increased by 71 per cent (at current exchange rates) between 2004 and 2007.[7]

Foreign exchange markets are much larger, more liquid, and less regulated than all other financial markets. But at the same time the foreign exchange market is a leading and broad indicator of status as an IFC. Its volume of business depends on the presence of many banks, openness to international trade and having a large international business base generally.

Equally important is the policy environment: Not only freedom of currency convertibility and capital mobility, but also broader market-friendly policies — as Singapore critically did forty years ago when, upon request, agreed to grant tax exemption to non-residents' deposit income (which HK had refused on fiscal grounds. It thereby gained first-mover advantages in the new Asiadollar market and was well placed to profit from petrodollars following the 1973–74 oil crisis — and gave Singapore a particular edge on foreign exchange, which it has continued to retain and develop ever since.

Because of the lack of a central organizing body, the exact size and scope of the global foreign exchange markets are not known. But the Bank for International Settlements (BIS) conducts a triennial survey of the foreign exchange markets — or more precisely, it leads, designs and coordinates an enormous effort conducted in participating jurisdictions by their central banks and monetary authorities. The latest such survey was conducted in April 2007, with the participation of fifty-four countries or territories, and its preliminary results were announced in late September 2007. The results from these surveys are the acknowledged prime source of data and information on the matter.

As mentioned above, the BIS 2007 Survey shows that there has been a huge increase in activity in foreign exchange markets in 2004–07, which at 71 per cent even exceeds, but also compounds with, the also very large 57 per cent global growth of the previous triennium, 2001–04.[8] This large increase in foreign exchange trading was probably fuelled by increased activity by investor groups, including hedge funds, whose intensive search for profit in and out of markets was encouraged by the recent low levels of financial volatility, which played well into their already low levels of risk aversion. These recent sharp increases more than reversed the substantial fall in global trading volumes that took place between 1998 and 2001.

Foreign exchange trading takes place through several different sub-markets. The so-called "traditional foreign exchange markets" consist of spot transactions, outright forwards, and foreign exchange swaps. It is these that are reported in analyses and in the BIS data on the foreign exchange market. Foreign exchange trading is also embodied in derivatives, first and foremost in foreign exchange options, which we will not be looking at in this chapter.

As among the components of traditional foreign exchange market, the BIS data reveal that swaps were the strongest performers in this period, in contrast to the previous triennium when spot transactions and outright forwards were the stronger. However, the focus here will be on the trends and locational structure of the totals. Consider Table 2.15.

As much as the size and vitality of the sector, the geographical distribution of foreign exchange trading is of particular interest here — what that distribution looks like and how is it evolving.

Table 2.16 lists daily foreign exchange transacted in the largest markets and the region, including shares and ranks. Three points in time are shown: 1995 for comparisons with the market structure that existed prior to the Asian financial crisis; 2004 to assess the state of current growth in each market; and the present.

Interesting changes can be seen first of all among the market leaders at the top of the table: Numbers 1 and 2 remain the same — U.K. and U.S. — throughout the period. Nevertheless the United Kingdom has consistently

Table 2.15
Global Foreign Exchange Market Turnover
(Daily averages, in April, in US$ billion)

	At current exchange rates		Constant exchange rates[b]	
	volume	growth[a]	volume	growth[a]
1989	590	—	675	—
1992	820	40	880	30
1995	1,190	45	1,150	31
1998	1,490	25	1,650	43
2001	1,200	(–20)	1,420	(–14)
2004	1,880	57	1,950	37
2007	3,210	71	3,210	65

Notes: a. Percentage, over the three-year period. b. April 2007 exchange rates.
Source: BIS.

Table 2.16
Geographical Distribution of Foreign Exchange Market Turnover
(Daily averages, in April, in US$ billion, percentages, and ranks)

	2007			2004			1995		
	rank	amount	share	rank	amount	share	rank	amount	share
U.K.	1	1,359	34.1	1	753	31.3	1	464	29.5
U.S.A.	2	644	16.6	2	461	19.2	2	244	15.5
Switzerland	3	242	6.1	8	79	3.3	6	87	5.5
Japan	4	238	6.0	3	199	8.3	3	161	10.3
Singapore	5	231	5.8	4	125	5.2	4	105	6.7
Hong Kong	6	175	4.4	6	102	4.2	5	90	5.7
Australia	7	170	4.2	7	81	3.4	9	40	2.5
France	8	120	3.0	9	64	2.7	8	58	3.7
Germany	9	99	2.5	5	118	4.9	7	76	4.8
Korea	17	33	0.8	15	20	0.8	—	4[a]	0.2[a]

Note: a. April 1998.
Source: BIS.

been gaining market share all along, in fact quite considerably so, and it now represents more than one-third of the world total. Its growth in these three years exceeds the entire size of the German market share, despite the latter being a much larger economy, a major trading power, and boasting the seat of the European Central Bank — whose currency, the euro, is exchanged in greater volumes in London than in all Eurozone countries combined. The second place, the United States, having also increased its market share sharply between 1995 and 2004, showed a considerable decline of almost three points in the last triennium.

On its part, Japan showed a healthy growth in business since the last survey, of 20 per cent over the period. This, however, was not enough to fend off the challenge from Switzerland, which more than trebled its volume transacted to jump five places to number three in the listings. Switzerland's spectacular performance in this period begs an explanation which we do not have. We can only note that the Swiss public release of the results of the survey mentions that "This development is also due to trading desks for spot transactions having been shifted to Switzerland."[9] Whatever the cause for such relocation may have been, attracting it is what building up a world class financial centre is all about.

Besides Japan, Singapore and Hong Kong were also overtaken by Switzerland. But in fact their growth in business was very strong in the triennium: 85 per cent and 72 per cent respectively. Both increased their global market share in the process: Singapore by a fair 0.6 per cent of the world market and Hong Kong an additional 0.2 per cent. But all three East Asian main players remain at well below the market shares they had in 1995, which placed them as participants numbers 3, 4 and 5 in this sector at that time.

In search of explanations for relative market shares, one factor to be looked at is the extent to which there is a link between the currencies that are transacted and the venue where this is done. The link is not tight: we referred above to the euros' trading taking place more in London than in Euroland. Surely the same applies to the U.S. dollar, which is very strong as U.S. participation is in foreign exchange transactions, with close to 17 per cent of the global total last April, this is nowhere the participation in such transactions of the U.S. dollar itself, which is involved in a massive 86.3 per cent of all transactions at present. While this connection is not true for the leading venues and currencies, one might wonder if it might be truer for others.

Table 2.17 presents the numbers for a range of currencies, to better shed light on the point. There are not many surprises from this table, nor significant changes over time. However, two main observations seem to arise: One, the loss in the share of the third-most important currency in the last three years, the yen, after having held its level through much of the period covered. This loss, however, is pure measurement, as it is likely to

Table 2.17
Currency Distribution of Foreign Exchange Market Turnover

Currency	1992	1995	1998	2001	2004	2007
U.S. dollar	82.0	83.3	87.3	90.3	88.7	86.3
euro	—	—	—	37.6	37.2	37.0
Japanese yen	23.4	24.1	20.2	22.7	20.3	16.5
U.K. pound	13.6	9.4	11.0	13.2	16.9	15.0
Swiss franc	8.4	7.3	7.1	6.1	6.1	6.8
Australian dollar	2.5	2.7	3.1	4.2	5.5	6.7
Canadian dollar	3.3	3.4	3.6	4.5	4.2	4.2
Swedish krona	1.3	0.6	0.4	2.6	2.3	2.8
Hong Kong dollar	1.1	0.9	1.3	2.3	1.9	2.8
Norwegian krone	0.3	0.2	0.4	1.5	1.5	2.2
New Zealand dollar	0.2	0.2	0.3	0.6	1.0	1.9
Mexican peso	—	—	0.6	0.9	1.1	1.3
Singapore dollar	0.3	0.3	1.2	1.1	1.0	1.2
Korean won	—	—	0.2	0.8	1.2	1.1

Notes: Percentage shares in daily trades, April.
Shares add to 200 per cent.
Two currencies in each trade.
Source: BIS.

reflect the downward movement of the yen in this period and not a fall in volume of use.

Second, and this is the main lesson drawn from this table, is to note the very weak relationship that seems to exist between the use of currencies and the location of financial activity. Important as it is as a currency, the sterling is numerically not the star that London is among venues. Similarly, Hong Kong and Singapore have greater shares of trade in foreign exchange than their currencies do. Interestingly, Korea shows the opposite relation. Finally, the sharp ascent of the Australian dollar over the period is noted, more than doubling the market share of its currency — in this case whilst also increasing its participation as a location for currency trading.

6. BOND MARKETS

East Asia's financial structure has traditionally been unique among major areas of the world in its significantly lower reliance on bond rather than other forms of government and particularly, corporate finance. This picture is changing, however, perhaps more than is commonly recognized. Bond finance has been growing very significantly throughout the region and now has broadly comparable levels of operation relative to GDP compared to other regions of the world — which does not mean that the sector cannot still develop and grow considerably, as will be argued below. But first things first: Is the sector weak in the region?

While Bank financing has long been the pillar of Asian financial systems, the 1997–98 financial crisis in Asia prompted considerable reconsideration of the role of bond markets in the region's economic progress, which had historically and until recently continued to be inadequate. It was recognized, and we should stress, that bonds are important. They are not merely one additional source of financial intermediation and funding — which they are, and a rich one — but have a critically important role to play in the overall financial architecture of a modern and complex economy. Well-developed bond markets provide participants with useful information on interest rates;[10] allow better risk management;[11] lowers funding costs; and introduce enhanced competition to the banking sector.

But the fact is that East Asia's present level of overall (public and private) funding from bonds is no longer unusually low (see Table 2.18, which contains data for 2005).

It is Japan and not the United States or a European country that has, by a wide margin, the largest bond market as a share of GDP in the full list, which includes twenty-six industrial, emerging and East Asian economies. With the only exception of the United States at number 2, Japan's bond ratio is over twice as large as any other country's. But not only Japan has a large bond sector in the region: Korea, Malaysia and Singapore have higher total bond ratios than do all non-Asian emerging markets on the table, with the first two of being among the leaders.

Some numbers on past evolution will confirm the impressions noted. But first, how does bond finance compare to bank and equity finance? Even if East Asian bond finance has reached similar levels to those in other regions relative to GDP, has it also reached some balance with equities and bank lending, sectors that are so highly developed particularly in the more advanced countries in East Asia? See Table 2.19.

In terms of shares of bonds in overall finance, the East Asian countries' numbers are comparable to those in other regions. One striking exception is Hong Kong. Looking at column 1 of the table, Hong Kong's bank credit relative to GDP is one of the largest, behind only the United Kingdom and Mexico, and close to both. But even with such large numbers for banking, that sector is not even close to dominating the scene as far as financing in

Table 2.18
Bonds Outstanding as a Share of GDP
(Selected Countries, 2005)

	Bond Market Capitalization / GDP		
	Private[a]	Public	Total: Public + Private
1. China	10.4	15.2	25.2
2. Hong Kong, China	17.8	9.1	26.9
3. Indonesia	2.4	16.6	19.0
4. Japan	42.4	150.2	192.6
5. Korea, Rep. of	52.8	25.3	78.1
6. Malaysia	52.2	38.2	90.4
7. Philippines	0.3	38.4	38.7
8. Singapore	18.8	39.2	58.0
9. Thailand	20.2	21.1	41.3
10. Australia	39.3	12.6	51.9
11. Canada	18.7	51.3	70.0
12. France	41.4	53.8	95.2
13. Germany	34.1	41.0	75.1
14. New Zealand	—	22.2	22.2
15. Spain	42.0	38.9	80.9
16. Sweden	42.8	42.2	85.0
17. Switzerland	32.3	32.3	64.6
18. United Kingdom	15.9	31.1	47.0
19. United States	111.8	46.3	158.1
20. Brazil	12.0	44.6	56.6
21. Chile	19.9	17.2	37.1
22. Mexico	4.8	22.1	26.9
23. Czech Republic	5.9	46.1	52.0
24. India	1.0	32.9	33.9
25. South Africa	10.8	31.3	42.1
26. Turkey	—	49.1	49.1

Note: a. Financial institutions and corporations.
Source: Beck et al. (2000) database, from BIS, World Bank and IMF.

Hong Kong is concerned: The real giant is its stock market (column 2), which is very large in absolute terms, and more so relative to the size of the Hong Kong economy. The territory's market capitalization as a share of GDP is thus several times higher than the next places on the table.

Nevertheless it must be recognized that Hong Kong's relative smallness in bonds relative to equities and lending is not only due to the bigness of

Table 2.19
Relative Composition of Finance: Bank Lending, Equities and Bonds
(Selected East Asian and Other Countries, 2005)

	1 Private Bank Credit/GDP	2 Stock Market Capitalization/GDP	3 Bond Market Capitalization[b]/GDP	4 Share of Bonds in total = 3/(1+2+3)
Hong Kong	141.9	528.1	26.9	3.7
Japan	98.0	93.8	192.6	50.1
Korea	89.1[c]	72.9	78.1	32.5
Malaysia	103.0	143.6	90.4	26.8
Singapore	96.5	163.4	58.0	18.2
Australia	101.8	113.5	51.9	19.4
France	90.4	85.2	95.2	35.2
Sweden	106.3	110.9	85.0	28.1
Switzerland	161.6	242.4	64.6	13.8
United Kingdom	155.4	134.7	47.0	13.9
United States	46.1	134.6	158.1	46.7
Czech Rep.	33.1	28.4	52.0	45.8
Brazil	29.0	50.8	56.6	41.5
Mexico	145.9	26.8	27.7	13.8
South Africa	80.1	213.5	42.1	12.5

Notes: a. Financial institutions and corporations.
b. Private + Public.
c. 2004.
Source: Beck et al. (2000) database, from BIS, World Bank and IMF.

these, but to the fact that the bond market has not taken off in earnest in the territory. One reason for this is evident from Table 2.18: The only single-digit entry for public bond issues in the whole list is Hong Kong's. This in turn deprives the territory of the strong catalytic effects that large volumes of sovereign bond issuance have in Singapore or indeed, the United States. Such issues provide a basic volume of activity and momentum to their respective markets, and also help set the pricing. Nevertheless, the figures in Table 2.19 indicate that Hong Kong has the depth of liquidity, the market talent and expertise, and the banking and financial infrastructure needed to handle a much greater volume of prime bond issues and trading than it has attracted to date.

Let us briefly turn our attention to the evolution of the bond business over the last decade. Table 2.20 shows very clearly how much the situation has changed in those ten years throughout the region. With the only exception of Malaysia, which by 1995 already had a higher bond/GDP ratio than the rest of the region (but still grew by a further 40 per cent over GDP in the next decade), all the other East Asian economies on the list roughly doubled their bond debt outstanding relative to GDP.

Despite the region's growth in bond finance in recent years, with the exception of Japan's, the region's bond markets are young and not very deep. One problem in particular is the fact that yield curves in some cases are short, certainly shorter than in mature markets, a situation that notably affects Hong Kong whose bond market is extends only to ten years (see Figure 2.4, showing yield curves for all countries in the region plus the United States). Hong Kong's lack of depth arises because of its heavy reliance on short-term bank deals and absence of longer sovereign issues to benchmark. Singapore's bond market yield curve is longer, extending to fifteen years, led by the issuance of longer-term government bonds, while China's and Japan's yield curves are long, extending to thirty years.

Table 2.20
Bond Finance 1995–2005: Shares in GDP
(Totals outstanding: Public, Corporate and Financial)

	1995	2000	2005	% Growth (2005 on 1995)
Hong Kong	14.1	25.4	27.0	91
Japan	86.8	124.2	192.5	121
Korea, Rep.	40.0	52.6	78.1	95
Malaysia	65.6	78.4	90.4	38
Singapore	25.5	43.0	58.1	128
Australia	48.4	49.3	51.9	7
France	66.2	80.7	84.8	28
Sweden	100.9	91.5	84.0	(–17)
Switzerland	66.7	65.9	64.6	(–3)
United Kingdom	47.0	50.7	47.0	0
United States	138.9	145.1	158.1	14
Czech Rep.	15.0	42.5	52.0	3.5
Brazil	28.8	49.5	56.5	96
Mexico	12.2	13.4	26.9	120
South Africa	64.8	47.9	42.1	(–35)

Figure 2.4
Benchmark Yield Curves — LCY Bonds, 2006

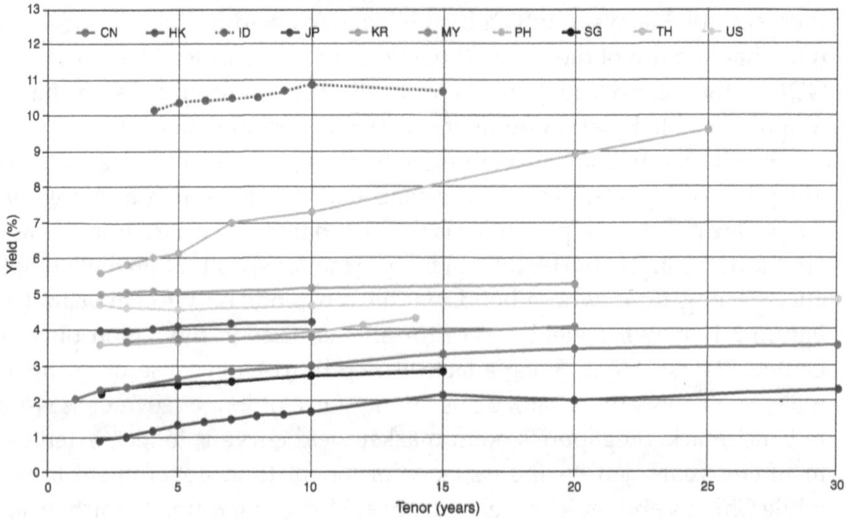

Source: Reuters.

7. CONCLUDING REMARKS

The relative structure, growth and prospects of international financial centres (IFCs) is a topic of considerable interest in Asia, and rightly so, given the size of the stakes and the fluid nature of the industry. The region's phenomenal and sustained economic growth and its substantial tradition of financial excellence seem to have convinced many people that its leading financial centres can only move forward towards the top of the global leagues — the question being only which one will get there first and how fast. The well publicized announcement last year and ratified since then in a sequence of major reports on the industry prepared for the City of London,[12] to the effect that Hong Kong and Singapore are the undisputed occupants of positions three and four in the highest firmament of IFCs, only reinforced among many observers in the region, the perception that ultimate success for one of its leading centres is at hand if not inevitable: Graduation into the top elite of world finance. The reality is complex, however, and the true challenge might be a different one from what many believe it is.

As noted at the outset of this chapter, the locational structure of financial industry in Asia is unusual. The rest of the world is used to having dominant players in London and New York, but neither Tokyo nor Singapore or Hong Kong meet that description, nor is Shanghai likely to get there, despite its formidable ascent which has yet to play itself out in full.

I happen to believe that the delivery of financial service exhibits strong economies of scale in many ways. Once a successful operation gets established, with a strong leadership and headquarters and an efficient back office, the sky is the limit. In addition, finance is all about trust, and clients and associates prefer to feel that they are dealing with the strongest and the best. Scale is appreciated. All this speaks of continuing concentration, among banks and operators but also among locations where business is done. In that light, how is the locational structure of financial industry to unfold in East Asia?

One conclusion I do draw from the above reasoning is that East Asia's present distribution of business may be unsustainable in the long run: The premium for further consolidation will be high. With China and the East moving from their present status as a very important economic area of the world, to their future as first-tier power houses, the business case for such consolidation is likely to become irresistible. But, does that need to take the form of consolidation within those present, with Hong Kong, Tokyo or Singapore taking the global mantle? Not necessarily. This would mean one of them actually beating London and New York and not only its regional peers at the hottest game to come, namely, to take pride of place as the financial centre for the core global needs of this region.

The leading banks are all headquartered in London and New York, and it is they who are benefiting the most from the relentless concentration taking place in world finance. We saw above that in area after area and indicator after indicator, Asia's position of strength in the spectrum of financial centres is relative, and most often not growing in relation to the dominant world players. If this is the trend at present, there is no basis to confidently predict it will change in future but rather, perhaps the contrary. Business is increasingly global and anonymous, not needing physical proximity for its conduct. The staggering increase in the last three years in forex trade, to its latest recorded (April 2007) US$3.2 trillion per day, seems to have been caused in significant measure by the expansion of *algorithmic investments* by hedge funds and other institutional investors. Internet banking too, is taking off. With all these qualitative changes in the way financial business is conducted, it could well happen that the lions' share of global business with this geographical area is increasingly done by global giants from headquarters elsewhere.

The point of all this speculation is to stress that that the common question of who in East Asia will be the next global financial leader is not important. The key concern should be with the real possibility that all the centres in the region end up relative losers in the long run, assured of a fair amount of regional and local business but not the lion's share of future exponential growth.

Of course, the scenario just described is the bearish one for the issues at hand. The more common bullish possibility is also real — that one or other of the leading regional financial centres will gradually grow into an equal of today's two global giants, across the board or in selective sectors of finance. In any case, the region can be assured of a large fraction of its own financial business, as the well-known "time difference" factor demands a full array of financial service providers to be located in East Asia itself, as does the "local knowledge" factor — local and regional providers of finance will always have an advantage when it comes to the needs of medium-size business and local markets. But none of this speaks for the bulk of mega-business in future global markets, which can perhaps increasingly be located in only the fittest and the best, wherever these may be located.

For this reason the topic of this conference is extremely appropriate and timely. It is incumbent on the financial centres of East Asia, and on us their observers, to identify ways of making business in the region better and stronger, in order to identify ways to collectively survive and win.

With proper cooperation and aggressive betterment of the business infrastructure in East Asia, the region's FCs can create a superbly nimble and effective network that can operate as the most efficient of IFCs: A global network-IFC. For the same reason that it is perfectly possible to service much of the higher-end financial needs of the region from London or New York, mentioned earlier, it is equally feasible to do that servicing from a network of locations in Asia, constituted as a collective mega-IFC. This probably requires an aggressive and wise mixture of competition and cooperation among the region's FCs: Competition as at present, because that is the mother of enhanced creativity and efficiency, and cooperation to bring markets and pull scale together wherever possible, thus increasingly becoming a magnet that can match the power of the global leaders.

What would that cooperation need to be, to ensure the region does not lose out in future waves of consolidation? An excellent instance of cooperation that has delivered very good results actually on the ground has been the region's Asia Bond Initiative that created the Asia Bond Fund, which Hong Kong was very involved in. Joint development of the regional bond market is a natural area for cooperation, and schemes to further enlarge the scale and impact of these initiatives would be highly desirable. A second excellent area of potential cooperation would be among stock exchanges in the region, with dual listings and other forms of cooperation. Shanghai and Hong Kong have been showing the way here and there is no reason the same could not happen in a deliberate and systematic way across national borders too. The striking recent marriage between NYSE and Euronext should serve as inspiration for the bold and powerful steps that the challenges ahead require.

But the vision and objective for the region should be broader: To effectively create an East Asian Financial Area through infrastructure and regulatory integration, cooperation and harmonization: a common integrated space for financial operators in the region. This could include the following.

Recommendations

i. Place the highest priority on the creation of an integrated infrastructure and payments system in the region. This is a *sine-qua-non* condition for seamless and unified business to be possible among geographically separate centres, as simple and unified as it is within single-market regions in North America or Europe.
ii. Regulators and industry should work together and aggressively towards the development and adoption of common codes and standards at the regional level, consistent with international best practice, appropriate for the region, and above all common;
iii. Create a working group among financial industry participants and regulators to identify core elements and stumbling blocks towards the establishment of uniform regulatory frameworks, which would be a common basis to be further developed, implemented and administered separately by each jurisdiction;
iv. Work towards the adoption of other practical measures to facilitate intra-regional business such as facilitating regional recourse to

arbitration and the fullest cooperation (operational + technical) among supervisors;

v. Beyond the above essentially technical steps, make it a priority to negotiate effectively and speedily the fullest freedom of financial business establishment across the region, in particular among and starting with its major centres. The renewed vigour with which several countries and jurisdictions in the region are negotiating (broad, WTO-compliant) Free Trade Agreements provides an excellent opportunity to move forward the intra-regional liberalization agenda in the all-important financial sector.

Such a scheme of cooperation would effectively create a single economic space in the region for matters of financial industry. The region's operators, whether domestic or "guest", would gain profitability through larger scale and avoidance of duplication. This means adding together the separate strengths of the region's financial centres, in a context that might otherwise be evolving towards the increasing development of the top tier of global business elsewhere.

With cooperation firmly in place to expand scope within the region, yet in a relationship of vigorous competition among its centres to maximize incentives and creativity, East Asia's financial industry would gradually re-organize itself into complementary, specialized and efficient niches in different locations. Collectively they would have — sector by sector — a leading global role, effectively adding to a global financial centre based not in a city but in a region and network, spread out as much as the region is vast. Present individual powerhouses big and small would all have a place in this more cohesive whole, as activities go to places in pursuit of the human and locational resources that those have to offer.

Notes

This chapter is part of a research on international financial centres underway at Lingnan University that also includes Professors Chen Lin, Ping Lin, Xiandong Wei, and Yifan Zhang. The author thanks his collaborators and the university for encouragement and support, Chen Lin for helpful suggestions, Dr Esmond Lee of the HKMA for valuable discussions on regional financial infrastructure, Betty Ngai and Luk Ying Wa for research assistance, and his students in his courses on IFCs for their interest and contributions. Views expressed and any errors or omissions are the author's alone.

1. City of London, 2008.
2. BIS, Triennial Central Bank Survey of Foreign Exchange and Derivatives Market Activity in April 2007, Preliminary Global Results, September 2007.
3. International Financial Services (IFSL) is a private financial industry organization in London. Reference from IFSL's "Market Trends Europe vs. U.S. 2006", October 2007.
4. Admittedly this is a comparison between lists referring to different years, but Table 2.10 is the latest information available under this criterion. However, if the same comparison is made between this table and the ten or fifteen largest banks in 2003, the comment still stands but with a different pair of banks, namely, HSBC and BNP Paribas.
5. Think of ten regions with identical levels of over all concentration among 100 banks, but with different distributions of market shares to individual banks. The banks' shares in the sum of the regions (the larger "country") are the average values of their shares in the various regions. The numbers at the country level converge towards the mean (more sharply the more the banks differ in their respective regional strengths.) But the strength of competition in High Street has not changed with the mere erasing of the borders.
6. Own estimate based on World Federation of Exchanges information.
7. April-to-April. BIS' Triennial Survey Preliminary Global Results, September 2007.
8. These figures refer to growth at current exchange rates and correspond to growth of 65 per cent (2004–07) and 36 per cent (2001–04) when volumes are measured at constant exchange rates.
9. "Turnover in foreign exchange and derivatives markets in Switzerland — 2007 Survey" (p. 2). Swiss National Bank, <http://www.snb.ch/en/iabout/stat/statpub/umdev/id/statpub_umdev_hist>.
10. The bond market produces a yield curve, a market-determined term structure of interest rates, which serves as a benchmark for pricing bank loans, credit risk, and equity shares.
11. Barry Eichengreen (2004, p. 12) has put it very effectively: "...equity finance encourages risk taking, since holders of equity stakes share in super-normal returns whereas their losses are truncated on the down side, while debt holders, who do not share in exceptional profits, encourage risk aversion."
12. City of London Corporation (2008).

References

Asian Development Bank. *Asian Bonds Online*, from <http://asianbondsonline.adb.org/administrative/abm_overview.php>, 2007.

Bank for International Settlements (BIS). *Triennial Central Bank Survey of Foreign Exchange and Derivatives Market Activity in April 2007*, Preliminary Global Results, September 2007. <http://www.bis.org/publ/rpfx07.htm>.

BIS. *Locational Banking Statistics*, September 2007. <http://www.bis.org/statistics/bankstats.htm>.

Bareau, Paul. "The International Money and Capital Markets". In *International Financial Centres*, edited by Richard Roberts, vol. II, pp. 26–42. Aldershot: Edward Elgar, 1994.

Barth, James R., Gerard Caprio, Jr. and Ross Levine, 2004, "Bank Supervision and Regulation: What Works Best?". *Journal of Financial Intermediation* 13 (2004): 205–48.

———. *Rethinking Bank Regulation: Till Angels Govern*. New York: Cambridge University Press, 2006.

Beck, Thorsten, Asli Demirgüç-Kunt and Ross Levine. "A New Database on Financial Development and Structure". *World Bank Economic Review* 14 (2000): 597–605.

City of New York with McKinsey and Co. *Sustaining New York's and the US' Global Financial Services Leadership*. New York, 2007.

Corporation of London. *The Competitive Position of London as a Global Financial Centre*. London: Z/Yen Limited, 2005.

City of London Corporation. *The Global Financial Centres Index 3*. London: Z/Yen Limited, 2008. <http://www.zyen.com/Activities/On-line%20surveys/GFCI.htm>.

Eichengreen, Barry. *Financial Development in Asia: The Way Forward*. Singapore: Institute of Southeast Asian Studies, 2004.

International Financial Services (IFSL), *Banking*. London. <http://www.ifsl.org.uk/uploads/CBS_Banking_2006.pdf>, March 2006.

———. *Financial Market Trends Europe vs. US 2007*. London, October 2007. <http://www.ifsl.org.uk/uploads/RP_Europe_vs_US_2007.pdf>.

Jao, Y.C. "Hong Kong and Shanghai as International Financial Centres: Historical Perspectives and Contemporary Analysis". Working Paper, University of Hong Kong, 2003.

Jiang, G., N. Tang, and E. Law. "The Costs and Benefits of Developing Debt Markets: Hong Kong's Experience". BIS Papers no. 11, 2001. <http://www.bis.org/publ/bppdf/bispap11h.pdf>.

Jones, Geoffrey. "International Financial Centres in Asia, The Middle East and Australia: A Historical Perspective". In *International Financial Centres*, edited by Richard Roberts, vol. I, 1992, pp. 301–24. Aldershot: Edward Elgar, 1994.

Lamberte, Mario B. "Developing the Fledgling Debt Securities Markets in Southeast Asia". In Freeman, Nick J., *Financing Southeast Asia's Economic Development*. Singapore: Institute of Southeast Asian Studies, 2003.

Plender, John. "London's Big Bang in International Context". Ibid., pp. 87–96.

Robbins, Sidney M., and Nestor E. Terleckyj. "The Rise of New York as a Money Market". In Roberts, Richard, *International Financial Centres*, vol. II, pp. 137–62.

Roberts, Richard, ed. *International Financial Centres*, vols. I to IV. Aldershot: Edward Elgar, 1994.

Sagaram, J. P. A., and J. Wickramanayake. "Financial Centres in the Asia-Pacific Region: An Empirical Study on Australia, Hong Kong, Japan and Singapore". *Banca Nazionale del Lavoro Quarterly Review* 58(232) (2005): 21–51. From ProQuest database.

Weithers, Tim. *Foreign Exchange: A Practical Guide to the Fx Markets*. John Wiley & Sons, 2006.

Wright, C., F. Haddock, and J. Lee. Three Local Markets Compared. [Electronic version]. *Asiamoney* 12, no. 5 (20010: 29–32. From EBSCOhost database.

3

SINGAPORE AS A LEADING INTERNATIONAL FINANCIAL CENTRE
Vision, Strategies, Roadmap and Progress

Tan Khee Giap

1. SINGAPORE EVOLVING TO BE A LEADING INTERNATIONAL FINANCIAL CENTRE: HISTORICAL ACCIDENT OR PROACTIVE ROLE OF THE GOVERNMENT?

After decades of rapid economic expansion, with gross domestic product (GDP) averaging 8.4 per cent growth per annum for Singapore throughout the 1970s and 1980s, it has become apparent that the high efficiency of the export-driven manufacturing sector is not matched by the increasingly internationalized but unsophisticated financial sector.[1] However, as recounted by Dr Goh Keng Swee, then the deputy prime minister of Singapore and also undeniably the first architect of the financial centre, that the government did not initially plan to develop Singapore as an international financial centre (IFC).

Although developing a financial centre was part of the government's overall industrialization policy strategy since the 1980s, its potential as a full-fledged IFC only became apparent to policymakers in the late 1980s. In fact the sector was initially meant to provide the necessary financial infrastructure support to foreign direct investment (FDI) brought in by multinational corporations (MNCs) which Singapore has successfully attracted since the establishment of the Jurong Industrial Park after its independence in 1965.[2]

Tax exemptions and tax incentives such as pioneer industry (PI) status, operational headquarters (OHQ) status, and business headquarters (BHQ) status were introduced for MNCs. Singapore's robust international financial services were therefore developed due to the financial requirements of MNCs and growing demand from regional entrepôt trade to help build up precious foreign exchange earnings through export drives to boost economic growth, and using MNCs to facilitate the much needed essential technology upgrading and management skill transfer by investing in physical and human infrastructure.

IFC is often defined as a location that provides facilities for clearing and settlement on international payment between globalized parties: Where large values of foreign exchange are traded, cross-border pooling of deposits and disbursement of loans are allowed, and cross-border securities issues and other international financial trading are being managed and transacted. It is not unusual to find that almost all financial centres portray themselves as IFC, but clearly, not all are. Financial centres can be further classified under onshore financial centre (such as Tokyo, Frankfurt, Paris and Shanghai), offshore financial centre (such Singapore and Hong Kong) and global financial centres (such as London and New York).

Over the past decades, Singapore has faced various internal and external shocks to its financial system. Internal disturbances include the Pan-El incident in 1985, the brief economic recession in 1986, and the collapse of Barings Bank in 1995. Singapore did also go through several external shocks which include the international monetary crisis in 1971/73, the stagflation in 1974/75 induced by the oil-price hike, the global stock crash of 1987. Other external shocks include the substantial contraction of offshore financial activities in 1992 after the imposition of the capital adequacy ratio requirement and East Asian financial turmoil that began in 1997.

The way in which the Singapore government carefully structured and nurtured the unique dichotomized financial and banking system into onshore and offshore distinction ought to be recognized. Specific features or mechanisms that allowed the financial system to cope with shocks and cushioned against the adverse effect of swift capital flows could be identified. Because of the government's conscious effort to adopt English as the medium of instruction in education establishments and to develop English as an effective business language, coupled with ideal geographical location and advantageous time zone, international financial services grew rapidly, together with manufacturing, as twin engines of growth for decades. Hence the Singapore government did play a proactive role, at least in the initial stage in guiding the financial sector development.

As the financial sector continued to expand throughout the 1980s and 1990s, the government decided to further fine-tune this engine of growth through a series of consistent financial reforms and liberalization drive, more so in the aftermath of the 1997 Asian financial crisis, especially when many potential up-and-coming financial centres and institutions in East Asia encountered setbacks and retreated. In retrospect, the post-1997 liberalization is yielding dividends that have consolidated Singapore further as a leading international financial centre in Asia.

According to ISEAS-NTU (Institute of Southeast Asian Studies-Nanyang Technological University), Overall Progress Ranking on Financial Reforms and Liberalization of ASEAN 10+5 Economies, Singapore has been continuously ranked as the economy which has made the most progress in terms of financial reforms and liberalization in 2004 and 2005 (see Table 3.1). The ISEAS-NTU index is meant to provide peer pressure by ranking progress made in financial reforms and liberalization in fifteen Asian economies, namely the ten members of Association of Southeast Asian Nations (ASEAN-10) plus mainland China, Hong Kong Special Administrative Region, Korea, Japan and Chinese Taipei. The ISEAS-NTU Index was constructed based on more than 100 financial indicators covering four major categories, that is banking institutions' stability and soundness, financial markets development and liberalization, regulatory authorities' policies and management efficiency and financial corporate governance.[3]

Section 2 appraises generally benefits and costs of an international financial centre. Section 3 traces the successful recipe in terms of policies, factors and conditions which led Singapore to be a leading international financial centre. Singapore's financial sector development is revisited in section 4 in terms of policy sequencing and liberalization drive. Section 5

Table 3.1
2007 Update of ISEAS-NTU Overall Progress Ranking on Financial Reforms and Liberalization of ASEAN 10 + 5 Economies

Economies	STD Value	2005	STD Value	2004
Singapore	0.6735	1	0.6264	1
Hong Kong, China	0.5688	3	0.5129	2
Japan	0.5995	2	0.4665	3
South Korea	0.5001	4	0.4416	4
Thailand	0.3439	6	0.3416	5
Chinese Taipei	0.2735	8	0.3082	6
Malaysia	0.3251	5	0.2654	7
Indonesia	0.1712	9	0.2128	8
China	0.3151	7	0.0580	9
Philippines	0.1062	10	0.0576	10
Vietnam	–0.5152	11	–0.4313	11
Cambodia	–0.6667	12	–0.5681	12
Myanmar	–0.7897	13	–0.6738	13
Laos PDR	–0.8630	14	–0.7335	14
Brunei	–1.0692	15	–0.8843	15

Source: Tan and Chen (2007).

critically appraises the international competition, constraints and challenges that would affect Singapore's status as a leading IFC. Some tentative concluding remarks based on recommendations made and lessons learnt are provided.

2. BENEFITS AND COSTS ANALYSIS: WHY SINGAPORE ASPIRES TO BE A LEADING INTERNATIONAL FINANCIAL CENTRE?

Singapore has a per capita GDP of US$29,838 in 2007, with GDP size expanded rapidly from US$21 billion, in 1987 to US$95 billion in 1997 and US$112 billion in 2007. Between 1987 and 1997, the GDP grew by an average of 9.3 per cent per annum, compared to the relatively lower growth of 3 per cent per annum from 1998 to 2003 due to the Asia financial crisis and the outbreak of Severely Acute Respiratory Syndrome (SARS), thereafter the economy recovered to grow at above potential level, averaging 7.4 per cent per annum from 2004 to 2007.

According to the projections by Asian Research Centre at Nanyang Technological University, the potential output growth for Singapore for the period from 1998 to 2025 is estimated to be 5.5 per cent per annum. Between 1997 and 2007, inflation or the consumer price index grew at an average of 0.8 per cent and with unemployment rate hovering at around 3.3 per cent. Financial services accounted for 13 per cent of Singapore's GDP, and its share of employment is approximated to have been about 5 per cent in 2007. It is thus a vital sector with spillover and multiplying effect. The positive economic externalities of the IFC cannot be underestimated as it allows Singapore to expand its economic space beyond its small physical size and reinforces its regional, if not global, political significance.

The IFC directly supports manufacturing activities, maintaining the attractiveness of Singapore as a regional operational headquarters for MNCs. It also indirectly enhances Singapore as a regional logistic, transportation and tourism hub. The financial centre allows Singapore to be interconnected to regional economies and stay relevant globally, one of the critical engines for extending Singapore's external economy.

As evident by many international yardsticks, Singapore has been ranked consecutively since 1994 as the world's second freest economy, according to the 2008 rankings by *The Heritage Foundation* and *The Wall Street Journal*. In terms of the world competitiveness scoreboard, Singapore was ranked second-most competitive economy after the United States of America, according to the 2007 *IMD World Competitiveness Yearbook*. Singapore is also ranked as the best in perceived corporate governance, most politically stable, and government with the highest integrity in Asia, according to evaluation in 2007 by Political and Economic Risk Consultancy.

In summary, the benefits of IFC include a more resilient and diversified economy with employment creation; better access to capital markets that facilitates capital financing, enhanced corporate and personal tax revenues from MNCs and highly paid business professionals; increased direct foreign investment portfolios and other investment flows; and greater internationalization of the local economy, which enables it to be better plugged into the globalization process.

In the context of East Asia financial crisis, amongst other causes, it is often argued that swift opening up of domestic financial markets, greater cross-border transactions, freer flows of capital across national boundaries and capital account convertibility create added risks which can lead to tumultuous financial markets. These negative arguments are not dismissed as irrelevant and in fact, the true extent of their impact still remains an open verdict. Nevertheless, it is postulated that such financial tumultuousness can be mitigated and coped with via carefully formulated policies, taking into account positive factors and creating conducive conditions through a series of consistent, broad-based and long-term reform programmes.

The malignancy of East Asian financial turmoil comes from the twin crises, combining the externally driven currency crisis with the internally induced banking crisis. In other word, it is capital account shortfall coupled with domestic credit contraction, which is distinct from the traditional current account crisis being caused by the deterioration of domestic macroeconomic performance such as inflation, fiscal deficits and low saving rates. The vulnerable and precarious banking institutions and financial systems were further typified and exacerbated by double mismatches also referred to as currency and maturity mismatches.[4]

Although it is widely acknowledged that the East Asian financial crisis was essentially private sector-induced, it is believed that the governing authorities played the most critical role in creating, confronting and overcoming the crisis. Therefore the respective regulatory authorities clearly should also be held responsible for the imbalance-growth between the real and financial sectors as well as the ensuing systemic-wide financial tumultuousness.

Regional governments often like to direct resources to promote financial centres and fasten the pace of financial liberalization. It is often being overlooked that speedy capital growth through non-market oriented promotions such as pre-approved loans, directed lending, non-competitive-priced borrowings and non-market evaluation assets are sure recipes for financial market instability.

Financial sequencing and policies spacing between domestic and external financial market liberalization are typically ignored. Unsophisticated local corporations and indigenous financial institutions, in the midst of exuberant growth, actually went into high financial leverage or gearing without fully grasping the risks incurred. Regulatory authorities in particular, did not realize or understand the grave implications of hasty financial liberalization, and therefore failed to put in place the necessary institutional safeguards. Gaping distortions in money market activities, currency funding exposures due to government interventions and caused by activities which are not reflected by market-oriented business considerations certainly contributed to maturity and currency mismatches.

In summary, it is often argued that potential costs of IFC include losing control over domestic monetary conditions, risks of volatile and speculative capital movements, and intense foreign competition that tends to dwarf domestic financial institutions that are still at their infancy. Retrospectively, Singapore's experience is an interesting case study to look at. In terms of resiliency, the IFC evidently stood the test well and minimized those costs mentioned when compared to the rest of the East Asian economies in terms of economic fundamentals and financial indicators ten years since July 1997 when the Asian financial crisis struck. The next section will account for and explain how Singapore as an IFC has avoided the textbook cases, adopting instead unconventional approaches to fine-tune the financial system and institutions which avoided or mitigated the potential costs encountered.

3. SUCCESSFUL RECIPE: POLICY DESIGNS, FAVOURABLE FACTORS AND GENERAL CONDITIONS WHICH LED TO EMERGENCE OF A LEADING INTERNATIONAL FINANCIAL CENTRE

It is useful to conduct an in-depth study to identify the success recipe in terms of policy designs, factors and general conditions which led Singapore to emerge as a leading international financial centre. By policy designs we mean approaches adopted or pursued by regulatory authorities that are advantageous or expedient, directly or indirectly, that have contributed to the development of the financial sector. Favourable factors refer to facts or influences that have helped to alleviate the financial system and financial institutions from being paralysed or weakened. General conditions refer to circumstances or environment demanded or required as a prerequisite to render financial stability.

It is important to take note that these policy designs, favourable factors and general conditions may seem unorthodox and sometimes not as relevant now as they used to be, but they are nevertheless critical or useful to kick-start, develop and expand the financial sector in the early stages, but only to be relaxed or modified as the financial sector deepens. It is thus not wrong to say that the IFC would not be what it is today if not for the unorthodox approaches taken and if their effectiveness simply reflected the prevailing circumstances or conditions then in the international financial environment.

3.1. The Dichotomized Financial System: Conceptual Framework and Rationales of the Two-tier Financial Entity

The terms Asian Currency Unit (ACU) and "Domestic Banking Unit" (DBU) are potentially confusing. It is not known why these terms were coined in Singapore and became the subject of legislation and guidelines. Very often, the ACU and the DBU are misunderstood as currency units like the ECU in Europe. Sometimes they are mistaken for demarcated financial markets. In fact, both are simply accounting conventions for financial legal entities established within financial institutions and registered to operate according to specific guidelines laid down by the Monetary Authority of Singapore (MAS). Technically, what distinguishes the ACU from the DBU is that the former is allowed to deal in any currency except the Singapore dollar. The two-tier financial entity serves to encourage foreign capital inflows to stay within the minimum regulated offshore financial sector, that is the ACUs, while it also cushions foreign capital outflows which are in the first instance discouraged but not prevented to flow into the domestic financial sector, that is the DBUs.

Such accounting conventions for financial legal entities being established within financial institutions and registered to operate according to strict guidelines are facilitated by comprehensive information reporting on financial activities by banks. Such available pools of information matrix are later being fully utilized by the regulatory authority for the purpose of subsequent policy setting and fine-tuning. This shows that from the early stage of development, when the authority had very little experience, it focused on establishing an extensive matrix of data and monitoring information on financial activities within the two-tier financial system.

Clearly such dichotomized financial system assumes a unique role where financial institutions are expected to observe not just letters but also spirit of all rules, regulations and guidelines laid down by the regulatory authority. Such "uneven handed" relationship between financial institutions and regulatory authority are expected to prevail at least through the initial period of financial development before the rules of the game can clearly, and are ready, to take shape. It is within this overall context that such conditions tend to give more emphasis to the micro approach of protecting individuals, products and projects in contrast to the systemic risks monitoring as the financial system and institutions matured.

3.2. Setting Prudential Safeguards and Directing Fiscal Incentives

The MAS, tasked with at times seemingly contradictory objectives of developing and regulating financial markets, was able to steadily expand and consolidate financial activities through a series of effective policies such as prudential safeguards, incentive measures and the unorthodox, non-internationalization of the local currency. By requiring high capital adequacy ratio of 12 per cent in excess of the 8 per cent minimum set by the 1988 Basle Capital Accord signified the conservative attitude adopted by MAS, yet indigenous banks in particular operate at around 20 per cent capital adequacy ratio reflective of their risk adverse attitude, given the protected and lucrative domestic financial sector resulting from the tightly scrutinized and monitored internationalization of financial intermediation by the regulatory authority. Such one-size-fit-all capital adequacy ratio was abandoned since 2000 as indigenous banks are now allowed to maintain individual capital adequacy ratio according to the bank's respective risk profile.

Incentives refer to measures that help to promote market development, strengthen market forces and stimulate participants' interest. To spur greater participation in the ACUs, the concessionary corporate tax on income was reduced from 40 per cent to 10 per cent in 1973. This immediately rendered participation in the DBU relatively less attractive. Although the corporate income tax was steadily reduced to 25 per cent in 1999 and 17 per cent by 2007, it is still much higher than the 10 per cent imposed on the ACU. The success of fiscal incentives can be seen from changes in the shares of "out-out" transactions and "out-in" transactions when comparing Singapore's two-tier financial system with Thailand's Bangkok International Financial Facilities (BIBF). While "out-out" transactions in Singapore's ACU market have exceeded 90 per cent since 1994, the pattern in BIBF market is relatively low ranging from 16 per cent to 43 per cent.

3.3. Gradual Internationalization of the Singapore Dollar

From the perspective of deterrence to currency speculation, having a definite distinction between residents and non-residents enables the authority to demarcate the financial activities of financial institutions between the DBU and the ACU. The key essence of the policy lies in the restrictive usage of the Singapore dollar for non-residents and restrictive circulation of Singapore dollar within Singapore's geographical boundary. However, as the strength of indigenous financial institutions and the local economy has grown over time, MAS has gradually relaxed the limit on Singapore dollar financing to non-residents and foreign financial entities. This approach is known as gradual internationalization of the Singapore dollar.

The evolution of the policy of discouraging internationalization of the Singapore dollar can be traced from the policy directives below:

- 1978: MAS abolished all exchange controls.
- 1983: Issued MAS Notice 621 which codified the policy of discouraging internationalization of the Singapore dollar.
- 1992: Amendment to MAS Notice 621, which allowed extension of Singapore dollar credit facilities of any amount to non-residents where the Singapore dollar funds were used for activities tied to economic activities in Singapore.
- 1998: The new MAS 757 replaced MAS 621 which reaffirmed the basic thrust of the policy to discourage internationalization of the Singapore dollar but would minimize need for banks to consult MAS. Some activities in relation to arranging Singapore dollar denominated equity listings and bonds issues of foreign companies were relaxed to foster the development of the capital market in Singapore.
- 1999: Key amendments made to MAS 757: (i) Allow banks to transact Singapore dollar interest rate derivatives with non-residents freely. This followed the launch in September 1999 of the Singapore dollar interest rate futures on (then SIMEX) Singapore Exchange where participation was opened to residents and non-residents; (ii) Allow banks to arrange Singapore dollar denominated equity listings for foreign companies freely. Provided the proceeds were converted into foreign currency before being used outside Singapore.

- 2000: Key amendments made to MAS 757: (i) Allow banks to lend Singapore dollars to non-residents for investment purposes in Singapore. This would allow non-residents to obtain Singapore dollar funding for investment in Singapore dollar denominated equities, bonds and real estates and hence broaden investors base for Singapore dollar denominated assets; (ii) Allow banks to extend Singapore dollar credit facilities to non-residents to fund offshore activities, as long as the Singapore dollar proceeds were first swapped into foreign currency before being used outside Singapore.
- 2002: Key amendments made to MAS 757: (i) Exempt all individuals and non-financial entities from the Singapore dollar lending restrictions of MAS 757. This recognized that such entities were not usually the prime drivers of destabilizing Singapore dollar currency speculation; (iia) Allow non-resident financial entities to transact freely in asset swaps, cross-currency swaps and cross-currency repos, Such transactions were viewed as forms of Singapore dollar lending (iib) Allow non-resident financial entities to lend any amount of Singapore dollar denominated securities in exchange for both Singapore and foreign currency denominated collateral. Previously, lending of Singapore dollar denominated securities exceeding S$5 million had to be fully collateralized by Singapore dollar collaterals; (iic) Allow non-resident financial entities to transact freely in Singapore dollar denominated foreign exchange options. Previously such transactions were allowed only if they were supported by underlying economic and financial activities in Singapore.
- 2004: Key amendments made to MAS 757: (i) Non-resident and non-financial issuers of Singapore dollar denominated bonds no longer required to swap/convert the Singapore dollar proceeds into foreign currency before remitting abroad; (ii) MAS renamed the policy of "non-internationalization of Singapore dollar" as "lending of Singapore dollar to non-residents".

Put another way, the primary concern or thrust is not with internationalization *per se*. In fact Singapore's move to liberalize and deregulate is a gradual process instead of the "big bang" approach. Relaxation of policy directives have shifted gradually over time from resident to non-resident financial entities but still restrictive to circulation within Singapore until 2004. In any case, the republic's economic circumstances, institutional features, and monetary policy designs do impose certain constraints which would limit the impact of a full relaxation on internationalization of the Singapore dollar.

3.4. "Nurturing" Domestic Banking Institutions for "Strategic Interests" and in Preparation for Regional Expansion

On the asset management side, measures such as imposing a ceiling on Singapore dollar credit facilities for resident non-bank customers of offshore banks are perhaps more effective in preventing foreign encroachment on DBUs. Consistently MAS has denied that such a ceiling poses a constraint to offshore banks since "every foreign bank has excess of up to $150 million in Singapore dollar loans and it is not fully utilized." Such argument is technically valid since the credit ceiling has been steadily revised upward over the years, but the issue remains as to why there is a need to set a ceiling to begin with.

A rough calculation suggests that an increase in the limit by US$30 million can increase the stake of offshore banks in DBUs by a collective US$3 billion. As can be seen, the ceiling has been raised since the 1970s, very gradually at the outset but in more generous increments since the mid-1990s. Foreign banks tend to consider the argument as a vicious cycle. Credit facilities are not fully utilized because the ceiling itself has effectively capped the potential market for each foreign bank so that its management board is unwilling to commit resources in the DBU. In effect, the ceiling discourages foreign participation even if that is not its stated purpose. For many offshore banks, however, the ceiling is not a problem since most of their syndicated loans are dollar-denominated and their clients' fund requirements are mostly denominated in foreign currencies.

On the liability management side, the relative inaccessibility of local deposits to restricted banks and offshore banks also tends to discourage foreign participation in DBUs. Both offshore banks and restricted banks are not allowed to accept fixed deposits of less than S$250,000 per deposit and savings deposits from non-residents. Offshore banks were not allowed to accept savings deposits, fixed deposits, and other interest-bearing deposits in Singapore dollars from Singapore residents. Other restrictions include limits on the number of branch premises; exclusion from the Network for Electronic Transfers, Singapore (NETs), and limits on the number of automated teller machines (ATMs) allowed. These factors have, quite naturally, discouraged offshore banks from participating in DBUs. The unequal treatment of foreign banks in the domestic sector, where they are excluded from electronic point-of-sale systems and the shared ATM network and are restricted from branching, was perceived by some quarters as constituting a cartel to keep them out of DBUs.

The core activities of a bank revolve around the efficient management of its assets and liabilities. To maximize profit, banks must not only acquire a portfolio of assets that offers the highest yield, but also raise the required funds while minimizing the costs of borrowing. In fact it is not uncommon for indigenous banks to request from MAS the permission to launch long-term non-negotiable certificate of deposits which are reserve free in order to match a specific long-term funding requirement. It appears that the conspicuous inertia of foreign banks when it comes to participating in DBUs is not explained by the interplay of market forces and competition. Rather, it can be perceived as a result of the government's policy-inspired regulations to "nurture" indigenous banks and to insulate the domestic financial sector from foreign participation.

Crucial factors that helped shape the banking industry's assets-liabilities structure and corporate sector's financial requirements can be attributed to the policy to "nurture" the domestic banking institutions. Such a strategy to deliberately nurture indigenous financial institutions, while justifiable in "strategic national interests", nevertheless discourages competition and does not make financial services more efficient. After decades of nurturing by MAS, major indigenous banks have grown in size and are among the top twenty banks in Asia based on Tier 1 capital. Although the limit on foreign shareholding on indigenous banks was raised from 20 per cent to 40 per cent in the 1990s, such restriction was totally relaxed by 2000, and these indigenous banks have since grown bigger and made significant presence into the regional banking scene through a series of mergers and acquisitions, but they are still considered too small when compared with global players.

4. DEVELOPMENT OF THE FINANCIAL CENTRE: POLICY SEQUENCING AND LIBERALIZATION DRIVE

If one were to carefully examine the underlying principles of Singapore's regulatory framework and the way in which it has evolved over time, it becomes clear that the governing authorities have consistently opted for a liberalized financial environment based on market forces and high capital mobility, creating general conditions conducive for financial sector resiliency.

4.1. Liberalizing the Pricing Mechanism for Basic Monetary Aggregates in the 1970s

In June 1967, almost two years after Singapore's independence in August 1965, the Board of Commissioners of Currency, Singapore (BCCS) started issuing Singapore dollars which were fully backed by gold and foreign reserves. Following this was the introduction of the Banking Act of 1970, which took immediate effect when the MAS began operating in January 1971. Singapore formally abolished the cartel system for exchange-rate fixing in July 1972 and terminated the currency interchangeability between the Malaysian ringgit and the Singapore dollar in May 1973 but maintained par interchangeability with the Brunei dollar.

In July 1973, MAS removed the cartel system of foreign exchange quotation among banks and allowed the Singapore dollar to float "freely". Unofficially though, this floating system was managed. In 1981, MAS officially adopted a managed-float regime, creating a basket of currencies based on the value of trade with Singapore's major trading partners. The Ministry of Trade and Industry (MTI), which was then in consultation with MAS, would decide the future worth of the basket of currencies or the value of the Singapore dollar vis-à-vis the upper and lower bands of the weighted basket of currencies. MAS have since been authorized to manage-float the Singapore dollar within this band, which has been widening gradually in the 1990s.

The abolition of the cartel system of interest rate determination in 1975 allowed banks to quote their own interest rates on deposits and advances to customers. MAS, however, had to be informed, at least one working day in advance, of any change in the prime lending rate, the rates paid on all types of non-bank customer deposits, and the rate charged on overdraft facilities. Reliance on the market mechanism to regulate precious financial resources would ensure both efficiency and competitiveness in credit allocation and capital mobility.

Capital account liberalization in Singapore took full effect in 1978 with the complete abolition of exchange controls. Residents could now participate fully in ACU asset-liability activities and foreign exchange transactions. MAS were quite prepared to liberalize the capital account at this early stage of financial development. Certainly, it did not intend to deal with capital flows through exchange controls since ample safeguards could be installed by legislating incentives that would not hamper the healthy expansion of the offshore financial sector.

4.2. Re-structuring the Framework for Monetary Policy in the 1980s

It is widely accepted in the literature and among central banking authorities, and confirmed by international experience, that the monetary authority cannot persist in trading inflation against higher economic growth. Although the dominance of money supply is widely recognized, money supply targeting has not been very successful worldwide because of the long and unexpected lag in monetary impact. In fact, decreasing number of countries still peg their currencies to a single currency or a basket of currencies or in terms of shares in world trade. More countries appear to be moving toward a flexible, independent floating exchange regime, in which the authorities only act to "smooth" fluctuations but not to target a particular level.

Singapore has adopted an exchange rate arrangement whereby MAS concentrates on a single nominal anchor instead of monitoring several intermediate targets or control measures at the same time. Singapore will also not maintain an official peg of any sort as this could lead to unrealistic exchange rates. Macroeconomic stabilization by MAS since the 1980s has been dominated by monetary policy, essentially exchange rate management. Does the republic's dichotomized financial system facilitate such management? Does the demarcation of financial activities between the DBU and the ACU, coupled with the segregation between local and foreign banks, make exchange rate management more effective by helping to regulate liquidity in the domestic financial sector? These are interesting issues to consider. An affirmative answer connotes rejection of the hypothesis of the triad of incompatibilities, which argue against the coexistence of exchange rate stability, free capital mobility, and monetary autonomy.

Singapore's long-standing budgetary policy is to maintain operating and development expenditures at levels that can be financed with government revenues. The role of active fiscal stabilization in Singapore is therefore somewhat curtailed, even in the short run. The MAS has adopted the exchange rate as the moving nominal anchor for monetary policy since the early 1980s:

> The Authority's ability to pursue independent monetary and interest rate policies is constrained by the open nature of the economy and the close linkage between domestic and international financial markets. In this setting, the Authority concentrates on an exchange rate policy. The Singapore dollar exchange rate is based on a managed float system, in which it is allowed to fluctuate within a target band. This target band is based on a trade-weighted basket of currencies of Singapore's major trading partners. The Authority manages the float within the band mainly through its foreign exchange operations.[5]

The unusual features of consistent budget surpluses and a huge but forced net contribution to the CPF rendered liquidity management and the implementation of exchange rate policy rather unique. Conventional channels and instruments for regulating liquidity flows in an economy under monetary policy, such as open-market operations through treasury bills and bonds, variations in reserve requirements, or the discount-window approach, do not play an active role in Singapore.

The more important, if not the most frequent, means of regulating liquidity in the banking system appears to be intervention by MAS through the foreign exchange market, currency swaps, and direct deposit injections or withdrawals in the money market. Compulsory CPF contributions and domestic surpluses from government agencies such as the statutory boards and ministries are channelled to MAS as part of official reserves for investment by the Government Investment Corporation (GIC). Hence, the banking system periodically experiences substantial liquidity drains. MAS often purchases U.S. dollars and sells Singapore dollars in the currency swap market, in amounts that depend on its exchange rate objective.

If MAS wishes to see a stronger Singapore dollar, the offsetting transactions in the currency swaps would be less than the initial liquidity drains from the banking system. If the objective were a weaker Singapore dollar, the offsetting transactions would exceed the initial liquidity drains. Since Singapore is a price taker when it comes to domestic interest rate movements, growth in the money supply would therefore be totally subservient to the exchange rate policy if MAS were "actively" pursuing its exchange rate objective. On the other hand, if MAS were merely "guiding" the exchange rate movements, money supply could retain its dominance in a monetarist world.

The official objective of a strong exchange rate policy is to contain imported inflation and keep domestic price increases low, for sustained economic growth. Rapid economic expansion in the post 1985/86 years has presented another task for exchange rate management, which is to regulate the economy when it overheats. However, MAS also recognizes that with full employment in Singapore, "any attempt to hold down the Singapore dollar artificially would only buy a temporary improvement in competitiveness. It would be quickly undermined by higher inflation." If there is a sharp rise in worldwide inflationary pressure, MAS admits that it may be difficult to engineer "an offsetting sharp appreciation of exchange rate without causing short-run competitive and adjustment problems". An economic system of highly flexible wages and swift price adjustments will have limited scope for monetary policy. Given the widespread year-to-year adjustments in wage contracts under the National Wages Council's tripartite arrangement, exchange-rate policy may be able to exploit only a very short-term trade-off, lasting no more than a year, between inflation and trade competitiveness.[6]

In Singapore, money supply manages to retain its dominance in the real economy and inflation is still essentially a monetary phenomenon. MAS seems to have no long-term ability or intention to "target" the exchange rate and its "guiding" policy serves only to smooth fluctuations in the short-run through liquidity management. Despite the absence of capital control and with high capital mobility, the Singapore dollar still remains as one of the most stable currencies. The "impossible trinity" of exchange rate stability, free capital mobility, and monetary autonomy would have been difficult to achieve if liquidity management in the DBU were frustrated by the money multiplier which tends to become more unpredictable if capital flows are not contained within the ACU.

Exchange rate management would have been less effective if the short-term exchange rate target were neutralized by a significant pool of Singapore dollars outside Singapore or with non-residents, outside the jurisdiction of MAS. Speculative attacks on the Singapore dollar in the foreign exchange market would have been difficult to quell if liquidity in the local inter-bank money market were controlled by the full-licence banks that have no long-term business interests of Singapore at heart. This must be the essence of the dichotomized financial system. Being able to identify correctly the monetary transmission mechanism and restructured the framework of monetary policy appropriately since the 1980s have therefore paved way for financial and banking stability.

4.3. Deepening Financial Markets Further and Revamping Bond Activities in the 1990s

After three decades of preparation to lay down the building blocks to develop Singapore as a world-class financial centre, an important policy reform milestone was announced by MAS in July 1999. Amongst the key strategic thrusts of policy reforms included the further development of the depth and breadth of capital markets in debt, equity and derivatives. Such strategic thrusts would support efforts to promote a vibrant asset management industry. This is a turning point in the sense that Singapore would now aim to be not just a centre for regional fund sourcing but also aspire to be a global fund management centre.

The latter objective to increase trading volume is to be achieved through a two-pronged approach: Firstly, by introducing new products into the Singapore International Monetary Exchange (SIMEX) such as the MSCI Singapore stock index futures contract, the Dow Jones Thailand stock index futures contract and the Euroyen LIBOR futures and options contract and secondly, by forging strategic international linkages by making SIMEX as part of the global electronic trade alliance with the Chicago Mercantile Exchange and the Societe des Bourses Francaises as the demutualization and merger of Stock Exchange of Singapore (SES) and SIMEX.

As for longer term capital bond market development, similar to the situation in other Asian countries, the bond market in Singapore, in particular the corporate bond market, is clearly underdeveloped. MAS had attempted on several occasions since the 1980s to revamp the Singapore government securities market but ended with little progress. Notwithstanding the absence of an active market to raise long-term funds, Singapore was able to avoid a double mismatch. If Singapore's domestic corporate bond market had been bigger or more liquid as comparable with those in developed countries, its financial system would have been much more resilient and complete.

An inspection of relevant data reveals that almost all corporate bonds listed on Singapore's stock exchange are Asian dollar bonds denominated in U.S. dollars, and that there are virtually no issues of Singapore dollar denominated bonds, particularly long-term bonds of over five to seven years' maturity. Issuers are limited to GLCs and large enterprises. As for the secondary market, there is lack of liquidity and limited trading activities, in sharp contrast to the stock market. Trading turnover ratio in the bond market, including government bonds, is only a few per cent compared to the 20 per cent to 30 per cent in the stock market. The scale of issues in the government bond market is growing, but like the corporate bond market, trading is sporadic at best.

Lack of interest from institutional investors explains why the secondary market is not developed for Singapore bonds. The Central Provident Fund (CPF), a compulsory savings pension system, mainly invests its funds in government bonds, and the CPF Board has purchased nearly 80 per cent of the outstanding government bonds. Commercial banks come next at a little less than 20 per cent. The CPF Board channelled household savings into long-term government bond investments and retains most of the bonds until maturity. Because banks set aside government bonds to fulfil MAS mandatory liquid asset reserve requirements, those bonds are also typically not traded.

On the other hand, the government constantly runs a surplus and is not necessarily obliged to issue additional government bonds. The issuance of government bonds has continued in order to provide the CPF Board with an investment vehicle; the development of the bond market was of less importance. A portion of the CPF, siphoned off by the government through the issuance of government bonds, was diverted to foreign investment through the GIC. The maintenance of such a system to increase net foreign assets was required in order to limit the supply of Singapore dollars. Looking at it from a different perspective, the bond market was a type of intermediary through which the CPF Board's risk management function relating to investment assets was transferred to the GIC.

The fact that businesses could raise funds from other sources such as the use of internal reserves, bank loans, or equity finance, coupled with the lack of interest among citizens for bond investments and the limited need for corporate bond issuance, explains why the corporate bond market failed to develop. From the investors' point of view, it is believed that the CPF Board and financial institutions buy-and-hold attitude in a market with few bond issues further impeded the development of bond trading skills, and portfolio strategies of the institutional investors.

Financial liberalization and reform programmes were beginning to be implemented vigorously in Singapore immediately after the East Asian currency crisis. One of the main focus set to become the subject of reform is the Singapore dollar denominated bond market. One of the objectives of the reform effort is to mitigate or avoid the problem of double-mismatch and this was accomplished by expanding the options available for raising long-term funds. The significant shift must be the intake of both domestic and overseas investment funds by making the domestic bond market more substantial and further developing Singapore as an international financial centre. The objective was to do away with the "fund-raising in Singapore" and "fund-managing in Hong Kong" syndrome which was prevalent at the time, with the intention of promoting "Singapore for both fund-raising and fund-managing".

The relevant policy has been implemented since 1998 and three major measures were put into practice. First was the periodic issue of ten-year government bonds to create a benchmark in the bond market. This made it possible to draw both long-term and short-term yield curves for the bond market, and that contributed to increased bond trading and assists the pricing of corporate bonds. Secondly, the issuance of bonds denominated in Singapore dollars by government agencies, foreign businesses, and international agencies was approved to increase bond issues. Government agencies actually issued bonds totalling S$2.3 billion and foreign corporations (particularly U.S. entities) along with international agencies such as the International Financial Corporation issued bonds totalling S$2.85 billion. What is significant here in relation to the non-internationalization policy of the Singapore dollar is the issuing of bonds by foreign businesses and international agencies in Singapore dollars.

Up to this point, MAS had prohibited foreign issuers from issuing Singapore dollar denominated bonds in order to prevent the outflow of Singapore dollars to the extent possible. However, in order to remove the constraint in connection with the development of the local bond market, the Singapore dollar was gradually relaxed to make it an easier currency to use. Again, one interpretation is that this led to the diversification of potential investments for domestic savings. If the range of investment vehicles denominated in Singapore dollars is expanded, it helps alleviate exchange risks incidental to overseas investment. Nevertheless, foreign currency swaps are required in the event that Singapore dollars raised by foreign issuers are to be used overseas and in this context there is no change regarding the basis of non-internationalization policy of the Singapore dollar.

Moreover, so as to generate investment in the bond market by individual retail investors that had been at a rather low level, the purchase of bonds issued by government agencies using CPF savings was permitted. In fact, S$10 million of the S$300 million JTC medium-term bonds issued in November 1998 were sold to individual investors.

Authorization to purchase government agency bonds through CPF accounts that cover all workers in Singapore expanded the investor base, and this is expected to energize the secondary market. If the primary bond market can expand through the vitalization of the secondary market, this would certainly stimulate corporate bond issues by domestic companies, thereby eliminating or mitigating double mismatches. When encouraging the Singapore dollar listing of foreign companies on the Singapore Exchange (SGX), MAS nevertheless is still in control to judge whether the economy and the respective governing authorities can cope with the liberalization, and work out carefully calculated steps and measures with ample safeguards.

4.4. Challenges from Cross-border Financial Activities, Cyber-banking and Further Deregulation beyond 2000

In the aftermath of the East Asian financial turmoil, MAS realized what were some of the system weaknesses revealed by the crisis and recognized the major challenges posed by cross-border financial activities and cyber-banking. After three decades of financial development and consolidation, MAS felt Singapore was ready and it was timely to make a bid to be the leading financial centre in Asia. Unlike many regional financial centres in the post crisis era, MAS took a bold step ahead in 1998 to deregularize further, albeit through a steady and incremental approach.

The global banking industry has gone through a series of lending excesses over the past three decades which include the international bad debts of the 1970s, energy and real estate crisis of the 1980s and Asian emerging markets of the 1990s. For the year 2000 and beyond or the new millennium, ways have been cleared to erase financial barriers in the creation of financial supermarkets. This significant U.S. financial sector reform is supposed to lead to major improvements in financial services, promote financial innovations, lower capital costs, create greater variety of financial products for consumers and strengthen international competitiveness. Historic legislations were passed by U.S. lawmakers to repeal the 1933 Glass-Steagall Act and the 1956 Bank Holding Company Act.

Intensified competition worldwide had led to a series of M&As which began in the United States and subsequently took place amongst European and Japanese banks. The Financial Service Modernization Act of 1999 set the train of M&As, moving across bank and non-bank financial institutions, producing vast service-based conglomerates. The main rationales for M&As are essentially over capacity, to realize cost savings, greater business synergies, to allow cross-selling of services and, of paramount importance, Web-based Internet technology-driven consolidation.

Overcapacity in the banking industry leads to lowering of the lending criteria and irrational pricing of credits which can weaken the financial system. M&As will therefore necessarily mean substantial loss of jobs at least in the shorter term, further investment and super-heading the new technology advancement, responding to demand for specialists in newer businesses under a new competitive environment and coping with the mammoth task of business consolidation and management restructuring. From the investors or consumers' perspective, intensified competition had led to increasing emphasis for high growth/high yield financial instruments. Greater financial deregulation worldwide and freer flows of financial information enhance financial innovations and complex financial products with cross-border financial investments. Hence financial institutions in Singapore were not spared in the 2007 U.S. subprime credit crisis, although with limited losses.

Wealth accumulation in Asia after prolonged years of robust growth have significantly changed investors' expectation towards the returns from Western traditional pension funds. In meeting this more sophisticated demand by the new high net worth Asian individuals, commercials banks are shifting their traditional financial intermediation of deposits taking-corporate lending businesses emphasis to investment portfolios, fund managing and private banking. Hence Singapore witnessed the rapid growth of "target" funds, boutique fund managers and private banking facelift with very tailored-made structured financial products to cater for the individual investor's requirements and expectations.

Such changing landscape in the global banking industry is changing the approach in which central bankers think about supervision in view of the worldwide trends of convergence amongst financial institutions and blurring of product boundaries. It is therefore rather logical to look into the model of an Omnibus Act to streamline and consolidate the existing supervisory role, regulating structure and financial services legislation which are deemed to be more cost effective and prevent regulatory arbitrage. Examples of possible changes include a single authorization or licence for all financial institutions and a bottom-up approach where capital is required for different regulated activities within a financial institution.

As the demarcating lines between bank and non-bank financial institutions such as securities firms and insurance companies are blurring, competition and market encroaching from non-bank financial institutions — which are also strong, branded market players, to commercial banks in terms of the traditional financial intermediation, are intensifying. Web-based online financial services (OFS) with virtual branch and specialist services outsourcing such as mortgage processing companies, are becoming new marketing and sales channels where contracting or closure of brick-and-mortar branch networks are to be expected.

In Asia, Hong Kong and Singapore are amongst the leaders in the provision of OFS. In Singapore, OFS including commercial banking, securities brokerage services and insurance services have been gaining momentum over the recent years by indigenous banks. MAS announced in July 2000 its approach to the licensing, regulation and supervision of Internet banking in Singapore. For effective banking supervision, regulatory authorities ought to seriously take into account the characteristics and impact of OFS. Issues pertaining to maturity and currency mismatches may turn ambiguous since electronic money that cuts across borders and is more fluid in nature, may attract further gapping risks and invite greater currency exposure which are even harder to understand, assess and tract.

5. COMPETITIVENESS AND CONSTRAINTS: CAN SINGAPORE CONTINUE TO BE A LEADING INTERNATIONAL FINANCIAL CENTRE?

In conclusion, Singapore has indeed built up a tested and credible dichotomized financial system with effective policy instruments. A preliminary and more pragmatic approach to financial liberalization is to work according to the established regulatory framework by considering changes from within, in a gradual manner. In the early stage of financial development, tight or "high-handed" micro supervisory approach adopted by the regulatory authority to financial institutions are to be expected, especially when MAS is pushing ahead on uncharted ground in turbulent periods.

As domestic financial institutions regionalize and their financial activities are increasingly internationalized, their participation in offshore financial activities would increase accordingly, although Singapore is still unlikely to do away with the dichotomized financial system in the foreseeable future. Since 1999, MAS has encouraged mergers and acquisitions of local banks and enticed foreign banks to compete in the domestic banking sector. DBU and ACU are likely to continue to operate on the basis of a non-level playing field in segregated financial entities but the segregation would be and is increasingly blurred between local and international players. As reaffirmed by the then Chairman of MAS and Deputy Prime Minister Lee Hsien Loong in 1997, "so far, this approach has promoted rather than hindered our growth". Such strategy is crucial to systemic stability as Singapore's external economy expands, as its regional funding role improves, as its status as a major financial centre is further enhanced, and as swift fund flows become the norm for capital markets which are globally integrated.

The authority's effort to "nurture" indigenous banks into bigger international players, initially through domestic market protection over decades, was discontinued since 1999. The attempt by MAS to entice foreign competition into the DBU with approval of half a dozen or so full-licensed banks, is meant to "force" modernization and innovation of indigenous banks but not to do away with the demarcation approach to "cushion" fund flows. In the context of a financial liberalization thesis and an economic development strategy, it is to be noted retrospectively that the "nurturing approach" adopted did entail a necessary trade-off. In exchange for nurturing indigenous banks to become sufficiently large for international competition, Singapore indeed had paid a price and is perhaps still suffering from the outcome of protectionist measures which must necessarily be lower quality, fewer choices and less competitive financial services for consumers.

Given the policy on restrictive usage of the Singapore dollar for non-residents and partly due to the lack of the natural need to borrow through government bond issuance, the rudimentary domestic capital market may well be just another price Singapore has to face under the dichotomized financial system. The sequencing approach adopted for financial deepening also involves a necessary trade-off: The relatively underdeveloped domestic long-term capital market during the early stages of development in exchanging for an orderly and sustainable growth environment. While the policy dilemma is recognized, to the MAS, the Singapore dollar is already "internationalized" as far as its monetary policy allows. All impediments to capital market developments have been removed, and the policy is reduced to its essence of discouraging speculation on the Singapore dollar with the latest 2004 amendments to MAS Notice 757. Statutory boards and GLCs are also being encouraged to raise funds directly through market bond issuances instead of resorting to government funding, though the progress made is far from satisfactory.

Prima facie evidence appear to suggest that the hypothesis known as the "triad of incompatibilities", that is, the non-coexistence of exchange rate stability, free capital mobility and monetary autonomy, does not hold, at least in Singapore. Three strands of empirical results which do not lend support to the hypothesis include. Firstly, the three decades-long relative exchange rate stability of the Singapore dollar under the "smoothing" exchange rate management by MAS continued to prevail. Secondly, strong econometric evidence of "dominantly active" impulses from both the broad and narrow money aggregates in affecting the real economy was detected.[7] Thirdly, high level of capital mobility was statistically verified particularly in the category of "other investments" as classified by IMF, which includes all other capital transactions of the private sector which are mainly, but not exclusively, bank lending and depositing.[8]

In the bracing international environment of volatile fund flows, important policy implications under the dichotomized financial system surely must come from the remaining restrictive usage of the local currency within geographical Singapore, which is basically equivalent to "throwing sand into the wheels" of perfect capital mobility. The regulatory authorities can then check on "unusual movements" in sources and uses of funds, thus have some "leverage" on the local currency but not to restrict capital movements under the two-tier financial entity.

The post-crisis challenges for regulating authorities must be to ensure balanced-sustainable economic growth, enforce effective regulation on financial institutions and to cope adequately with internationalized fund flows resulting from electronic transfers and globalization. In its mission and objectives, MAS has always pledged commitment to the promotion of sustainable non-inflationary economic growth. It acts as a banker and financial agent to the government by protecting the value of its accumulated reserves and developing a competitive and progressive financial services sector through prudential oversight.

> MAS is the central bank of Singapore. It formulates and executes Singapore's monetary and exchange rate policies. As banker and financial agent to the government, it manages the country's official foreign reserves and facilitates the issuance of government securities. As supervisor and regulator of

> Singapore's financial services sector, MAS has prudential oversight over the banking, securities, futures and insurance industries. It is also responsible for the development and promotion of Singapore as an international financial centre.[9]

Prior to the 1997 Asian financial crisis, many Asian countries or economies aspired to be amongst the major IFCs, notwithstanding the obvious lack in economies of scale of the financial activities and duplication of regional financial services. The post-Asia financial crisis effort in 1999 and 2004 to further liberalize Singapore as an international competitive financial centre appears to have paid off. Total assets under management (AUM) have consistently registered double-digit growth since 2000, reaching S$900 billion in 2006 (See Table 3.2). Fund mangers have added more functions such as global research capability, regional trading desks and centralized middle- and back-office settlement functions in Singapore.

Investment professionals have also grown in tandem from 1,300 in 2005 to 1,600 in 2006 as private banking services and the wealth management industry took off strongly, with robust growing Asian economies coming from China, India and the Middle East since the late

Table 3.2
Central Provident Fund (CPF) Board Holdings of Singapore Government Securities (SGS), CPF Members' Balance and Fund Management Industry

(In S$ billion)	Holdings of SGS	Members' balance	Size of FMI
■ 1995	$45	$66	$86
■ 1996	$52	$73	$125
■ 1997	$57	$80	$124
■ 1998	$60	$85	$151
■ 1999	$63	$88	$274
■ 2000	$61	$90	$276
■ 2001	$89	$92	$307
■ 2002	$94	$96	$344
■ 2003	$101	$104	$465
■ 2004	$108	$112	$571
■ 2005	$115	$120	$720
■ 2006	$119	$126	$900

Source: MAS Annual Report.

1990s. Going by investment classes, equities constitute to 55 per cent of the total assets under management, followed by 17 per cent in bonds and 12 per cent in money market instruments (See Figure 3.1).

Figure 3.1
Investment of Funds by Instruments

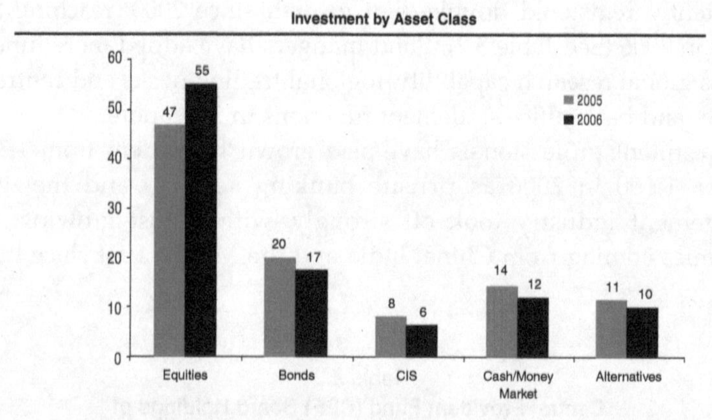

Source: MAS, Singapore

In the effort to better deal with international capital movements, empirical studies to identify components or sources of investment fund flows in each economy as classified by IMF under the three broad categories of direct investment (DI), net portfolio investment (PI) and other net investment (OI) would be useful. Research findings after the 1997 Asian financial crisis on ASEAN-5 and twenty-two-member economies of the World Trade Organization have revealed that the source of volatility indeed could be traced to the OI category. Contrary to the general perception, PI and DI in most economies are rather stable.[10]

The important policy implication is that non-internationalization of the local currency under the dichotomized financial system in which the offshore and onshore financial activities are demarcated, may be a useful tool to consider for those relatively small open but high growth export-oriented economies.

Some useful lessons to be reminded of are as follows: Firstly, curbing financial activities directly will be a costly process while direct and massive intervention in the marketplace tends to cause distortion. It may be more efficient and less arbitrary to find a resilient financial structure to better deal with capital flows. Secondly, instead of trying to fend off excessive capital inflows or outflows, it may be more pertinent for policy authorities to ensure that economic conditions and the political environment are not created to attract excessive inflows or exacerbate volatile outflows. Thirdly, while waiting for international monetary reforms to take shape, individual economies should seek initiatives to buffer their own system by working within the requirements of the international financial community and global monetary order. A regional initiative towards core principles for effective banking supervision consistent with Basle Initiatives may be the more realistic and efficient way of pushing ahead.

We should also be more careful in the formulation of policy strategies and in the direction of resources by regional authorities to promote growth of financial centres. The relevant financial centres in the region should explore and compete based on comparative advantages of the respective economies in Asia instead of pursuing policies of unwarranted duplication. It may be more productive to seriously consider sequencing and spacing of reforms in the area of financial structure and financial institutions. It may be warranted to review the effectiveness of checks and balances on excesses within the regulatory and other relevant governing authorities instead of being overly concerned with or complaining about what could well be the dynamic behaviours and consequences of a more integrated financial market pricing mechanism. The phenomenon may well represent the new global financial order that we all must learn to live with.

Alternative options to consider are perhaps not the totally *laissez faire* market-driven system currency-pegged exchange rate regime of Hong Kong which has proven to function well only during normal times, or the total market insulation approach of capital controls adopted by Malaysia which is a short-run remedy to buy time but with long-run costs. Given Singapore's experience, restrictive usage of the local currency for non-residents under a trade-weighted basket of managed float exchange rate regime in which the offshore and onshore financial activities are demarcated, could be useful for relatively small open but high growth export-oriented economies. Such a middle-path approach may help to preserve greater stability with sustainable growth as Malaysia, Thailand, Philippines and Indonesia have gone some way along this direction since the 1997 Asian financial crisis.

Retrospectively, failure to appropriately judge members' readiness prior to the advice on capital account liberalization by international agencies in the past is a serious policy oversight. Weak financial institutions and rudimentary financial system can only evolve through a gradual process of financial liberalization consistent with economic development. Effective mobilization of domestic savings through extensive network of financial intermediaries may be an important source of funding for investment projects. Given the recent trends of convergence within the global banking industry, for efficiency and streamlining of regulation, an Omnibus Act for all financial institutions may be the inevitable way forward. The ongoing developments of Internet-driven online financial services do pose some challenge to regulatory authorities in terms of effective fund flow supervision, although its impact is not as serious as it was initially conjectured. The more fruitful approach is perhaps not to attempt to regulate or control these activities but to allow the market to dictate instead. However, the effective monitoring of their impact on financial services and financial institutions would call for a more comprehensive financial information system. In this sense we may concur with some market observers that "it is a fallacy to speak of the wisdom of the marketplace at all times" especially where efficiency of the marketplace prevails through regulations and institutions set up by the international policy authorities and financial agencies.

Notes

1. Tan, K.G. "Coping with Capital Flows and Dealing with Capital Controls", paper prepared for the "First Conference on Pacific Basin Financial Markets and Policies", organized by New Jersey Center for Research in Financial Services and Review of Pacific Basin Financial Markets and Policies, Rutgers University, U.S.A., being held at The World Trade Institute, 25–26 March 1999, One World Trade Center, 55th Floor New York, USA.
2. Goh, K.S. Speech delivered at the Second Reading of the Monetary Authority of Singapore (Amendment) Bill 1984, 24 August 1984, Singapore Parliament.
3. Tan, K.G. and Chen, K. "ISEAS-NTU Overall Progress Ranking on Financial Reforms and Liberalization of ASEAN 10+5 Economies", prepared for the inaugural launch on 10 March 2006, Institute of Southeast Asian Studies (ISEAS), Singapore.

4. Asian Development Bank Institute, "Asian Policy Forum Report", by Asian Policy Forum Secretariat, July 2000.
5. Monetary Authority of Singapore, *Annual Report 1981/82*.
6. Teh, K.P. and Shanmugaratnam, T. "Exchange Rate Policy: Philosophy and Conduct over the Past Decade", in *Public Policies in Singapore: Change in the 1980s and the Future Signposts*, edited by Linda Low and Toh M.H. (Singapore: Time Academic Press, 1992).
7. Chen, K. and Tan, K.G., "The Nominal Anchor for Monetary Policy in Singapore: Exchange Rate Targeting or Guiding?". Paper prepared at Pacific Economic Outlook/Structure Specialists Meeting, 27–28 September 1996, Osaka, Japan.
8. Tan, K.G., "Coping with Capital Flows and Dealing with Capital Controls". Paper prepared for the "First Conference on Pacific Basin Financial Markets and Policies", organized by New Jersey Center for Research in Financial Services and Review of Pacific Basin Financial Markets and Policies, Rutgers University, USA held at The World Trade Institute, 25–26 March 1999, One World Trade Center, 55th Floor, New York, USA.
9. Monetary Authority of Singapore, *Annual Report 1997/98*.
10. Tan, K.G., "Coping with Capital Flows and Dealing with Capital Controls", op. cit., and Kono, M. and Schuknecht, L., "Financial Services Trade, Capital Flows and Financial Stability", Staff Working Paper ERAD-98-12, Economic Research and Analysis Division, World Trade Organization, 1998.

References

Asian Development Bank Institute. "Asian Policy Forum Report". Asian Policy Forum Secretariat, July 2000.

Chen, K. and Tan, K.G. "The Nominal Anchor for Monetary Policy in Singapore: Exchange Rate Targeting or Guiding?". Paper prepared at Pacific Economic Outlook/Structure Specialists Meeting, 27–28 September 1996, Osaka, Japan.

Goh, K.S. Speech delivered at the Second Reading of the Monetary Authority of Singapore (Amendment) Bill 1984, 24 August 1984, Singapore Parliament.

International Monetary Fund. "Issues in International Exchange and Payments Systems". IMF Publication Services, Washington D.C., 1995.

Kono, M. and L. Schuknecht. "Financial Services Trade, Capital Flows and Financial Stability". Staff Working Paper ERAD-98-12, Economic Research and Analysis Division, World Trade Organization, 1998.

Lee, S. L. Speech delivered at the SESDAQ Tenth Anniversary, 4 November 1997, Westin Stamford Hotel, Singapore.

———. Speech delivered at the Official Launch of the MAS Electronic Payment System, 13 August 1998, Monetary Authority of Singapore.

Monetary Authority of Singapore, *Annual Report 1997/98*.

Tan, K.G. "Coping with Capital Flows and Dealing with Capital Controls". Paper prepared for the "First Conference on Pacific Basin Financial Markets and Policies", organized by New Jersey Center for Research in Financial Services and Review of Pacific Basin Financial Markets and Policies, Rutgers University, USA held at The World Trade Institute, 25–26 March 1999, One World Trade Center, 55th Floor, New York, USA.

Tan, K.G. and Chen, K. "ISEAS-NTU Overall Progress Ranking on Financial Reforms and Liberalization of ASEAN-10+5 Economies". Prepared for the inaugural launch on 10 March 2006, Institute of South East Asian Studies (ISEAS), Singapore, 2006.

———. "2007 Update on ISEAS-NTU Overall Progress Ranking on Financial Reforms and Liberalization of ASEAN-10+5 Economies". Unpublished manuscript, Asian Research Centre, Nanyang Technological University, Singapore, 2007.

Teh, K.P. and Shanmugaratnam, T. "Exchange Rate Policy: Philosophy and Conduct over the Past Decade". In *Public Policies in Singapore: Change in the 1980s and the Future Signposts*, edited by Linda Low and Toh M.H. Singapore: Time Academic Press, 1992.

4

PROMOTING TOKYO AS AN INTERNATIONAL FINANCIAL CENTRE

Sayuri Shirai

Japan's economic power is widely recognized worldwide, thanks to it being the world's second largest economy (US$4.4 trillion equivalent GDP in 2007) and having a high per capita income (US$34,000 in 2007). According to Flow of Funds accounts, the amount of total assets held by resident financial intermediaries was about US$25 trillion at end-2007 (of which, US$13 trillion was held by deposit taking institutions, US$4 trillion by pension funds and insurance firms, and US$7 trillion by other financial institutions). This substantial financial wealth was the second largest after the United States, where in the same year the total financial assets recorded were US$62 trillion.

Relative to its economic power, however, Japan's financial and capital markets have not realized their full potential. This is so in terms of providing diverse, innovative financial products and services at reasonable cost, giving domestic and foreign entities greater access to diverse sources of finance, and creating an active and self-disciplinary environment for the wholesale market. This chapter analyses the performance of these markets (until mid-2007) and discusses the possibility of promoting Tokyo as a top international financial centre. The chapter is in four sections. Section 1 briefly provides background information and issues associated with the Tokyo market. Section 2 looks at the Japanese version of a "Financial Big Bang" launched in 1996 and its impact on financial and capital market developments. Section 3 takes an overview of the current financial and capital markets in Japan. Finally, section 4 reviews the visions proposed most recently by the Japanese Cabinet (led by the then Prime Minister Shinzo Abe) and discusses the recent initiatives as well as agenda remaining.

1. BACKGROUND

1.1. The Period of the 1980s

The period of the 1980s was a time when the Japanese economy was in great shape, reflected by its persistent current account and trade account surpluses and high economic growth driven by TFP (total factor productivity) growth (which exceeded 4 per cent and was higher that those of the United States and United Kingdom). At the same time, a strong yen and the rising asset values of banks, securities firms, and insurance companies (reflected in their high stock values) encouraged them to move their assets out of the country, particularly to the United States and Europe. This helped Japan to become the world's largest external creditor. In the domestic capital market, stocks were being actively traded and Japan's market capitalization had become the largest in the world, accounting for about one-third of the world market capitalization — far beyond its relative GDP size (13 per cent of global GDP). A number of overseas banks and securities firms rushed in and opened branches and offices in Tokyo to expand their financial operations, while overseas firms attempted to list their stocks on the Tokyo Stock Exchange. Also, this was the time when Ezra Vogel published his well-known book entitled *Japan as Number One*, which boosted Japanese confidence.

In retrospect, Tokyo was indeed not only the biggest international financial centre in Asia, but also had the potential to become one of the top three global financial centres in the world, along with New York (whose main advantages arose from being in the largest economy with deep financial/capital markets) and London (whose main advantages arose from various cross-border transactions in diverse currencies). In those days, there was debate about whether Japan's financial and capital markets should be actively promoted to become a more competitive international financial centre — by introducing comprehensive and drastic reforms, as had already been done in the United Kingdom in 1986 (the so-called "Big Bang"). This debate reflected a concern that relative to the sizes of GDP and market capitalization, the Japanese financial sector had not been as efficient and so was not as attractive as those of New York and London. Despite active discussions, the Japanese government did not take the opportunity to undertake reform, mainly because of resistance coming from the banking, securities, and insurance industries.

1.2. Background Behind the Financial Big Bang Initiative

It took another decade before the Japanese government finally launched its comprehensive reforms. In 1996, the Cabinet of then Prime Minister Ryutaro Hashimoto announced its intention to introduce the "Japanese version of a Financial Bing Bang". It set up a clear goal of promoting Tokyo to become an international financial centre comparable to those of New York and London. This decision was motivated by the awareness that during the so-called "lost decade" (ten-year economic stagnation beginning in 1991) of the 1990s, Japan's financial and capital markets had rapidly waned as they suffered from the effects of the collapse of financial bubbles (the Nikkei Index and the urban land price both declined by about 60 per cent in the 1990s) and the resultant accumulation of non-performing loans. By 1994–95, the non-performing loan problems were first revealed through so-called "*Jusen*" or non-bank financial companies specializing in housing loans; this led to the government having to implement financial counter-measures of JP¥680 billion (US$6 billion) in 1996.[1]

The injection of public money invited harsh criticism (by Japanese citizens) of the supervisory and inspection capacities of Japan. Some claimed that excessive regulations by the Ministry of Finance (particularly to avoid excessive competition) and inadequate disclosure requirements resulted in not only weakening the soundness of financial institutions but also in limiting competition. Such a regulatory framework deterred banks from advancing financial skills and offering diverse financial and product services. It is true that the regulations imposed on the Japanese financial and capital markets had been more stringent than those in London and

New York. In these cities, deregulation has promoted competition and lowered commission fees, thus encouraging financial institutions to develop new financial products and services in order to increase new sources of income. Moreover, Japan's deflation caused by a growing excess of demand for goods and services added to the deterioration of non-financial firms' profitability, thereby increasing non-performing loans and dropping stock values further. The plunge of Tokyo's presence as an international financial centre was in stark contrast to the high-technology and knowledge-intensive manufacturing and software industries, which had managed to maintain and even strengthened international competitiveness throughout the 1990s. In response to the criticism, a series of structural reforms focusing on deregulation (as described in section 2) has been implemented under the catchphrase of "Japan's version of the Financial Big Bang".

1.3. Reasons for Promoting Tokyo as an International Financial Centre

Against such a background, it may be worthwhile to re-examine why Tokyo should even become one of the top international financial centres in the first place. There are at least the following four reasons that have been widely pointed out.

First, it is becoming increasingly important for Japan to utilize its substantial financial assets more efficiently to better cope with challenges posed by its rapidly progressing aging society. The ratio of population of people equal to or over sixty-five years old already accounted for 20.2 per cent in 2005, and is expected to reach 31.8 per cent in 2030 and 39.6 per cent in 2050. This makes Japan the most rapidly aging society in the world. As of end-2007, household financial assets reached about US$14 trillion, the second largest after the United States where household assets registered US$45 trillion. However, for a long time these assets have not been efficiently utilized. This is evidenced by the fact that half of these funds have been allocated to deposits and cash without really being channelled into stocks and investment trusts. Moreover, given that the Japanese government has gradually reduced public pension benefits and postponed the eligibility age under tight pension budgets, households need to seek alternative and more diversified ways of accumulating assets for use after retirement. Given that higher returns mean higher risk, the domestic financial and capital markets should play a greater role in providing risk money for households.

Second, the promotion of the financial and associated business sectors is regarded as a crucial economic growth strategy by the Japanese government. Currently, Japan's GDP growth rates have been constraint by sluggish TFP growth. The TFP growth rate has been only about 0.7 per cent (of which, according to the Cabinet Office, 1.3 per cent came from the manufacturing sector and a mere 0.1 per cent by the tertiary sector) — the level being nearly half of TFP growth in the United States. Thus, the key for raising TFP and GDP growth lies in the tertiary sector, which already accounts for about 70 per cent of GDP and total employment. The manufacturing sector, despite its past and present role as an engine for growth, has been constantly shifting its production and marketing locations to the United States and rapidly growing emerging markets such as China, India, and Russia. Thus, the main source of future economic growth depends increasingly on the tertiary sector. Taking an overview of the experiences of the United States and United Kingdom, it is clear that the financial (although excessive risk-taking actions leading to the current crisis), business (that is law, accounting, consulting, and information provision), and communication sectors have been the main contributors to their successes.

Third, Tokyo could potentially become a common Asian platform to support current and future trends of growing populations and economic sizes in neighbouring Asia. The abundance of funds in Japan and its advantageous location confirm Tokyo's potential role to provide Asian governments and corporations with greater access to diversified and stable financing sources. Asian investors with rising wealth would also benefit from portfolio diversification and innovative financial products and services if Tokyo would be able to meet their needs. The development of better financial infrastructure that would enable smooth cross-border financial and capital transactions could enable Asian funds to circulate within the region and thus enjoy greater regional investment returns — instead of making their funds take detours through the United States and Europe. It is widely known that prior to the recent global crisis, Asian funds were invested largely in financial assets (through U.S. and European financial intermediaries and settlement systems) in the United States and Europe, which in turn re-invest them back into Asia.

Fourth, related to the point raised above, if overseas financing and investment activities by Japanese financial institutions expand again, especially in Asia, they could be positioned as key players to promote the development of regional foreign exchange and financial markets conducting direct exchange rate transactions in yen and other Asian currencies. Japan's domestic financial institutions have finally recovered from the collapse of the bubbles by reducing their holdings of nonperforming loans and improving their financial intermediary capacity domestically and globally. Thus, they are in a position to able to take on this role. Also, encouraging Japanese banks to make yen- or local-currency denominated loans and to issue financial bonds in the region will increase overseas use of the yen as well as promoting regional bond market development — just as development of the international banking market in Europe contributed to the internationalization of the euro. Because Japanese firms are increasing foreign direct investment (FDI) in Asia, the parallel role of Japanese banks is becoming important. If Japanese banks could establish financial networks in the region, overseas Japanese firms, their affiliates, and their partner companies would be able to develop efficient cash management mechanisms involving a networking system to pay just net gains from mutually held credits and liabilities. This would facilitate business activities and reduce operating and financial costs for all involved.

2. JAPANESE VERSION OF THE FINANCIAL BIG BANG AND ITS IMPACT

2.1. Overview of the Financial Big Bang

The then Prime Minister Hashimoto announced in November 1996 a basic policy of reforming Japanese financial and capital markets to become "free, fair, and global" to upgrade Tokyo to a level comparable to those of the London and New York markets by the year 2001. A broad list of measures with specific time schedules was subsequently announced in June 1997.

By the word "free", the Japanese government meant to promote market principles and competition. This included (a) a reduction of the entry limitations in the banking, securities and insurance sectors through allowing the establishment of financial holding companies, (b) a removal of the separation of banking businesses between short- and long-term businesses, (c) a liberalization of fees and commissions in the brokerage and insurance businesses, and (d) a liberalization of asset management regulations. In particular, the one that had caught the attention of the public was the approval of establishing financial holding companies, under which financial institutions would be able to provide comprehensive and diverse financial services for the benefit of investors. The word "fair" referred to a market with greater transparency and equitable rules through a strengthening of disclosure requirements, self-responsibility principles, and enforcement rules. Finally, the word "global" reflected the government's intention to align the accounting systems with global standards, establish better and more cooperative global supervisory capacity, and rationalize taxation in line with global trends. To adapt into the new regulatory framework, moreover, a Financial Supervisory Agency was established by splitting it from the Ministry of Finance in 1998, with the mandate of inspecting and supervising financial institutions and conducting surveillance over securities transactions. The Securities and Exchange Surveillance Commission (SESC) was transferred from the authority of the Ministry of Finance to the Financial Supervisory Agency. In 2000, the Financial Services Agency (FSA) was renamed after the Financial Supervisory Agency by taking over the function of planning the financial system from the Ministry of Finance. The FSA is currently operating as an external organ of the Cabinet Office.

The Financial Big Bang basically had two parts: One related to foreign exchange transactions and the other to cross-entry deregulation and strengthening of competition. The first part of the reforms was undertaken in 1997, while the second part of the reforms was implemented gradually from mid-1997 to 2001.

As for the first part of the Financial Big Bang, the government introduced a new Foreign Exchange Law in 1997 (with effect from April 1998). Prior to the revision, authorized banks had monopolized the foreign exchange market, while being responsible for examining documents (that is, letter of credits, shipping bills) to check the reasons for the entities' engagement in trading foreign exchanges.[2] The new law indicates a shift from a prior-checking system to an ex-post reporting system. Now, foreign exchange business can be performed freely by institutions other than authorized foreign exchange banks. No permission is needed before starting foreign exchange business; the submission of only an ex-post report is needed. Foreign deposit accounts can be opened freely both domestically and abroad with only the requirement of subsequent notification. This revision means that companies (such as exporters, importers, and trading firms) and individuals are able to purchase, sell, lend, and borrow foreign currencies without going through authorized banks.

The second part of the reform did not begin until the middle of 1997. The major changes and reforms are listed below:

Year 1997

- Lifting of a ban on options transactions in specific stocks as well as trade and intermediation of unlisted securities by securities companies.
- Introduction of Cash Management Accounts placed with securities firms.
- Lifting of a ban on a sales of investment trusts through renting floor space in banks.
- Removal of a ban on the issuance of subordinated bonds by commercial banks.
- Permission for issuing perpetual bonds.
- Law permitting the establishment of financial holding companies.

Year 1998

- Liberalization of regulations related to floating-rate term deposits and the depositing period for CDs.
- Deregulation of investment advisory and other asset-management services.
- Introduction of corporate-type and private-placement investment trusts.
- Introduction of link bonds.
- Liberalization of non-life (property) insurance premium rates as well as stock brokerage commissions.
- Deregulation of a series of cross-entry barriers — including the sale of insurance by securities companies, sales of investment trusts by banks themselves, trading of over-the-counter derivatives by banks and securities companies.
- Full liberalization of securities derivatives.
- Shift from a licence system to a registration system regarding securities business.
- Shift from a licence system to an approval system regarding investment trust firms.

Year 1999

- Further liberalization of cross-entry barriers — such as the issue of stocks and secondary trading business by banks securities subsidiaries; and pension trust business by securities companies trust subsidiaries.
- Introduction of wrap accounts placed with securities firms.
- Permission for issuance of straight bonds by commercial banks.
- Introduction of a discount broker system.

Year 2001

- Introduction of ETFs (linked to stock indices).
- Introduction of real estate investment trusts (J-REITs).
- Liberalization of regulation on participation in third-sector fields (sickness/medical insurance) by domestic life and non-life insurance companies.
- Liberalization of non-life (property) insurance premium rates.
- Partial permission for sales of insurance at bank counters (full permission to be implemented by end-2007).[3]
- Permission for banks to hold insurance subsidiaries.

Additionally, the Tokyo Stock Exchange since 1999 has required firms on its Mother's Section (section for venture firms) to release quarterly financial reports and since 2004 all other firms listed on other sections must do so — a tightening of disclosure rules by shifting from the release of biannual reports. Furthermore, in an effort to align the Japanese accounting system with international standards, consolidated accounting and cash flow statements were introduced in 2000. Moreover, the mark-to-market based accounting system was introduced for evaluations of financial assets in 2001 and on cross-holding shares in 2002, thereby making it difficult for firms to hide losses through subsidiaries.[4]

2.2. Impact of the Financial Big Bang (Until Mid-2007)

Since then, the financial and capital markets have seen many changes. First, financial transactions have grown, as investors become more accustomed to the concepts of risk and returns. Japanese private (institutional and households) investors have increased holdings of stocks, and recently foreign assets, with a widening of interest rate differentials. The Financial Big Bang has provided households with a wider range of choices over their asset portfolios, helped by declines in brokerage commissions (particularly for Internet transactions), insurance premiums, and monthly bank fees.

Second, investment asset management businesses have boomed. For example, the asset sizes of investment trusts for individual and institutional investors as well as investment management contacts for institutional investors have been expanding. Real estate investment business has also been growing. In particular, J-REITs, which were introduced in 2001, have become popular. This is because the low interest rates have enabled them to obtain low-cost finance for purchases of real estate, and at the same time, provide investors with higher returns than other assets, such as bonds. Some real estate investment funds, including foreign funds, participate in development projects (such as shopping malls, commercial facilities, and warehouses) from the beginning of projects by bringing in new financing sources procured through lower-cost securitization. Also, some real estate funds or investors have purchased hotels and resort facilities to improve operations and thereby increase profits. Other real estate investment funds have provided professional property management services to the office and commercial facilities they invested in and so have improved operational efficiency. Hedge fund investment has also expanded.

Third, several large city banks have merged with each other to form three financial holding groups (Mizuho Financial Group, Mitsubishi UFJ Financial Group, and Sumitomo Mitsui Financial Group) to provide full financial services. As the largest financial group, Dai-Ichi Kangyo Bank, Fuji Bank and Industrial Bank of Japan agreed to establish a bank holding company in 1999 and so established Mizuho Holdings in 2000. In 2002, it reorganized their banks into the Mizuho Bank (targeting individual customers and domestic firms) and Mizuho Corporate Bank (focusing on large firms and investment banking). Also, Yasuda Trust Bank joined the group as Mizuho Trust Bank; and, three middle-sized securities firms were consolidated into Mizuho Security. In 2003, the Mizuho Financial Group took over the operations of Mizuho Holdings. As the second largest financial group, the Bank of Tokyo and Mitsubishi Bank merged into the Bank of Tokyo-Mitsubishi in 1997; and subsequently, in 2001 the Bank of Tokyo-Mitsubishi, Mitsubishi Trust & Banking and Nippon Trust Bank established a bank holding company called the Mitsubishi Tokyo Financial Group. In 2002, Mitsubishi Trust & Banking merged with Nippon Trust Bank. In 2003, the Mitsubishi Tokyo Financial Group acquired Kokusai Securities and renamed it as Mitsubishi Securities. In 2005, the Mitsubishi UFJ Financial Group was formed by merging the Mitsubishi Tokyo Financial Group and UFJ Holdings.[5] Accordingly, the Bank of Tokyo-Mitsubishi and UFJ Bank merged as the Bank of Tokyo-Mitsubishi UFJ Bank. The Mitsubishi Trust & Banking and UFJ Trust Bank merged as Mitsubishi UFJ Trust & Banking. Mitsubishi Securities and UFJ Tsubasa Securities merged as Mitsubishi UFJ Securities. As the third largest financial group, Sakura Bank and Sumitomo Bank were merged to establish the

Sumitomo Mitsui Banking Corporation (SMBC) in 2001 and then established the Sumitomo Mitsui Financial Group (SMFG) in 2002. In 2003, Sumitomo Mitsui Card Company, SMBC Leasing Company, and The Japan Research Institute became wholly-owned subsidiaries of SMFG. In 2005, SMBC reached agreement with NTT DoCoMo on its credit card business. In 2006, SMBC Friend Securities became a whole-owned subsidiary of SMBC.

As well as these three mega-groups, Resona Holdings was established by three middle-sized city banks as a regional oriented group. It was originally established in 2001 as Daiwa Bank Holdings through consolidating the Daiwa, Kinki Osaka, and Nara Banks. The company was renamed as Resona Holdings after acquiring Asahi Bank in 2002. In 2003, the government injected public funds (about JP¥2 trillion) to this group because the bank's position was effectively insolvent. As a result of the government becoming the largest shareholder, this support effectively realized the nationalization of the bank, and the existing management was sacked. In 2004, the bank's new management achieved a profit and announced a business revitalization plan aimed at ultimate repayments of public funds received through achieving sustainable growth with a differentiated strategy. Based on the results, in 2006, it announced a new revitalization plan for the period through the end of March 2000.

Moreover, new types of banks that provide specialized financial services have emerged. The first was Japan Net Bank established in 2000 (an Internet bank established the former Sakura Bank in 1998 as a subsidiary, and now held by the SMBC and Yahoo Japan Corp. as major shareholders). In 2001, the following new banks emerged: IY Bank (established by the Ito Yokado Group focusing in real trade business) specializing in payment and settlement services for individual customers, Sony Bank (established by Sony Corp. in cooperation with SMBC and JP Morgan) providing services through the Internet to individual customers), and eBANK (established by trading firms, insurance firms, and information service firms) specializing in small-amount payments using the Internet and portable phones). In response to the emergence of these new types of banks, the Financial Reconstruction Commission and the FSA released a guideline on the measures for licensing and supervising new types of banks in 2000.

Fourth, banks have become "universal" in a sense that they have begun to deal with securities and sell insurance through teller windows. In particular, major banks have increased the ratio of net non-interest income to operating profits, offsetting a decline in net interest income. Main sources of net non-interest income come from fees and commissions associated with new financial services, such as sales of investment trusts, insurance and underwriting private placement bonds. As well, fee incomes have risen from formations of syndicated loans and the liquidation of assets. Recently, banks have gained profits by providing derivative instruments to small- and medium-sized firms in response to their growing need for hedging financial risks. Brokerage firms have also begun to offer financing and investment services.

Fifth, foreign investors have increased investment in Japanese financial assets, particularly the stock market. Foreigners have been net purchasers of Japanese equities since 2003. As a result of domestic banks' reduction in holdings of stocks under the "main bank system", foreign participation in the stock exchanges has jumped sharply, accounting for nearly 30 per cent of market capitalization in 2006. This participation ratio is greater than the United Sates (13 per cent) and is equivalent with the United Kingdom (33 per cent). While European and U.S. investors are major foreign investors, Asian investors have recently increased their presence. Also, some foreign banks and securities firms have enlarged their operations in Tokyo as their profit and business size has expanded. Also, the number of buy-out funds and resultant M&As has been growing, as exemplified by the case of the Long-term Credit Bank of Japan (nationalized in 1998, taken over by the U.S. buy-out group Ripplewood in 2000, reborn as Shinsei Bank in the same year). The move that a domestic bank became under foreign control was the first time in the Japanese history.

Sixth, the revision of the Foreign Exchange Law has encouraged trading firms to establish financial subsidiaries in Tokyo. As large trading firms have already financial subsidiaries in London and New York, this has enabled them to conduct financial trading twenty-four hours a day. In addition, the transaction costs of foreign exchanges, particularly those involving yen/U.S. dollar, have declined, as evidenced by a decline in the bid-ask spread. The difference between spreads quoted by Japanese and non-Japanese quoters has narrowed as well (Ito and Melvin 1999).

2.3. Macroeconomic Perspectives on the Financial and Capital Markets since the Financial Big Bang

Since 1996, a little more than ten years has passed. Contrary to the initial expectation, nevertheless, it can be said that the vision of promoting

Tokyo to become one of the world's top international financial centres has not materialized yet, as described in the details in Section III. The attractiveness of Japan's financial and capital markets has remained small in proportion to its economic size. From a macroeconomic perspective, this reflects at least the following four factors:

First, the Bank of Japan (BOJ) has not yet been able to fully normalize its monetary policy. In March 2006, the BOJ abandoned its so-called "quantitative easing" monetary policy that had been instituted for the five years following March 2001. This meant a shift of the monetary policy target — from the outstanding current account — balance held at the BOJ back to the conventional uncollateralized overnight call rate. The restoration of the original target of uncollateralized overnight call rate indicated the explicit use of a short-term interest rate, which had been in effect "zero" since March 2001 under the quantitative easing monetary policy. In July 2006, subsequently, the BOJ terminated its "zero interest" policy by raising the target uncollateralized overnight call rate from virtually 0 per cent to 0.25 per cent and the basic loan rate from 0.1 per cent to 0.4 per cent. In February 2007, furthermore, the BOJ raised the target uncollateralized overnight call rate from 0.25 per cent to 0.5 per cent and the basic loan rate from 0.4 per cent to 0.75 per cent.

However, the BOJ had not since been able to raise its target short-term interest rate, contrary to its wishes. This is a clear contrast to the rest of the world, where the majority of central banks raised their target interest rates from 2004–05 to mid-2007. The growing interest rate differentials have promoted the so-called "yen carry trade" (borrowing in yen at low interest rates to invest in higher-yielding non-yen instruments) and the undervaluation of the yen. In such circumstances, Japan's financial and capital markets functioned simply as a provider of short-term finance for the yen carry trade, not as a place to manage and invest yen-denominated financial assets for overseas funds. A series of factors — such as (a) the inactive use of the yen as an investing currency, (b) a withdrawal of Japanese banks and institutional investors from cross-border operations together with a decline in their credibility and reputation during the Lost Decade, as well as (c) a decline in the Japanese government's creditworthiness (due to its growing public debt and fiscal deficits) — all contributed to this phenomena. In other words, Japan has been unable to exploit rapidly growing global financial activities and obtain more income arising from the provision of diverse financial services to the world. It is ironic that the Japanese public appears not to be bothered with this fact, notwithstanding Japan's economic size and position as the largest external creditor country.

Second, low interest rates, while easing firms' access to funding, have led to a narrowing of the spread on corporate bonds. Interest rates have been low in real and nominal terms on the one hand, and in short and long terms on the other. This makes it hard for investors to obtain returns that could be justified on the basis of their investment risks. This indicates that the persistence of exceptionally low levels of interest rates has weakened the capacity of the bond market to distinguish issuing firms by the degree of their creditworthiness and so to properly price them. In addition, there are growing concerns that the prolonged low levels of interest rates might be promoting unproductive and excessive investment activities, thereby lowering capital productivity growth and slowing down the necessary structural reforms needed for firms to become viable. As a result, Japan's corporate bond market has remained small, accounting for only 7 per cent of the global bond market (although this partly reflects that non-financial firms use accumulated retained earnings for financing their investment).

Third, households as well as institutional investors (pension funds, insurance firms, and investment trusts) continue to prioritize the guarantee of principal over high returns — thus preferring bonds to stocks. Their low risk appetite also contributes to the underdevelopment of the wholesale market, where diverse professional market players compete with each other to create new and innovative financial products and services to institutional investors. The markets for securitization and derivatives have been growing but not as rapidly and remarkably as those of other global financial centres.

Fourth, Japan's financial and capital markets have not yet been internationalized. Indeed, they reversed course towards internationalization and now have become more or less "local" because of their limited cross-border activities. There are less than 100 foreign banks (over 200 foreign banks in New York and London). There are still less than thirty overseas firms listed on the Tokyo Stock Exchange. A number of overseas hedge funds and other investment funds with strong interest in Japan as an investing market continue to place their operating strongholds in Hong Kong or Singapore that have offered them preferential tax treatments and low-cost infrastructure as well as limited regulations on financial businesses. Foreign workers engaging in financial services in Tokyo account for less than 5 per cent, and there are shortages in the financially skilled labour market, including those with a good command of English. By contrast, the Hong Kong and Singapore financial and capital markets have increased their presence as regional international financial centres in Asia, notwithstanding their small economic sizes. In September 2008, the City of London released the Global Financial Center Index and rated Singapore and Hong Kong consecutively as the third and fourth international financial centres, following London (first) and New York (second). Tokyo was rated only seventh, something of a shock to the Japanese government and its political leaders.

3. PERFORMANCE OF JAPAN'S FINANCIAL AND CAPITAL MARKETS (UNTIL MID-2007)

3.1. Trends of the Stock Market

Size of Market Capitalization

In the 1980s, the stock market capitalization of the Tokyo Stock Exchange was the largest in the world. Its market capitalization accounted for more than 30 per cent of the world market capitalization. It dropped from 33 per cent in 1990 to 10 per cent in 2005 (see Figure 4.1). The size of the market capitalization of the Tokyo Stock Exchange was the second largest after the New York Stock Exchange as of end-2006. Nonetheless, the gap between the New York Stock Exchange and the Tokyo Stock Exchange has widened over the period, as evidenced by the increase in the market capitalization ratio of the former to the latter from 0.9 times in 1990 to 3 times in 2005. This suggests the rapid growth of the former relative to the latter. The stock market capitalization of the Tokyo Stock Exchange expanded only 1.6 times between 1990 and 2005 — lagging behind the growth of the New York Stock Exchange (5 times). The sluggish growth of the Tokyo Stock Exchange is also pronounced compared to other stock exchanges, including the Nasdaq (11.6 times), London Stock Exchange (3.6 times), Hong Kong Stock Exchange (12.7 times), and Singapore Stock Exchange (7.5 times).

Liquidity of the Market

Relative to the size of its market capitalization, the liquidity of the market has been low. In 2006 the total value of share trading on the

Figure 4.1
Share of Market Capitalization of the Top Three Stock Exchanges
(Percentage of World Total, 1990–95)

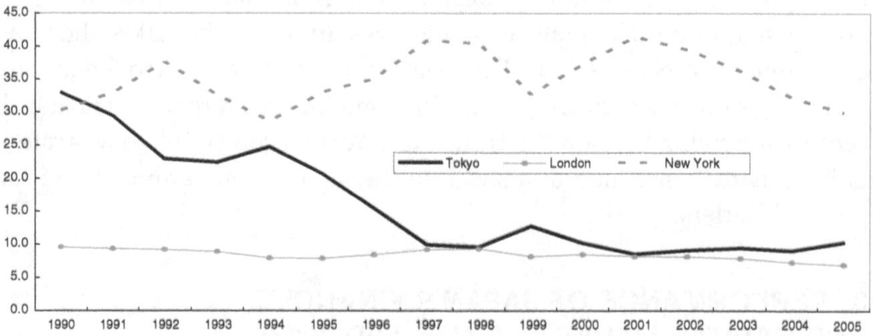

Source: Prepared based on data compiled by the World Federation of Exchanges.

Tokyo Stock Exchange was the fourth largest in the world, following the New York Stock Exchange, Nasdaq and London Stock Exchange (see Figure 4.2). In particular, the expansion of trading in the two stock exchanges in the United Sates is remarkable notwithstanding the severe damage caused by the information technology (IT) bubbles in the early 2000s. The growth rates of share trading value in Tokyo between 1991 and 2006 have been highly volatile and remained more or less sluggish until 2002 (see Figure 4.3). The growth rate for 2006 was 33 per cent, but still ranked only thirty-second in the world.

Growing Presence of Foreign Investors and the Low Risk Appetite of Domestic Investors

What is remarkable is that foreign (non-resident) investors have increasingly played an important role in activating transactions in Japan. Between 2000 and 2006, the monthly average volume of shares traded in the Tokyo Stock Exchange increased 2.6 times for domestic investors, but that of foreign investors expanded even further by a scale of 3.85 times. Over the same period, the monthly average turnover value (valued in yen) grew 3.4 times for foreign investors, while that for domestic investors expanded 2.4 times (IMF 2007).

Figure 4.2
Total Value of Share Trading on Major Stock Exchanges
(US$ billion, 1990–2006)

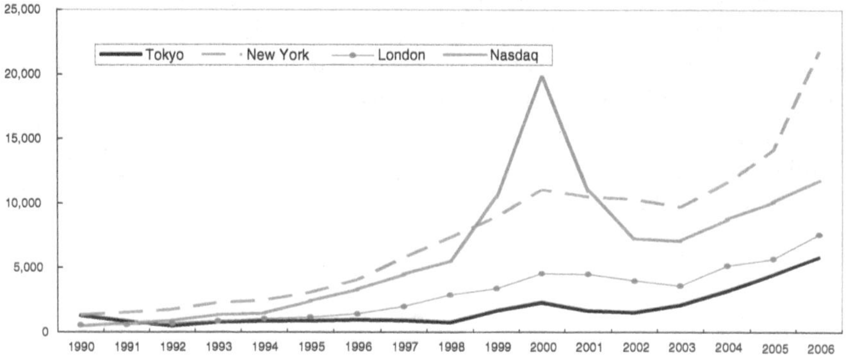

Source: Prepared based on data compiled by the World Federation of Exchanges.

Figure 4.3
Growth Rates of Share Trading Value on Major Stock Exchanges
(Percentage, 2001–06)

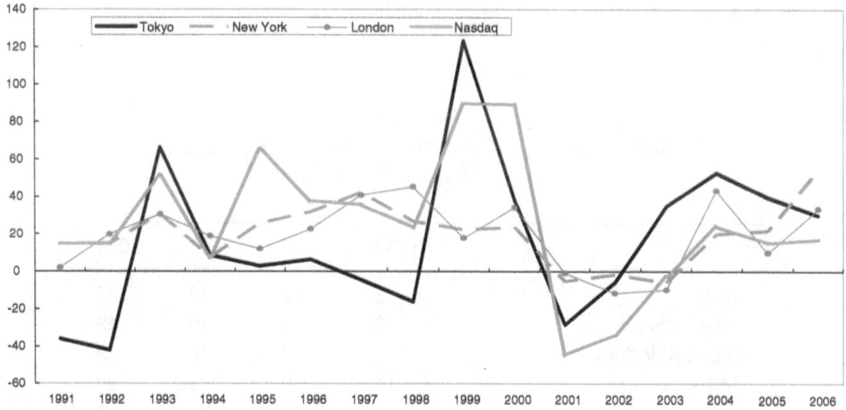

Source: Prepared based on data compiled by the World Federation of Exchanges.

Japanese assets held by foreign investors increased from JP¥204 trillion (US$1.9 trillion) in 1996 to JP¥343 trillion (US$3 trillion) in 2006. Over this period, the ratio of stocks to total Japanese assets held by foreign investors increased from 18 per cent to 44 per cent (see Table 4.1). Foreign investors increased their investment mainly in publicly traded stocks. As a result, foreign investors accounted for 27 per cent of market capitalization in 2005 (see Table 4.2). Meanwhile, foreign investors' investments in private bonds and other structured instruments still represent less than 5 per cent of foreign investments in Japan, reflecting the generally small size of these financial markets (IMF 2007).

Table 4.1
Japanese Assets Held by Non-Residents
(1996 and 2006)

	1996 (JP¥ trillion)	2006 (JP¥ trillion)	1996 (% of total)	2006 (% of total)
Stocks	37	149	18	44
Bonds	28	60	14	18
FDI	3	13	2	4
Loans and Other Investment	136	117	67	34
Total	204	343		

Source: Prepared based on the data compiled by the Ministry of Finance.

Table 4.2
Ratio of Foreign Investors to Market Capitalization
(Percentage, 1991–2005)

	1991	1996	2001	2005
Japan	6	12	18	27
United States	6	7	10	13
United Kingdom	13	24	32	33
Germany	11	9	14	20
Korea	—	13	37	40

Source: Prepared based on the data submitted to the Financial System Council, FSA.

By contrast, households' holdings of stocks have accounted for less than 20 per cent of their financial assets throughout the period, notwithstanding their increased holdings (see Figure 4.4). In 2006, households' holdings of stocks accounted for 12 per cent of their total financial assets — much lower than those of the United States of 31 per cent (see Figure 4.5). Japanese households continue to hold over half of their financial assets in the form of deposits and cash even after the Financial Big Bang had been implemented. This phenomenon appears puzzling, since their behaviour has not changed much despite the nearly zero interest rates in place since the second half of the 1990s. This feature is also unique from the standpoint of global experiences, as households' holdings of deposits and cash account for only 13 per cent in the United States, 25 per cent in the United Kingdom, 31 per cent in France, and 36 per cent in Germany. Thus, it is clear that households have not been the major contributors to the recent increase in the market capitalization as well as to the issuance of stocks by non-financial firms.

Moreover, major domestic institutional investors have been reluctant to invest in stocks (as well as foreign securities) as compared with bonds. There is a strong preference toward bond investment, as seen in Table 4.3.

Figure 4.4
Composition of Japanese Household's Financial Assets
(Percentage of Total, 1990–2006)

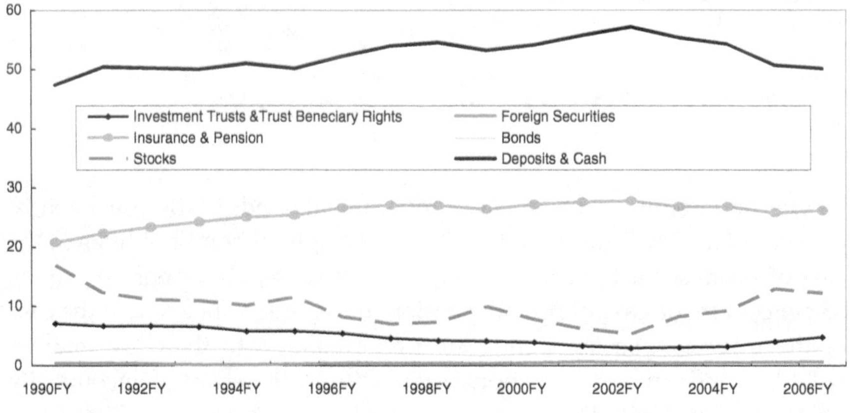

Source: Prepared based on the flow of funds accounts compiled by the BOJ.

Figure 4.5
Composition of Households' Financial Assets in Japan and the United States
(Percentage of Total, 2006)

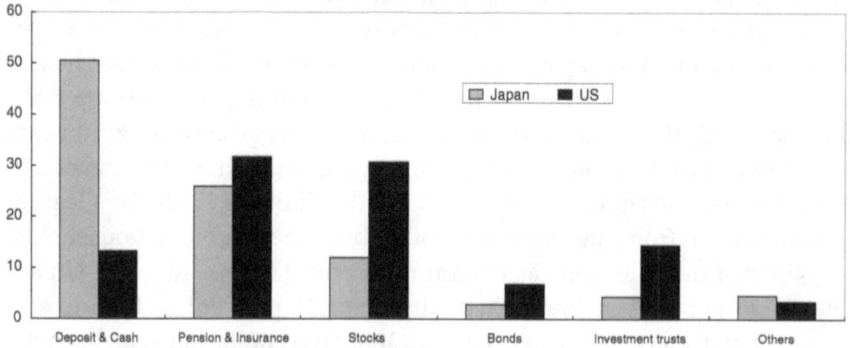

Source: Prepared based on the flow of funds accounts of the BOJ and Federal Reserve Board.

Table 4.3
Asset Composition of Major Institutional Investors in Japan
(Percentage of Total, March 2007)

	Deposits & Cash	Stocks & Investment	Bonds & Others	Foreign Securities
Social Securities Funds	3	14	43	15
Pension Funds	6	31	33	25
Insurance	1	12	54	11

Source: Prepared based on the flow of funds account compiled by the BOJ.

Of the bond holdings, the Japanese government bonds (JGBs) are the most popular bonds. JGBs account for 72 per cent of total bond holdings in the case of social security funds (largely consisting of public pension funds), 67 per cent in the case of private pension funds, and 57 per cent in the case of the insurance sector. Bonds are preferred due to their low market volatility and are seen as more secure assets in terms of income. By contrast, in the United States, pension funds as a whole invest 49 per cent of their assets in stocks and investments (including foreign stocks) and only 14 per cent in bonds. Institutional investors there, such as insurance firms, pension funds, and college funds, have been globally actively investing in stocks and other risky assets.

The conservative investment attitude seen in Japan is affected partly by regulations on investment portfolios. For example, the Government Pension Investment Fund (GPIF) — which was established in April 2006 as an independent administrative institution with the mission of managing and investing the Public Pension Reserve Funds by taking over the old Government Pension Investment Funds — possesses investment assets of US$789 billion at end-2007. But the GPIF has only been required to achieve the following portfolio by the end of March 2009 (11 per cent in domestic stocks, 8 per cent in foreign ones, and 9 per cent in foreign stocks), while allocating 67 per cent to domestic bonds.[6] By contrast, public pension funds in other countries tend to allocate more funds to domestic and foreign shares, as in the case of Canada (25 per cent for domestic stocks and 39 per cent for foreign stocks) and Sweden (16 per cent for domestic stocks and 42 per cent for foreign stocks). In the United States, the two best-known public-defined benefit pension funds in the United States, CalPERS (the California Public Employees' Retirement System and the California State Teachers' Retirement System, invest more than 40 per cent in domestic stocks and more than 20 per cent in foreign stocks.[7] There are a number of diverse professional investment management firms (or asset management firms) in this country that these institutional investors could call on for advice.

It should also be noted that other Japanese investors are also conservative. For example, while investment trusts allocated 44 per cent of their assets to foreign securities, they largely consist of bonds, not stocks.[8] Also, their holdings of domestic stocks and investments account for only 26 per cent and domestic bonds for 12 per cent. U.S. investments trusts, on the other, hand, allocate more than 50 per cent of their assets to stocks and investments, while only 36 per cent to bonds. Thus, it is certain that Japanese domestic investors on the whole have been very conservative.

It has also been pointed out that domestic investors' unwillingness to hold a large amount of stocks reflects the sluggish returns experienced from the 1990s to early 2000s, which have been lower than those from bond investments. The average return on domestic bonds achieved 6.3 per cent in the 1990s, while that on stocks was –4.2 per cent (Pension Fund Association, 2007). It is also attributable to the policy of Japanese firms to pay smaller amounts of dividends from their profits as compared to firms in the United States and Europe. A series of corporate scandals and false accounting practices added to the low risk appetite of households. It is likely to take a while for households to feel more comfortable with the idea that in the long run stocks' returns are on overage higher than other financial assets (such as bonds, deposits) and thus investors would be better off taking greater risks in their investments.

Inactive Listings by Foreign Firms

The Tokyo Stock Exchange permitted the listing of foreign stocks in 1973 in line with the process of capital account liberalization launched by the government. It has targeted mainly blue-chip firms in the United States and Europe. Transactions have been performed in yen and financial reports are required to be released in Japanese. Many foreign firms decided to list their stocks in the Tokyo Stock Exchange for the purpose of raising their reputation in Japan because its market capitalization was then the largest in the world, as well as expanding business in then booming Japan. Double listings — listings on both the stock exchange of their home countries and the Tokyo Stock Exchange — have been commonplace.

The number of listings grew rapidly in the 1980s, reaching the peak of 127 firms in 1991. Since then, the number has dropped to a mere 25 firms by 2006, ranking it only the twentieth in the world (see Figure 4.6). Among those listed foreign firms, there are only three firms from Asia — far below the New York Stock Exchanges (72 Asian firms out of 451 foreign firms) and London Stock Exchange (39 Asian firms out of 343 foreign firms).

Compared with the share of foreign investors in market capitalization, the share of foreign firms in the issuer base represents a large gap and supports the view that the Tokyo market has not really been internationalized. The decline took place in part because some foreign firms — such as Apple Computer, Daimler Chrysler, and Deutsche Bank — delisted their shares in the face of economic stagnation and declining market size in Japan. It was also because some foreign firms increased recourse to public offering without listing (POWL) or obtaining funds from Japanese institutional investors without publicly listing — for the purpose of avoiding stringent disclosure requirements imposed — by the Tokyo Stock Exchange and so enjoying lower issuing costs. Unlike publicly listed stocks, the transactions for these issues are made in local currencies,

Figure 4.6
Number of Foreign Firms Listed in Major Stock Exchanges, 2006

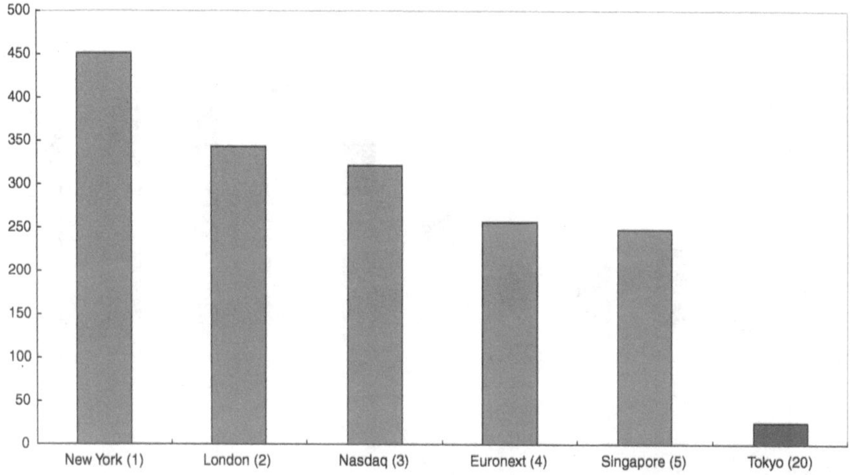

Source: Prepared based on data compiled by the World Federation of Exchanges.

not in yen. Since 2003, the number of POWLs reached 36 (16 from China) and procured JP¥762 billion (US$6.6 billion), according to the information provided by the Tokyo Stock Exchange (2007).

Furthermore, the number of newly listed foreign firms was just 1 firm each in 2005 and 2006 (while the number of newly listed domestic firms was 98 and 113, respectively). By contrast, the number of newly listed foreign firms was 19 in 2005 and 28 in 2006 in the New York Stock Exchange (while the number of newly listed domestic firms was 127 and 100, respectively). The performance of the London Stock Exchange is even more remarkable, as evidenced by the number of newly listed foreign firms, recording 21 in 2005 and 32 in 2006 (while the number of newly listed domestic firms registered 605 and 544, respectively).

3.2. Trends of the Bond Market

Japan's bond market has been dominated by the JGBs, as shown in Figure 4.7. Because of the deterioration of the fiscal balance since the collapse of the financial bubbles, the outstanding value of government

Figure 4.7
Size of Outstanding Bond Issued
(US$ billion, 1998–2007)

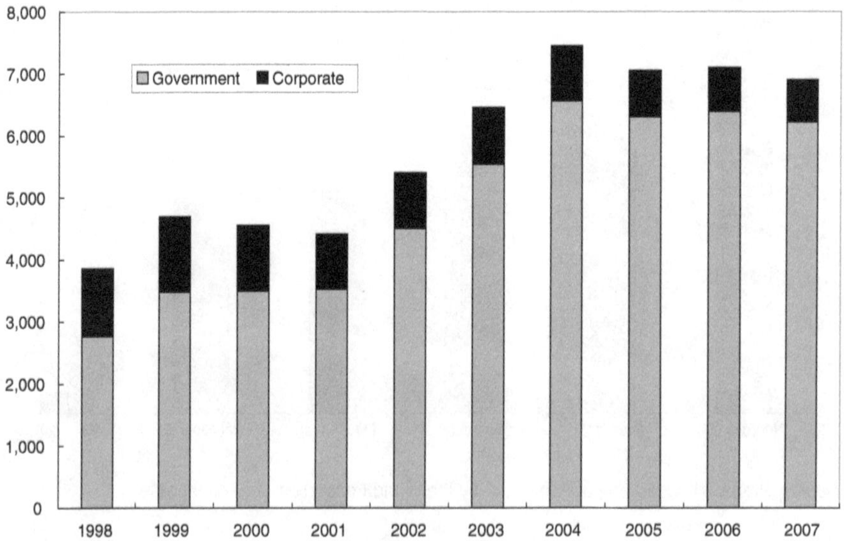

Note: The data for 2007 refers to the figure as of June.
Source: Prepared based on data from Asian Bonds Online.

bonds issued increased from US$2.8 trillion in 1998 to US$6.2 trillion in 2007. Accordingly, the ratio of government bonds to total outstanding bonds issued rose from 70 per cent in 1998 to 90 per cent in 2007. Japan's total outstanding public debt (including bonds) is the largest in the world. Despites its huge debt, the government has so far found it relatively easy to find investors — mainly from domestic sources thanks to the conservative investment attitude of domestic investors.

Figure 4.8 indicates that the public and public-related sector (including the Central Government, the Bank of Japan, Public Pensions, Postal Savings, and Postal Life Insurance) held 54 per cent of the outstanding JGBs issued as of September 2006 (Figure 4.8). Households held only 4.5 per cent. It may be said that households indirectly support the Government through making deposits and purchasing insurance, which in turn invest in the JGBs. Meanwhile, foreign investors held only 5 per cent. This investor composition differs from the United States, where the federal government depends on foreign investors for 44 per cent of its marketable treasury

Figure 4.8
Composition of Outstanding Issuance of JGBs by Investors, June 2006

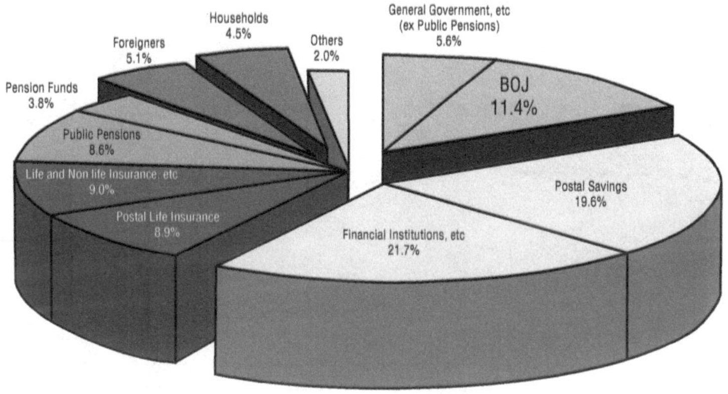

Source: Ministry of Finance <http://www.mof.go.jp/english/bonds/ir/ir070308b.pdf>.

securities. The share of government bonds held by foreign investors is also high in other countries; France (29 per cent), Germany (47 per cent), and United Kingdom (27 per cent) (IMF 2007).

By contrast, the corporate bond market has hardly developed. This is mainly because recently firms tend to raise funds by issuing stocks, as well as the traditional way of borrowing from banks (Figure 4.9). The financing position of the corporate sector has shifted from a net deficit to a net surplus since the late 1990s, reflecting the efforts to reduce leverage and the low demand for credit. The presence of too many banks and intense competition, together with low interest rates, has eased firms' borrowing costs from banks and thus reduced the need to issue corporate bonds.

The outstanding corporate bonds issued is recorded as US$682 billions in June 2007 — far below the size in the United States where US$3.2 trillion was issued as of December 2006. The majority of issuers have been firms with investment grade (90 per cent of total bonds). Namely, the market for bonds with below-investment grade, commonplace in the United States (accounting for more than 50 per cent of total bonds), has hardly emerged. The Government Pension Investment Fund (GPIF) requires that the credit

Figure 4.9
Major Sources of Liabilities by Non-Financial Firms
(JP¥ trillion, 1990–2006)

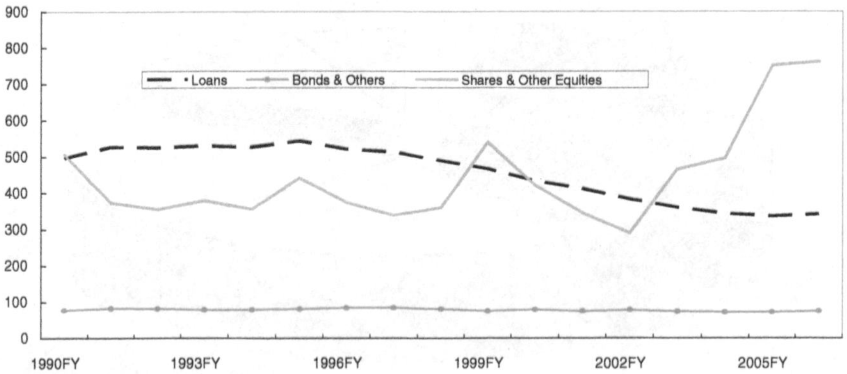

Source: Prepared based on the flow of fund accounts compiled by the BOJ.

ratings of the bond issuers they invest in should be equal or above BBB. Such a management policy has adversely affected the behaviour of private institutional investors as well. This has contributed to the lack of diversity in the corporate bond market and also hindered skill development in the market regarding the evaluation of risks and returns. These factors partly explain why corporate bond market liquidity has been low (for example as compared with the JGBs). The low liquidity makes it difficult for investors to transact bonds without affecting prices. It has also been pointed out that low interest rates have narrowed the spreads on corporate bonds, which makes it difficult for investors to acquire returns that could be justified by the risks they are undertaking.

3.3. Trends for ETFs and Securitized Markets

The types of financial assets listed on the Tokyo Stock Exchange are limited. As of end-2006, there were only eleven listed ETFs on the Tokyo Stock Exchange; all of which were related to stock indices. This number is smaller than the New York Stock Exchange (135) and London (39). It is even lower than the Korea Stock Exchange (12) and the Singapore Stock

Exchange (13). Since ETFs are securities that track an index, a commodity, or a basket of assets and trade like a stock on the stock exchange, a wide range of ETFs can be created. Indeed, there are a large number of ETFs that have been listed on overseas stock exchanges, but not on the Tokyo Stock Exchange. These include a wide range of commodity indices (for example, agriculture, gold, sliver, petroleum, and grains), REIT indexes, and funds.

The markets for securitized bonds, such as mortgage-backed or asset-backed securities, and collateralized debt obligations (CDOs) have been growing (see Table 4.4). In particular, mortgage-backed securities have been rapidly expanding. However, the size of the mortgage-related securities were just US$77 billion (of which, J-REITs accounted for 25 per cent), which is much smaller than that in the United States of US$5.8 trillion in 2006. The size of the securitized bond market as a whole also accounts for just 3 per cent of GDP. Also, liquidity in the secondary market is low. It has been indicated that the lack of information for third parties about the products available makes it difficult to properly analyse risks.

Markets for ETFs and securitized bonds could be expanded if the requirements imposed on public pension funds for portfolio management were loosened. Tight portfolio regulation has resulted in an unimpressive

Table 4.4
Outstanding Securitized Securities Issued in Japan
(US$ billion, 1995–2006)

	Mortgage Backed	Asset Backed	CDO	Total
1995	0	0	0	0
1996	0	0	0	0
1997	1	0	0	1
1998	5	0	0	5
1999	8	0	0	8
2000	9	0	0	10
2001	17	2	0	19
2002	26	5	1	32
2003	34	22	3	48
2004	43	13	8	64
2005	55	25	17	97
2006	77	36	27	139

Source: Prepared based on Asian Bonds Online.

return performance and has thus affect the sustainability of the public pension system. Public pension funds in the United States and Europe actively invest in various securities by utilizing asset management funds, hedge funds, private equity funds, and other types of funds. Tight regulation in Japan hinders the development of investment trusts and various other funds as well as the increase in human resources with professional skills.

Moreover, the market for credit derivatives (that is, credit default swaps) has been growing worldwide. The notional principal outstanding for all credit derivatives reached over US$20 trillion worldwide at end-2005. Credit default swaps provide a useful tool of hedging credit exposure for banks (thus reducing credit concentration and freeing up credit lines), and at the same time, providing useful credit pricing information. This emergence has created an environment where banks lend and sell through securitization — a change from the past when banks traditionally lend and hold credit until maturity. So far, Japan's market for credit derivatives has been inactive because of (a) a lack of market volatility and liquidity in the corporate bond/loans secondary markets, (b) a too tight credit spread (thus no incentive to hedge with credit derivatives), and (c) regulatory factors such as an accounting mismatch (between accrual-based accounting for loans and market-based accounting for derivatives hedging instruments) and regulation to limit big loans to a borrower (International Swaps and Derivatives Association (ISDA), 2007). There are also a limited number of brands associated with credit derivatives.

3.4. Cross-Border Market Developments and Internationalization of the Yen

Capital Inflows and Outflows

Japanese investors have increasingly been paying attention to the possibility of overseas investments being lucrative. Their holdings of foreign assets have almost doubled from 2000 to about US$5 trillion in 2006. However, foreign assets have concentrated largely in debt securities rather than stocks — a sharp contrast to the fact that Japanese assets held by foreign investors concentrate largely on stocks (Figure 4.10). Loans and bonds account for 40 per cent of total foreign assets held by Japanese investors in 2006, because of investors' risk-averse attitudes (Table 4.5).

Figure 4.10
Composition of Japan's Foreign Assets and Liabilities
(Percentage of Total, 2006)

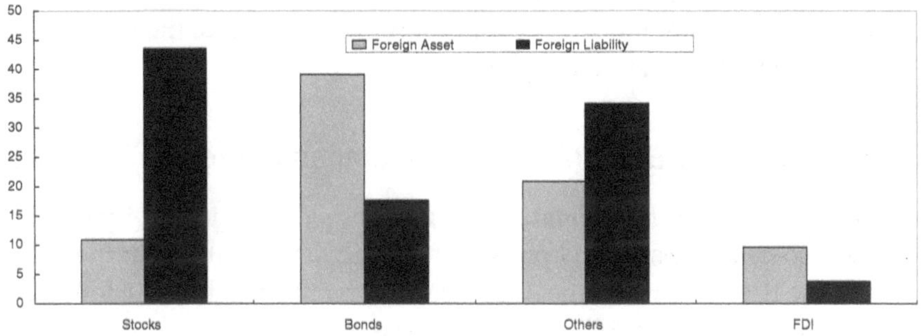

Source: Prepared based on data compiled by the Ministry of Finance.

Table 4.5
Foreign Assets Held by Japanese
(1996 and 2006)

	1996 (JP¥ trillion)	2006 (JP¥ trillion)	1996 (% of total)	2006 (% of total)
Stocks	18	61	8	19
Bonds	91	218	6	11
FDI	30	53	10	10
Loans and Other Investment	144	117	47	21
Foreign Reserves	25	106	8	19
Total	308	558		

Source: Prepared based on data compiled by the Ministry of Finance.

Among holders of foreign assets (excluding FDI, trade credits and official foreign reserves), banks have remained major investors and account for 53 per cent of foreign investment in securities and credits. But their investments mostly reflect lending operations, owing to easier provisioning regulations abroad and an extension of "relationship banking" to the foreign subsidiaries of domestic clients (IMF 2007). Pension and life insurance companies as a group are the next largest investors (14 per cent) but their investments are constraint by the internal exposure limit as indicated above. Households increasingly invest in foreign assets, but do so mostly through mutual funds. The expansion of investment trusts, though to a lesser extent compared with the United States, is assisted by the deregulation of sales of mutual fund products at bank branches in 1998 and subsequently at the branches of the Japan Post in 2005. Indeed, sales through bank windows account for more than half of the total assets under investment trust management.

Yen-denominated Bond Markets (Samurai and Euro-yen Markets)

The market for yen-denominated foreign bonds (bonds issued by foreign entities, so-called "Samurai bonds") in Japan was liberalized in the early 1970s. The first issuer was the Asian Development Bank in 1970, followed by the World Bank in 1971. The major issuers of Samurai bonds have shifted from foreign governments (such as those of Greece, Turkey, and Hungary in the first half of the 1990s) to the private sector from the United States and Europe (recently also increasing from Asia). Foreign securities firms that have operational activities in Japan (such as Goldman Sachs and Merrill Lynch) have increased the issue of Samurai bonds. This trend is evident notwithstanding that there was a large-scale issue by the governments of Argentina and Brazil in 2000. Major investors of Samurai bonds are domestic investors.

Furthermore, the euro-yen market emerged in 1979 to circumvent stringent issuing procedures and disclosure requirements, as well as withholding taxes imposed on interest income. The first issuer was the European Investment Bank. The euro-yen issue by nonresident entities other than foreign governments and international organizations (that is, foreign firms) — as well as by resident (domestic) firms — was liberalized in 1986. The gap between the markets for Samurai bonds and the euro-yen bonds has rapidly widened since the second half of the 1980s. This reflected greater liberalization of issuing terms in the euro market and no withholding tax imposed on interest income of euro-yen bonds (see Figure 4.11). Since then, issuing terms in Tokyo have also been liberalized (for example, by easing the eligibility criteria of issuers' rating from equal or over A to equal and over BBB in 1994) have become almost comparable to those of the euro-yen market. But, the cost related to issuing bonds (such as lawyers' fees required to prepare contractual documents, the requirement of preparing documents in Japanese and its English translation), has remained high, hampering the increased diversification of foreign issuers (Iijima 2005). The euro-yen bond market

Figure 4.11
Yen-denominated Foreign Bond and Euro-Yen Bond Markets
(JP¥100 million, 1970–2003)

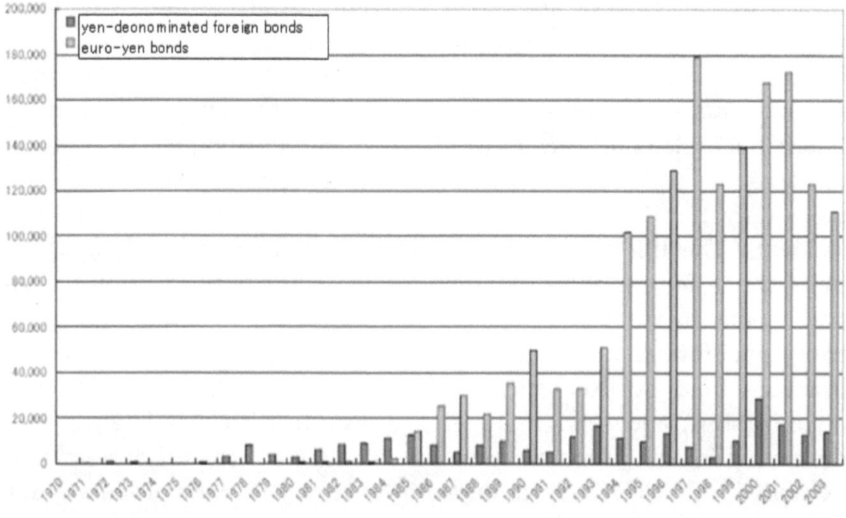

Source: Iijima, T., 2005.

has also declined in recent years, after experiencing a surge in 2000 (that is, by the issue of international organizations). Major investors of euro-yen bonds are also Japanese investors.

Moreover, the share of both Samurai-bonds and euro-yen bonds outstanding has declined from 17–18 per cent in 1994–95 to less than 1 per cent in 2005. This reflected that issuing volume of yen-denominated bonds has declined while the issuing volume of other currencies-denominated bonds has rapidly grown. The emergence of the large euro market in 1999 has made it easier for European governments to raise funds within Europe, thereby reducing the need to seek recourse to other markets, including the yen market. Also, the lack of investment demand for yen-denominated bonds by foreign investors (due to low interest rates) has helped lower the issue of yen-denominated bonds by foreign entities both in the Japanese and euro markets.

Tokyo Offshore Market

In 1986, the Tokyo offshore market was introduced as a platform for out-out financial transactions. In the offshore market, disclosure requirements related to the issuance and resale of securities are usually exempted; regulation on foreign exchange management is limited; tax exemption on interest and dividend incomes is provided; and statutory reverse requirements are exempted. The Tokyo offshore market refers to an International Banking Facility (IBF), where participating banks establish IBF accounts separately from the accounts for general markets and use them only for IBF-related transactions with both non-residents and residents. The IBF-type approach differs from that in London, where transactions for residents and non-residents are fully integrated. The participants in the Tokyo offshore market consist mainly of domestic banks and financial institutions approved by the government, foreign branches held by domestic banks, sovereign entities, international organizations, and foreign firms. The activities such as lending and depositing in any currencies have been conducted. The offshore market expanded in the 1990s. Since then, however, the market particularly for the yen has shrunk rapidly (see Figure 4.12).

Traditional Foreign Exchange and OTC Markets

For traditional foreign exchange markets (including spot transactions, outright forwards, and foreign exchange swaps), the United Kingdom is the world's most frequently traded marketplace (see Table 4.6). The ratio of the turnover in the United Kingdom to world turnover expanded from 27 per cent in 1992 to 34 per cent in 2007. The United States is the second-most active marketplace with its share growing from 16 per cent in 1995 to 19 per cent in 2004, but declining somewhat to 16.6 per cent in 2007. By contrast, Japan has reduced its share rapidly from 11 per cent in 1998 to 6 per cent in 2007, losing its ratio in the foreign exchange market vis-à-vis the United Kingdom and the United States (and recently Switzerland).

Among the foreign currencies used in foreign exchange markets, the U.S. dollar has remained the most actively traded currency, being on one side of 86 per cent of the transactions that sum to 200 per cent for two-way transactions in 2007 (Table 4.7). The ratio increased somewhat from 82 per cent in 1992 to 89 per cent in 2004, and declined somewhat to 86 per cent

Table 4.6
Geographic Distribution of Reported Foreign Exchange Market Turnover
(Daily Average in April; in US$ billion and Percentage, 1992–2007)

	1992		1995		1998		2001		2004		2007	
	Amount	% Share	Amount	% Share	Amount	% Share	Amount	% Share	Amount	% Share	Amount	% Share
Japan	120	11	161	10	136	7	147	9	199	8	238	6
United States	167	16	244	16	361	18	254	17	461	19	664	17
United Kingdom	291	27	363	30	637	33	504	31	743	31	1,359	34
Singapore	74	7	105	7	139	7	101	6	125	5	231	6
Switzerland	66	6	87	6	82	4	71	4	79	3	242	6
Germany	55	5	76	5	94	6	88	6	118	5	99	3
Hong Kong	60	6	90	6	79	4	57	4	102	4	175	4
Australia	29	3	40	3	47	2	52	3	81	3	170	4
Total	1,076	100	1,572	100	1,968	100	1,612	100	2,406	100	3,989	100

Source: Prepared based on BIS, 2007.

Figure 4.12
Yen- and Foreign Currency-denominated Offshore Market
(JP¥100 million, 1986–2004)

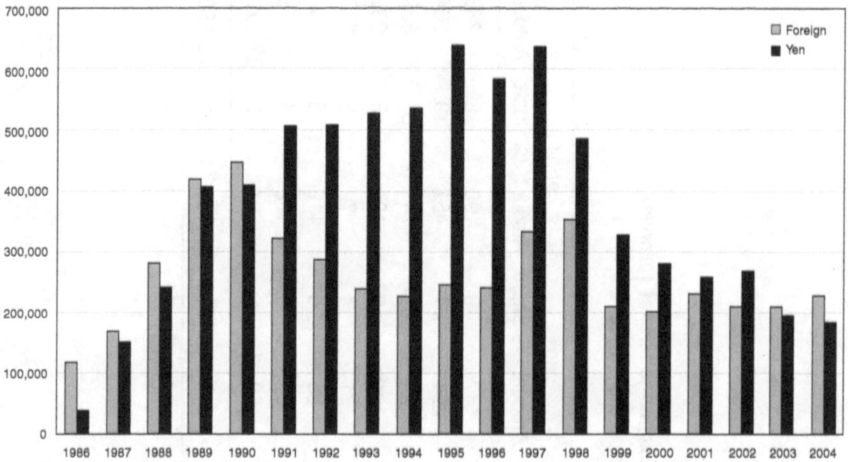

Source: Iijima, T., 2005.

Table 4.7
Currency Distribution of Reported Foreign Exchange Market Turnover
(Percentage of Average Daily Turnover in April, 1992–2007)

	1992	1995	1998	2001	2004	2007
US dollar	82	83	87	90	89	86
Euro	—	—	—	38	37	37
Deutsche mark	40	36	30	—	—	—
French franc	4	8	5	—	—	—
ECU and other EMS currencies	12	16	17	—	—	—
Yen	23	24	20	23	20	17
Pound Sterling	14	9	11	13	17	15
All Currencies	200	200	200	200	200	200

Source: Prepared based on BIS, 2007.

in 2007. The euro is the second-most traded currency, taking over the position of the Deutsche mark and accounting for 37 per cent in 2007. The yen is the third-most frequently used currency (17 per cent), followed by the pound sterling (15 per cent). The ratio of the yen declined from 23 per cent in 1992 to 17 per cent in 2007, while that of the pound sterling rose moderately from 14 per cent to 15 per cent over the same period. Among foreign currency pairs, the U.S. dollar/euro pair has remained the most-actively traded pair and accounts for 27 per cent of global foreign currency turnover (summing to 100 per cent), followed by the U.S. dollar/yen pair (13 per cent) and the U.S. dollar/sterling pair (12 per cent), as shown in Table 4.8. The share of the U.S. dollar/yen pair has declined during 1995–2007, while that of the U.S. dollar/sterling has rapidly expanded.

A similar pattern is also observed for the case of the foreign exchange OTC market as well as OTC interest rate derivatives. The United Kingdom was the world's most actively traded market place for exchange OTC and OTC interest rate derivatives during 1998–2007, expanding the average April turnover from US$171 billion to US$1.1 trillion and its share in global turnover from 36 per cent to 43 per cent (Table 4.9). The United States was the second most active markeplace with turnover growing from US$90 to US$607 billion and its share from 19 per cent to 24 per cent over the period of 1998–2007. By contrast, Japan's market has not grown much despite its position as the third-most active market; the turnover grew only from US$42 to US$88 billion while its share dropped from 9 per cent to 4 per cent.

Among foreign currencies, the U.S. dollar is the most-actively transacted one-side currency in the foreign exchange OTC market (including forward and swaps contracts). The euro is the second-most traded one-side currency in the foreign exchange OTC market, but is the most frequently used denomination currency for interest rate derivatives (followed by the U.S. dollar). The yen is the third traded one-side currency in the foreign exchange OTC market (followed by the sterling pound), but the fourth denomination currency for interest rate derivatives (after the pound sterling).

The above observations suggest the importance of the United Kingdom and United States in the foreign exchange and OTC derivatives markets. In terms of currency, the U.S. dollar remains the dominant transaction currency, followed by the euro. By contrast, the presence of Japan as a market place as well as the yen as a transaction currency has been declining. This makes it difficult for Japan to play an increasingly important role in

Table 4.8
Reported Foreign Exchange Market Turnover by Currency Pair
(Daily Averages in April, in US$ billion, Percentage, 1995–2007)

	1995		1998		2001		2004		2007	
	Amount	% Share	Amount	% Share	Amount	% Share	Amount	% Share	Amount	% Share
US dollar/euro					354	30	501	28	840	27
US dollar/yen	242	21	257	18	231	20	296	17	397	13
US dollar/sterling	78	7	118	8	125	11	245	14	361	12
US dollar/deutsche mark	51	4	58	4	—	—	—	—	—	—
US dollar/ECU	18	2	17	1	—	—	—	—	—	—
US dollar/other EMS	104	9	176	12	—	—	—	—	—	—
US dollar/other	200	17	338	23	349	30	532	29	1,061	36
All currency pairs	1,137	100	1,430	100	1,173	100	1,773	100	3,081	100

Source: Prepared based on BIS, 2007.

Table 4.9
Geographic Distribution of Reported OTC Derivatives Turnover
(Daily Average in April; in US$ billion and Percentage, 1998–2007)

	Total (US$ billion)				% Share			
	1998	2001	2004	2007	1998	2001	2004	2007
Japan	42	22	39	88	9	3	3	4
United States	90	135	355	607	19	18	24	24
United Kingdom	171	275	643	1,081	36	36	43	43
Germany	34	97	46	93	7	13	3	4
France	46	67	154	183	10	9	10	7
Total Turnover	475	764	1,508	2,544	100	100	100	100

Source: Prepared based on BIS, 2007.

Asia, with a view to reducing the region's heavy dependence on the U.S. dollar and making progress toward future common exchange rate arrangements. Asian countries use various types of exchange rate arrangements. However, the local currencies in many countries have remained linked, to a significant extent, to the U.S. dollar and this is particularly so on a day-to-day trading basis.[9] The common adherence to the U.S. dollar reflects the dominance of the U.S. dollar in trade and capital transactions as an invoice currency as well as foreign exchange, financial and capital markets as an intermediary currency.

4. GOVERNMENT VISION FOR THE TOKYO MARKET AND THE REMAINING AGENDA

4.1. The Vision of the Government for Revitalization of the Tokyo Market

There are two types of government documents with respect to the revitalization of the Tokyo market. The first report — called "Interim Summary Issues (Phase 1)" — was released by the Study Group on the Internationalization of Japanese Financial and Capital Markets of the FSA in June 2007. The second report is called "Toward the Establishment of Truly Competitive Financial and Capital Markets (the interim report)" prepared in April 2007 by the Working Group on Financial and Capital Markets of the Council on Economic and Fiscal Policy (CEFP).[10] The essence of this report is reflected in the "Direction and Strategy for the Japanese Economy 2007" (drafted by the CEFP and adopted subsequently by the Cabinet in June 2007). While the reports overlap each other and stress a vision of developing the Tokyo market into a top international financial centre, the latter is written within the broader perspective of seeing the revitalization of the financial and capital markets as an engine for Japan's growth strategies.

In the first report by the study group of FSA, attractive markets are defined as those that could offer diverse products and services (particularly markets for high-yield bonds and credit-related products), accommodate various market players; and fulfil market functions underpinned by strict self-discipline of market participants. It identifies regulatory environmental issues that should be tackled to develop Tokyo as an attractive market. Those include: (1) further clarification of rules, enhancement of information on laws/regulations in English and Japanese, improvement of regulatory authority's skills, enhancement of collaboration with overseas authorities, and enhancement of roles and functions of self-regulation; (2) review of the penalty system and enhancement of the dispute resolution system; (3) review of firewall regulations for banking and securities business; and (4) overhaul of the financial and securities tax system with the aim to minimize the distortion of the market by the tax system.

Suggested measures to increase financial assets include a diversification of products tradable at exchanges and an expansion of trading opportunities for shares of foreign firms' in Japan, such as Japan Depository Receipt [JDRs]. The JDRs refer to ownerships of foreign stocks that are issued by Japanese depository banks and can be traded like shares of foreign firms, but carry prices in yens and pay dividends in yen. Infrastructure-related measures cover a stimulation of transactions among professionals, as well as improvements in the security, efficiency, and convenience of settlement systems in response to the advancement of the IT industry and growing cross-border financial and capital transactions. The report also stresses an enhancement of the Japanese version of 401K (defined contribution pension plan) system, as demonstrated by the Individual Retirement Account (IRA) in the United Stats and Individual Savings Account (ISA) in the United Kingdom. The IRA refers to a retirement plan account that provides some tax advantages for retirement savings in the United States. Meanwhile, the ISA refers to an account which can be used to hold many types of savings and investment products (for example, cash, life insurance and stocks and shares). There are strict rules regarding the maximum amount allowed for each component and the overall amount that can be invested in any one tax year. The returns earned in an ISA (capital growth and income) are tax-free.

In the second report prepared by the working group of the CEFP, a clear and detailed vision for upgrading Tokyo as an international financial market is described in detail, as shown in the Box. In particular, the report stresses measures to promote diversified financial assets that could be listed on stock exchanges — such as commodity futures to be included in investment trusts and the ETFs. At the same time, it is pointed out that the organization of existing multiple commodity exchanges should be reviewed given that they are being left behind the global expansionary trends observed in overseas exchanges. For example, their role in price-making has been lost to other countries. To strengthen the governance of these exchanges, it is important not only to increase competition and merge among domestic exchanges, but also to shift these exchanges from a membership system to a joint-stock corporation and eventually list their shares. Once these measures are implemented, the regulatory environment should be adjusted accordingly. For example, restrictions should be imposed on the re-employment of officers in the supervisory agencies at the exchanges. The need for permission regarding listed products from the minister in charge must be abolished and should be left to the self-regulation of the exchanges.

To further develop the J-REIT market, moreover, the report stresses that overseas real estate should be included. There are no legal stipulations forbidding the inclusion of overseas real estate as management assets for J-REITs in Japan. However, there are no established methods for evaluating overseas real estate. As a result, stock exchanges have forbidden such listings by issuing listing provisions. As well, a JDR should be permitted to increase shares from Asian countries, such as China and India.

A creation of a market for professionals with limited regulations and greater emphasis on the principle of self-responsibility should also be considered to promote innovation in financial products and services. Such a market enables firms to raise capital through the issue of specialist securities (including debt, convertibles and depositary receipts) to professional or institutional investors. This type of market is already demonstrated by the Professional Securities Market (PSM) in London, following EU deregulation in 2005. The PSM is a listed, exchange-regulated market, where issuers benefit from a flexible and pragmatic approach to

Towards the Establishment of Truly Competitive Financial and Capital Markets

(1) To Turn the Tokyo Market into a Common Asian Platform

- Create new financial products by incorporating gold spot and commodity futures as assets in investment trusts and ETFs, as well as overseas real estate as an eligible asset for J-REIT investment.
- Amend the Financial Instruments and Exchange Law as well as Commodity Exchange Law that would enable the establishment of comprehensive exchanges covering financial and commodity futures (and possibly, electricity and emissions), and the establishment of commodity exchanges under a stock exchange holding company.
- Establish government and ministerial ordinances related to the JDRs.
- Strengthen payment and settlement systems by (a) promoting their international harmonization with respect to English notation and SWIFT (Society for Worldwide Interbank Financial Telecommunication); (b) reducing settlement times from three days to one day;[11] (c) advancing infrastructure (financial Electronic Data Interchange (EDI)), and (d) improving crisis management systems (for example, backup systems and Business Continuity Plan).
- Establish markets for professional investors and prepare differentiated regulations applicable to professional and general investors.
- Improve secondary markets and information provision with respect to securitization products and syndicated loans by formulating disclosure criteria at the initiative of industry groups.
- Promote convergence of accounting standards and allow disclosure by Japanese firms based on International Financial Reporting Standards (IFRSs).[12]
- Implement English language disclosure (of laws), provision of information in English, and establish specialist English-speaking contact points in government agencies and exchanges.
- Attract foreign participants by reviewing regulatory and taxation systems.
- Legislate Public Company Law with the aim at strengthening the governance of companies in the capital market.[13]
- Strengthen Tokyo's overall capacity as a global financial centre by improving human resources, the regulatory environment, physical access to international financial markets, and business infrastructure including airport access.

(2) Promoting Innovation by Participants

- Revision of firewall regulations on banking, securities, and insurance.
- Permission for special licences to enable narrow banking (specializing in

continued on next page

settlement operations) and captive insurance company (specializing in underwriting the issuance of a specific organization).

- Increased freedom of investment for public pension funds (such as GPIF) and strengthen fiduciary duties.
- Integration of taxation applied to various financial asset incomes and introduction of individual investment accounts to promote securities investment.
- Improve the basic abilities of the public to understand and utilize financial knowledge.
- Develop professionals with expertise in finance (for example, include finance-related topics to the subjects in choice of bar exams, introduce CPA exams, modify civil service exams, establish courts that specialize in handling finance).
- Creation of an environment to secure top talent from overseas.

(3) Improving the Transparency and Predictability of Regulatory Supervision

- Deregulation of markets for professionals and full protection of individual investors.
- Strengthen the function of the Securities and Exchange Surveillance Commission (SESC) (review the modalities of planning/design/supervision/inspection, and strengthen the SESC's independence and its quasi-judicial function).
- Utilize regulatory and supervisory methods based on principles.
- Improve no-action letter system (scope of items, anonymity, and flexible timing of public announcements) and introduce Safe Harbour Rules.
- Foster dialogue between financial supervisory authorities and financial business people.
- Enhance functions and structure of self-regulatory organizations (that is, Japan Securities Dealers Association, stock exchanges) without generating regulatory duplication.
- Promote personnel exchanges between government and private sectors and prevent conflicts of interest.
- Introduce cost-benefit analysis into regulations.

regulatory requirements, and institutional investors gain the assurance of investing in listed securities. To introduce such a market in Tokyo, professional market participants must establish firm compliance and internal governance and satisfactorily accept the disciplines of professional liability. The rules regarding the fiduciary duty of institutional investors that manage the assets of ordinary investors need to be clarified as well.

4.2. Recent Initiatives by the Government and Stock Exchanges

The Financial Supervisory Administration (FSA) announced a "Plan To Enhance the Competitiveness of Financial and Capital Markets" in December 2007. The programme includes plans (1) to vitalize the capital markets (through an increase in diverse exchange-traded products, a review of securities taxes, a strengthening of the self-regulatory operations by exchanges, a creation of a market for professional investors); (2) to improve business environment (through a deregulation of firewalls with a better management system to cope with the conflicts of interest arising from the removal); (3) to introduce a better regulatory environment (through an emphasis of principle-based regulation, improvement of staff supervisory capacities, greater collaboration with foreign exchanges); and (4) to increase financial professionals and improve urban infrastructure. These initiatives are to establish Tokyo as a global IFC which attracts more foreign investors and capital and at the same time, serve as the market for foreign corporations to raise funds from. In line with the continued efforts and new initiatives by the government, several new measures and initiatives have been implemented since 2006.

Regarding the cross-entry barriers, further deregulations have been launched. First, the bank agency business system — through which non-bank financial institutions can perform intermediating functions, such as depositing and lending — has been allowed since 2006. In response, a few securities firms and insurance firms have established their bank business agencies. For example, the bank business agency established by the Nomura Securities, the largest securities firm in Japan, has begun to intermediate depositing and remittance services on behalf of its affiliated Nomura Trust Bank. Second, the FSA allowed banks and insurance firms to conduct a part of fund businesses (that is, constructing/offering/investing in the funds targeting own loan credit and the funds investing in preferred stocks) through their own subsidiaries from end-September 2007, not only through already approved, separately managed banks under the financial holding firms. Such a move is likely to expand the market for funds.[14] The Bill for Amendment of the Financial Instruments and Exchange Law passed the Diet in June 2008, which would allow revamp the firewall regulations among securities firms, commercial banks, and insurance firms possibly in 2009. This move is a promising step toward developing a more efficient, attractive and fair financial and capital markets.

The Osaka Securities Exchange, one of the largest stock exchanges in Japan (Tokyo, Osaka, and Nagoya), has begun to list the gold-price-linked ETF in August 2007. This is the first commodity-linked ETF listed in the Japanese stock exchanges. The Tokyo Stock Exchange, meanwhile, listed Korean KODEX 200 ETF in November 2007, while the Korean Stock Exchange listed KODEX Japan ETF (TOPIX 100) on the Korean Exchange in February 2008. In April 2008, moreover, the Tokyo Stock Exchange listed China A-Share Panda CSI 300 Index ETF. Reflecting the efforts to increase diversity, there are fifty-six ETFs listed on the Tokyo Stock Exchange and ten on the Osaka Securities Exchange as of September 2008. Regarding the JDR, Tata Motors Ltd is expected to list a JDR on the Tokyo Stock Exchange in 2009 and make a debut as the first Indian firm on the exchange.

From May 2007, the provision of the Corporation Law allowed a foreign firm to merge or acquire a Japanese firm through its subsidiary in Japan in an effective "stock swap" (under the so-called Triangular Mergers). This enables a foreign firm to complete acquisitions in Japan using their parent firms' shares. Suppose a foreign firm wishes to merge a Japanese firm operating in Japan through this system, it needs to establish a subsidiary in Japan and needs to get approval from the (merged) Japanese firm's shareholders at the general meeting. Also, certain disclosure requirement on the foreign firm and shareholders' rights must be satisfied. Then, Japanese shareholders of this merged Japanese firm can exchange their shares with the shares of the parent firm of the foreign subsidiary. If the foreign firm is already listed on the Tokyo Stock Exchange, it would be easier for the foreign firm to obtain approval at the general shareholders' meeting for a triangular merger. Using this scheme, Citigroup announced in January 2008 that Citigroup Japan Holdings Ltd and Nikko Cordial Corporation had signed a definitive share exchange agreement. Consequently, Nikko Cordial became a wholly-owned subsidiary of Citigroup in a US$4.8 billion stock swap deal.

Moreover, in line with the government's vision, the Ministry of Economy, Trade and Industry (METI) announced in June 2007 its intention to introduce detailed strategies in the near future to improve the competitiveness of the commodity markets (such as listing oil and metals) under its jurisdiction; thereby, promoting inflows of capital from domestic and Asian sources. The measures include an introduction of a 24 hour-transaction system and the loss cut rule, an expansion of listed products, deregulation on price setting and position, and an enhancement of the settlement system. The Ministry of Agriculture, Forestry, and Fisheries (MAFF) has also begun to examine a strategy to revitalize the grain and food commodity markets under its jurisdiction.

As for a market for professionals, the Financial Instruments and Exchange Law passed in June 2006 (taking effect in September 2007) with the aim to protect investors by requiring listed firms to make quarterly information disclosure and internal control reports, and covering a wide range of financial products and services under the same regulation. The law has also distinguished general (retail) investors and professional (qualified institutional) ones with respect to user protection; and implemented stricter counter-measures against unfair trading on retail investors regarding sales promotion (such as exemption of requirement to provide investors with written explanations about risks). By extending this view, the FSA began to examine if such a distinction could be applicable as well to the market itself, as already demonstrated in the United Kingdom and the United States. As well, the permission for information disclosure only in English and a simplification of the audit certification prepared by auditors were considered. These reviews were realized by passing the Bill for Amendment of the Financial Instruments and Exchange Law (passed the Diet in June 2008), which would allow an establishment of new exchange markets exclusively for professional investors (which can be exempted from current disclosure requirements and instead become subject to the rules set by exchanges), separating from retail investors. In anticipation of the passing of the bill, the Tokyo Stock Exchange and London Stock Exchange announced plans in October 2007 to establish a new stock market for domestic and Asian emerging innovative firms in 2009 to help them raise venture capital in a less severe regulatory environment. Keeping in mind the successfully Alternative Investment Market (AIM) introduced in 1995 (that allows emerging firms to list their shares under a more flexible regulatory system than that applied to the existing main market) in the London Stock Exchange, foreign firms will be permitted to submit financial statements in English and use internationally-accepted accounting IFRSs.

Finally, the FSA introduced some elements of the principle-based regulation in April 2008 by presenting the concept of "optimal combination of rules-based and principles-based supervisory approaches". Through extensive discussions with representatives of relevant financial firms, it announced key principles, which would become the cornerstones of principles-based supervision.

4.3. Important Agenda Remaining

Incentives to Promote the Entry of Foreign Entities

Some measures to promote important foreign players (such as hedge funds and other types of funds) could be considered. Hedge funds are likely to provide new sources of financing for Japanese firms, support a robust economy by providing additional liquidity to the market, and improve the market's corporate culture through promoting sound governance of portfolio companies.[15] The United Kingdom and Singapore have successfully attracted hedge funds with preferential treatments. In the case of the United Kingdom, the tax authority created an Investment Manager Exemption that allows the profits of an eligible nonresident hedge fund not to be included in the United Kingdom's tax net. It only taxes the profits of the agent, the U.K. investment adviser, rather than the profits of its principal, the offshore head fund. Singapore created a hospital regime for fund managers to setting up operations there to manage hedge funds. Considering these global moves, Japan's tax regime could be revised to make it clear that hedge fund managers' activities, within certain guidelines, do not cause the funds they manage to become subject to tax. The International Bankers Association (IBA) (2007) claims that hedge fund managers should be permitted a broader range of discretionary activity in Japan without the risk of the managed funds being deemed to be a permanent establishment. Moreover, it claims that the laws that aggregate partnership holdings for purposes of determining whether such partnerships exceed large-scale thresholds and are thus subject to taxation of gains should be considered for review.

Furthermore, different regulations could be applied to different investment vehicles. In the United States, for example, hedge funds are not subject to the same regulations as other investment vehicles due to the limited numbers of investors (although the recent global crisis indicates better-designed regulations over hedge funds are necessary). By contrast, in Japan, a licence is required to act as an investment company so hedge funds would also be subject to periodic disclosure requirements. Also, the government should focus on Asian firms through special government incentives and better marketing.

Abolition of Cross-Entry Regulations

The already-implemented Bill for Amendment of the Financial Instruments and Exchange Law includes the removal of distinctions between banking, securities and insurance. While the detailed new measures are yet to be seen, the abolition of cross-entry barriers needs to be implemented with appropriate measures to contain conflicts of interest. Since the Financial Big Bang in Japan, cross-entry barriers have been deregulated by allowing the establishment of financial holding firms, but separate management of various financial businesses has remained a requirement. The concerns over conflicts of interest and possible abuses exercised by banks have deterred the move toward the integration of various financial services or a universal banking system for a long time. The United Kingdom has already made much progress in this area. Even the United States, which used to maintain the stringent Glass-Steagal (GS) Act of 1933, passed the Gramm-Leach-Bliley Act in 1999 to replace some parts of the GS Act. While the regulatory arbitrage between commercial and investment bankings must be minimized, the global trends towards integrated financial services concur with the view that integration would encourage greater efficiency by allocating resources and managing risks at a lower cost.

There are some other entry deregulations that have been demanded by foreign market players. For example, allowing asset management companies to place orders on behalf of overseas affiliates as well as promoting off-shore funds for related companies without additional licensing have been suggested. Furthermore, certain investment activities of investment advisers, such as stock lending, could be considered for deregulation. Currently, separate licences are required for hedge funds and for the advisers to such funds, discouraging fund professionals to establish operations in Japan.

Notes

1. The government later introduced emergency financial measures in the face of the failure of Hokkaido Takushoku Bank and Yamaichi Securities in 1997. The total public funds amounted to JP¥47 trillion, of which JP¥9.7 trillion was allocated for purchasing NPL by RCC (Resolution and Collection Corporation), JP¥18.6 trillion allocated to dealing with deposit guarantees of bankrupt banks, JP¥12.4 trillion allocated for improving the capital base of viable banks, and JP¥5.9 trillion allocated to other measures including the nationalization of banks.
2. In 1980, the Foreign Exchange and Foreign Trade Control Law of 1947 was revised to liberalize cross-border transactions, but capital and financial transactions required prior application and approval. Furthermore, foreign exchange transactions were required to be performed through authorized banks. In 1984, the euro-yen bonds were allowed to be issued by resident firms

and foreign firms (foreign governments and international organizations were already permitted to issue euro-yen bonds in 1979) in the euro market for the purpose of internationalization of the yen. An offshore market for the yen was established in Tokyo in 1986.

3. The liberalization of sale of insurance products through bank windows will be fully implemented by the end of 2007. Currently, banks are allowed to sell savings-type insurance products. By the end of 2007, other insurance products — such as health, elderly care, term life, whole insurances — were permitted to be sold through bank windows.
4. The recent global financial crises have lead to the loosening of some of these requirements in 2008, following the movements in the United States and Europe.
5. UFJ Holdings was established in 2001 by merging the Sanwa Bank, Tokai Bank, and Toyo Trust & Banking. In 2002, Sanwa Bank and Tokai Bank were merged into the UFJ Bank; and, Toyo Trust & Banking was renamed as UFJ Trust Bank. In addition, Sanwa Security and Tokai Security were merged into UFS Capital Market Securities in 2001 and merged with Tsubasa Securities in 2002 by forming UFJ Tsubasa Securities. It became the fourth largest financial group.
6. The GPIF is the largest pension fund in the world in terms of the size of assets. It is followed by Government Pension in Norway (US$2.4 trillion), ABP in Netherlands (US$2.3 trillion), National Pension in Korea (US$2.1 trillion), and CalPERS (US$1.9 trillion).
7. However, the Federal Old-Age, Survivors, and Disability Insurance (OASDI) in the United States, which is financed by payroll taxes, invest most of their reserved funds in non-marketable treasury securities.
8. As of end-2006, the amount of assets held by investment trusts reached US$7 trillion in the United States, while that of Japan reached only US$888 billion.
9. For example, McKinnon and Schnabl (2002) showed that high frequency (day-to-day) linkage to the U.S. dollar has become as robust after as it was before the crisis. Using the Swiss franc as a numeraire for measuring exchange volatility for any East Asian country, the exchange rates of each of the nine East Asian currencies were regressed on the U.S. dollar, the Japanese yen, and the German mark (as a leading currency for the European currency system, representing the euro) and for three periods: pre-crisis (from February 1994 to May 1997), crisis (June 1997 to December 1998) and post-crisis (January 1999 to April 2002). The nine East Asian currencies include the Chinese yuan, Hong Kong dollar, Indonesian rupiah, Korean won, Philippine peso, Singapore dollar, Taiwan dollar, Thai baht, and Malaysian ringgit. The study indicated that degree of linkage to the U.S. dollar declined during the crisis period, the weights of the U.S. dollar have again become close to unity and stable after the crisis.

10. The CEFP is a consultative organ placed within the Cabinet Office for the purpose of facilitating full exercise of the prime minister's leadership and sufficiently reflecting the opinions of private-sector experts in economic and fiscal policy formation. The CEFP is headed by the prime minister, and includes the chief cabinet secretary, the minister of state for economic and fiscal policy, other relevant ministers, governor of the Bank of Japan, and four private-sector experts.
11. In Japan, settlement time is T+3 for both treasury bonds and stocks, while that for treasury bonds is T+1 and T+3 for stocks in the United States.
12. The International Bankers Association (IBA) (2007) has recommended that the government and exchanges should relax the review process for acceptance of documents using the IFRSs and ease the Japanese SOX regulation applied to foreign firms which have already filed equivalent reports in other major markets. Currently, Japanese firms are allowed to adopt consolidated balance sheets based on U.S. accounting standards (U.S. GAAP), but not on International Financial Reporting Standards.
13. The Public Company Law is recommended by the Japan Association of Corporate Directors (JACD). It is pointed out that the benefits include a simplification of double regulations caused by the Financial Instruments and Exchange Law and Company Law (in principle by integrating the latter into the former), an establishment of full-scale management systems over subsidiaries through better internal controls and risk management, and a possibility of (consolidation-based) dividend payment (JACD 2007).
14. However, they are not allowed to establish buyout funds for the purpose of avoiding corporate controls by banks and insurance firms. The maximum amount allowed to invest in ordinary shares is 5 per cent (of outstanding issued stocks) for banks and 10 per cent for insurance firms. The same regulation is applied to their own subsidiaries as well.
15. According to the TASS Database, the residence of hedge funds is concentrated on the United States (52 per cent), the United Kingdom (19 per cent), Bermuda (6 per cent), France (3 per cent), and Hong Kong (1 per cent). Japan accounts for only 0.4 per cent, which is smaller than Hong Kong, Singapore, and Australia. The factors, such as the residence of investors, tax benefits, and regulations, have affected this geographical contribution.

References

American Chamber of Commerce in Japan (ACCJ). "Nihon no Kinyu-Shihon Shijyo no Kokusai Kyousouryoku no Kyoka nitsuite". Materials submitted to the FSA committee, 6 March 2007.

Bank for International Settlement (BIS). Triennial Central Bank Survey, "Foreign

Exchange and Derivatives Market Activity in April 2007 Preliminary Global Results", September 2007.

Council on Economic and Fiscal Policy (CEFP). "Toward the Establishment of Truly Competitive Financial and Captive Markets". The First Report of the Working Group on Financial and Capital Markets, 20 April 2007.

European Business Council in Japan. "Promote Tokyo as a Global Financial Centre", Documents submitted to the FSA committee, 6 March 2007.

Financial Services Agency (FSA). Interim Summary Issues (Phase 1), "The Study Group on the Internationalization of Japanese Financial and Capital Markets", June 2007.

Iijima, Takao. "Kinyu Big Bang to Asia Saiken Shijo", Keio University, KUMQRP Working Paper Series, DP2005-039, 2005.

International Bankers Association (IBA). "Recommendations to Promote Tokyo as a Global Financial Center". Materials submitted to the Committee of FSA, 16 March 2007.

International Monetary Fund (IMF). "Japan: Selected Issues", July 2007.

International Swaps and Derivatives Association (ISDA). "Recent Developments in Credit Derivatives Market and the Challenges for Japan". Materials submitted to the FSA committee, 10 May 2007.

Ito, Takatoshi and Michael Melvin. "Japan's Big Bang and the Transformation of Financial Markets". NBER Working Paper no. 7247, 1999.

Japan Association of Corporate Directors (JACD). "Kokai Kaisyaho Youkouan toha nanika", 2007.

McKinnon, Ronald and Gunther Schnabl. "Synchronized Business Cycles in East Asia: Fluctuations in the Yen/Dollar Exchange Rate and China's Stabilizing Role". Mimeo, 2002.

National Institute for Research Advancement (NIRA). "NIRA Asia Kinyu Platform Syoiinkai Teigen", 23 February 2007.

Pension Fund Association (PFA). "Wagakuni Kinyu-Shihon Shjyo no Kokusaika nitsuite". Materials submitted to the FSA committee, 1 March 2007.

Tokyo Stock Exchange. "Tokyo Syouken Torihikijyo Gaikokukabu Shijyo nitsuite". Materials submitted to the FSA committee, 1 March 2007.

5

CAN TOKYO BECOME A GLOBAL FINANCIAL CENTRE?

Masahiro Kawai*

1. INTRODUCTION

In the late 1980s, London, New York, and Tokyo were the top three global financial centres, and Tokyo was challenging the leading role of New York in global finance. Today, however, the consensus view is that London and New York are the only two genuinely global financial centres. Other centres such as Frankfurt, Hong Kong, Singapore, and Tokyo are national and/or regional centres and, according to Z/Yen Limited (2005), are not likely to challenge the dominance of London or New York. A view is even emerging that if a third global financial centre is to develop, it is most likely to be Shanghai, which would surpass the regional financial centres of Tokyo, Singapore and Hong Kong.

The weaknesses of Tokyo as an international financial centre are often identified as the lack of a business-conducive regulatory environment and the absence of available expertise and talent (see Z/Yen Limited, 2005; and International Bankers Association [IBA], 2007). This chapter explores the prospects for Tokyo to become a global financial centre. It argues that even if Tokyo does not become a truly global financial centre, Japan's efforts to improve Tokyo's profile as a competitive international financial centre are part of a healthy competition among Asian cities, which will be good for Japan as well as Asian and global finance.

2. FEATURES OF FINANCIAL CENTRES

According to the most recent British biannual survey conducted by the City of London in September 2008 (Y/Zen Group, 2008), the world's ten most important financial centres, ranked in descending order of importance, are London, New York, Singapore, Hong Kong, Zurich, Geneva, Tokyo, Chicago, Frankfurt and Sydney. This shows that East Asia hosts three of the top ten financial centres. Other Asian cities that ranked in the top fifty are Shanghai (34th), Beijing (47th), Seoul (48th), Mumbai (49th), and Osaka (50th).[1]

Financial centres are financial intermediation hubs for overall economic activity for a nation, a region, or the world. Each country tends to have at least one national financial centre that provides a national intermediation function in mobilizing and reallocating funds for the country's residents. A national centre usually hosts a stock exchange, a central bank, a supervisory authority, and headquarters of other public and private financial institutions. A national centre can become a regional financial centre for a group of geographically proximate countries by providing the necessary physical infrastructure (especially telecommunications and transport links); a stable regulatory, supervisory and legal framework; political stability; and business-enabling climates, thereby attracting regional financial institutions and supporting service providers. A regional centre serves for residents of the host and neighbouring countries.

A regional centre can grow to function as a global financial centre if it offers deep and liquid financial markets for global players — in addition to national and regional players; becomes a hub for global financial information; has a reservoir of highly educated and well-trained professionals (for investment banking, law, accounting, and information and communications technology [ICT]); provides a conducive, responsive regulatory environment; and ensures economic freedom supported by unambiguous legal certainty.[2] If the centre successfully creates agglomeration of financial activities and international consumers and suppliers — through critical mass, sufficient scale and the cluster effect — the transaction cost of conducting business can be reduced substantially, thereby further attracting more global players to do business.

London and New York rank first and second, respectively, as global financial centres. London's strength lies in three aspects: (i) its amenable and collaborative regulatory environment, (ii) its liberal immigration policy that makes it easier to recruit and retain international professionals and experts, and (iii) the authorities' philosophy of providing a responsive and business-friendly regulatory environment. These equip London with the reputation of a cosmopolitan city and the so-called "Wimbledon effect", that is, the equal opportunity for local and overseas participants to trade and deal. New York also has similar strengths, but lags behind London in terms of the regulatory balance, the legal environment and skilled professionals (City of New York and the United States Senate 2006). New York's biggest advantage is its ability to serve as the financial centre for the world's most dynamic, liquid economy, the United States.

Although Tokyo ranks seventh as a global financial centre, this ranking does not quite match Japan's economic size or potential. Given that Japan has the world's second largest GDP, the world's second largest stock market in terms of capitalization, top-class amenities (including a number of Michelin-rated restaurants) and an efficient transport system, Tokyo should rank among the top five or even top three centres globally. Partly because of its decade-long economic stagnation in the 1990s, its too-restrictive regulatory and supervisory framework and the absence of high-calibre international professionals, Japan has not been able to maximize its economic and financial potential to become a truly global financial centre. As a result Tokyo has been overtaken by Singapore and Hong Kong as Asia's international financial centre.

Singapore and Hong Kong, two of Asia's small economies, have created well-functioning international financial centres by finding a niche and attracting foreign financial institutions that provide competitive financial services for their neighbouring and global clients. Unlike large countries, these small open economies have the advantage of being able to adopt a very liberal policy stance toward financial services as they do not have many sensitive interests to protect, such as agriculture and poor farmers. Being former British colonies, they have also inherited English as their business language, market-friendly institutions, and strong administrative capabilities.

3. DETERMINANTS OF FINANCIAL CENTRE DEVELOPMENT

There are several determinants of the development of a financial centre.

First, the development of a major financial centre is closely linked to the economic power of the country that hosts it. Shifts of global financial centres in history — from Amsterdam to London in the years around 1800 and from London to New York in the 1920s — have been closely linked to shifts in the economic power of the countries hosting these centres (Cassis 2005). A similar force was behind the rise of Tokyo as a global financial centre in the 1970s and 1980s. Japan's remarkable industrialization and economic growth beginning in the 1960s helped expand the country's domestic financial activities, facilitate the accumulation of wealth, and encourage firms and financial institutions to invest abroad. Tokyo attracted a large number of foreign financial institutions in the 1980s, reflecting impressive economic expansion and financial sector liberalization and opening. The world's financial leadership even appeared to be shifting from New York to Tokyo. Such judgements were, however, premature. First, Japan's asset price bubble in the real estate and stock markets caused overestimations of Japan's financial power. Second, the asset price bubble burst in the early 1990s, damaging the health and stability of Japan's financial sector significantly. Third, the United States economy experienced spectacular growth in the 1990s, while the Japanese economy went into a long stagnation in the post-bubble period. This led to the sudden decline of Tokyo as a global financial centre.

Second, government can play a critical role in the development of an international financial centre: It can make a conscious effort to make the country's national centre a regional and global financial centre by focusing on the essential elements of international financial centres. These elements include presence of an enabling, competitive environment for financial intermediation and innovation while preserving financial system stability; availability of skilled international professionals through liberal immigration policy; offering of high-quality business infrastructure (ICT and transport links); and provision of attractive environments for doing multinational business through tax and other incentives. Singapore and Hong Kong — without the kind of economic power held by the major industrialized countries — have been able to ascend to the status of top Asian financial centres because of their focused policy efforts to provide liberal, business-friendly environments and credible institutional arrangements (including legal, supervisory and regulatory frameworks) for global financial institutions' multinational businesses. The presence of trust and confidence in the financial system is an essential element that cannot be achieved without ensuring legal certainty of transactions, that is, rule of law. At the same time, government needs to protect small consumers and investors, while providing freedom for wholesale service providers and professional investors. Maintaining this balance would be important for a government seeking to build a top-notch international financial centre.

From this perspective, the political economy aspect of financial sector reform is an important factor behind creating a competitive financial services industry. Incumbent firms that benefit from the existing system have no incentive to embark on reforms. For example, commercial bankers who benefit from an oligopolistic market structure would resist opening of the market to foreign banks or development of corporate bond markets. However, a severe crisis can create opportunities for significant policy reforms. Financial crises in New Zealand and Australia, for example, prompted financial liberalization and opening. East Asian crisis-affected countries — Thailand, Indonesia, Malaysia and Korea — were forced to pursue reforms in the crisis resolution process under International Monetary Fund (IMF) and/or World Bank programmes (Kawai 2000).[3] Japan's financial crisis, which occurred over an extended period without a currency crisis, did not change the financial sector's business practices immediately and rapidly; they began to change steadily as a result of the introduction of decisive reform measures.

4. THE TOKYO "FINANCIAL BIG BANG"

Following the decline in Tokyo's status as an international financial centre, the Japanese authorities began their efforts to reverse the trend. Japanese Prime Minister Ryutaro Hashimoto announced a five-year plan in November 1996 for financial system reforms, the so-called "Financial Big Bang". The principal objective of the reforms was to turn Tokyo into a world-class international financial centre on par with New York and London. The plan's idea was to encourage a transfer of savings for investments, make Japan's financial markets more "free, fair and global", and create a competitive financial services industry. From 1997 to 1998, the government announced the details of the "Financial Big Bang" policy and began implementation of its key elements between 1998 and 2001.

Under this policy, the authorities pursued further liberalization of a financial system still highly regulated explicitly by the law or implicitly by entrenched practices; enticement of domestic savers to place money in capital markets rather than in bank deposits; and greater openness of the financial markets to international competition and further internationalization of Japanese financial activities. For these purposes, they sought to break down barriers separating banking activities, securities transactions and insurance businesses; lifted the last remaining foreign exchange controls; brought the accounting system into line with international standards; and strengthened the powers of the agencies monitoring the financial system.

However, the worsening of the Japanese banking system, which culminated in a systemic crisis in 1997–98, prevented the full realization of the impact of the Financial Big Bang. The authorities' efforts had to be focused on the resolution of bank non-performing loans (NPLs), the restructuring of failed banks, and the restoration of a sound banking system. In 2001, the Financial Services Agency (FSA) was created as a new external agency of the Cabinet Office to regulate Japan's financial services industry.[4] The FSA and its predecessor encouraged banks to put in place reliable risk management systems and introduced a better bank insolvency procedure, which improved bank soundness. It took several years to overcome the banking system crisis; NPL ratios were reduced to a comfortable level and adequate capitalization of banks was ensured (Kawai 2005). The Japanese banks, particularly the big ones, became healthy and solid and were once again ready to operate in the international banking markets.

From a longer-term perspective, the "Big Bang" reforms have been successful in revitalizing Japan's financial markets. Breaking down barriers among various sectors and opening the market to foreign institutions and to new products resulted in healthy competition. Financial holding companies were introduced. Foreign securities firms and insurance companies have expanded their business operations in Japan over the last ten years, although the presence of foreign commercial banks in Tokyo has generally been flat. More innovative services and products, such as retirement planning and income products, have been made available to consumers.

5. FSA REGULATORY REFORM

With the restoration of a sound banking system, the authorities became able to refocus their emphasis from the stability of the financial system to its vitality. In December 2004, they announced the "Programme for Further Financial Reform" which aimed to create a vibrant financial system that would be led by the private sector — rather than the public sector — and would be superior in its convenience, price advantage, diversification, international nature, and reliability. One of the most significant features of this programme was to increase transparency, predictability, and efficiency of regulation and supervision and harmonize Japanese regulations with international standards.

More recently, the authorities began to place top priority on policies for strengthening the competitiveness of Japan's financial markets. For this purpose, in December 2007, the FSA announced the "Plan for Strengthening the Competitiveness of Japan's Financial and Capital Markets". The key aim of this policy package was to streamline the regulatory environment so that markets can become reliable and vibrant and the financial services industry can be vitalized. This was accompanied by further relaxing firewall regulations among banking, securities, and insurance businesses; broadening the scope of business permitted to banking and insurance groups; and supplementing these with stronger internal control systems in financial firms and groups.

To improve the regulatory environment, the FSA has been putting in place what they call "better regulation" initiatives, which aim at achieving financial system stability, protecting consumers, and creating a fair, transparent, and vibrant market. The "better regulation" initiatives have focused on: Optimal combination of rules-based and principles-based supervisory approaches; timely recognition of priority issues and effective response; greater emphasis on financial firms' voluntary efforts; and improvement of transparency and predictability of regulatory actions (see the Box). Such a policy direction is highly welcome as an emerging worldwide trend is the move toward principles-based regulations that automatically adapt to changing circumstances. This approach also has the benefit of being more transparent over time as it generally requires less interpretive guidance than previous approaches. Securities, banking, and insurance regulators in major developed countries are moving in the direction of harmonization of issues that affect multiple industries — such

Box: FSA's "Better Regulation" Initiatives

The Japanese Financial Services Agency (FSA) has been pursuing initiatives for "better regulation". With a growing need for regulation to place a greater emphasis on self-responsibility and voluntary efforts by financial firms, these initiatives attempt to improve the quality of financial regulation and supervision in order to enhance its effectiveness, efficiency, consistency, and transparency. The "better regulation" initiatives centre on four pillars:

- Optimal combination of rules-based and principles-based supervisory approaches;
- Timely recognition of priority issues and effective response;
- Greater emphasis on voluntary efforts by financial firms and providing them with incentives; and
- Improvement of the transparency and predictability of regulatory actions.

To address the first pillar, in April 2008, the FSA agreed with the relevant parties on fourteen key "Principles in the Financial Industry" which constitute the cornerstones of principles-based supervision.* The principles are to play a guiding role for financial firms in exercising best practices and to serve as a basis for the interpretation of rules. The principles-based supervision encourages voluntary efforts by financial firms in line with explicitly stated principles, thereby ensuring maximum freedom and flexibility in business management of financial firms. With the recognition that there are areas where rules-based supervision tends to be more effective relative to principles-based supervision, the FSA has taken the view that there is an optimum combination of rules-based and principle-based supervision approaches. A good balance between these two types of supervision needs to be achieved.

With regard to the second pillar, given that financial market conditions are changing fast, the FSA has decided to take a proactive approach to promptly identifying areas of potential risks in the financial sector and allocating its administrative resources intensively to these areas so that it can address the most pressing issues of the time. This will improve the effectiveness of FSA supervision and responsive policies.

For the third pillar, the FSA has already taken incentive-compatible approaches in its regulatory framework. This includes implementation of Basel II and the Financial Inspection Rating System, which provide financial firms with incentives for voluntary efforts. The FSA will make further steps to encourage voluntary actions by financial firms through provision of incentives to them.

continued on next page

Regarding the fourth pillar, pursuit of fair and transparent financial regulation and supervision has always been one of the FSA's core principles of conduct. To further improve the transparency and predictability of regulatory actions, the FSA has compiled and published collections of cases in which supervisory action was taken; conducted a review of the no-action letter system; and compiled FAQs (frequently asked questions) regarding interpretation of laws and regulations.

Under these pillars, the FSA has been enhancing its dialogue with financial firms, disseminating information more widely, strengthening cooperation with foreign authorities, and improving research functions to promptly grasp market developments.

* The "principles" are a set of key codes of conduct or general rules that are an underlying basis of statutory rules such as laws and regulations, and should be respected when financial firms conduct their business as well as when the FSA takes supervisory actions.

Source: FSA, 2007.

as risk management, reserve requirements, capital adequacy, accounting, and disclosure — by using the principles-based approach.

6. CONCLUSION: TOKYO'S CHALLENGES AND OPPORTUNITIES

For Japan, where the population is rapidly aging, demand for better financial services is growing because of the need of a rising portion of the population to maximize the rates of return on their wealth to support them after their retirement. Japan's massive savings need to be channelled into high-return investment opportunities while managing risks. That would include investing abroad, but so far Japanese investors have invested mostly in bonds and equities in developed country markets; Japan's portfolio investment in emerging Asia has been limited. Given the dynamic growth opportunities in emerging Asia, Tokyo should be able to intermediate Japan's savings for emerging Asia's investment, including for the ever-rising infrastructure investment needs, but this requires a substantial change in public policy toward greater freedom and openness in financial services.[5] Development of private banking and asset management, like in Zurich and Geneva, for Japanese wealth-holders is key. This requires accumulation of regional financial information and knowledge, analytical capabilities and innovative business environments.

Tokyo has a great deal of potential for re-establishing itself as Asia's leading international financial centre and even as a global financial centre. Tokyo has almost everything it needs to be a leading international centre for a long time to come (IBA 2007):

- The largest pools of savings liquidity in Asia;
- A highly educated workforce; and
- A "world-class city" with a dynamic urban environment supported by the best public infrastructure of the world's "mega-cities", and good public safety.

The biggest advantage of Tokyo is its deep pool of savings and financial assets that can be invested in emerging Asia, the world's fastest growing region — particularly by attracting more listings in the Tokyo Stock Exchange from emerging Asia. Tokyo offers the tremendous advantage of having a highly educated, literate workforce. Tokyo has the best infrastructure of all the world's "mega-cities", an excellent quality of life and a high degree of personal safety.

Building on these advantages, Tokyo can make efforts to overcome its weaknesses; that is, the lack of a conducive, responsive regulatory regime capable of promoting financial innovation and the absence of abundant financial-sector professionals and supporting talent. The regulatory and supervisory reforms undertaken so far since the creation of the FSA are laudable, but the FSA could further improve the country's regulatory framework — or make its "better regulation" even better — by forming a comprehensive strategy to transform Tokyo into a competitive, global financial centre and strengthening the core principles of consistency, effectiveness, efficiency and transparency (IBA, 2007). In particular, a consistent regulatory approach covering financial conglomerates and all product offerings — including, for example, deposits, insurance, commodities and securities transactions — would be needed for both regulators and market participants. The current regulatory philosophy is often criticized as too restrictive and business-unfriendly despite improvements, and it needs to change to one that nurtures competition and innovation.

Several other factors hamper Tokyo's efforts to become a top-notch international financial centre. Language, corporate culture and social attitudes are major impediments. Tokyo must find ways to overcome these obstacles.

First, English is unlikely to replace Japanese in Tokyo even as the business language. But more English-speaking professionals and supporting experts can be made available if sufficient incentives are given. More foreign experts should be brought in to Tokyo, and many more Japanese supporting staff should be trained to do business in English. Second, Japanese corporate culture, particularly its human resource management practices, is not conducive to competition and innovation. Essentially, Japanese financial institutions have not maximized the potential of their employees' expertise. Japanese professionals who were hired by foreign financial institutions after the Japanese institutions they worked for failed have been doing excellent work. There is no doubt that Japanese professionals have adequate knowledge and skills, though there is room for improvement and further training. A key reason for Japanese institutions' low performance is that many of them do not offer an attractive incentive scheme for high-performing experts, yet still provide implicit lifetime employment until the age of fifty-or-so years old, even though the lifetime employment practice has long been discredited. In contrast, many foreign institutions liberally reward outstanding performers and let go underperformers. How a financial institution organizes its business practices and manages human resources can make a huge difference in terms of its performance. A big challenge is how to adapt the corporate culture of Japanese financial institutions to the new market environment.

Third, there are social concerns about the opening of the labour market and the provision of favourable treatment to the financial sector. If the labour market is opened to financial-sector professionals and supporting service experts, there will be an increased demand for English-speaking personnel such as office support staff and household workers. This is a big social challenge for Japan due to its historic insularity. Also there is a strong social resistance to favouring the financial services industry. A widely held view is that the government should not further favour the financial industry — through the provision of tax and other incentives — over other industries such as manufacturing. Japan needs to overcome these social concerns.

Combined, these factors amount to an enormous challenge for Japan to face. Japan can never become an England, a United States, or even a Hong Kong or a Singapore. Taking into account the constraints described above, the country needs a comprehensive strategy to transform Tokyo into a world-class international financial centre. Otherwise Japan's financial services may start migrating elsewhere — to Hong Kong, Singapore and Shanghai. The rapid rise of China may transform Shanghai into the largest Asian financial centre — and, over the next ten to fifteen years, a global one — if the government commits to completing market-oriented reforms including the establishing of a clear rule of law, financial market liberalization, capital account opening, and creation of a market-based regulatory regime.[6]

Healthy competition among Asian financial centres — particularly Tokyo, Shanghai, Singapore, and Hong Kong — can help improve the quality of Asia's financial intermediation services, facilitate Asian financial integration, and expand financial trading, dealing and businesses in Asia. Developing a truly global financial centre in Asia — particularly in its time zone — is beneficial for Asian savers and investors as well as for global financial players as it allows diversification of global financial transactions into the tri-polar regions (Europe, North America and Asia) and reduces risks due to time zone differences. In this sense, Japan's efforts to improve Tokyo's role as a competitive international financial centre are important not only for Japan, but also for Asia and the world, because it encourages healthy competition among Asian cities to develop and deepen the respective financial markets, which benefits all consumers of financial services.

Notes

Editor's Note: This chapter is based on a paper submitted by the author after the conference in which he elaborates the remarks he made as one of the panelists of the conference. It has been inserted here as a supplement to Professor Shirai's chapter on Tokyo, in view of the very substantive content of the paper.

*The author is thankful to Patricia Decker for her careful editing work. The findings, interpretations, and conclusions expressed in the paper are entirely those of the author alone and do not necessarily represent the view of the Asian Development Bank, its executive directors, or the countries they represent.

1. Seoul ranked 42nd in the September 2007 survey, but did not rank within top fifty in the March 2008 survey.

2. Economic freedom can nurture financial innovation and competition, and market-based regulation and supervision can ensure the overall integrity of the financial system.
3. Although Malaysia did not go to the IMF for liquidity assistance, it received a World Bank adjustment loan which facilitated financial and corporate sector restructuring and reforms.
4. In June 1998, the Financial Supervisory Agency had been created, taking over the functions of supervision and inspection of the financial system from the Ministry of Finance (MOF). The MOF retained the function of policy planning and created a new Financial System Planning Bureau by consolidating the policy planning functions of the Banking and Securities Bureaus. In December 1998, the Financial Reconstruction Commission (FRC) was established as a parent body of the Financial Supervisory Agency, taking charge of oversight of the financial industry. In July 2000, the Financial Services Agency (FSA) was launched, integrating the functions of the Financial Supervisory Agency and the Financial System Planning Bureau of the MOF. In January 2001, with the abolition of the FRC in conjunction with the reorganization of the central government ministries, the FSA became an external agency of the Cabinet Office, absorbing the crisis response function of the FRC.
5. If Tokyo could intermediate emerging Asia's savings for the region's investment, it would be even better, but this would not be easy.
6. Although China will likely host a competitive international financial centre, Shanghai, in the near future, India is not. The consensus view is that India will remain an inexpensive back office and IT centre and develops it own national financial centre, like Mumbai, but it will not challenge the existing top international financial centres (Y/Zen Limited, 2005).

References

Cassis, Youssef. *Capitals of Capital: A History of International Financial Centres, 1780–2005*. Geneva: Pictet & Cie, 2005.

City of New York and United States Senate. "Sustaining New York's and the US' Global Financial services Leadership". McKinsey & Company and New York City Economic Development Corporation, New York, 2006.

Financial Services Agency (FSA). "Plan for Strengthening the Competitiveness of Japan's Financial and Capital Markets" (21 December 2007). Government of Japan, Tokyo.

International Bankers Association (IBA), Japan. "Recommendations to Promote Tokyo as a Global Financial Centre" (16 March 2007), Tokyo.

Kawai, Masahiro. "The Resolution of the East Asian Crisis: Financial and Corporate Sector Restructuring" *Journal of Asian Economics* 11 (2000): 133–68.

———. "Reform of the Japanese Banking System". *International Economics and Economic Policy* 2, no. 4 (December 2005): 307–35.

Z/Yen Limited. *The Competitive Position of London as a Global Financial Centre.* Corporation of London [title changed in January 2006 to the City of London, or the City of London Corporation] (November 2005), London.

Z/Yen Group. "The Global Financial Centres Index 4". City of London (September 2008), London.

6

MAKING AUSTRALIA A SUPPLIER OF FUND MANAGEMENT TO THE WORLD

Nicholas Gruen

> At any half-decent lunch in the City of London a few decades ago, the cabbage was overcooked and the conversation was about cricket. Today's financiers eat their brassica puréed, with seared scallops and a cumin jus, while chatting about the property they own back home in the Auvergne or New England. And they — and the businesses that pay their wages — are wealthier and more successful than ever.
>
> Britain's most lucrative industry owes its dynamism to many things, including globalization, innovation and the good fortune to be based in an old imperial trading city that sits handily between Asia and the Americas. But there was nothing pre-ordained about London's success as a financial centre: It happened largely thanks to an inspired piece of state intervention twenty years ago that opened the doors to foreign talent and foreign capital.
>
> *The Economist*, 19 October 2006

> We don't mind paying Australian tax. We don't want tax breaks on our profits in Australia. We'll pay the going corporate rate. What we can't live

> with is the Australian government taking a cut of our investors' money on the way through. Foreigners won't invest with us and we can't build serious capacity to export fund management from Australia if there's even a hint of sticky fingers. If we can't get that certainty, we'll just keep doing it from Dublin.
>
> CEO of a foreign-owned Australian fund manager

EXECUTIVE SUMMARY

Australia's funds management industry is, remarkably, the fourth largest in the world. Already managing A$1 trillion (about US$640 billion) in assets and growing fast, it is sophisticated, capable and cost competitive. Government policy — in this case compulsory superannuation — has been an important driver of its growth.

Yet official statistics have less than three per cent of its revenue coming from exports — that is, foreigners paying Australia's industry to manage their money.

There is a parallel in its own recent past. In the 1960s Australia had capable and competitive manufacturing. Government policy too was important in driving its growth, in this case, trade protection.

But while manufacturers and policymakers in Japan, Korea and Taiwan turned their eyes towards world markets with great vigour from the 1960s and 1970s on, Australia remained complacent. It took until the late 1980s to reduce protection and start the long and arduous process of learning to export.

In funds management the policy issues are quite different,[1] but the basic story is similar. Exports are always welcome of course — a nice bit of icing on the cake — but Australia has not pursued them with the single-mindedness of others.

Exporting is not easy. A global fund is domiciled in one country, holds assets in other countries and may have investors from several other countries as well. Add the network of bilateral tax treaties to this heady mix and the complexities are enormous.

If we were limited to a single finding from this research, if this report stands for a single proposition, it is this: Global fund management should be thought of as a joint-product between fund management firms and their regulators (including taxation authorities).

Of course tax authorities and regulators must continue delivering on their central mission — protecting consumers, vouchsafing market integrity and tackling tax evasion and avoidance. But those officials in the countries which most successfully export fund management do this with assiduous attention to the specific needs of their global fund managers.

This is not a rationalization for tax avoidance or some special plea for favours for global fund managers operating in Australia. Just as it exempts exports from GST (like other countries) so there is a general global understanding here and in other countries that global funds should be "tax neutral" or "tax transparent".

Thus here and amongst Australia's developed world competitor countries, it is accepted that the firms that manage global funds should pay company tax on their profits wherever those profits are earned. On the other hand, the principle of tax transparency calls for investments within a global fund not to be directly taxed on account of the domicile of the fund. After all, the returns from the investments will often have already borne company tax at source and will generally bear income tax in the investors' home country.

For this reason, Australia has spent recent years trying to extricate global fund managers from inadvertent taxation. A raft of recent changes to the tax and regulatory treatment of Australian domiciled funds has removed many of the worst problems of unintended tax burdens on Australian domiciled global funds.

However, difficult trade-offs are sometimes required between tax neutrality for global funds and preventing avoidance in Australia's domestic tax system.

The financial entrepôts in the developed world, like Ireland and Luxembourg, have successfully established global financial service centres from far more modest bases than Australia's own financial services industry. They have done so by:

- aggressively courting financial services exporters with low rates of corporate taxation;
- having a radical commitment to tax transparency, if necessary at the cost of anti-avoidance measures like Australia's own "Controlled Foreign Corporations" regulation; and
- assiduously meeting the industry's regulatory needs — for instance, for investment vehicles that optimize tax transparency.

This chapter argues that, though it may be cost beneficial from the perspective of the national economy, the first of these strategies — direct and discriminatory assistance to financial services exports — is the least important of the three strategies.

While Australia may never be primarily a financial exporter, it can aspire to export financial services far more than it does. And given the natural advantages provided by its base, it can expect substantial increases in exports if it rises to the challenge of the financial entrepôts in the other two respects.

Even if it were to be implemented vigorously rather than in the half-hearted manner in which it has so far been practised, Australia's policy of "minimum effective regulation" is of little assistance.

It puts little emphasis on the responsiveness of existing regulation and so offers little assistance in optimizing tax transparency for Australian domiciled global funds. For this is an ongoing task of responding to emerging problems and seizing opportunities. Consider the contrast offered by the financial entrepôts.

When the European courts held that one of Luxembourg's unique private wealth management vehicles breached the Treaty of Rome, a new regime — the *Société de Gestion de Patrimoine Familial* (SPF) — was developed and introduced in just four months.

Similarly Ireland's regulators worked closely with major global funds and in competition with Luxembourg to produce an innovative regime which is more tax transparent than companies and trusts in specific circumstances particularly related to the pooling of funds — the so-called Common Contractual Funds (CCFs). Industry figures suggests that with a similar regime Australia would manage billions more in pension assets right now.

It is however a "chicken and egg" problem that is all too familiar in industry economics. Regulation is, in substantial part, standard setting. And firms and regulators at the forefront of standard setting can gain "first mover" advantages. The complex regulatory and tax problems faced by global funds are solved first and faster in the financial entrepôts for whom it is "core business".

A good analogy is provided by the American state of Delaware — a corporate regulatory entrepôt which has opened up an apparently unassailable lead amongst U.S. states as a corporate domicile of preference. It offers an elaborate regulatory and judicial infrastructure devoted to meeting corporate needs — most particularly the minimization of regulatory uncertainty. Delaware's jurisdiction comes complete with specialist courts and an enviably deep stock of judicial and regulatory precedents.

In a similar way the financial entrepôts are marketing their own regulatory prowess. Their regulatory structures are not just a set of sovereign commands and protections, but a value-added service which meets core regulatory objectives while maximizing flexibility and minimizing uncertainty.

If Australia is to succeed in becoming an exporter of funds management services, tax and regulation must be more responsive to opportunities and developments as they emerge. This chapter describes this as a "co-evolutionary" regulatory regime in which regulators and industry work together on the common goal of improving regulatory and tax competitiveness and optimizing tax transparency whilst upholding the broad prudential, consumer protection and anti-tax avoidance goals of regulation.

Despite several years of hard work in helping deliver better tax transparency to Australian domiciled global funds, uncertainty continues to frustrate major investment in Australian domiciled global fund management capability.

When Australian firms receive advice on regulatory or tax arcana — say, whether a particular transaction crystallizes a capital gain — they are often told "probably not". Meanwhile Ireland's regulators answer "no" with a deep stock of precedents to back them up and/or an ability to deliver regulatory changes where necessary.

Australia should:

- Identify *bona fide*, export-ready fund managers and consider offering them an alternative to the current generic policies that fail to address the specific problems associated with exporting financial services.
- Consider establishing a specialist agency to accelerate deliberations upon the regulation of managed funds and be willing to foster collaborative arrangements between regulators and financial service providers.
- Develop an export culture in government and industry, with a focus on achieving higher recognition and better representation for the Australian industry in Asian markets. It must strive to be recognized as a credible financial centre in the Pacific. Financial services should be accorded a higher priority in trade negotiations, particularly with Asian countries to which Australia might become a substantial exporter of fund management and fund management expertise. Until Australia can demonstrate a more energetic pursuit of export orientation, these countries will continue to look to other centres.

Finally what is at stake? It is not immediately apparent why, at a time of labour shortages Australia should prefer the jobs generated in this industry over those already existing elsewhere. On further inspection however, finance employees get paid nearly twice as much as others — and even controlling for higher skill levels, finance employees still earn far more.

That helps explain why, from about the time they became major centres of global fund management, both Luxembourg's and Ireland's economic trajectory headed sharply north. Ireland went from being the poor man of Western Europe to being Europe's second wealthiest economy. The wealthiest? In the 1970s when it decided to become a global financial centre, Luxembourg was one of the wealthier countries. Today it is the richest by a country mile.

OTHER PEOPLE'S MONEY: MAKING AUSTRALIA A FINANCIAL SERVICES EXPORTER

1. Australia's Comparative Strengths as a Financial Centre

On paper there are good reasons for expecting Australia to be a very competitive centre for international finance. Table 6.1 below itemizes those attributes regarded as desirable for a financial centre — as enumerated by Deloitte, in a review of Ireland's attractiveness for the Irish government (2004). It then enumerates Australia's strengths relative to Ireland. The scale is the number of stars out of five, with one being bad and five being outstanding.

Table 6.1
Australia and Ireland Compared

Characteristic	Ireland	Australia
Taxation	*****	***
Availability of skilled labour	****	****
Relative cost	***	****
Political stability	****	*****
History and infrastructure	***	****
Access to a large market	*****	***
Strong financial regulation and financial stability	****	*****
Regulatory flexibility	*****	***

Of course, the impressionistic measurements set out above cannot capture the full detail of economic life in the two locations, yet the indicators are highly suggestive that Australia's fund managers should be competitive exporters. All the prerequisites are there as far as Australia's political stability and the credibility and capability of our regulators are concerned. Indeed, one substantial pension fund managed from Australia on behalf of an Asian government agency gave that agency the choice of setting up an entity subject to Australian Securities and Investments Commission's (ASIC) regulatory control (together with the higher costs this would entail) and a lower cost entity without ASIC supervision. The holder of the funds plumped ASIC supervision.[2]

The most important advantage Ireland has over Australia is access to the European Union that its membership of the union brings. This has been crucial in its success, particularly given ongoing efforts within the EU to unify Europe's financial markets.

On the other hand, at least over the longer term, Australia has its own advantages — both small and large. It operates in the Asian time zone, giving it unique advantages in an area that is much less developed than most European markets. Two decades of compulsory superannuation have seen Australia acquire an expertise in funds management for pension provision that is in many respects at the frontier of world best practice, not to mention a population with the greatest per capita exposure to managed funds in the world![3]

However Australia's industry is remarkably inward oriented, overwhelmingly serving the needs of Australian investors. Even where it is acquiring a reputation overseas — as has Macquarie Bank, for instance — this is generally for its growing skill in investing its hoard of superannuation savings in offshore markets, rather than in helping to manage the funds of those in other countries.

It is worth being reminded that financial services can be traded in four basic ways: Cross-border trade (where domestic consumers purchase services from a foreign supplier located abroad); commercial presence (where a foreign supplier merges with or acquires a domestically owned institution, or establishes an affiliate, typically a branch or a subsidiary for example, to exploit an already-established brand); consumption abroad (where domestic consumers purchase services outside the territory of their country); and movement of persons (where foreign persons supply services to domestic consumers in the territory of a country). Cross-border

Figure 6.1
Australia's Funds Management Cluster

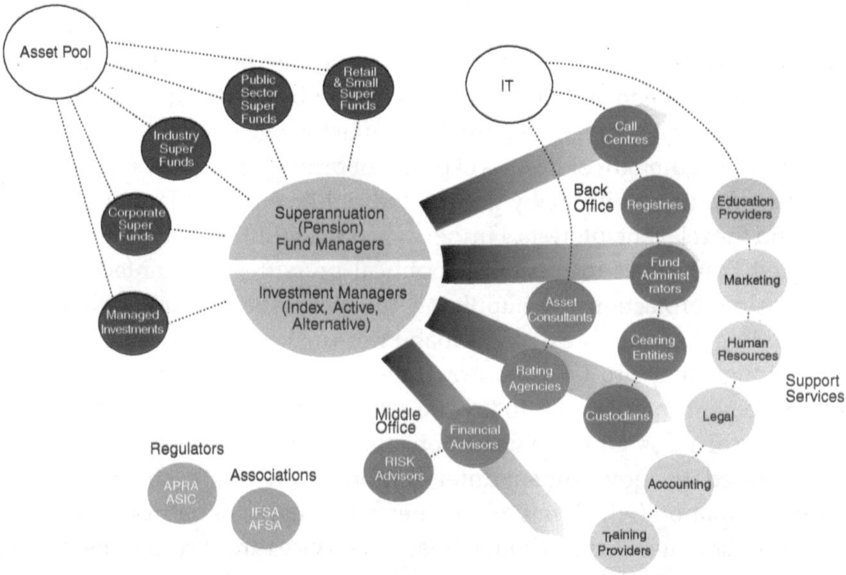

Source: *Axiss*.[4]

trade and commercial presence are the most common forms of trade in financial services.

2. Parallels with the Past

In certain respects, the situation in which Australia's fund managers find themselves today is not unlike the situation in which manufacturers found themselves in the 1960s. Much of Australia's manufacturing was capable and sophisticated, particularly by comparison with its peers in the region, even if it was not necessarily at the technical frontier. It had grown up partly because of its unique circumstances — as a developed country in a less developed region a long distance from other centres of technical sophistication (conferring a degree of natural advantage). Government intervention had also played its part, particularly in providing protection from imports.

This pattern of government intervention also presented risks to its further development. For just as Asian countries like Japan, Korea and Taiwan were turning the eyes of their industry to export markets, Australian manufacturers preferred the comfort of their protected home market. So when Australia engaged the world in trade negotiation, little attention was given to the idea that it might become substantial exporters in some specialized niches of sophisticated manufacturing.

Australia thought of itself as exporter of primary products and importer of manufactures, with lobby groups and political parties largely oriented around the relevant interests. Further, when structural adjustment pressures exerted themselves in the 1970s, political pressures all pointed towards increasing protection for supplying the domestic market, rather than expanding Australia's existing capabilities further into export markets.

Though they are far from exact, the parallels with the state of fund management in Australia today are nevertheless striking. The industry has critical mass and sophistication. Its development has been greatly accelerated by government intervention — in this case compulsory superannuation (which has also conferred a degree of natural advantage on local fund managers). Though financial services are of course mentioned in Australia's negotiations with other countries, they receive far less prominence than export market access for its agricultural products.

Certainly the fact that Australia's industry is not built on protection from offshore competition augurs well for its expansion into exports. However, the rapid and ongoing growth of the domestic market as a result of the continuing effects of compulsory superannuation risks dulling the urgency with which the country tackles the transition to export.

3. Outline of the Discussion to Follow

The following sections explore the parallels drawn in more detail regarding the transition to export orientation. Before doing so, it is appropriate firstly to document the policy efforts made to date. Next discussed will be tax and regulation — surely a critical input into financial services and certainly one Australia must get right to manage the transition to export orientation. In this context, the kinds of policies that were responsible for establishing financial centres elsewhere will be explored, with a focus on Ireland and to a somewhat lesser extent, Luxembourg.

It is hoped that, having thus sketched some of the distinctive policy problems of exporting financial services, we can return to the analogy we began with without doing violence to the differences between exporting manufactures and financial services. There follows some tentative suggestions from which might be built the next stage of work, which should lead to concrete policy recommendations.

4. Progress so Far

As was discovered with manufacturers, where an industry has grown up predominantly servicing the domestic market, there can be important barriers to export. In the case of manufacturing, tariffs indirectly raised costs for all exporters — by increasing Australia's exchange rate — but also directly (by increasing the costs of inputs). For this reason, schemes like duty drawback remitting tariffs on inputs to export were introduced. However, they were administratively cumbersome, and did little to establish an export culture, so long as high levels of protection remained. By contrast, as shall be seen below, the successful Asian countries were enormously energetic in fostering an export culture throughout their industries. In many ways they liberalized trade on behalf of exporters.

In finance there are no tariff barriers to the development of an export culture, but there can be tax and regulatory barriers. In particular, many of Australia's regulatory and tax avoidance measures have been designed in a context in which it did little exporting of financial services. As a result, many measures have been taken that impose taxes on the investments of foreigners and/or otherwise constrain the options of those interested in exporting financial services.

The industry has been active in proposing reforms to remove tax and regulatory burdens to export flows, and the government has responded in ways that are well regarded both by the local industry and internationally. Klein and Seddon of PricewaterhouseCoopers (writing for International Tax Review) commented (2005) that the reforms of the previous five years had

> made Australia much more attractive as a jurisdiction for locating holding companies. When the Australian tax system of five years ago is compared to the system that exists today as set out in [Table 6.2] below, it is very clear the extent of reforms as they affect foreign investors.

They offered the following table.

Further, since that time there have been numerous additional changes seeking to further extricate Australian managed funds from taxation on income streams from foreign-owned assets.[5]

To explore what arrangements might improve the "export friendliness" of Australia's tax and regulatory structures as they affect financial services, the nature of regulation itself is briefly discussed. It is argued that though the current focus on "minimum effective regulation" is a helpful principle

Table 6.2
Tax Snapshot — Then and Now

	2000	2005
Corporate tax rate	36%	30%
Treaty network	Extensive.	Extensive — Recently concluded treaties with the U.S. and the U.K. reducing withholding tax on dividends, interest and royalties.
Conduit relief for foreign income	Limited — No Australian tax payable on some non-portfolio foreign dividends received by Australian companies where on-paid to foreign shareholders.	Broader — Proposal to create a foreign income account for Australian companies, which should allow most foreign-sourced income (not limited to dividends) to be distributed to non-resident shareholders free of Australian tax.
Inbound capital gains tax	Foreign shareholders subject to capital gains tax on most shareholdings, but treaty relief may have been possible in some circumstances.	2005–06 federal budget proposes that foreign shareholders should only be subject to capital gains tax where there is a substantial interest in real property.
Outbound capital gains tax	Australian companies were subject to capital gains tax on disposal of shares in foreign subsidiaries.	Australian companies generally only subject to capital gains tax on the disposal of shares in foreign subsidiaries to the extent that the foreign subsidiaries hold passive assets.
Controlled foreign company (CFC) rules	Extensive and complex. Anomalous taxing of income arising from a number of common commercial transactions.	Extensive, but now less likely to result in Australian taxation, particularly for CFCs resident in comparably-taxed jurisdictions. Several anomalies resolved.

Source: Klein and Seddon (2005).

in the appropriate contexts, it is not particularly helpful in addressing the question of regulatory responsiveness. Subsequent sections argue that regulatory responsiveness appears to be one of the characteristics of successful global financial centres and that it is one that Australia should seek to emulate.

5. The Inevitability of Regulation

Both here and abroad, business activities are becoming progressively more regulated. This is self evidently true in finance (see Figure 6.2) and, at least by the crude measure of the volume of regulation on the statute books, is true more generally.

It appears that Australia's current "regulation review" measures — which focus on "gatekeeping" to prevent excessive regulation being passed — have enjoyed limited success. This has also been the case in other countries (Fiorino 1997).

In the context of this review, perhaps it is worth posing the question, "Is less regulation always better?"

Figure 6.2
Pages of Australian Government Primary Legislation
(Estimate)

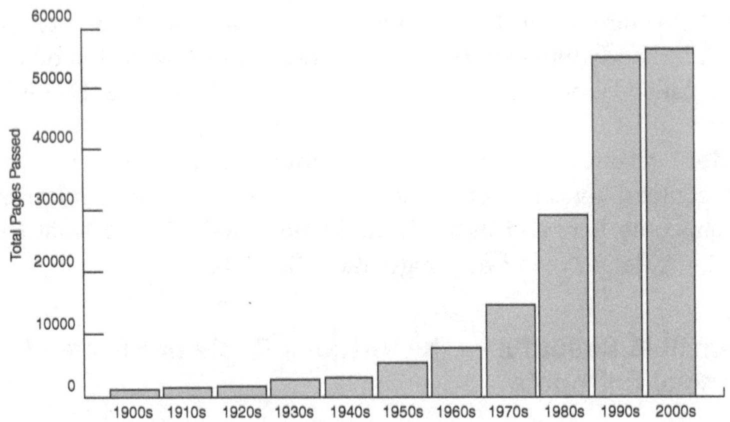

Source: Regulatory Taskforce (2006), p. 5.

Firstly, arrangements which most would accept have somewhat rationalized Australia's regulatory arrangements and improved their quality — such as the reforms following the Hilmer and Wallis reports — have done so at the expense of hundreds of additional pages of regulation! So the mass of regulation may grow — as software programs grow — as a result of increased functionality and/or attention to quality and detail.

Secondly, if regulation is inevitable and it is complex — as much regulation is — then it is important for it to be responsive. As argued below, some of the most responsive regulators are those in the most successful financial centres — and responsive regulation frequently involves more, rather than less regulation. The need for responsiveness is demonstrated even more clearly when considering what we call "regulatory dovetailing" in a subsequent section.

Fund management seems to be a paradigm case of an industry in which extensive regulation is so inextricably tangled up with the industry that it should be regarded as a "joint product" between service providers and regulators. A worthwhile analogy arises with information and communication technologies, where individual firms compete with each other but do so within the context of common standards which are often provided collectively.

A recent study illustrates the significance of this issue for finance relative to many other areas of goods and services. In a study of the competitiveness of four of the great financial centres of the Western world (London, New York, Frankfurt and Paris), three of six attributes of competitiveness relate to regulation — the competence, responsiveness and light-handedness of regulation or regulators— with the other three being skilled labour, tax and attractive living and working (Deloitte 2004, p. 33).

More recently, in an attempt to improve the regulation of risk management, concern about the financing of terrorism and corporate scandals both here and in the United States has unleased what Deloitte called a "tidal wave" of new regulation. See Table 6.3.

6. Small is Beautiful — the Virtuous Circle of Successful Financial Entrepôts

It is noteworthy how many major exporters of financial services are small-country financial entrepôts. To some extent Switzerland has been in this

Table 6.3
Recent Developments in the Regulation of Finance since 2000

Area	Regulations	Detail
Capital adequacy	Basel II, EU Capital Adequacy Directive, Insurance Directive	New capital adequacy regulations are being introduced to help prevent against corporate failures. For example, Basel II (due to come into force by the end of 2007) focuses on the amounts of capital a bank will be required to set aside in order to carry out different type of business (operational/credit risk assessment). Although it only applies to banking, it influences other sectors by influencing regulators viewpoints.
Corporate governance	Sarbanes-Oxley, Turnbull Review, Financial Conglomerates Directive, IAASA	Across the globe, the movement towards improved corporate governance is gathering pace with an unprecedented number of initiatives undertaken or planned for implementation over the coming years. In the United States, the Sarbanes-Oxley Act will drive tougher and more transparent financial reporting and disclosure in public companies operating in the United States. Furthermore, it will significantly influence legislation in other countries.
Anti-money laundering	Patriots Act	Anti-money laundering legislation is focusing organizations on the need to be wary of unusual transactions. In the United States, the Patriots Act 2001 requires suspicious transactions of US$5,000 or more to be reported adding to the administrative burden.
Financial reporting	IFRS	Financial reporting standards continue to be reviewed and updated. In particular the drive towards a unified set of accounting standards continues. This is not merely an accounting issue but extends into systems and management information matters.

Source: Deloitte (2004), p. 22.

category for over a century — as banker to the wealthy of Europe and now the world. Financial entrepôts to emerge since Switzerland include Singapore and Hong Kong in Asia from the 1960s on, and in Europe, Luxembourg from the late 1970s and Ireland from the late 1980s.

Box 6.1 Luxembourg Becomes a Global Financial Centre

While among the smallest EU countries, Luxembourg's successful policies have given it a reach that extends well beyond its borders. Following the steel crisis of the 1970s, Luxembourg managed the transition to a financial services-based economy because of its (i) advantageous tax and regulatory regime; (ii) early financial market liberalization; and (iii) responsible financial policies. These policies generated a virtuous growth cycle in the "golden 1980s and 1990s", permitting the public sector to accumulate substantial wealth. Relying to a considerable extent on foreign labour and capital, this growth steadily raised the country's profile in the global financial system. Luxembourg's international banking industry is comparable in size to those of Hong Kong ... and Singapore, while its investment fund industry (IFI) has become the second largest worldwide.

Source: IMF (2006).

From an early stage in their development as a financial centre each of these countries has actively courted the role of financial entrepôt. In some countries — such as Ireland — tax breaks have been important in establishing the centre in the first place.[6] But even here, over time, Ireland was able to augment its competitiveness with critical mass as policymakers focused on a regulatory/tax mix suited to financial services exports. Today none of these financial entrepôts are low-cost locations, each having high wages and high property prices (in part as a result of their success as financial service exporters).

As is illustrated below, regulators of financial entrepôts often understand their role in the context of competition with other financial centres. A close analogy can be drawn with the competition for corporate charters between states of the United States (see Box 6.2).

Given the complexity of regulation, and indeed of other countries' tax and regulatory structures (see below), tax and regulatory policy will often involve difficult trade-offs. Most particularly, governments have tax and regulatory objectives to raise revenue, prevent tax avoidance and deliver various safeguards for their own nationals that they have no reason to extend to foreigners. Yet it will often be difficult to quarantine foreigners from such action. Of course sometimes Australian regulation is valued by foreigners — as for instance in the example above, where a foreign super fund happily accepted ASIC supervision of the management of its pension fund in Australia. Australia's potential as an exporter of funds management

Box 6.2 Delaware: Regulatory Services Entrepôt

It is instructive to add one further location to the list of entrepôts, though here the entrepôt is in corporate law and regulation rather than finance.

Amongst American states, Delaware is relatively small but over the twentieth century, it established itself as a major exporter of corporate governance services. In effect it sells its regulatory services to U.S. corporates. In return for franchise fees to domicile their corporation in Delaware — they–are typically higher than those of other states — American corporations gain access to what Roberta Romano describes in the following terms:

> Delaware offers a superior product, including a substantial stock of legal precedents, expert judiciary and administrative services and a commitment to continued statutory responsiveness.
>
> Firms typically locate in Delaware when contemplating substantial corporate restructuring particularly where there is uncertainty as to the effect of other states' regulations. Some argue that Delaware's competitiveness in regulation is a symptom of a 'race to the bottom' in corporate governance with Delaware privileging the interests of managers over shareholders. However if this were the case one would expect changes of domicile in Delaware to be accompanied by reductions in share prices (as shareholders lose protections available in other states). Econometric research finds no such effect — if anything the opposite.

See Romano (1993), p. 1909; Romano (2002), pp. 6, 8, 76; Romano (1985), p. 226.

services must be built on a foundation of sound domestic regulation. Beyond this, however, tax and regulatory requirements can operate to raise costs and produce undesirable and unintended consequences which can close off export possibilities in the face of competition from others "getting it right".

Thus, there are usually important trade-offs between preventing domestic tax avoidance (particularly by use of offshore tax vehicles) and ensuring that such measures do not catch in their net foreigners to whom one is exporting *bona fide* financial services. Those trade-offs will differ depending on the relative size of financial exports compared with financial services supplied to the domestic market and compared with the size of the economy generally.

In particular, domestic authorities may introduce tax or regulatory requirements to counter tax avoidance. Some of these, such as regulation to prevent the use of foreign tax havens, can end up obstructing and/or taxing the activities of foreigners who are legitimately seeking to purchase (that is, import) financial services from another country. Where the financial services industry is not particularly export-oriented, this is of minor political importance. As a consequence, the expansion of financial exports is suppressed, but there is a limited political constituency to raise objections and the domestic industry gets on with servicing the domestic market.

By contrast, in a financial centre with substantial exports, there will be much more political pressure on the government to regulate in ways that do not obstruct legitimate export activity. The effect will be strengthened in a financial entrepôt where financial exports expand to become an indispensable component of the country's balance of payments.[7] Thus Ireland, for instance, has no controlled foreign corporation regime as Australia, and many other countries have established regulations to tackle tax avoidance using offshore tax havens. Presumably there is a case for doing something like this in Ireland, but it is outweighed by the potential cost to Ireland's financial services exports.

As it shall be seen in the subsequent section on "regulatory dovetailing", the presence of financial exporters provides regulators with feedback and intelligence about market developments which can be used to design regulatory innovations to capture further export market share.

As the financial centre's exports expand, a virtuous circle is thereby set up. Where fiscal exports are substantial, tax and regulatory proposals that impede exports will encounter political opposition, particularly if financial exports loom large as a source of export revenue for the country as a whole — as they do for financial entrepôts. In that case, nothing will be done that will seriously jeopardize financial exports. Investors in the financial centre know this. The financial entrepôt has the ultimate credibility with investors in the financial centre, for once firms have invested in a location, they are always hostage to opportunistic behaviour from their host country. If they invest in a financial entrepôt they know that the centre, and if it is not large, the country in which it is located, is also hostage — if not to the success of the investing firm itself, then at least to the industry of which it has become a part.

These ideas on the virtuous circle of tax and regulation in a financial entrepôt are illustrated in Figure 6.3.

Box 6.3 On the Stability and Credibility of Ireland's Tax and Regulatory Structure

Q: You wouldn't be concerned if a more left-wing government was elected?

I think that everyone in Ireland is very aware of the role of foreign direct investment and of the success of the current regime and, yes, our business survey confirms that our members are confident the government and the political parties in Ireland are very supportive of the current tax regime, because it is so central to Ireland's success.

Fraser Logue, Director of Operations at the Irish subsidiary of Abbott Diagnostics and 2006 President of the American Chamber of Commerce in Ireland, cited in *International Taxation Review,* March 2006.[8]

Figure 6.3
The Virtuous Circle of Tax and Regulation in a Financial Centre

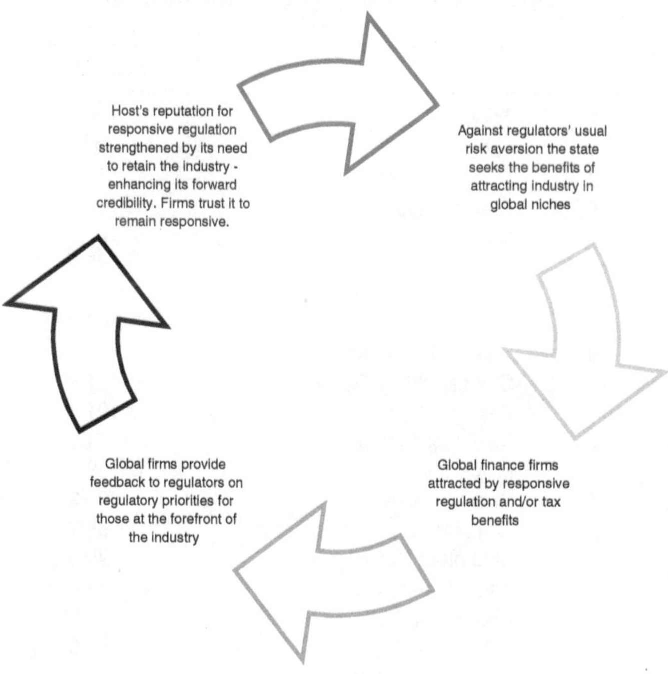

7. The Costs of Exporting Fund Management

It has been mentioned that though tax incentives were important in the establishment of Ireland as a financial entrepôt, Ireland and other recognized global financial centres were now high-cost locations. Table 6.4 shows the costs of living — and so to some extent the cost of purchasing inputs to service provision in various great cities of the world. The number of financial centres in the list is notable, with Sydney — easily Australia's most expensive city — falling well below others including Dublin on the list.

Melbourne has lower costs again (see Figure 6.4).

A look further will also show that the costs of production in Ireland and Luxembourg are not particularly low by comparison with other European centres which purchase their financial services.

The following things stand out from Figure 6.5. Firstly, although global financial centres are not among the highest-cost suppliers, nor are they

Table 6.4
Mercer Cost of Living Survey 2004 Top Cities

Rank	City	2004 Index
1	Tokyo, Japan	130.7
2	London, U.K.	119
3	Moscow, Russia	117.4
4	Osaka, Japan	116.1
5	Hong Kong	109.5
6	Geneva, Switzerland	106.2
7	Seoul, South Korea	104.1
8	Copenhagen, Denmark	102.2
9	Zurich, Switzerland	101.6
10	St. Petersburg, Russia	101.4
11	Beijing, China	101.1
12	New York City, U.S.A.	100
13	Milan, Italy	98.7
14	Dublin, Ireland	96.9
15	Oslo, Norway	96.2
16	Shanghai, China	95.3
17	Paris, France	94.8
18	Istanbul, Turkey	93.5
19	Vienna, Austria	92.5
20	Sydney, Australia	91.8

Source: Mercer, cited in Deloitte (2004).

Figure 6.4
The Competitiveness of Melbourne as a Financial Centre

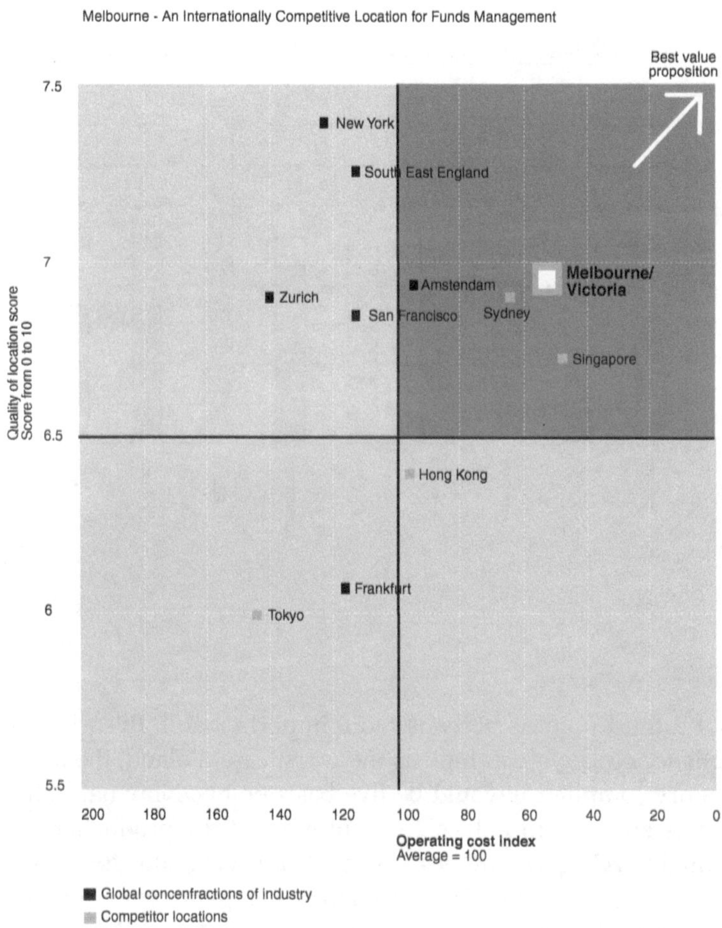

Source: Victorian Government (2004), p. 13.

among the lowest. Luxembourg, Ireland and the United Kingdom sit between 47 and 57 basis points, compared with outliers as low as 42 (Sweden) and 84 (Poland). Secondly it is notable that regulatory compliance costs are low in the financial exporters.[9]

Figure 6.5
Comparison of Total Production Costs for Equity Funds by Member State Based on Current Average Fund Sizes

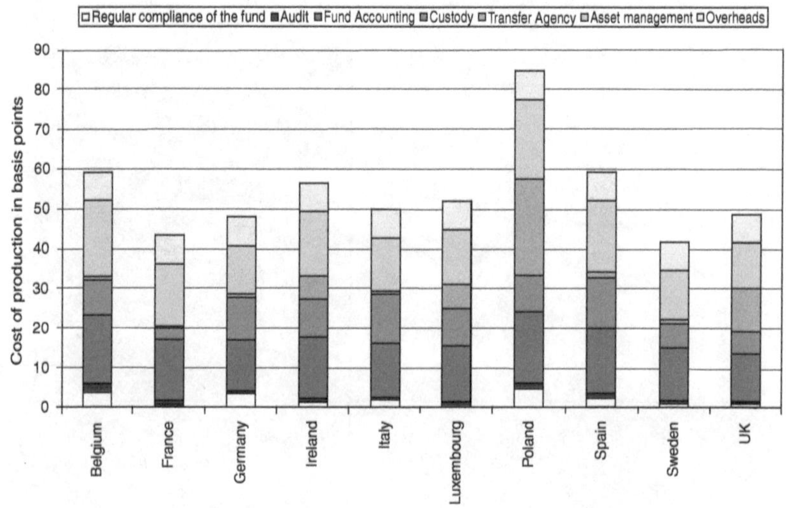

Source: CRA (2006), p. 8.

But a third point is perhaps more important still. Even if regulatory compliance costs were as high as the worst case, Poland, the total cost of regulatory compliance would be five basis points. Now naturally, funds managers are keen to reduce costs throughout the production chain, so they might well gaze enviously at such a saving. But it is unlikely to provide the explanation for the relative competitiveness of the major global financial centres.

But what if direct regulatory compliance costs are really the tip of the iceberg, the only economic aspect of the costs of regulation that is conceptually and practically easy to measure? As argued here, apart from regulating to deliver the safeguards they are there to deliver, financial exporters want their regulators to facilitate their legitimate export activities with the maximum of flexibility and minimum of obstruction. The very low levels of cost involved in regulatory compliance are at least suggestive of such flexibility.

8. "Law as a Product" and Regulatory Dovetailing

The complexity of regulation as experienced by the regulated entity will often extend well beyond the particular regulation in question. It can extend not only to other regulation imposed by the same government, but also to regulation imposed by other governments — or by non-government agencies with regulatory influence like standards boards. In this case the efficacy and functionality of any regulation cannot be judged on its own but only in relation to other regulations.

The multiplicity of sources of regulation and the efficiency with which they interface with each other has been one theme of discussion regarding roles and responsibilities under Australia's federation. Conflicting regulatory and tax demands from different levels of government within the federation has been of some significance in financial services — for instance, in the case of taxes on financial transactions such as share purchases and banking deposits or withdrawals, though these issues have diminished in significance since the states rationalized some of their financial taxation.

Of much greater import for a global financial centre however, is the way in which its own tax and regulatory structure interfaces with the international jigsaw of regulation and taxation within which all international financial services firms find themselves. The complexities are immense.

To provide competitive after tax returns funds must take into account tax and regulation in the countries that are host to their investors, the countries that host the assets in which the fund invests and in the country in which the fund is domiciled.

Funds are often domiciled in tax havens to address these complexities (and simply to avoid tax). But this often triggers anti-avoidance measures in countries that host investors and/or high levels of withholding tax from countries that host the investments. Thus for instance, a European investor seeking exposure to American assets may not be advantaged by investing in a (zero taxed) Cayman Islands trust holding such assets. Though avoiding Cayman Islands taxation, the investments in the trust will generally attract taxes (such as income withholding taxes) from the United States.

Thus a critical aspect of financial regulation in a global financial centre is optimizing investors' taxation and investment options — considering the jigsaw of arrangements they face in their own country, in the country hosting the investments they have, and the country in which their fund is domiciled. As Deirdre Power of Deloitte (2005) puts it:

> Multinationals have been lobbying for many years for investment fund structures that allow assets to be pooled in an efficient manner. The holy grail is to have a fully tax-efficient structure that is totally tax neutral with no drag on performance. Essentially, the structure and its investors must be exempt from tax in the location in which the fund is domiciled for tax purposes. In addition, a pooling fund vehicle should be considered tax transparent by the tax authorities of the investor location, investment location and fund location.

Note that, although financial centres do sometimes assist investors to avoid tax, the search for tax-transparent arrangements described above is better described as a search for a rational way through the maze of inter-country tax arrangements in an attempt to ensure that the global pooling of assets and globalization of the funds management supply chain does not entangle the investor in multiple layers of taxation.

It is fairly obvious that in a context like this, how the existing tax and regulatory structure interfaces with the corresponding tax and regulatory structures of other countries is a highly complex optimization problem which does not call for the kind of minimalism suggested by "minimum effective regulation". A more promising way to think of the challenges posed by financial exports is the co-evolution of business and regulation as a complex adaptive system (Beinhocker 2006).

9. The Co-evolution of Business and Regulation in Global Financial Centres: A Case Study

Certain hummingbirds have long curved beaks that give them an evolutionary advantage in supping nectar from orchards with long curved apertures. But which evolved first — the long beaks or the long apertured orchids? In fact neither could have evolved on its own. They co-evolved, each making the other's evolutionary pathway possible.[10]

To some extent this phenomenon of co-evolution can be seen going on in global financial centres as financial firms locate within a business and regulatory ecology that is congenial to them, and then provide rich feedback to their host regulators on how to make the centre more congenial still. Generally, both the firms and the regulators have a common interest in capturing more of the global financial market. Locally domiciled firms then acquire first -mover advantages in operating within the new regulatory structures, and in influencing their further development and evolution.

Regulatory and tax innovations are often at the heart of the establishment of financial centres in the first place — as in the case of Ireland and Luxembourg — or of an existing financial centre receiving a new lease of life — as in the case of London's "Big Bang". This process of innovation typically continues as the incumbent firms within the centre provide feedback to the regulator and the regulator identifies with its firms' aspirations to capture more global market share.[11]

The response of Ireland and Luxembourg to the "joint optimisation" problem of dovetailing its own financial tax and regulation with the tax and regulatory regimes of other countries provides an excellent case study in regulatory responsiveness or the co-evolution of financial centres and financial regulation. Regarding the examples discussed in the boxes below, in each case regulators are seeking what Deidre Power referred to as the "holy grail" in global asset management — to give locally domiciled firms access to the greatest degree of transparency regarding tax levied in other countries.

The story of Ireland's development of Common Contractual Funds (CCFs) is an ever clearer example of the regulatory ecology developed within an aggressive global financial centre in which regulators search with financial service providers for mutually beneficial regulatory structures. Having done much to attract global financial firms to Ireland, the Irish government responded quickly to compete with a legal structure available in Luxembourg which was designed specifically to facilitate tax transparent pooling of funds.

10. The Industry's Assessment — 'Even the Hint of Sticky Fingers...'

An explanation is offered now on why the Australian funds management industry has not responded more vigorously to the reforms made at their request since 2000 (as enumerated above). Some in the industry concede that the buoyancy of the local market, driven by compulsory superannuation, has encouraged many firms to focus on servicing domestic needs — rather than exploring export possibilities.

Yet several companies that consider themselves well placed to export financial services are moving slowly. These firms are often subsidiaries of

Box 6.4 A Special Vehicle for Private Family Wealth Management in Luxembourg

On 20 November 2006 new legislation defining the characteristics and conditions of the *Société de Gestion de Patrimoine Familial* (or SPF) was laid before the Luxembourg Parliament. It was introduced just four months and one day after the European Commission declared that an earlier vehicle (the Luxembourg 1929 Holding Companies regime) violates the EC Treaty state aid rules (Article 87).

The new legislation rescues the essence of the earlier structure as a passive vehicle for the management of wealth by requiring that the new vehicles only be used to acquire, hold manage and dispose of financial assets but prohibiting their use to engage in commercial activity.

SPFs are exempt from Luxembourg's corporate income tax, municipal business tax and net-worth tax and from Luxembourg withholding tax on distributions. Though the vehicle is exempt from tax at the level of the entity, income is fully taxed once it is distributed to the private investor if the investor is resident in Luxembourg and is not taxed in Luxembourg if it is held by a non-resident.

In a way that illustrates how the authorities provide regulation as a service to the firms domiciled there Luxembourg charges a subscription tax at a rate of 0.25 per cent applicable on its share capital, subject to a minimum of €100 (US$130) and a maximum of €125,000 a year.

Source: Samantha Nonnenkam, 2006–07, Atoz, Luxembourg.

foreign firms, with a substantial and highly capable "footprint" in Australia from which is managed smaller offices in Asia. These firms would like to build further capacity in Australia to export fund management into Asia. Yet there remains a sense of unease that Australia's financial exports may still not be "safe" from regulatory and tax imposts. As one CEO put it, "we have advice that certain tax provisions shouldn't hit the holdings of foreign investors in our funds, but we can't build our business around that. We need to know that they won't."

The CEO of another foreign-owned fund manager that manages most of its Asian offices from its Australian headquarters puts a similar point this way:

Box 6.5 Northern Trust Describes its Joint Search for a 'Tax Transparent' Entity for Asset Pooling

In 2001, two multinational companies approached Northern Trust to participate in a consortium to identify a practical solution for cross-border pension pooling… . The group identified two major barriers: Unfavourable withholding tax regimes threatened to create significant tax drag, negating the benefits, and in some countries local pension investment restrictions prohibited participation. The consortium examined multiple vehicles, investor countries and investment countries with a view to finding a vehicle that would accommodate multi-manager funds and multiple investment mandates. Moreover, the solution needed to be tax-neutral, that is, the plans investing through the pooled vehicle should pay the same tax rate they would when investing directly.

In 2002, Northern Trust implemented cross-border pension pooling for two multinational clients, using Irish Unit Trusts. While the initial focus was global bonds, the vehicles now support fourteen different investment mandates, including fixed income, equities and fund of hedge funds. Pension plans from fourteen different countries participate, including plans in Europe, North America, Asia and Africa. Each subsidiary retains control over asset allocation, deciding whether or not to participate in the mandates offered. In practice, the pooling vehicles support global investment mandates of interest to the majority of subsidiary pension plans, while each plan's domestic investment mandates usually remain outside the pool.

The chief drivers have been enhanced governance and risk management. The company can leverage the firm's pension and investment expertise across a large pool of assets, implement a consistent investment strategy across all country plans, and establish greater consistency in investment manager selection and monitoring. The benefits to the subsidiary pension plans, particularly the smaller ones, can be considerable. They can achieve manager diversification and gain access to specialised investment mandates. At the same time, economies of scale in investment management, administration, custody, and audit translate to lower fees. The corporation as a whole benefits from more efficient administration through the elimination of multiple manager selection and monitoring processes across the globe and consistent, enhanced reporting from a single global custodian.

The Irish Unit Trust (IUT), however, does not offer an effective solution for all asset classes. Since U.S. equities normally constitute about 50 per cent of a global equity mandate, an investor (such as a Dutch or U.K. pension plan) who is exempt from withholding tax on U.S. dividends will resist subscribing to a global equity IUT that must pay withholding tax on U.S. equities. The resulting tax drag would overwhelm any cost benefits to be derived from pooling. To find a solution for U.S. and global equity mandates, the consortium needed to identify a vehicle that tax authorities around the globe would recognise as "tax transparent", that is, the tax authority would "look through" the vehicle and apply the tax rate as if the investors were investing directly into the market. A Belgian pension plan could pay a different tax rate than a U.K. pension plan, depending on the tax treaties between the investor country and the investment country.

Luxembourg and Ireland emerged as attractive domiciles for cross-border pooling. Recognized as the most highly regulated of the offshore markets, these domiciles minimize taxes on investment vehicles. Moreover, pension funds from around the world commonly invest in Irish- and Luxembourg-domiciled funds. Initial research suggested that the legal structure of the Luxembourg FCP (*Fonds Commun de Placement*) fulfilled the requirements for tax transparency. Ireland, however, lacked a similar vehicle. The Irish government acted quickly to fill the void. Eager to position Ireland to compete for multinational assets, in May 2003 the Irish government established a new vehicle, the CCF (Common Contractual Fund), specifically to support cross-border pension pooling. Similar in legal structure to the FCP, the CCF had one major competitive advantage.

The Luxembourg FCP was subject to a 1bp (one basis point) annual subscription tax, the Taxe d'Abonnement. When Northern Trust, acting in partnership with a multinational client, alerted the Luxembourg authorities to this issue, the government moved to eliminate the tax in the case of multinationals that use the FCP as a cross-border pension pooling vehicle.

Having established that both the CCF and the FCP could work, Northern Trust undertook the lengthy process of turning theory into practice. Tax authorities in a number of countries were asked to review draft management regulations and confirm the tax transparency of both vehicles. With close cooperation from two clients and assistance from Deloitte and Touche, Northern Trust began the detailed tax work required to support cross-border pooling for global equity mandates in both Ireland and Luxembourg.

At the same time, Northern Trust enhanced its operating platform to support tax-transparent vehicles. In order to support tax withholding and regulatory and tax reporting, the system needs to track income, capital gains and withholding tax at the investor level. At the most detailed level, the system

continued on next page

Box 6.5 — *cont'd*

must be able to track each investor's share of each holding (for example, attributing 2,532 shares of XYZ stock to Investor A and 1,488 shares of XYZ stock to Investor B.) Investors reap an added benefit. This solution can provide full asset detail and risk and performance reporting at the investor level, services not normally available with other pooled funds.

Years of focused effort are about to bear fruit. Two Northern Trust multinational clients are preparing to launch tax-transparent, cross-border pension pooling vehicles in 2005, one in Ireland and one in Luxembourg. The initial launch will focus on various global equity mandates, with a view to adding other asset classes at a later date.

Kathy Dugan (2005).

> We don't mind paying Australian tax. We don't want tax breaks on our profits in Australia. We'll pay the going corporate rate. What we can't live with is the Australian government taking a cut of our investors' money on the way through to them. Foreigners won't invest with us and we can't build serious capacity to export funds management from Australia if there's even a hint of sticky fingers. If we can't get that certainty, we'll just do it from Dublin.

11. From Domestic Capability to Export Orientation

Compulsory superannuation has seen Australians become either the heaviest, or among the heaviest per capita investors in managed funds in the world, depending on the sources used. Returning to the analogy drawn earlier with export orientation in manufactures, it should be noted that what characterized success in the transition from inward to outward orientation was not the orderliness of the policy transition, but the energy with which it was pursued.

As economists tried to compare the evidence of development success with their theories, they found that many of the most successful exporting countries did not embrace liberal trading policies. Jagdish Bhagwati offered this suggestion for understanding the difference between failure and success:

> Instead of the chaotic selectivity of the incentive policies for "import substitution" which seems to be the main focus of our trade-theoretic analysis, a more *important* inhibition on growth may in practice be the speed with which import substituting industrialisation is geared toward "export promotion"…. [T]he key to success is not the absence of detailed, selective and target-oriented export promotion. . . . The distinguishing feature of superior export performance seems to be the pursuit of "indiscriminate" and "chaotic" but *energetic* policies to promote exports from industries which have been nurtured under protection in the first place (emphasis in original).[12]

Of course we are not advocating chaotic policies. But energy nevertheless counts for a lot. And in all matters trade-offs have to be made. The fact that Australia's financial services sector remains so lacking in export focus, given its apparent competitiveness on capability, skill and cost, suggests that greater vigour is needed to allow the industry to reach its considerable potential.

12. Next Steps

This section sketches out some ideas for policy progress suggested by the analysis in this chapter.

At the outset, it is worth mentioning that Australia is not in the position of a financial entrepôt that has constrained its own energies in pursuing tax avoidance wherever it threatens its financial exports. It begins from a point at which its financial services industry is heavily inwardly oriented, and so is in a weak position to insist that its own requirements for international tax transparency from Australia should take precedence over other policy goals.

For that reason, Australia may need to target its actions more carefully — to ensure that exporters are free to thrive whilst minimizing the extent to which special arrangements for them constrain its own abilities to meet other policy objectives, such as preventing tax avoidance.

Greater Use of Specialist Vehicles

Australia has a penchant for simplicity in policy — once captured in Paul Keating's memorable description of his department's preference for "long clean lines of policy". Other things being equal, of course simplicity, consistency and neutrality between different corporate forms is desirable. It simplifies policymaking and reduces distortions.

But things are far from equal. The research here has argued in another context (Lateral Economics 2006) that the desire to unify the top marginal rate of taxation with the corporate rate is one example where long clean lines of policy will generate far more costs than benefits — by tying progress that is urgently needed (reducing the rate of corporate taxation) to progress that is less urgent (reducing the top marginal rate of personal taxation).

The demand for consistency across a wide range of circumstances can weigh down the speed and decisiveness with which Australia deals with legal and regulatory challenges as they arise. Its approach to corporate vehicles such as companies and trusts tends to value consistency of approach between the large and the small, between the foreign and domestically owned, between those focused on the domestic market and those who are exporting. And this consistency may be weighing it down in targeting solutions to specific problems.

For this reason, Australia should give renewed attention to the scope to deliver better tax transparency institutions for financial service exporters by distinguishing between large corporate entities and smaller ones controlled by a small number of people. Where there was a concern that a new privileged class of corporate entity might create opportunities for avoidance, access to such an entity might be mediated administratively rather than legislatively. That is, businesses could have access to the regime only if, in the opinion of an administrator, they were a *bona fide* fund manager of a given size with an established reputation in the industry.

If Australia sought to establish entities that were particularly useful for exporters, it could also limit them to funds that had, or undertook to achieve, some minimum level of export orientation — say 20 per cent — and/or export growth over time. It should also consider giving such funds guarantees that foreigners investing in them would be exempt from any and all Australian capital gains and/or dividend withholding tax by virtue only of the fund being domiciled in Australia (though the manager of the fund would continue to pay tax on the profits they earned).

Lessons from Offshore Banking Units (OBUs)

In this regard it is important to take into account experience with earlier efforts to promote financial service exports in the past, particularly Offshore Banking Units (OBUs). Though many firms have taken advantage of the

OBU structure and its tax concessions appear substantial on paper, they have not led to a strong expansion of financial service exports. The industry reports that this is because they cannot be accessed unless export activity is effectively quarantined from services supplied to the domestic market.

One can understand the logic of this from the perspective of the authorities. Yet at least until such time as Australia becomes a major exporter of financial services, the major gains from export are likely to come from pooling funds and infrastructure between the domestic and export markets. It is for this reason that it has been suggested above that if Australia sought to target some regime for financial service exporters, it should limit it to those with some minimum level of export orientation, rather than quarantine exported financial services altogether.

An Agency to Accelerate Change

Although there has been a great deal of activity in removing impediments to exports in the last six years — activity that is ongoing — the impression still remains that regulatory change can be slow compared with the financial services entrepôts. The case for establishing a well resourced agency which is able to accelerate the speed with which tax and regulatory matters concerning exports can be deliberated upon, if necessary with private rulings should be investigated. Axiss has already built up substantial expertise in the area of promoting Australia as a financial centre and could perhaps be expanded to become a policy advocate within the Australian bureaucracy for measures to facilitate financial service exports.

Choice of Special Regimes

Once it is satisfied that it has identified a set of financial service providers who are *bona fide* exporters, Australia should consider widening the choice of regimes they can use. In addition to providing "law as a product" — that is collaborating with them to arrive at arrangements which facilitate their export of financial services — it could even "free ride" on the efforts of others. Thus we could announce that it would recognize the Irish Common Contractual Fund (CCF) regime (or consider recognizing any other regime proposed by an export-oriented financial centre) for use with Australian funds that were identified/designated as export-oriented funds. It could legislate to ensure that its courts recognized the regime (and possibly any precedents generated in Irish courts). It could also retain the right to modify some rule or precedent if it felt that it did not suit Australia's purposes.

The analysis here has also drawn attention to the limited benefits that dividend imputation offers foreigners (2006). Australia should explore the scope to make its tax regime friendlier to increased investment by foreign companies — the kind of companies that would be instrumental in making Australia a global financial centre. At some cost to revenue, it could give *bona fide* exporters of financial services (and at a greater cost to revenue it could give all firms) the choice between the existing corporate rate with dividend imputation or a lower rate — say 25 per cent.

An Export Culture in Government and Industry

Several industry leaders have expressed the view that to get good access to Asian markets, Australia must achieve higher recognition in those markets. And particularly in Asia, that means achieving higher profile representation. Accordingly, it is important for ministers of high ranking — sometimes the treasurer — to actively promote Australian financial service exports in Asia. Consideration should be given to the appointment of a minister assisting the treasurer with special responsibility for supervising the tax and regulatory arrangements for financial services exporters and for promoting Australia's financial service providers in offshore markets.

Given its size and potential, financial services should be accorded a higher priority in trade negotiations — particularly with Asian countries to which Australia might become a substantial exporter of fund management and fund management expertise (in the establishment of Asian countries' domestic financial service industries).

13. Conclusion: What Is at Stake

To summarize the "in principle" case made so far, it is surprising how little Australia exports financial services. Australia is a world leader in the management of pensions and sophisticated fund managers. New trends such as the move towards hedge funds have not taken long to take root in the Australian industry.

The sophistication of Australia's financial sector rivals any in the Pacific region, at a time of continuing high growth and growing prosperity in

Asia. China and India look bent on adding their combined population of over two billion more people to the list of prosperous people on earth — all closer to our time zone than the financial centres of Europe and the United States. In these circumstances the prospects for Australia's financial sector to export its services should be bright indeed. So far as a country, it has performed badly in this regard.

Where it is competing against city states in the region that have already made the transition from manufacturing to services entrepôts, the tax structure that Australia had five years ago may be a sufficient explanation for its poor performance. Indeed, if one were planning to locate substantial capacity to manage global funds on behalf of foreign investors in Australia, there remains the substantial risk of "sticky fingers" — that is, of taxation being taken not just from the profits of the fund manager and the pockets of its employees (as one would expect), but from the portfolios of foreign investors. Given the presence of vigorous competitors seeking to attract global fund managers, it is fairly clear to see why they would succeed at Australia's expense.

But Australia appears to be turning that culture around. Further study is necessary to be completely confident of this finding. It certainly seems plausible that Australia could become very successful in competing for global fund management of foreigners' money if investors felt as secure from Australian tax and regulatory obstacles to efficient management having their funds managed from Australia as they do having their funds managed from a competing financial entrepôt.

While Australia will not in the short term become the Dublin or Luxembourg of the Pacific, the prize for doing so over time is substantial. Some of the worlds' richest cities are financial entrepôts, and no financial centre is anything but wealthy. This is not surprising when one considers the remarkable fact that in Australia average incomes in the finance sector — including those employed part-time — are nearly twice the average paid in other industries.

However successful Australia is, its own financial exports will never become as large a share of our economy as they are in Dublin and Luxembourg. But then just some of their prosperity could make a large contribution. Figure 6.6 shows them both as the stand-out economic performers of Europe. Over the last twenty years they are the only countries to clearly outperform Australia's per capita growth within the OECD.

As the figure illustrates, both economies "took off" as they became financial entrepôts. Ireland's success is built on more than its financial

Figure 6.6
Per Capita Income per Year in Selected European Countries

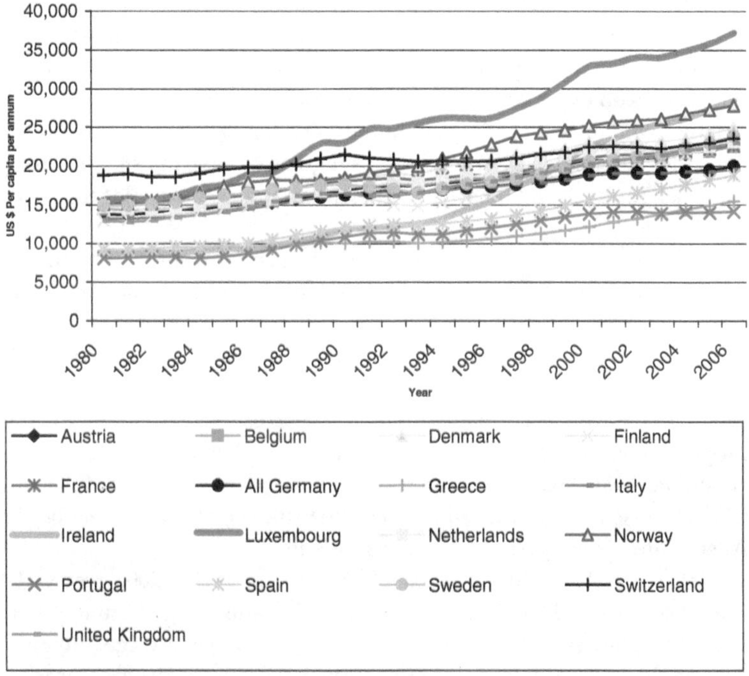

Source: Groningen Growth and Development Centre at <www.ggdc.net>.

sector. It has been successful in attracting other industries which have grown quickly. It has also pursued successful education policies and received unusually high subsidies from the EC for a time. But success in the financial sector is a huge part of Luxembourg's success, and no small part of Ireland's. Financial services comprise around a-third of Luxembourg's GDP and over 10 per cent of Ireland's.

Given current salaries, if Australia were able to lift the proportion of the economy accounted for by financial services from its current 7.8 per cent of GDP to Ireland's level of 10 per cent then at current rates of salary, average wages would rise by over A$600 per year.

Notes

1. It should be clear that the stark contrast between the government policy involved in driving superannuation and that involved in driving manufacturing means that there are contrasts as well as parallels in the policy issues involved in exporting — most particularly that compulsory superannuation poses no direct costs on exports, whereas trade protection does.
2. Lateral Economics Interviews with industry, January 2007.
3. A smaller advantage is that Australia's regulators have not shielded the public from hedge funds, as they have in Europe and America (Jacobs and Black, 2006).
4. Accessed at <http://www.axiss.gov.au/index.cfm?event=object.showcontent&objectid=B3E06210-D9D9-4294-55C7053DD55A3BF3> on 30 January 2007.
5. Tax Laws Amendment (2006 Measures No. 4) Bill 2006 was introduced into Parliament on 22 June 2006. This bill implements the government's 2005–06 budget announcement and has two main features. First, it narrows the range of assets on which a foreign resident is subject to Australian CGT to real property and the business assets (other than Australian real property) of Australian branches of a foreign resident. Second, the integrity of the narrower CGT tax base is strengthened by including rules covering indirect holdings of Australian real property by foreign residents.

   Tax Laws Amendment (2006 Measures No. 1) Act 2006 received Royal Assent on 6 April 2006. In part, this act implements the government's 2005–06 budget announcement to exempt from income tax the non-wage foreign income (and equivalent capital gains) of people here on temporary entry visas who are first-time tax residents of Australia for a period of four years.

   Tax Laws Amendment (Loss Recoupment Rules and Other Measures) Act 2005 received Royal Assent on 14 December 2005. In part, this act allows an Australian company that receives foreign income to pay dividends to foreign shareholders free of Australian tax.

   These details are excerpted from the Treasury's webpage updating the ongoing results from the Review of International Taxation Arrangements. Accessed on 1 January 2007 at <http://www.treasury.gov.au/content/int_tax_review.asp?ContentID=760&titl=Review%20of%20International%20Taxation%20Arrangements>.
6. Though the low corporate tax rate of 10 per cent was an important part of its success, it was an equally important part of the Irish strategy that it not be seen as a tax haven. This was not just to avoid friction with Brussels but also because throughout the world, countries' impose withholding taxes on income paid to foreigners — which taxes are reduced where reciprocal tax treaties exist. See for example, Jennings, John. "For Ireland's IFSC — The Road is Still

Rising to Meet It", 17 March 1997, National Underwriter Property & Casualty-Risk & Benefits Management Edition, accessed via Factiva.

7. Haggard makes a somewhat similar point about country size and the political economy of reform (1991, p. 30).
8. While these comments are made about tax, they would apply equally well to regulatory matters. Accessed on 30 January 2007 at <http://www.internationaltaxreview.com/includes/specialfeatures/PRINT.asp?SID=616508&ISS=21458&PUBID=224> (subscription required).
9. It is possible that regulatory compliance costs are as low as they are in France because of the preponderance of bond trusts in France.
10. When he visited Madagascar, Charles Darwin predicted that a moth of particular dimensions existed based on the size and shape of a flower he saw there. It was discovered forty years later.
11. The comparison with Delaware remains pertinent. "In the competition for corporate charters among U.S. states, the leading incorporation state, Delaware, engages in significant and continual legal innovation". Romano, "Law as a Product", p. 240.
12. Similarly, here is Anne Krueger describing the Koreans' "pragmatic" approach:

> [W]hen export performance was deemed satisfactory, policies were left unaltered; when however it appeared that export growth was faltering, changes were instituted until satisfactory performance was again observed.... The means chosen [to encourage exports] varied pragmatically in accordance with the degree of success then being achieved.... As those urged to export protested at various disabilities or disadvantages, means were found for removing such disadvantages; when exports lagged, new incentives were introduced or the value of existing incentives increased in order to spur export performance (1979, pp. 85, 92–94).

References

Adams, F., Gerard, Shachmurove, and Yochanan. "Trade and Development Patterns in the East Asian Economies", *Asian Economic Journal* 11, no. 4 (1997): 345–59.

Anthony Klein and Norah Seddon. "Australia as An Investment Location". *International Taxation Review* (July 2005). Accessed on 30 January 2007 at <http://www.internationaltaxreview.com/?Page=22&ISS=17502&SID=523293>.

Beinhocker, Eric D. *The Origin of Wealth: Evolution, Complexity, and the Radical Remaking of Economics*. Boston: Harvard Business School Press, 2006.

Charles Rivers Associates International (CRA). "Potential Cost Savings in a Fully Integrated European Investment Fund Market". By Wilsdon, Tim and Malcolm, Kyla. London, United Kingdom, Brussels, Belgium, 2006. Accessed 25 January at <http://ec.europa.eu/internal_market/securities/docs/ucits/expert-group/extstudies/finrep280906-1.pdf>. See also <http://ec.europa.eu/internal_market/securities/ucits/index_en.htm> more generally.

Deloitte. Study on the Future of the International Financial Services Sector in Ireland. IDA, September 2004. Available at <http://www.idaireland.com/uploads/documents/IDA_Publications/Deloitte_Report_on_International_Financial_Services_Industry.pdf>.

———. Study on the Future of the International Financial Services Sector in Ireland September 2004. Accessed 25 January 2007, at <http://www.finfacts.ie/biz10/Deloitte_Report_on_International_Financial_Services_Industry.pdf>.

Dugan, Kathy. "Tax-transparent Pooling: New Tools for Efficient Management". *International Investment and Securities Review* 2005. Accessed 25 January 2007 at <http://www-ac.northerntrust.com/content/media/attachment/data/article_reprint/document/euromoney_dugan_2005.pdf>.

European Commission Staff. Commission Staff Working Document Accompanying the White Paper on Enhancing the Single Market Framework for Investment Funds: Executive Summary to the Impact Assessment. Accessed at <http://ec.europa.eu/internal_market/securities/docs/ucits/whitepaper/executive_summary_en.pdf> on 24 January 2007.

Fiorino, Daniel, J. "Strategies for regulatory reform: forward compared to backward mapping". *Policy Studies Journal* 25, no. 2 (1997): 249–65.

Haggard, Stephan. *Pathways from the Periphery: The Politics of Growth in the Newly Industrializing Countries*. Ithaca, Cornell University Press, 1991.

IMF. *Luxembourg*: 2006 Article IV Consultation — Staff Report, accessed 30 January 2007 at <http://www.imf.org/external/pubs/ft/scr/2006/cr06164.pdf>.

Jacobs, David and Susan Black. "Recent Developments in the Australian Hedge Fund Industry". *Reserve Bank Bulletin*, November. Accessed on 31 January 2007 at <http://www.rba.gov.au/PublicationsAndResearch/Bulletin/bu_nov06/rec_dev_aus_hedge_fund_ind.html#f1>.

Kahan, Marcel. "The Demand for Corporate Law: Statutory Flexibility, Judicial Quality, or Takeover Protection?". *Journal of Law, Economics, & Organization* 22, no. 2 (2006): 340–65.

Kenen, P.B., ed. *International Trade and Finance: Frontiers for Research*. Cambridge University Press, Cambridge, 1975.

Krueger, A.O. *The Developmental Role of the Foreign Sector and Aid*. Cambridge, Mass: Harvard University Press, 1979.

Lateral Economics. "Tax Cuts to Compete", CEDA Information Paper No. 85, 2006. <http://www.lateraleconomics.com.au/outputs/CEDA%20Tax%20cuts%20to%20compete.pdf>.

Nonnenkam, Samantha. "Luxembourg: Vehicle for private wealth management introduced, International Tax Review, December 2006 – January 2007,

Luxembourg. Accessed 30 January 2007 at http://www.internationaltaxreview.com/Default.asp?Page=10&PUBID=35&ISS=23172&SID=668631&TYPE=20>.

Power, Deirdre. *The Irish Solution to the Asset Pooling Dilemma*, Deloitte. Accessed 25 January 2005, at <http://www.internationaltaxreview.com/?Page=22&PUBID=224&ISS=14555&SID=496589&SM=&SearchStr=CCFs>.

Regulation Taskforce. *Rethinking Regulation: Report of the Taskforce on Reducing Regulatory Burdens on Business*. Report to the Prime Minister and the Treasurer, Canberra, January 2006.

Romano, Roberta. "Law as a Product: Some Pieces of the Incorporation Puzzle". *Journal of Law and Economic Organisation* (1985): 225–83.

———. *The Genius of American Corporate Law*. Washington, D.C.: AEI Press, 1993.

———. *The Advantage of Competitive Federalism for Securities Regulation*. Washington, D.C.: AEI Press, 2002.

Rossi, Jim. "Book Review: *Bargaining in the Shadow of Regulation: Regulatory Bargaining and Public Law*". Cambridge University Press, 2005. Accessed at <http://www.abanet.org/antitrust/at-source/05/09/Sep05-TomainRev9=27.pdf> on 24 January 2007.

Victorian Government. The Victorian Government's Action Plan for the Financial Services Industry, Melbourne. Accessed 25 January 2007 at <http://www.diird.vic.gov.au/corplivewr/_assets/main/lib60046/financial_services_industryplan.pdf>.

Williamson, Oliver E. "Credible Commitments: Using Hostages to Support Exchange". *American Economic Review* 73 (1983): 519–40. Accessed 1 February 2007 at <http://links.jstor.org/sici?sici=0002-8282%28198309%2973%3A4%3C519%3ACCUHTS%3E2.0.CO%3B2-J>.

7

BUILDING THE SHANGHAI INTERNATIONAL FINANCIAL CENTRE
Strategic Target, Challenges and Opportunities

Xu Mingqi

When Deng Xiao Ping made his inspection tour of Southern China in 1991 he pointed out to Shanghai officials that Shanghai had been an important international financial centre where currency had been convertible. He hoped Shanghai could regain its financial centre status in the future. The following year, the Communist Party of China (CPC) Fourteenth Congress made a resolution to build Shanghai into an international financial centre and stressed that it would be the national strategy to do so. Since then, fifteen years have passed, and the questions now are: What has been achieved and what is the specific target of Shanghai as an international financial centre? This chapter will try to discuss these issues and provide a clear view of Shanghai as an international financial centre.

1. STRATEGIC TARGET EVOLUTION OF THE SHANGHAI INTERNATIONAL FINANCIAL CENTRE

Although the strategy to build Shanghai into an international financial centre was set as early as 1992, the concrete target and when and how to achieve the target was not clear in the early days and is yet still gradually evolving. Table 7.1 gives a chronological view of the events that are gradually shaping the strategic targets of the Shanghai international financial centre.

From Table 7.1, it can be seen that the strategic target of a Shanghai international financial centre is gradually becoming concrete and clear. By now Shanghai is already the most important financial centre in China, and basic elements for a financial centre have been already established. According to the Eleventh Five-year Plan, the overall construction of a Shanghai international financial centre can be divided into three stages. The first stage is to set up and consolidate the national financial centre status. The second stage is to become an Asian regional financial centre, and the third stage is to emerge as a global financial centre.

As Table 7.2 shows, from 1992 to 2001, the first stage target was fulfilled, and Shanghai has already emerged as the most important domestic financial centre in China. The market foundation has been improved step by step. Now it is in the second stage of becoming an Asian regional financial centre.

Up to now, Beijing, Tianjin and Shenzhen have all proclaimed their intentions to develop into a financial centre in China, bringing about competition among these cities that want to be financial centres. This kind of competitions is good to some extent. Because China is a big country, differences between regions are comparatively big. For this reason, there is room for some cities to emerge as regional financial centres. For instance, Beijing is the political centre and headquarters of state financial institutions. It could be the financial policy centre of China but not necessarily the business transaction centre before the headquarters of state financial institutions could move to other cities. Statistics shows that the added value created by the financial industry was RMB112.6 billion and 12.5 per cent of total GDP of Beijing in 2007. The value was a bit lower than RMB120.9 billion of Shanghai, but the share of GDP was higher than 9.9 per cent of Shanghai. However, if those headquarters' profits surrendered by their branches and subsidiaries were deducted, its real financial activities are far behind. So there could be room for further development of the financial industry in Beijing. Recently, the Beijing municipal government formulated a blueprint of financial sector development. It seems to have quietly dropped the target to compete with Shanghai to develop into an international financial

Table 7.1
Strategic Evolution of the Shanghai International Financial Centre

1991	In early 1991, Deng Xiaoping put forward the idea to build Shanghai into an international centre as he said: "Shanghai was the financial centre in the past and was the place where currency was convertible. In the future Shanghai should still be the same."
1992	CPC 14th Congress adopted the strategy of building Shanghai into a Dragon Head and Three Centres (International Economic Centre, International Financial Centre and International Trade Centre)
1994	In April 1994, Central Government set up the unified Foreign Exchange Trading Centre in Shanghai, and in 1996, the Shanghai inter-bank loan centre was also set up in Shanghai.
2001	State Council approved the municipal development plan of Shanghai, and the International Economic Centre, International Financial Centre, International Trade Centre and Sea Transportation Centre plans were reiterated.
2001	Shanghai municipal government made a blueprint of the Tenth Five Year Plan in which is contained a section on building Shanghai into an International Centre.
2002	Shanghai municipal government puts forward a target of Four Basic Implementations to realize the Four Centres, and preferable policy was adopted by Shanghai towards financial institutions setting up branches and subsidiaries in Shanghai.
2004	Shanghai municipal government announced the Action Plan to Promote a Shanghai International Financial Centre. A strategy target of five years for foundation building, ten years for framework construction and twenty years to achieve the basic aim was formulated.
2005	Pudong New Area district government announced the Action Plan for 2005–2007 Modern Service Industry Development in which it put forward a concrete target to have 450 financial institutions in Pudong by the end of 2007. In the same year, the state council approved Pudong as one of three trial areas for comprehensive reforms and the financial centre function was reiterated.
2005	POC, China's central bank set up its second headquarters in Shanghai
2005	MNCs in Pudong were allowed to carry out the reform of autonomous handling of their foreign exchange funds.
2006	Shanghai municipal government announced the blueprint of the Eleventh Five Year Plan of Building a Shanghai international financial centre.

Source: Compiled by author according to chronological events in China concerning the Shanghai financial centre.

Table 7.2
Financial Market Element Concentration in Shanghai since 1990

Marketplace	Content	Founding Year	Status or scale
Shanghai Securities Exchange	Main capital market (equity, bonds)	1990	80% of total trading turnover of China
Foreign exchange trading centre	Foreign exchange	1994	Head office of national trading market
Inter-bank loan centre	Money market	1996	National centre for interbank trading
RMB bond trading centre	Money market	1997	National centre for bond trading
Shanghai Futures Exchange	Rubber, copper aluminum and fuel oil	1999	60% of futures trading volume of all China
Shanghai Gold Exchange	Gold market	2002	The only gold market
Note market service centre	Provide note transaction information and service	2003	Principal note pricing system in China
Shanghai petroleum market	Futures transactions	2006	The only petroleum futures market in China
China Financial Futures Exchange	Financial derivatives transactions	2006	The only derivative market in China

Source: Compiled by author.

centre. Instead, it defined the aim of its financial sector development as that of a financial centre city with international influence.

As for Tianjin, although it is still trying hard to develop its financial sector and wants to emerge as a financial centre in the northern part of China, it has become aware that it is not going to compete with Shanghai to become an international centre. It will probably concentrate on over the counter (OTC) business and private equity (PE) and some other corporate financial activities. Its target is to develop the financial sector's added value to 6 per cent of Tianjin's GDP by 2010. It can therefore be seen that Tianjin will have some competition with Beijing to see which will become the most important financial centre in the northern part of China.

Shenzhen is a financial centre in the southern part of China. Its securities market is an important part of China's stock market although its volume is only 20 per cent of the total capital. In May 2004, the second board of the stock market for small- and medium-sized enterprises' (SMEs) fund-raising was opened in Shenzhen. This gives Shenzhen strength as a financial market. Financial institutions are concentrated in Shenzhen just next to Shanghai. It has also the advantage of being adjacent to Hong Kong, which provides more business opportunites. However, this advantage also becomes a constraint for its future development into an important international financial centre, as Hong Kong will overshadow Shenzhen for a rather long time.

2. THE OBSTACLES AND CHALLENGES SHANGHAI FACES

There are a lot of comparative advantages and policy preferences for Shanghai to emerge as an international financial centre. Shanghai is the biggest economic metropolis and culturally the most open city in China, as it was historically the biggest foreign concession city before the Communist Party took power in China. It has a long history of international trade and finance and was the biggest city in the Far East in the 1930s. It is situated at the mouth of the Yangtze River and connects directly to the most developed Yangtze River Delta area. Until now, Shanghai port has handled one-fourth of China's international trade and contributes about 15 per cent of the fiscal revenue of all of China. It is believed that these elements are the reasons that the Chinese government have made the building of Shanghai into an international financial centre a national strategy. As China is growing, with its aggregate economy ranking fourth in the world, its financial strength is also becoming one of the largest in the world. With this background, Shanghai is bound to play an important role in China's financial system, representing China in competition with other countries' international financial markets, and it will inevitably become an important financial centre in the Asia-Pacific region in the future.

However, the Shanghai international financial centre is facing a lot of challenges, and there are still some obstacles ahead.

The first challenge — administrative control and the lack of market mechanism in financial resources allocation — has made it difficult for the financial centre to fulfil its function full-scale. The Chinese financial system is still undergoing market-oriented reform and, comparatively speaking, the financial sector is lagging behind the other sector reforms. China continues to maintain a strong government control over financial activities and transactions. State-owned commercial banks allocate credit not just according to market principles. Government orientation still plays a role in making loans. The Big Four Banks are vertically organized according to administrative layers and managed according to each branch's administrative ranking. Thus cross-regional flow of funds and capital are limited. Even after three of the Big Four Banks were listed on the capital market and invested in by foreign strategic investors, their operation mechanisms still remain almost the same. Capital market IPOs and re-issuance of shares by listed companies are controlled directly by the China Securities Regulatory Commission. Under these malfunctioning financial market conditions, the financial centre can only play a very limited role in resource allocation, and its function as the hub of funds accumulation and channelling is limited. This is the most important reason that many people believe Beijing is a more important financial centre in China than Shanghai. The headquarters of the Big Four state banks are located in Beijing and all headquarters of regulatory commissions and important securities companies are located in Beijing as well. Beijing has been the centre of administrative financial resource allocation in China until now. All of this leads to some unhealthy competition among the big Chinese cities for the status of international financial centre. Not only Beijing, but cities such as Tianjin, Shenzhen, and even Dalian, Guangzhou have put forward blueprints to be international financial centres and asked for preferential policy treatment from the central government because people still believe that administrative measures and policy undertakings will deliver the things that a financial centre needs most. In fact, the market mechanism in financial resource allocation is the most important thing for a city with a comparative advantage to emerge into a financial centre. So further financial system reform and market mechanism improvement are the most important conditions for Shanghai's international financial centre status.

The second challenge is that the low degree of internationalization of the local financial markets prevents Shanghai from having much influence in the Asia-Pacific region. Although Shanghai is the most important financial centre in China, and the market volume of some financial activities is big enough to compete with other financial centres in the region, Shanghai has little direct influence on other markets. For instance, by the end of September 2007, capitalization of listed companies on the Shanghai Securities Exchange exceeded RMB19.5 trillion, which was bigger than that of Hong Kong. It is already the sixth largest securities exchange in the world. Banks in Shanghai held RMB2.5 trillion deposits, and their stock of loans was RMB1.8 trillion by the end of June 2007. Shanghai's share of deposits and loans for the whole of China is 10 per cent and 7 per cent, respectively, and is considerably higher than that of other regions and cities. Total insurance premiums in Shanghai are also much higher with RMB40.7 billion in 2006, ranking fourth in China.[1] However, the impressive scale of financial transactions in Shanghai is mainly achieved domestically with little international impact. The most important reason for this is the capital account control and limited convertibility of the Chinese renminbi (RMB).

Rather strict nominal control measures constrain cross-border financial transactions and capital flows. If a financial market cannot accumulate capital worldwide and channel funds to where they are needed most worldwide, or at least in the Asia-Pacific region, it would be hard to say it is an internationalized market. This is the main reason for the weakness of Shanghai as an international financial centre in comparison with many other Asia-Pacific cities trying also to become international financial centres. Right now, there are 100 foreign banks operating in Shanghai. The absolute number is not small compared to many other cities in the region, but the assets owned by foreign banks only make up 14 per cent of total bank assets in Shanghai. This ratio is 69 per cent in New York and 50 per cent in London. The foreign bank assets share in total bank assets in Singapore is 75 per cent.[2] So the role played by foreign banks is quite different and we see the gap between Shanghai and other important international financial centres. Another example is that the Shanghai Securities Exchange is already the sixth largest in the world in terms of listed companies' capitalization volume. It has already reached some RMB19 trillion as it has grown rapidly since last year and capitalization value has doubled. Yet there is no foreign company listed on the exchange, and it is not yet open fully to foreign investors. This makes the Shanghai Securities Exchange a closed market with very limited influence on the world capital markets. Shanghai's capital market only passively absorbs external shocks at present. The last, but not least, example is the foreign exchange market. Daily trading volume of important international financial centres is very impressive. London is US$1.2 trillion. New York is US$565 billion. Singapore and Tokyo are all more than US$200 billion. Shanghai is the centre for foreign exchange transactions in China, but the daily turnover is only US$4.4 billion. Without opening the market to foreign financial institutions, the market has very limited international influence. Hence, internationalization is the most important element that Shanghai needs to develop into an international financial centre. Thus, speeding up the pace of capital account liberalization and the renminbi's full convertibility would be the most important step for building Shanghai into an international financial centre.[3]

The third challenge is the need to improve the legal system and other soft infrastructure to host international financial transactions. To have only the willingness and hope to become an international financial centre and trying to enjoy the benefits of being an international financial centre is not the way to move ahead. Sufficient infrastructure from hard to soft is required. Shanghai has been trying hard to construct enough hard infrastructure, from building first-class office space, to transportation and telecommunication facilities. However, in terms of soft infrastructure, it is not yet good enough to attract international financial transactions to be initiated and carried out in Shanghai. Usually, international banks will initiate a cross-border transaction in Shanghai and move to Hong Kong or Singapore to execute it with the contract governed by Anglo-Saxon legal terms. If Shanghai cannot establish suitable legal frameworks for international finance and implement them strictly in practice, it will be difficult for Shanghai to emerge as an international financial centre. Broadly speaking, a well-established culture of credit worthiness and legal structures of international standard are more important infrastructures for an international financial centre. In this regard, having only Shanghai municipal government's efforts is far from adequate. It needs central government efforts as well as the whole nation's efforts.

Some seemingly less important elements also need to be improved, such as human resources, business costs and government service efficiency. Shanghai is considered the primary pool for national human resources, and many talented people work in Shanghai. Multinational financial institutions will not find it very difficult to find their middle management employees in the local labour market. But high-ranking managers are usually in short supply and need to be found in the international market. This sometimes leads to extra costs for newcomers to Shanghai. China needs to enhance its own educational system and improve policies to attract overseas Chinese university graduates in the Western countries to come back and work in the Shanghai financial centre. However, the quantity of English-speaking qualified young graduates in Shanghai is not enough, and foreign financial institutions are complaining of not having enough qualified employees. As for those returning from abroad, *Hukou* (resident registration) and some other domestic problems, such as international travelling documents, their children's education, etc. also become obstacles to their settling in Shanghai. So there is much room for improvement in this regard.

As for escalating business costs, Shanghai is also meeting big challenges. Real estate price hikes and rising rents have driven Shanghai's business costs already to a world metropolitan level. The comparative advantage of low labour cost is diminishing. Government on the whole is supportive and friendly towards foreign investment, but bureaucratic measures are sometimes very annoying and are regarded by foreign institutions as an extra cost of doing business. If Shanghai is to compete with other cities in the region as an international financial centre, it must solve these problems as soon as possible. Otherwise, it may lose its comparative advantage and momentum as the candidate with the most potential to become an international financial centre in the Asia-Pacific region.

3. FUTURE MEASURES OF THE CHINESE CENTRAL AND SHANGHAI GOVERNMENTS

Consensus has been gradually reached among central government officials and the Shanghai government. All are aware that building the Shanghai international financial centre is the national strategy, and neither the Shanghai government nor the central government efforts alone will be enough. Both levels of effort and policy orientation need to go together. Recently, the Shanghai municipal government set up the Leadership Committee of Shanghai International Financial Centre. Members of the committee are mostly the heads of state financial regulatory commissions, from China Securities Regulatory Commission (CSRC), China Insurance Regulatory Commission (CIRC), China Banking Regulatory Commission (CBRC) to People's Bank of China (PBOC) with two Beijing-based think-tank leaders. The Shanghai mayor is the Chair. This committee is aimed at mobilizing all efforts from Beijing and Shanghai to promote the Shanghai

International Financial Centre. This move shows clearly the awareness of the importance of Beijing's support by the Shanghai municipal government. Hopefully, the committee will make a real contribution toward this end. In his recent inspection of Shanghai, Premier Wen Jiabao reassured the city of central government support to build Shanghai into an international financial centre and promised to give full policy backing. He urged Shanghai officials to work hard to realize the target of Four Centres, especially the international financial centre.

The Shanghai municipal government has gradually realized that the biggest obstacle in becoming an international financial centre is the lack of market mechanisms and financial market internationalization in China. The Shanghai financial centre could not become an international centre without real progress in these key aspects. So now the Shanghai government is trying hard to move in the right direction. In the previous plans drawn up by the Shanghai government, most of the efforts were put on infrastructure building and pure market scale enlargement. For instance, in the Eleventh Five-year Plan for Shanghai Financial Centre Development, one of the targets is that the capitalization volume of listed companies on the Shanghai Securities Exchange is to reach RMB7 trillion by the end of 2010. By the middle of 2007, this volume already exceeded RMB19 trillion. So even if all the targets set forth in the Eleventh Five-year Plan are fulfilled by the end of 2010, nobody can really be sure that Shanghai would be an international financial centre by then. The following targets were drawn in the Eleventh Five-year Plan, but the key indicators of market mechanism and internationalization were carefully avoided (see Table 7.3). The reason for this omission is clear. Reform and policy measures in further marketization and internationalization are not in the hands of the municipal government, and Shanghai cannot really take such initiatives on its own.

With reiterated support from Premier Wen Jiabao and central government officials, the Shanghai municipal government realized the important elements necessary for an international financial centre and tried to revise the Eleventh Five-year Plan. At present, new plans are being drafted and think-tanks such as the Institute of World Economy in Shanghai are involved in the policy recommendations. It is forseeable that China's financial market is going to open more widely and quickly so as to meet new challenges in international market conditions. In the process of opening and liberalizing Chinese capital markets, the speed of Shanghai's emergence as an international financial centre is going to accelerate.

Table 7.3
Main Targets in the Eleventh Five-year Plan for Building the Shanghai Financial Centre

Indicators linked with market volume	Indicators of financial institutions business scale
Direct financial transactions reach 25% of all China	Assets of financial institutions are 10% of all China financial institutions.
Total financial transactions reach RMB80 trillion	Deposits stock value reaches RMB4.5 trillion
Money market trade volume reachesRMB40 trillion	Loan stock value made by Shanghai Banks reaches RMB3.2 trillion
Shanghai Securities Exchange listed companies worth RMB7 trillion	Commercial entities acceptance ratio on credit cards reaches 70% and above
Shanghai Futures Exchange enters the top ten ranks of world futures exchanges	Card usage in consumption reaches 40% or above
Shanghai gold market becomes one of the important international gold markets	Insurance deepening ratio reaches 5% (insurance premium/GDP)
Non-listed equity market in Shanghai become nationwide market	Insurance density ratio (insured value per capita) reaches RMB4,000

Source: Shanghai Municipal Government Eleventh Five-year Plan for Building Shanghai International Financial Centre.

There are many plans and policy measures that are under discussion and will be undertaken in the future in building Shanghai into an international financial centre, especially those promoting internationalization of the Shanghai financial market. For confidentiality reasons, the timing of the proposed policy measures cannot be discussed. However, they are under discussion and hopefully will be adopted in the future.

The first measure is further opening the Shanghai securities market to both investors and fund-raisers. Until now, only China's B shares were open to foreign investors and through Qualified Foreign Institutional Investor (QFII). No foreign companies are yet allowed to be listed in either the Shanghai Securities Exchange or the Shenzhen Securities Exchange. In the future, the number of QFII will be expanded and more investment volume will be granted to them. Certain special investment funds will be allowed to invest in China's stock. More importantly, foreign companies will be allowed to list on the Shanghai Securities Exchange. By doing so, the Shanghai capital market will enter a real stage of internationalization.

Secondly, foreign government entities and international organizations will be allowed to issue bonds and other debt in Shanghai. Some big companies are in discussions to be allowed to issue bonds in Shanghai either denominated in renminbi or foreign currencies.

Thirdly, some foreign securities companies will be granted licences to provide intermediary services to Chinese portfolio investment abroad. Of course, foreign companies' entry to domestic intermediate or underwriting businesses will still be under some control in the near future.

The fourth measure is to expand the scope of QFII and allow domestic citizens to invest in foreign financial assets directly. Opening to the Hong Kong stock market is the first step. In the future, channels to invest in the U.S. or European market will also be introduced. By doing so, Shanghai financial markets will play a more important role in providing services to channel investment.

The fifth measure is to unify the A and B share markets and allow B shareholders to convert to A shareholders so as to open the A share market to foreign investors. Of course, this is only a proposal at present, and while the principle may stand, the way to handle it could be very different in the future. However, under the process of opening the financial markets, the problem of the separation of A and B share markets will be solved sooner or later. If this measure is adopted, as the biggest capital market in China, the Shanghai Securities Exchange will become competitive in the East Asian region in terms of scale and liquidity.

Sixth, in the process of the renminbi (RMB) currency's full convertibility, Shanghai will be the hub of RMB-denominated transactions. China is going to promote more RMB-denominated transactions in international trade, and banks in Shanghai will be asked to conduct RMB clearing and settlement for foreign trade transactions. If the internationalization of the RMB develops together with RMB's full convertibility, more financial transactions denominated in RMB will take place. Then Shanghai will have the potential to be the ideal place to centre all the pricing and clearing.

Seventh, open the Shanghai Foreign Exchange Trading Centre to more foreign financial institutions. Until now, only Chinese financial institutions and foreign subsidiaries registered in China have been allowed to execute transactions in the market. In the future, foreign entities with equivalent accounts in China will be allowed to enter the market. By doing so, the Shanghai foreign exchange market will get onto the real international market stage and will join the integrated world foreign exchange market. Of course, this may not be happen in the near future as the process of lifting all measures of foreign exchange control is gradual and the RMB's full convertibility is only progressing gradually.

And the last but not least measure is to improve infrastructure especially the so-called soft infrastructure. This includes improvement of the legal system and implementation of all regulations and laws, building a culture of credit worthiness by establishing a regionwide credit record for all economic entities and every citizen, and creating suitable living and working conditions for foreign financial institutions and their employees. The Shanghai municipal government and Pudong government are trying to introduce some local legislation and regulation according to international standards concerning financial contracts and implementation of contracts. The central government has already granted Pudong comprehensive reform rights to meet international standards. The "Yangtze Delta regional credit worth net" is under construction and will cover all entities' and individuals' credit record for fifteen cities in the region. It will provide inquiry services to goodwill customers. Regarding business cost control, the Shanghai municipal government is trying cut licensing procedures as much as possible to reduce costs connected with administrative measures. For other costs, such as rent and labour, the government cannot do anything directly. But lowering the income tax and other fees is under discussion. For transportation costs and enhancing the convenience of international travel, the Shanghai municipal government is also in discussions with central government departments to find a way to resolve some of the inconvenience.

On the whole, Shanghai is marching in the right direction to becoming an international financial centre. Right now, Shanghai is not yet an international financial centre and has not really joined the competition with other cities in the Asia-Pacific region, but its potential is enormous. It is because of this enormous potential that the pressure is on for other financial centres in the region. Right now only Hong Kong enjoys the status of international financial centre in China. Most of the financial flows in and out of China mainly pass through Hong Kong. Even before the Chinese RMB realizes full convertibility, Hong Kong will serve as offshore transactions centre of the RMB. So in the short run, Shanghai will not pose real competition to Hong Kong as an international financial centre. Shanghai and Hong Kong will complement to each other in financial functions. The former will act mainly as an "inward" influential financial centre with foreign institutions investing into China in the near future. Hong Kong will serve as an "outward" financial flow centre for China's external investment. However, by 2020, Shanghai could become one of the most important financial centres in this region and will really challenge other cities in Asia-Pacific including Hong Kong.

Notes

1. Statistics data are form Shanghai and China Statistics Bureaus.
2. New York data came from Nolan Murray. "Deposit growth in New York Bank Branches 2000–2005", 2005 and Federal Reserve website; London data was from <http://www. ifsl.org.uk/research/news.cfm>; Singapore data was from <http://www.mas.gov.sg/fi_directory/index.html>.
3. Foreign exchange data here are from: <www.sse.com.cn>; <http://business.timesonline.co.uk>; <http://asia.news.yahoo.com/070726/kyodo/d8qk8a2g1.html>; <http://www.euronext.com/fic/000/023/906/239063.pdf>.

8

THE KIWI THAT HAD TO FLY
Path Dependence and Evolutionary Niches among International Finance Centres

Roger J. Bowden

1. INTRODUCTION

Why should some small countries end up batting well out of their league in international capital markets? In some cases this might be due to location at geographical trading hubs, or from geopolitical accidents of history. In others it might arise from endowments of nature, most notably in the form of oil or gas reserves and the markets that grow up on the back of oil trading. Such cases may also feature what economists and political scientists call "path dependence", or "history matters", the idea that an outcome is going to be very dependent on the precise historical path taken to get there.[1] In the case of New Zealand, it could be said to arise because it has a rather odd and chronically unbalanced economy, that has in part arisen because of particular policy decisions or philosophies, most notably those concerning capital market deregulation, monetary policy, and to some extent, tax regimes. Natural endowments are also important, in this case of an equable climate and fertile volcanic soils, exploited by an extremely efficient farming sector; together with outstanding scenic features that underpin a growing tourism trade.

The combination has created a demand for capital that feeds heavily off the rest of the world, which in turn has projected Wellington into the international spotlight as the financial intermediary centre that facilitates the capital flows involved. In terms of the sort of capital markets that the man in the street might think about, such as the stock market, Wellington rates as no more than a small regional centre. Naturally we hope that will change, for one can always substitute cleverness for size and Kiwis have been remarkably innovative in creating trading and clearing platforms and the technology to drive them. But the flows in question are much larger than that. They originate in Japan and Europe and they end up financing the sort of spending and borrowing habits that calvinistic preachers used to think would consign us all to perdition. As it happens, they are unlikely to be proved right, because the economy can sustain our bad habits. The N.Z. economy is stronger than at any time since the Korean War, and looks set to become even stronger.[2] But it will continue to suffer from the problem of structural instability. Paradoxically, it is this that makes New Zealand of interest to world capital markets, for it creates an offshore market in high coupon debt instruments, together with the currency trading and derivatives necessary to support it.

The scheme of this chapter is as follows. Section 2 is an introductory background, setting out the scope of N.Z. capital markets, a menu that covers all the standard things — equities, debt, derivatives, and currency, a reasonably complete package if not a large one. The particular menu is not of central importance in the present context, but it is useful background for things that are. Monetary policy has central relevance for the way that our markets operate and this is also covered. Section 3 turns to the economic background. The objective is not to survey the economy as a whole, but to explain the origins of the structural imbalances that have such profound implications for the financial markets. Section 4 turns to the things that do stake out a claim for Wellington to be a world capital market, namely the attractions of N.Z. dollar denominated debt in Europe and Asia, and the swap trade that builds on the back. Section 5 comments on perspectives of regional competition and cooperation. It also adds something that might otherwise be forgotten in a discussion of this kind: the importance of human capital as a complement to financial capital. Whatever New

Zealand's macroeconomic sins might be, they are expiated by the skills of the people who work and trade in its capital markets, which have become a resource for the world at large. Section 5 concludes with some miscellaneous complements such as the time zone factor.

2. THE NEW ZEALAND CAPITAL MARKET: BACKGROUND

A little general information about the N.Z. capital markets may be useful at the outset, not because it is of any special importance for the current enquiry, but because it will help in understanding some of the historical background to subsequent developments that have assumed more centre stage. More detail can be found in the comprehensive survey in Bowden and Zhu (2005).[3]

2.1. Equity Markets

Most people, when asked to think of a capital market, would probably think of the stock market. New Zealand does have its own organized stock market, as freely functioning as normal and proper prudential processes will permit it to be. The New Zealand Stock Exchange (NZX) demutualized in early 2003, and is now run by NZX Ltd, which is a listed public company on the exchange itself. Headquarters are in Wellington, appropriately enough in a former woolshed on the waterfront, though much of the trading also takes place from Auckland offices of brokers and other registered traders. Its monopoly status as the only registered stock exchange is based in formal legislation, namely the Securities Market Act 1988, which at the same time formalized the status of the N.Z. Securities Commission as the official watchdog over the exchange and of the conduct of N.Z. securities markets in general. The rules of the exchange, called "participant rules", govern the conduct of listed companies as well as the trading process, and are established with supervisory oversight by the securities commission. They govern such things as share buy-backs, which must be offered publicly on the exchange in the first instance. The exchange operates an automated screen trading system called FASTER. In fact, the precursor N.Z. stock exchange (NZX) was one of the first countries in the world to introduce automated screen trading, originated over the years between 1988 and 1992. The innovative tradition has continued. At times it gets a bit cheeky: Recently the NZX has applied to set up an electronic network to record large off-market crosses in the Australian stock market, to the displeasure of the Australian Stock Exchange (ASX), who are finding out that preaching competition is one thing, but suffering it is another. The N.Z. stock exchange offers a number of equity derivatives or related products, such as warrants, options, convertible notes and trust or fund units, including equity options in conjunction with the Sydney Futures Exchange. It also operates an associated debt trading board for bonds, debentures and capital notes. Finally the NZX publishes the official stock price indices, notably the NZSX-50, which is the free-float based index most often used as a market barometer. It also runs a numbers of other index services, covering also commodities and other prices of importance for economic activity. A recent introduction is an index for the fixed side of interest rate swaps.

The N.Z. stock market was materially broadened by a number of privatizations of public enterprises, mostly in the late 1980s and early 1990s. These include utilities such as Telecom, two major airports, electricity and gas retailers, and Air New Zealand, as well as more exotic assets such as natural gas supply contracts, forestry cutting rights or on the debt side, state housing mortgages. Much of this equity soon disappeared, being taken over and absorbed, or in one or two cases collapsing, but some still remain wholly or partly in the public domain. About a dozen of the larger N.Z. companies are also quoted on the Australian Stock Exchange, and one or two on U.S. exchanges via the ADR (American Depository Receipts) market. There is appreciable foreign ownership of N.Z. stocks, with many larger companies majority owned offshore, extending to derived ownership of formerly public assets like forests. There is scrutiny of outright control of N.Z. domiciled companies by the Overseas Investment Office, formerly known as the Overseas Investment Commission, which does have the power to decline applications where it is judged that no economic benefit will accrue or on general national interest grounds. In practice, this has not been much of a constraint on foreign takeovers or majority control. The desired openness of our own capital markets represents a natural symmetry with outward capital movements. In this respect, most N.Z. funds have extensive holdings of offshore shares in response to both the limited availability of well traded local scrip and natural portfolio diversification. The N.Z. economy is a heavily cyclical one and international diversification protects against adverse states of the local economy, as well as to industrial sectors that are not well represented in the domestic economy. The industrial coverage of the N.Z. equity regimen is a bit sketchy, with little representation from growth sectors such as pharmaceuticals, electronics, or Internet software. To be sure, Kiwis are an innovative breed, and we have had some very successful developments along such lines: Smith Glaxo Kline originated from a N.Z. company, and more recent examples include Trade Me, a very popular online auction system along the lines of eBay, and Rakon, which makes silicon wafers. But such developments tend either to end up absorbed in offshore companies, or as private equity and therefore unavailable to general investors. As a result, the traded N.Z. stocks have a reputation of being more of the nature of cash cows, with a P/E ratio for the indexes only about half those of the corresponding U.S. indexes. This is not entirely a matter of growth prospects, for New Zealand also has a dividend imputation tax regime, under which corporate tax can be credited against personal tax on dividends, meaning that dividends are in effect taxed only once rather than twice as in the United States (the so called double taxation of dividends). There is less of an incentive to retain earnings as a tax shield.

Private equity plays a much larger role in New Zealand than one commonly finds in other countries. By this is meant not private equity funds, though New Zealand do have some such funds, but extensive ownership of assets that are traded only by private treaty. Of these, by far the most important is real estate, covering commercial, rural and housing. This is partly because in the commodity industries that drive New Zealand's economy, notably farming and horticulture, family ownership is predominant.[4] But in addition, New Zealanders have a love affair with home ownership, which as an investment class has been superior to company shares, especially once all sources of rewards are factored in including owner-occupied imputed rental. Unsurprisingly, this has lead to extensive investment in rental property, just as in Australia. New Zealand has one of the highest rates of home ownership in the world; the rate has only been dropping recently because of price competition from landlords buying to rent. The dispossession of young people from home ownership has caused some disquiet, and it has been mooted that the government should step in to control speculative housing, either by disallowing tax loss offset against other income or by introducing a capital gains tax. Neither looks likely to happen in the near future.

Indeed there is even more of a real estate motive in New Zealand, because of the absence of a capital gains tax, apart from short-term trading activities (when the investor is reclassified as a "trader"). By way of contrast, investments in most managed funds, such as equity or fixed interest products, incur corporation tax on all sources of income, including capital gains. The incentive is therefore to roll your own investment rather than employ a fund manager, for individual investors in shares do escape capital gains tax. Funds do enjoy economies of scale from which small investors can benefit, obtaining diversification access to many more stocks or assets than they could hope to on their own account. Rightly or wrongly, most people would like to think that fund managers have superior informational or expertise in selectivity or market timing, and there is some evidence to suggest that some N.Z. fund managers do have it.[5] Thus fund investment has grown in recent years, even if not quite as pervasively as in the United Kingdom or the United States, and recent government savings initiatives will create a taxation incentive for people to lock away savings in managed funds, which will be good for the sector. However it must still be said that a lack of confidence in their own trading abilities, or of faith in company management following some well-known historical debacles, drives NZ investors away from the equity market into the property market as the investment of first choice.

2.2. Debt Markets

Turning to the debt markets, New Zealand has a range of interest rate instruments with maturities dating out to about ten to twelve years. In major capital markets such as the United Kingdom or the United States the latter would be regarded as at most intermediate maturities. In that sense, New Zealand does not have long-dated bonds. Recent attempts by the author to induce the Treasury to issue long bonds under the name of "infrastructure bonds" to underpin retirement instruments,[6] did not bear fruit: Treasury promptly expropriated the name, but the maturity remained bogged down at about ten years. There is a fairly full range of government maturities up to that point. However, there is a shortage of volume, for in recent years the N.Z. government has been running very substantial budget cash surpluses and an early priority was in fact to retire government debt (net debt is now in fact negative). Much of the existing volume is held by institutions rather than private investors. The shortage of governments means that the market as whole is not well served with adequate pricing signals for fixed interest. This has some limiting implications for the way that monetary policy can influence the term structure. It could even be regarded as leading to a parallel high-quality market offshore, in the form of Uridashis and Eurobonds, a subject of central importance for the present enquiry. In the meantime, we note a further adverse exposure, namely that if there is flight to quality then there is likely to be insufficient scrip to satisfy the demand. Such a flight to quality duly occurred in late August 2007, just as it did with the rest of the world. One participant described the N.Z. debt market at the time as "completely dysfunctional", as banks and other financial institutions scrambled for cover. The N.Z. Debt Management Office, Treasury's debt manager, was forced to step in and make a special issue after a more or less routine NZ$150 million issue attracted bids of NZ$1billion. It was ironic that after struggling through the mid-1990s to pay back large amounts of debt, the N.Z. government found itself having to issue more at a time of massive budget surpluses. Such is the price of virtue.

It is possible to get coupon strips or zero-coupon bonds as OTC products off the back of government bonds, and there are very occasional issues into the N.Z. market of other high grade debt such as the World Bank. Proceeding down the credit scale, there are smaller volumes of local authority stock: Large regional authorities, city councils, hospital boards and the like, some of which are issued on tap. There is also a reasonably well traded market for corporate debentures, mostly issued by finance companies. Some of the finance company debentures have had undiversified or downright bad asset backing and unconvincing credit ratings. The latter has led in 2007 to some well publicized corporate failures, exacerbated by a flight to quality, with some unfortunate social consequences. There are issues from time to time of more structured debt products such as convertible notes and collateralized debt obligations, generally by major corporations such as Fonterra or Telecom NZ. Bond coupons are taxed at full income tax rates for the holder, as is accrued capital gain. For a further overview of the N.Z. bond market, see Bowden and Zhu (2005, ibid).

At the very short end there is a flourishing market in bank CDs, out to a year or so, formerly structured as bank bills, with ninety days as the most popular maturity. The Treasury issues T-bills in accordance with the government's liquidity needs, but these tend to be held by banks as rediscounting instruments with the central bank, and are also used by the latter for purposes of managing the liquidity in the system. Commercial bills are also popular with fund managers, with commercial paper as the unsecured version.

Turning to interest rate derivatives, exchange-based trading in N.Z. instruments has, after a fairly long history, now been taken over by the Sydney Futures Exchange, though listed as a distinct New Zealand based board. The bulk of volume is accounted for by ninety-day bank bill futures; the origins of the name referred to bank accepted bills, though as earlier noted, the latter are now effectively supplanted by bank CDs. There are much smaller volumes of three- and ten-year futures on government bonds. Settlement on the above contracts is in cash. Options do exist on all these contracts, settled in the relevant futures contract, but liquidity is poor, at best.

For OTC interest rate instruments, there is an active interbank market for bond options and for corporate treasury forward rate agreements (FRA's) though the latter are not very actively quoted for anything longer than eighteen months out, reflecting the lack of liquidity in the Sydney Futures Exchange. The predominant form of interest rate derivative is unquestionably interest rate and related swaps. These are well supported both in the domestic floating to fixed vanillas and also in the foreign exchange and currency swaps, which will be considered further below.

2.3. Monetary Policy and Foreign Exchange

The anchor to short interest rates is implicitly provided by the central bank, the Reserve Bank of New Zealand (RBNZ). The bank runs an inflation targeting regime, currently in the 1–3 per cent band. The control instrument is the Official Cash Rate (OCR), which is a rediscount rate applied to banks that are short end-of-day settlement funds. The clearing banks can rediscount using T-bills; or more recently, by means of foreign exchange swaps with the RBNZ as counterparty, as a response to a shortage of high quality government paper. There is no official reserve ratio. The RBNZ does not rely on attempts to control the supply of high-powered money, and indeed the M* family as a whole has become almost irrelevant. Indeed with the advent of an automated real-time gross settlement, subsequently modified, clearing bank cash reserves are extremely low by international standards. Changes to the OCR, if they are to take place, are announced by the governor at monthly intervals. There is naturally much market second guessing ahead of such pronouncements, for all short-term rates will rise or fall in sympathy, and that in turn has a profound influence on the N.Z. dollar. The drivers and dynamics will be reviewed in what follows, for they are at the heart of New Zealand's emergence as an internationally traded currency. Also of relevance will be the limited extent to which OCR changes impact further out along the yield curve. The N.Z. term structure is by no means a single factor model.

Finally, New Zealand has its own currency, the N.Z. dollar (NZD) which up to June of this year has been remarkably free of any attempts by the central bank to smooth or manage it, unlike some of its trading partners such as Japan or even Australia. New Zealand is an open country in terms of its export and import flows, so there is a fair bit of day-to-day underpinning to the spot market on this account. This extends into the forward market where many export operations routinely manage their exposures with foreign exchange hedges. OTC forwards are the preferred instrument for this purpose though NZD futures are also available on the Chicago Mercantile Exchange. Foreign exchange (FX) forwards do drive the spot NZD rates at certain times, just from the ordinary processes of covered interest arbitrage.

In recent years, FX trading has been dominated by capital account transactions. Short-term flows are very responsive to changes in the Reserve Bank's OCR, and the NZD has become a major speculative currency for this reason. Spot FX transactions also emerge from longer-term capital inflows, notably those connected with offshore issues of NZD denominated debt, which are discussed further below. Figure 8.1a illustrates spot trades where one leg is the NZD. Most of these are in either the U.S. dollar (USD) or the Australian dollar (AUD).There is also a flourishing market for third party-USD trades, in which the NZD is not directly involved, derived partly from time zone considerations. Figure 8.1b illustrates.

3. THE ECONOMICS OF STRUCTURAL IMBALANCE

The picture thus far is of a small but reasonably complete capital market, not terribly liquid in some respects, but one that on the whole functions quite freely as to price setting. New Zealand has a central bank, operating at arm's length from the government; a more or less free floating currency (though see below); locally owned trading and savings banks as well as foreign banks; a debt market; its own stock market; a futures market by proxy with the Australians; and well developed OTC derivative markets. In many of these, New Zealanders have been very innovative with respect to things like automated trading or clearing systems. Financial services companies such as Sunguard Treasury Systems started as small local operations but have spread their wings worldwide. Indeed New Zealand advertises itself to prospective offshore students in finance as the "world's smallest fully self-contained capital market", though some debate exists about whether Iceland might not qualify!

Figure 8.1a
Monthly Spot FX Trading Volume with NZD as Terms or Commodity

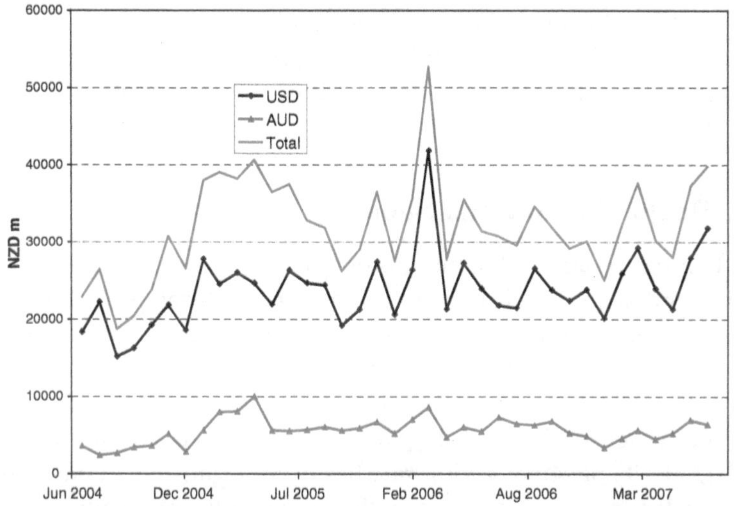

Figure 8.1b
Monthly Spot FX Trading Volume with USD as Terms or Commodity

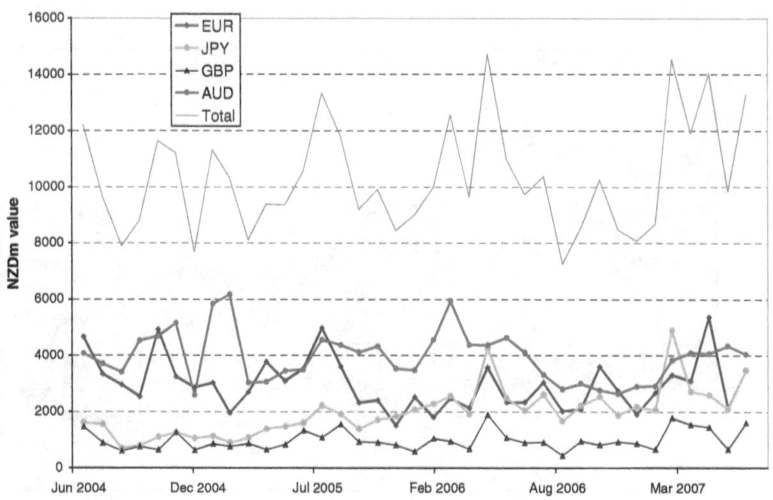

On the other hand, there is nothing in all this to suggest that New Zealand should be an object of interest to anything much except financial anthropology, were there to be such a discipline. That it has become of wider interest to the world as a whole follows as much from its weaknesses as from its strengths. What follows singles out the nature or origins of these problems, before proceeding to draw out their implications for the international financial markets.

3.1. Deplorable Savings Habits

It is helpful to start with a bit of economics, specifically the economics of saving and spending. Kiwis are just about the developed world's worst savers on personal account, no matter what income concept you use as benchmark (national income or flow of funds, etc.). New Zealand is even worse than Australia, Canada, and the United States, none of which are admittedly too flash either. Figure 8.2 pretty much says it all. Since the mid-1990s, its personal saving rate has been negative, and badly so.

Nor does corporate savings, in the form of retained earnings, do much to compensate. Corporate retained earnings took a bit of a slug when dividend imputation was introduced, twenty years ago. In countries like

Figure 8.2
Comparative Personal Savings Rates

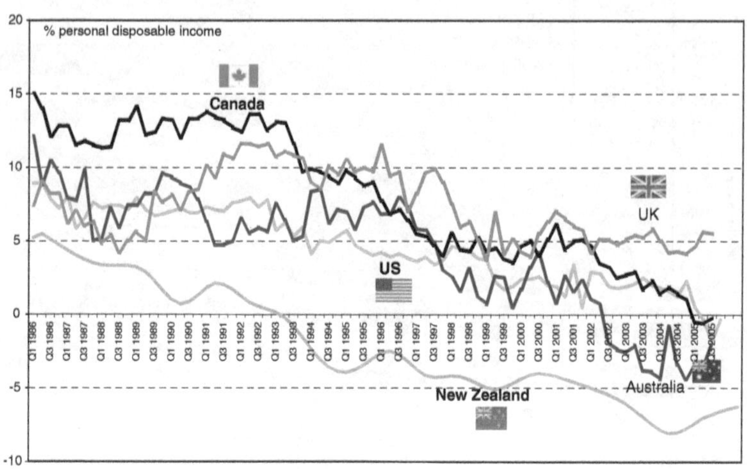

the United States or United Kingdom, company earnings are taxed twice, first in the form of company tax, and then again once received as dividends, in the form of personal tax. In New Zealand or Australia, that is no longer quite as true, because corporate tax can now be claimed as a credit against most of your personal tax. In the United States, shareholders actually prefer the firm to retain earnings as this shields them against the tax on dividends, and the same motivation induces companies to search more actively for productive activities. So one can expect to find higher rates of corporate savings in the United States, and this is just what happens. In recent years, N.Z. companies have not been retaining earnings they way that they probably should, and have acquired the general reputation as high dividend yield cash cows rather than growth stocks. New Zealand does have growth capital, located in primary industries, tourism (another major export earner) or education, but not enough to compensate.

This leaves government as the third arm of savings. In recent years the government has been running fairly large budget surpluses, arising partly as a consequence of some very good economic times. A fairly rigorous regime of goods and services tax (GST) on nearly all transactions has helped in this respect: A vacuum cleaner sort of effect. The official cash surplus is also a more mechanical consequence of fiscal creep, arising from the failure of the N.Z. government to index marginal tax rate markers in a progressive income tax (unlike neighbouring Australia). As a result, the government budget surplus has over the last three to four years been running at 5–6 per cent of GDP.

To some extent, the public surplus has compensated for the dismal savings record of the private sector. But there may be cause and effect involved to the contrary. The government has been squirreling some of the surplus away in the form of its National Superannuation Fund (NSF), a sovereign wealth fund that is rapidly moving into the international big league in terms of asset size. The NSF is intended to underpin the retirement of the baby-boomers, similar in this respect to the funded state schemes of countries such as Ireland, Norway, and more recently Australia (as the "future fund"). This has led to fears that Ricardian equivalence may be involved, and that the public is looking to the government to save on their behalf, rather than seeking to assure their own source of future retirement income support via long-term contractual or other forms of saving.

3.2. Macroeconomic (Im)balance

The obverse side of saving is investment. In the case of New Zealand there has not been a problem with aggregate investment expenditure as such. The housing market has been booming, driven by higher immigration flows as well as incomes, together with plentiful home finance (see below). Higher housing prices and Tobin's Q have combined to mean that new home building has been roaring along, and so too has commercial construction. Economic purists might grumble about the direction of the investment spending toward what are basically consumption rather than producer goods; but there is no doubting the strength of investment spending in the aggregate.

As every economics student knows, if there is an excess of local investment over locally generated savings, then it has to be made up with an inflow of foreign savings. In other words, the balance of payments has to fill the gap, in the form of a capital account surplus to match the current account deficit. Figure 8.3 shows that the current account deficit has exploded in recent years, now at about 10 per cent of GDP.

If investment is too high in relation to domestic saving, then this also connotes an inflationary gap, which can be expected to attract a great deal of attention from a central bank as rigorous in its inflation targeting as the Reserve Bank of New Zealand. Their major sources of concern as to the origins of the inflation have centred on the buoyant housing market. By progressively raising the OCR, the expectation was that this would flow into rates on house mortgage lending. In the event, things did not pan out quite as hoped. The only unequivocal outcome was that very short-term floating rates did rise in sympathy and that N.Z. short rates were maintained at rates radically higher than available funding rates offshore such as the United States or Japan; and particularly in the latter years, also higher than New Zealand's local comparator, Australia. Figure 8.4 illustrates.

3.3. Exchange Rate Consequences

As one might have expected from the scale of the interest rate divergences, there has been an incentive for the carry trade to fund in Japanese yen, alternatively euros or pounds, and invest in N.Z. dollar cash rates or CDs.

Figure 8.3
NZ Current Account Balances

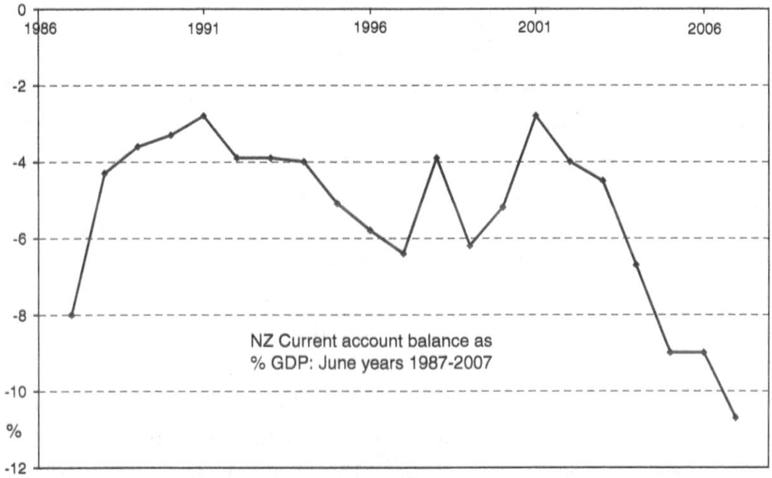

Figure 8.4
Comparative Short-term Interest Rates

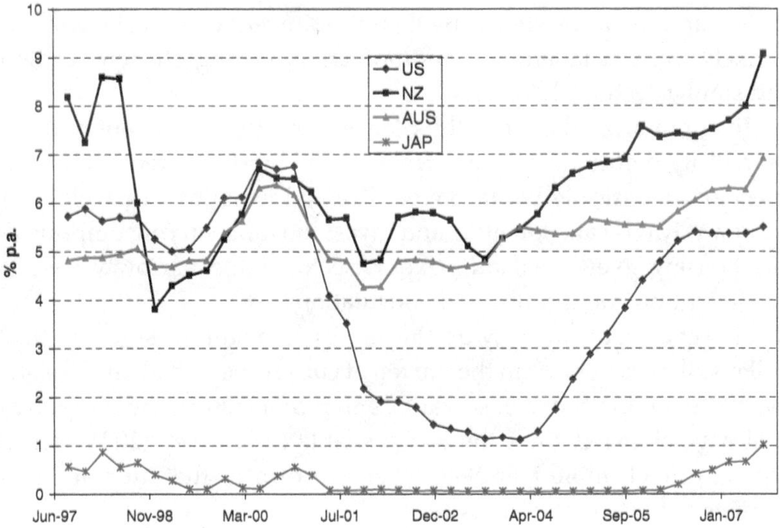

This remained a high-risk investment, because the NZX had by then acquired a reputation as one of the world's wobblier currencies,[7] though it must be remembered that the yen had also acquired similar dubious status in the aftermath of the Asian crisis. But as the N.Z. housing market continued to boom, and inflationary fears to grow, the RBNZ was also sending signals to the market about future tightening ahead, that is, likely future hikes in the cash rate. The effect was like a comfort blanket to the carry trade, sharply undercutting the risk to holding the N.Z. dollar.

At the same time, it became apparent that structural changes in world trade were likely to be of benefit to New Zealand. This was especially true of the relationship with China in respect of trade in dairy products. It became apparent that a stronger N.Z. dollar might in fact have some more fundamental underpinning. Moreover that the export base might also continue to narrow, underpinned in dairy, tourism, meat and forestry by the new relationships with the emerging economies of China and India, at the expense of export diversification away from the primary commodities sector. The effect would be to expose the economy to commodity price or other shocks from time to time, which might create continuing instability. This sort of thing would put New Zealand firmly on the map as a zone of interest to professional currency traders. That it might become so was put beyond all doubt by a rare central bank intervention on 10 June 2007, in which the RBNZ tried to sell down the NZD. Unfortunately it was still signalling monetary tightening at the time, and the carry trade was quick to pick up the inconsistency. By then the Kraken[8] had awoken, taking the unlikely form of Japanese grandmothers operating off doji candlesticks and similar technical analysis.

To summarize the story thus far, it is of a small economy projected beyond its merits on to the screens of the world currency traders. The effect arises basically because New Zealand is not at all a well balanced economy. Kiwis save too little, and invest too much in consumption assets like housing. New Zealand's export sector is too narrowly based, and dependent on commodity price fluctuations.

However, spot currency trading is less than half the story, for the N.Z. dollar still does not rate in the top ten of currencies traded on BIS statistics; though given the above observations on recent history, the position might well have changed since the last available BIS Survey (2004). The story becomes much more complete when we turn to the international debt markets and associated derivatives.

4. EUROKIWIS, URIDASHIS AND CONSEQUENCES

As a high interest rate currency, the N.Z. dollar was bound to attract attention from more traditional investors, with a requirement for higher coupons for fixed rate debt, or of floating rates for notes. The trade was to some extent helped along by New Zealand's history of substantial balance of payments deficits. But even without the existing pool, the trade has been enabled by the worldwide growth and sophistication of the cross-currency interest rate swaps industry. To be sure, there are other generic types of swap in which NZD features as one leg, such as foreign exchange or currency swaps.[9] These short-dated swaps can be used to structure forward agreement and remain popular between banks; their use was also noted above in the context of monetary clearing, and seems bound to grow in the NZD/USD context. In what follows, the label "generalized currency swaps" will sometimes be used to refer to the totality of all kinds of swap with a foreign currency amount or flow as one side. It thus includes narrow currency swaps, foreign exchange swaps and cross-currency interest rate swaps. It is the cross-currency interest rate swaps (CIRS), and associated transactions that they facilitate, that are the focus of special interest in the account that follows.

4.1. Some Structural Background

To understand just why New Zealand has become a major force (if that is the right word) in CIRS requires an appreciation of cognate structural and other trends of the last few years. The first of these has already been touched on, namely high interest rates, most notably at the short end but extending to some degree to further out along the yield curve. This helps to create the supply side and will be elaborated on in due course.

The complementary demand side also emerges out of remarks earlier made, in this case concerning the love affair of Kiwis with their houses, and with housing as an investment. Exploding house prices have been pretty much a worldwide phenomenon — everywhere and anytime there is a conjunction of what can be called the three *i*'s in house prices: Incomes, Immigration and Interest rates. In New Zealand, things are acerbated by its exposure to export price and volume shocks and the way that these translate into general economic activity. This used to be thought of as a cycle, but recently there have been signs that the export price boom has been more than just a temporary shock, and that good economic times are here to stay. The willingness of households to bear mortgage debt has been an indication both of the initial economic stimulus due to the upswing in commodity prices and the prevailing climate of economic optimism that ensued. As in the United Kingdom and other countries, home mortgage debt is also used to finance consumer spending. It is indeed difficult to disentangle one from the other. Either way, the volume of household debt rose sharply, not just in volume, but in terms of the implied debt servicing burden.

New Zealanders are not heavy credit card borrowers, and there is some finance company debt, especially for motor cars. But the bulk of this debt represents home mortgages. In addition New Zealand's poor personal savings record has meant that loan to valuation rates have been quite high, especially for newer entrants to home ownership, or for investors on higher marginal tax rates willing to gear up their tax deductible interest costs. Figure 8.5 illustrates.

Over the last few years the bulk of home mortgages have been written in terms of fixed rather than floating interest rates. There are some good economic reasons to do so. There is always going to be a motive just from simple risk aversion: If the rate is fixed, one knows in advance what the liability is every month, at least until the mortgage has to be refinanced. But in addition, the RBNZ has been hiking up floating interest rates via their OCR monetary instrument. This has created an inverted yield curve,

Figure 8.5
Household Indebtedness

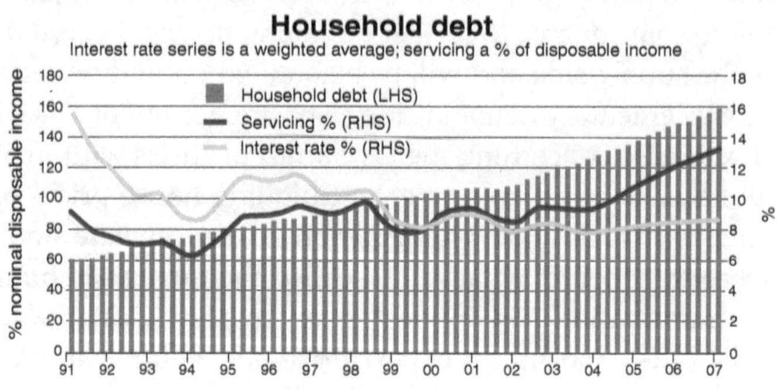

Source: http://www.rbnz.govt.nz/keygraphs/Fig5.html.

so that the typical three to five-year fixed rate is significantly lower than the floating rate mortgages.

4.2. Offshore NZD Funding: Eurodollars and Uridashis

All this adds up to a substantial demand for fixed rate mortgages. If New Zealand were a closed economy, a demand of this magnitude would drive up the fixed rate and equilibrate the volume to the demand. That it does not do so is due to the trade in eurodollar and uridashi bonds. N.Z. dollar denominated debt is popular in both markets, though from slightly different motives. The Kiwi eurodollar is the older of the two markets, with a greater variety of arrangements: Floating notes and zero coupon, as well as the more common fixed coupon. The uridashi bonds have been the growth market of recent years. Maturities are more uniformly shorter (typically two to three years), and the motive is simply the higher coupon relative to other available debt, including what the stylized "Japanese housewives" could ever have hoped to obtain locally. For both eurokiwi and uridashi, issuers very often have no intrinsic connection with New Zealand or N.Z. institutions, as Tables 8.1a and 8.1b make clear.

Figure 8.6 is a snapshot[10] from mid-2006 that adds both sources, eurokiwi and uridashi to get total issue volume. It also adds in the maturity profile for the years to come. The TWI is the trade weighted exchange rate. The strength through 2006 reflects two influences, one the carry trade earlier noted as the RBNZ tightened, and the second the demand for NZD that accompanied purchase of the uridashis, which had perforce to be unhedged so that the high NZD coupons could be enjoyed. The rush of issues from 2005–06 coincided with the strength of the N.Z. housing market and is driven partly by the demand for swaps off the back. It has created a future redemption/rollover shadow, which has occasioned some worry as to the consequences. The newspaper clipping illustrated as Figure 8.7 is fairly typical of commentary on the subject.

4.3. Cross-currency Interest Rate Swap Structures

It is the role of the CIRS market to bring the two above influences together, namely the demand for funds originating ultimately from N.Z. homeowners, and the supply originating with offshore demand for N.Z. dollar denominated debt and their high coupons. The basics are reasonably straightforward. The foreign debt issuers will receive fixed rate payments from NZ banks passing them through as coupons to the Japanese

Table 8.1a
NZD Uridashi Issues
(January 2006–May 2007)

Issuer	Arranger	Launch Date	Settle Date	Maturity Date	Amount	Issue Price per 100	Coupon	Years to Maturity
Swedish Export Credit Corp	Mizuho Investment	5-Jan-06	21-Jan-06	24-Jan-08	49	—	6.20	2.0
BNG	Daiwa Securities	6-Jan-06	25-Jan-06	25-Jan-08	655	—	6.00	2.0
CADES (France)	Tokai Tokyo	6-Jan-06	25-Jan-06	24-Jan-06	100.5	—	6.10	2.0
UBS	Takagi	6-Jan-06	27-Jan-06	26-Jan-11	16	79.61	1.00	5.0
CADES (France)	Tokai Tokyo	1-Feb-06	16-Feb-06	20-Feb-08	45	—	6.00	2.0
Instituto de Credito Oficial	Shinko Securities	3-Feb-06	16-Feb-06	15-Mar-08	157	—	6.05	2.1
European	Nomura	9-Feb-08	16-Feb-06	15-Feb-08	611	—	5.90	2.0
KfW	Mizuho Investment	10-Feb-06	24-Feb-06	25-Feb-08	59	—	5.90	2.0
World Bank	Toyota FS	16-Feb-06	24-Feb-06	25-Feb-08	14	—	5.93	2.0
UBS	Takagi	1-Feb-06	27-Feb-06	24-Feb-11	16	79.42	1.00	5.0
Rabobank	Daiwa SMBC	13-Feb-06	28-Feb-06	27-Feb-09	365	—	6.10	3.0
Rabobank	Daiwa SMBC	13-Feb-06	28-Feb-06	27-Feb-08	431	—	5.95	2.0
Kommuninvest	Shinko Securities	2-Mar-06	14-Mar-06	12-Jun-08	120	—	6.06	2.2
Inter-America Development Bank	Daiwa SMBC	2-Mar-06	16-Mar-06	13-Mar-08	761	—	5.67	2.0
Rentenbank	SMBC Friend	2-Mar-06	24-Mar-06	23-Oct-08	115	—	5.82	2.6
Swedish Export Credit Corp	Nikko Cord.	10-Mar-06	28-Mar-06	27-Mar-08	48	—	6.03	2.0
Kommunekredit	Shinko Securities	10-Apr-06	19-Apr-06	23-Apr-08	50	—	6.00	2.0
Landwirtschaftliche Rentenbank	SMBC Friend	10-Apr-06	27-Apr-06	26-Mar-09	150	—	5.70	2.9
World Bank	SMBC Friend	9-May-06	9-May-06	26-May-09	150		5.82	3.0
Eksportfinans	Tokai Tokyo	28-Apr-06	18-May-06	15-May-08	42	—	5.92	2.0
Municipality Finance	Shinko Securities	10-May-06	19-May-06	20-May-08	73	—	6.00	2.0

continued on next page

Table 8.1a — *continued*

Issuer	Arranger	Launch Date	Settle Date	Maturity Date	Amount	Issue Price per 100	Coupon	Years to Maturity
World Bank	Toyota FS	17-May-06	26-May-06	27-May-08	16	—	6.08	2.0
World Bank	SMBC Friend	26-May-06	2-Jun-06	15-Dec-08	8	—	5.70	2.5
EBRD	Daiwa Securities	31-May-06	9-Jun-06	12-Jun-08	500	100	5.80	2.0
Kommunekredit	Shinko Securities	6-Jun-06	14-Jun-06	16-Jul-08	77	—	6.25	2.1
Eksportfinans	Tokai Tokyo	19-Jun-06	30-Jun-06	18-Jun-08	39	—	6.16	2.0
Kommunalbanken AS	Shinko Securities	5-Jul-06	14-Jul-06	13-Aug-08	80	—	6.16	2.1
Eksportfinans	Tokai Tokyo	18-Jul-06	1-Aug-06	24-Jul-08	47.5	—	6.12	2.0
CBA	Nikko Cord.	20-Jul-06	3-Aug-06	4-Aug-08	10	100	6.35	2.0
World Bank	Shinko Securities	7-Aug-06	10-Aug-06	10-Sep-10	82		6.19	4.1
CADES (France)	Nomura	11-Aug-06	14-Aug-06	14-Aug-08	312	—	6.28	2.0
SEK (Sweden)	Tokai Tokyo	31-Jul-06	16-Aug-06	14-Aug-08	38.5	—	6.23	2.0
Inter-America Development Bank	Daiwa Securities SMI	17-Aug-06	25-Aug-06	26-Aug-08	419	—	6.00	2.0
Rentenbank	Shinko Securities	1-Sep-06	11-Sep-06	11-Sep-08	85	—	6.40	2.0
Kommuninvest	Tokai Tokyo	4-Sep-06	21-Sep-06	18-Sep-08	56.5	—	6.32	2.0
EBRD		20-Sep-06	2-Oct-06	29-Sep-08	566	—	6.12	2.0
Institutio de Credito Oficial	Shinko Securities	2-Oct-06	12-Oct-06	13-Nov-08	103	—	6.47	2.1
World Bank	Daiwa	4-Oct-06	16-Oct-06	16-Oct-08	282	—	6.05	2.0
Bank Nederlandse Gemeenten N	Tokai Tokyo	2-Oct-06	18-Oct-06	16-Oct-08	59	—	6.33	2.0
UBS AG	Takagi	10-Oct-06	30-Oct-06	27-Oct-11	16	78.86	1.00	5.0
Kommuninvest	Tokai Tokyo	1-Nov-06	16-Nov-06	17-Nov-08	87.5	—	6.56	2.0
Toyota Motor Credit	Shinko Securities	9-Nov-06	17-Nov-06	18-Nov-09	162	—	6.68	3.0
Municipality Finance	Ando Securities	23-Oct-06	21-Nov-06	21-Nov-16	60	63.17	1.00	10.0
Bank Nederlandse Gemeenten N	Daiwa Securities	9-Nov-6	23-Nov-06	20-Nov-08	570	99.98	6.32	2.0
World Bank	Nikko Cord.	16-Nov-06	30-Nov-06	19-Nov-09	39	—	6.30	3.0

EBRD	Daiwa	8-Dec-06	11-Dec-06	11-Dec-08	234	—	6.14	2.0
Kommunalbanken AS		18-Dec-06	18-Dec-06	18-Dec-08	85	—	6.42	2.0
KfW	ABN Amro	8-Dec-06	21-Dec-06	21-Jun-09	35	—	6.64	2.5
UBS	Takagi	11-Dec-06	22-Dec-06	21-Dec-11	7.85	78.48	1.00	5.0
World Bank		20-Dec-06	9-Jan-07	8-Jan-09	411	—	6.32	2.0
Bank Fukuoka	Daiwa	9-Jan-07	23-Jan-07	22-Jan-10	375	98.38	6.88	3.0
KfW	BNP	17-Jan-07	23-Jan-07	23-Jan-09	180		6.62	2.0
Toyota Motor Credit	Nomura	18-Jan-07	25-Jan-07	27-Jul-07	76		6.77	2.5
Eksportfinans	Tokai Tokyo	15-Feb-07	15-Feb-07	15-Feb-09	81		6.70	2.0
EBRD	Daiwa	5-Feb-07	15-Feb-07	15-Feb-09	417		6.48	2.0
IFC	Mizuho Investment	7-Feb-07	14-Feb-07	14-Aug-09	70		6.70	2.5
Rentenbank	Ando Securities	28-Feb-07	30-Mar-07	29-Mar-17	55	62.15	1.00	10.0
EFIC	Shinko Securities	28-Feb-07	9-Mar-07	9-Sep-09	65	—	2.50	2.5
Swedish Export Credit Corp	Tokai Tokyo	28-Feb-07	16-Mar-07	17-Mar-09	52	—	6.75	2.0
TMCC	Daiwa SMBC	28-Feb-07	13-Mar-07	26-Mar-09	640	—	6.88	2.0
UBS	Takagi	8-Mar-07	29-Mar-07	28-Mar-12	10	77.56	1.00	5.0
CADES (France)	Tokai Tokyo	4-Apr-07	18-Apr-07	16-Apr-09	51.5		6.97	2.0
Kommunalbanken AS	Mizuho Investment	4-Mar-07	16-Mar-07	16-Mar-09	34		6.70	2.0
Eksportfinans	Okasan	12-Apr-07	27-Apr-07	23-Apr-09	10.26		7.11	2.0
Inter-America Development Bank	Shinko Securities	12-Apr-07	13-Apr-07	14-Oct-09	87		6.95	2.5
UBS	Takagi	6-Apr-07	27-Apr-07	26-Apr-12	10	76.83	1.00	5.0
IFC	Rakuten	10-Apr-07	13-Apr-07	14-Apr-09	6		7.02	2.0
World Bank	Daiwa	23-Apr-07	2-May-07	23-Apr-09	385		6.68	2.0
Eksportfinans	Okasan	27-Apr-07	17-May-07	14-Apr-09	14.15		7.30	1.9
Eksportfinans	Tokai Tokyo	27-Apr-07	25-May-07	20-May-09	83.5		7.11	2.0
Kommunalbanken AS	Mizuho Investment	2-May-07	17-May-07	20-May-10	44		7.15	3.0
BNG	Shinko Securities	8-May-07	17-May-07	19-Nov-09	89		7.13	2.5

Source: Reserve Bank of New Zealand.

Table 8.1b
Eurokiwi Issues
(January 2006–May 2007)

Issuer	Arranger/Manager	Launch Date	Issue Date	Maturity Date	Amount	Issue Price per 100	Coupon	Coupon Paid	Fees	Credit Rating (Moody's/ S&P)	Years to Maturity
Societe Ge	SB CIB	3-Jan-06	3-Jan-06	3-Feb-09	22		Float				3.1
Rabobank	RBC Capital Markets	3-Jan-06	18-Jan-06	18-Jan-11	200	100.865	6.50	ann	—	Aaa/AAA	5.0
KFW	RBC Capital Markets	4-Jan-06	19-Jan-06	15-Jul-09	150	99.405	6.00	ann	—	Aaa/AAA	3.5
KFW	Fortis	4-Jan-06	24-Feb-06	24-Feb-09	50	100.96	6.50	ann	—	Aaa/AAA	3.0
KFW	TD Securities	10-Jan-06	20-Jan-06	17-Dec-07	100	99.925	6.25	ann	—	Aaa/AAA	1.9
European	TD Securities	11-Jan-06	24-Jan-06	15-Jul-09	100	99.225	6.00	ann	—	Aaa/AAA	3.5
Rentenbank	RBC Capital Markets	11-Jan-06	27-Jan-06	27-Dec-07	100	101.1	7.00	ann	—	Aaa/AAA	1.9
CAISSE D	Dresdner	24-Jan-06	24-Jan-06	24-Jan-08	101		6.10				2.0
European	RBC Capital Markets	24-Jan-06	10-Feb-06	10-Sep-14	100	102.471	6.50	ann	—	Aaa/AAA	8.6
Bank of N	RBC Capital Markets	25-Jan-06	3-Feb-06	3-Feb-06	150	Par	n BKBM+4	semi	—	Aa3/AA-	3.0
KFW	RBC Capital Markets	25-Jan-06	3-Feb-06	15-Jul-09	100	#VALUE!	6.00	ann	—	Aaa/AAA	3.4
Nordic Inv	UBS	2-Feb-06	23-Feb-06	23-Feb-09	100	101.095	6.63	ann	—	Aaa/AAA	3.0
KBC	KBC	3-Feb-06	3-Feb-06	3-Aug-06	23		6.50				0.5
HBOS	RBC Capital Markets	3-Feb-06	3-Feb-06	23-Feb-06	130		Float				3.1
KFW	TD Securities	6-Feb-06	15-Feb-06	17-Dec-07	100	100.015	6.25	ann	—	Aaa/AAA	1.8
EIB	TD Securities	6-Feb-06	17-Feb-06	15-Jul-09	100	99.615	6.00	ann	—	Aaa/AAA	3.4
Bank of N	TD Securities	8-Feb-06	16-Feb-06	16-Feb-10	150	Par	n BKBM+6	ann	—	Aa3/AA-	4.0
Bank of N	TD Securities	8-Feb-06	16-Feb-06	16-Feb-10	100	Par	n BKBM+6	ann	—	Aaa/AAA	4.0
Export De	RBC Capital Markets	8-Feb-06	23-Feb-06	23-Feb-09	200	100.933	6.50	ann	—	Aaa/AAA	3.0
Republic of	Deutsche Bank	9-Feb-06	22-Feb-06	26-Sep-08	70	99.64	6.00	ann	—	Aaa/AAA	2.6
Council of	Fortis	10-Feb-06	27-Mar-06	27-Mar-09	30	100	6.00	ann	—	Aaa/AAA	3.0
IBRD	RBC Capital Markets	13-Feb-06	27-Feb-06	15-Jul-09	200	101.325	6.38	ann	—	Aaa/AAA	3.4
EIB	RBC Capital Markets	13-Feb-06	28-Feb-06	10-Sep-14	100	101.99	6.50	ann	—	Aaa/AAA	8.5

ANZ Natio	ANZ National (Internat	14-Feb-06	14-Feb-06	17-Feb-11	150		6.82				5.0
CAISSE D	AMORTISSEMENT DI	15-Feb-06	15-Feb-06	20-Feb-08	45		6.00				2.0
IBRD	JP Morgan	21-Feb-06	21-Feb-06	26-Sep-08	12		6.06				2.6
Westpact	TD Securities	22-Feb-06	6-Mar-06	7-Sep-07	100	100.59	6.75	ann	—	Aa3/AA-	1.5
IBRD	Dresdner	23-Feb-06	23-Feb-06	25-Feb-08	14		5.93				2.0
BNP Parib	BNP Paribas	23-Feb-06	23-Feb-06	23-Feb-09	2		Float				3.0
BNP Parib	BNP Paribas	23-Feb-06	23-Feb-06	23-Feb-09	2		6.15				3.0
GECC	RBC Capital Markets	23-Feb-06	17-Apr-06	17-Apr-09	150	99.453	6.63	ann	—	Aaa/AAA	3.0
BNP Parib	BNP Paribas	3-Mar-06	3-Mar-06	14-Feb-14	7		Float				8.0
BNP Parib	BNP Paribas	3-Mar-06	3-Mar-06	14-Feb-14	7		Float				8.0
IBRD	BNP Paribas	9-Mar-06	9-Mar-06	13-Mar-09	15		5.58				3.0
IBRD	Dresdner	23-Mar-06	23-Mar-06	14-Mar-08	10		5.46				2.0
LWR	Dresdner	23-Mar-06	23-Mar-06	27-Jan-09	115		5.82				2.9
Bank of Ir	Barclays Capital	23-Mar-06	23-Mar-06	22-Mar-09	35		Zero				3.0
IBRD	Dresdner	29-Mar-06	29-Mar-06	14-Apr-08	15		5.46				2.0
Westpac	RBC	30-Mar-06	30-Mar-06	30-Mar-11	150		Float				5.0
CIBC (FR	TD Securities	6-Apr-06	20-Apr-06	20-Apr-11	150	Par	n BKBM+8bp			Aa3e/AA-	5.0
EIB	TD Securities	20-Apr-06	20-Apr-06	15-Jul-09	100		6.00			Aaa/AAA	3.2
LWR	Dresdner	26-Apr-06	26-Apr-06	23-Mar-09	140		5.70				2.9
BNP Parib	BNP Paribas	26-Apr-06	26-Apr-06	24-Apr-12	147		0.00				6.0
GECC		4-May-06	18-May-06	28-Sep-15	225	98.073	6.50	semi		AAA	9.4
EIB		9-May-06	18-May-06	10-Sep-14	100	101.14	6.50	ann		AAA	8.3
Anglo Irish	NAB	16-May-06	16-May-06	16-May-07	50		0.00				1.0
EIB		24-May-06	7-Jun-06	10-Sep-14	100	101.5	6.50	ann		AAA	8.3
IBRD	Dresdner	26-May-06	26-May-06	14-May-08	150		5.82				2.0
Danone F	Citigroup	27-May-06	27-May-06	29-Jan-08	253		5.92				1.7
EIB		31-May-06	15-Jun-06	15-Jul-09	100	99.338	6.00	ann		Aaa	3.1
IBRD	Dresdner	1-Jun-06	1-Jun-06	15-Dec-08	8		5.70				2.5
Kommune	Shinko	6-Jun-06	6-Jun-06	16-Jul-08	77		6.25				2.1
EIB		7-Jun-06	7-Jun-06	7-Sep-14	100	101.499	6.50				8.3

continued on next page

Table 8.1b — *continued*

Issuer	Arranger/Manager	Launch Date	Issue Date	Maturity Date	Amount	Issue Price per 100	Coupon	Coupon Paid	Fees	Credit Rating (Moody's/ S&P)	Years to Maturity
IADB	TD Securities	8-Jun-06	8-Jun-06	8-Jun-16	200	98.39	6.25				10.0
IBRD	BNP Paribas	21-Jun-06	26-Jun-06	14-Jan-09	8		5.82				2.6
IBRD	Dresdner	21-Jun-06	13-Jul-06	14-Jul-08	8		5.76				2.0
Bank of Ir	TD Securities	26-Jun-06	3-Jul-06	1-Jul-11	100	Par	n BKBM+8bp			Aa3e/AA-	5.0
Rentenbank	Mizuho	9-Jul-06	9-Jul-06	15-Oct-08	85		6.40				
IADB	TD Securities	10-Jul-06	19-Jul-06	19-Jul-11	100	100.04	6.13	semi		Aaae/AAA	5.0
IADB	TD Securities	15-Aug-06	15-Aug-06	15-Aug-11	100	99.775	6.25				5.0
Toyota	TD Securities	7-Sep-06	7-Sep-06	21-Sep-09	150		6.75				3.0
GECC	TD Securities	12-Sep-06	12-Sep-06	26-Sep-16	300	99.04	6.75			Aaa/AAA	10.0
Westpac	Barclays Capital	29-Sep-06	29-Sep-06	29-Sep-08	50		6.03				2.0
IBRD	JP Morgan	19-Oct-06	19-Oct-06	20-Apr-09	5						2.5
IBRD	JP Morgan	9-Nov-06	9-Nov-06	10-Nov-08	2						2.0
KFW	ABN Amro	21-Nov-06	8-Dec-06	2-Dec-09	100	99.73	7.00	semi		Aaa/AAA	3.0
IBRD	Dresdner	30-Nov-06	30-Nov-06	25-Nov-08	16						2.0
EIB	TD Securities	6-Dec-06	6-Dec-06	15-Jul-09	100		6.00				2.6
IBRD	Dresdner	7-Dec-06	7-Dec-06	25-Jun-09	13		6.06				2.6
CBA	CBA	11-Dec-06	11-Dec-06	11-Dec-11	20		0.00				5.0
GECC	RBCCM	12-Dec-06	8-Jan-07	8-Jan-10	100	100.365	7.25	semi	—	Aaa/AAA	3.0

Source: Reserve Bank of New Zealand.

Figure 8.6
Eurokiwi and Uridashi: Volume and Redemption Shadow

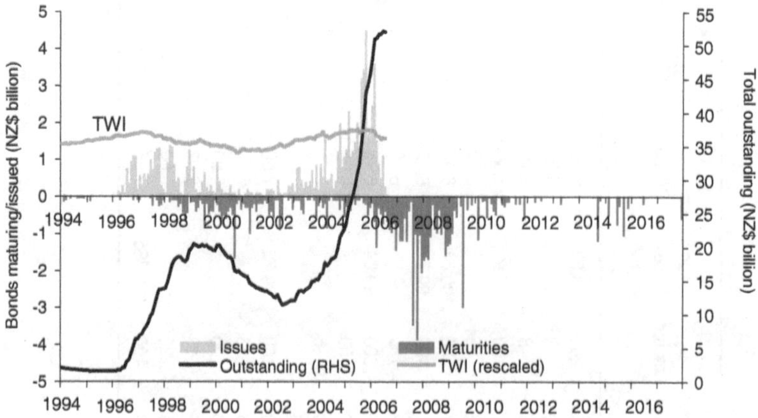

Figure 8.7
The Press in Worry Mode

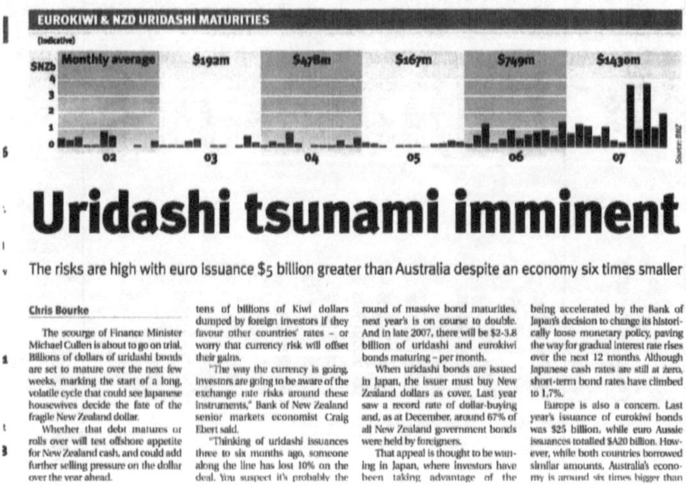

EUROKIWI & NZD URIDASHI MATURITIES

(Indicative)

$NZb Monthly average $192m $478m $167m $749m $1430m

Uridashi tsunami imminent

The risks are high with euro issuance $5 billion greater than Australia despite an economy six times smaller

Chris Bourke

The scourge of Finance Minister Michael Cullen is about to go on trial. Billions of dollars of uridashi bonds are set to mature over the next few weeks, marking the start of a long, volatile cycle that could see Japanese housewives decide the fate of the fragile New Zealand dollar.

Whether that debt matures or rolls over will test offshore appetite for New Zealand cash, and could add further selling pressure on the dollar over the year ahead.

tens of billions of Kiwi dollars dumped by foreign investors if they favour other countries' rates – or worry that currency risk will offset their gains.

"The way the currency is going, investors are going to be aware of the exchange rate risks around these instruments," Bank of New Zealand senior markets economist Craig Ebert said.

"Thinking of uridashi issuances three to six months ago, someone along the line has lost 10% on the deal. You suspect it's probably the

round of massive bond maturities, next year's is on course to double. And in late 2007, there will be $2-3.8 billion of uridashi and eurokiwi bonds maturing – per month.

When uridashi bonds are issued in Japan, the issuer must buy New Zealand dollars as cover. Last year saw a record rate of dollar-buying and, as at December, around 67% of all New Zealand government bonds were held by foreigners.

That appeal is thought to be waning in Japan, where investors have been taking advantage of the

being accelerated by the Bank of Japan's decision to change its historically loose monetary policy, paving the way for gradual interest rate rises over the next 12 months. Although Japanese cash rates are still at zero, short-term bond rates have climbed to 1.7%.

Europe is also a concern. Last year's issuance of eurokiwi bonds was $25 billion, while euro Aussie issuances totalled $A20 billion. However, while both countries borrowed similar amounts, Australia's economy is around six times bigger than

Source: *NZ National Business Review* article, March 2006.

housewives (or Belgian dentists,[11] etc.), in exchange for the preferred style and currency obligations (for example, floating USD). In turn, the N.Z. banks will receive their own fixed payments from their N.Z. mortgage customers. Figure 8.8 shows such a fairly typical arrangement.

The N.Z. leg of the CIRS is where the N.Z. banks come in. The swap spread, taken in the usual sense of the difference between the swap rate over the corresponding governments, climbed in late 2005 from just 15 basis points to 115 or more, reflecting the soaring demand from homeowners for fixed-price mortgage accommodation, and the corresponding willingness of their banks to supply fixed NZD through to the foreign institutions via the CIRS.

The conjunction of supply and demand on each side of the swap, together with a market clearing price, results in swap volume. Figure 8.9 plots the volume of home-based generalized currency swaps, that is, all types of swap incorporating the NZD as one leg and a foreign currency on the other. As the typical CIRS diagram (Figure 8.8) suggests,[12] the bulk of the business has the USD as the other leg (right-hand axis), though from time to time, there have been appreciable volumes in other currencies such as the Japanese yen. The growing volume through 2005–07 is clearly apparent.

Figure 8.8
Flows on a Typical Eurokiwi or Uridashi CIRS

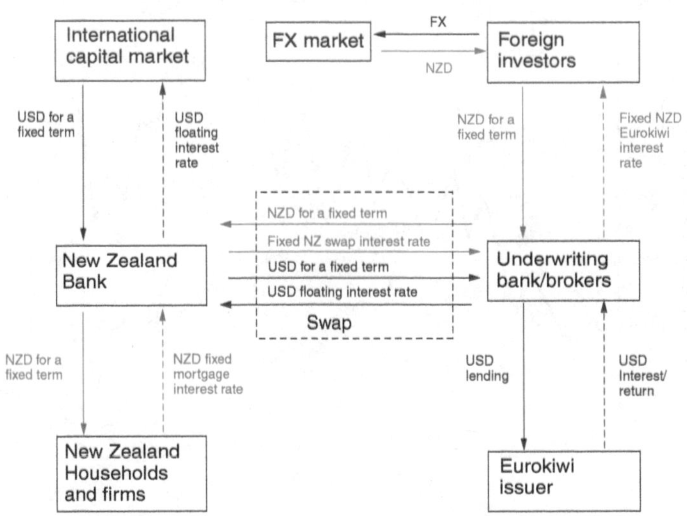

Source: Drage et al. (2005).

An appreciable amount of generalized currency swaps are also traded in the N.Z. market in which the NZD is absent from either leg; "third party" currencies, so to speak. Most of these have the USD on the one side, and of these, the majority involve the Australian dollar as the counterparty currency. Figure 8.10 plots the volume over the last few years.

To summarize the above discussion, there has in recent years been volume on an international scale in the market for offshore N.Z. dollar denominated debt, and in the derivatives that are used to convert the liabilities into those of the N.Z. banking system and ultimately of N.Z. homeowners. It is this trade, together with trading or positions in currency spot and forwards, that projects New Zealand onto the world markets.

5. THE REFINER'S FIRE: CONCLUDING REMARKS

5.1. Regional Perspectives

So far as regional competition is concerned, there is certainly some such, notably with the Australian markets. As earlier remarked, the recent attempt by the N.Z. Stock Exchange to construct an Australasian equity trading platform will stoke this particular fire. But frictions of this kind should not be allowed to obscure some cooperative synergies. New Zealand is too

Figure 8.9
Generalized Currency Swaps with NZD as One Leg

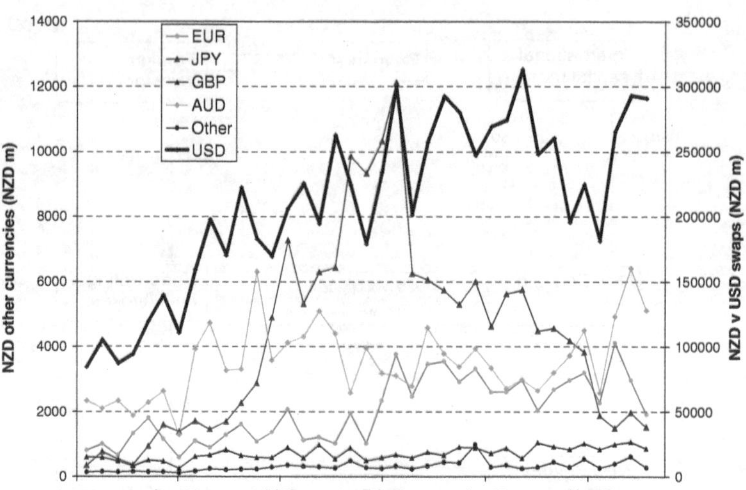

Note: Includes all types of swaps with foreign exchange as counter party.
Source: Underlying data from Reserve Bank of New Zealand.

Figure 8.10
Third-Party Generalized Currency Swaps

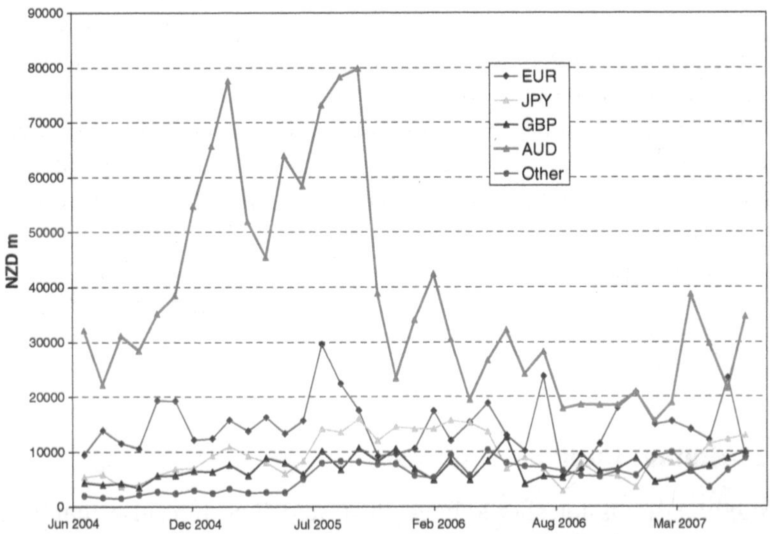

small to have an autarkic futures exchange, even though historically it did get established and proved rather innovative. It made much more sense for this to be developed further as a partnership between the Sydney Futures Exchange and the N.Z. Stock Exchange. Moreover, closer economic relationship (CER) agreements have done much to harmonize trade, regulatory, and taxation arrangements across the Tasman, and this will always help financial market integration, even if some taxation differences persist. But so long as the two Tasman countries continue to run separate currencies, there will always be a barrier to easy translation of financial capital from one to the other.

On the other hand, none of this is likely to impact adversely on just where New Zealand does contribute to international and Asian-Pacific capital market integration, namely the debt markets and the derivatives that handle the currency or interest rate risk. It is hard to see that New Zealand competes with anyone on such things. Indeed, a much better case can be made that NZD denominated liabilities add quite materially to the income and diversification possibility sets of investors across the Asian region. Where would the Japanese housewives be without their uridashis? Or their mothers without doji candlesticks, and the gyrations of the N.Z. dollar? Moreover, even N.Z. shares or similar assets can be quite useful to an equity or other balanced portfolio, for the N.Z. economy is not by any means synchronous in its business cycles with the U.S. or Japanese economies, nor even with the Australian.

To summarize, the N.Z. relationship with the rest of the APEC capital markets is not seen as zero-sum in character. Synergistic (positive sum) elements are associated with market completion benefits to the APEC capital markets as a whole. It is a matter of complementarity, rather than competition. To the extent that it does not happen now, it is a matter of improving investors' information sets, just as one would want to see N.Z. investors becoming more informed about the financial systems of Southeast Asia.

5.2. Human Capital

Preceding discussion should have illustrated, if nothing else, that the New Zealand economic environment has not been a calming experience. It has the world's wobbliest currency, and interest rates and stock prices are likewise highly variable. Chances are that all this will continue in the years ahead. Yet the odd thing is that it has come through the refiner's fire in good shape, and arguably much stronger for the experience.

Indeed, there is an important point underlying all this. A financial centre is not just a lot of screens and numbers, and nor are glass towers a necessary feature. What does make a market special are the people who work in it. The quality of the human capital is in fact more important than physical capital. In this respect, education is important and New Zealand pays a lot of attention to that aspect, particularly of the "learning by doing" variety. The VIAF programme has become one of the largest post-experience applied finance programmes in the world and its graduates have spread to all the major international financial centres.

But in addition, there is nothing like the refining fire of experience, and in this respect, New Zealand emerged as survivors. Learning how to cope with fluctuations has contributed a lot of valuable human capital in the general area of risk management. In the late 1990s, around the time of the Asian crisis, a number of large N.Z. corporates suffered major losses from ill-conceived hedging programmes, which have passed into case study history. Banks now pay a lot of attention to advising clients on how to deal with such problems, and in tailoring solutions, some of which call on exotic instruments like commodity-libor-exchange rate swaps. For instance, a local authority that runs a transport fleet has cost exposures to both oil prices (as diesel fuel) and the N.Z. dollar, both items highly volatile over all wavelet time scales. A bank would structure a swap under which the authority would exchange its floating exposures for a fixed NZD payment to cover both the N.Z. dollar and the oil exposure as the relevant Platt Singapore gas-oil reference rate. New developments like OTC milk futures are underway to help dairy companies or large farmer enterprises manage their exposure. Designing and pricing instruments of this kind is a first-class training experience for bank staff, and New Zealand takes a certain amount of credit from our academic role in preparing students for this sort of operational environment. As a result, some of our bank treasuries have become recognised training grounds for junior staff and a conduit for them through to the markets of London and New York: A case of "come to New Zealand and see the world".

In summary, one should not lose sight of the fact that it is people who run capital markets and people who trade in them, or manage positions. A further test of an international financial centre is the quality of the people who work there and their academic and experiential credentials. On that sort of criterion, New Zealand does not stack up too badly. After all, if opinion polls are to be believed, a home-grown Kiwi ex-FX trader from the New York markets now looks set to be New Zealand's next prime minister!

Finally, it is a truism that financial markets never sleep. A trader who has a position to lay off or develop further will operate well after the rest of the building has gone home, or may be forced to ask colleagues in the offshore offices to handle the position overnight. Some of the volume reported above in connection with generalized currency swaps will have originated in this way. Or colleagues offshore may ask N.Z. traders to manage positions into the new day. Until such time as Tonga[13] develops a financial market, New Zealand will always enjoy a place in the sun simply on time zone grounds: It is the first capital market to open each day and even if the caller is not fluent in English there are good chances of being able to find an expatriate from Japan or China on the premises.

Indeed that is a good note on which to conclude. Wellington as a city is virtually unrecognizable from when this author first started work as a humble clerk in the N.Z. Treasury. It is now a vibrant and cosmopolitan place. To be sure, the "Wellywood" movie industry has helped to project the city on to a world stage, as has the internationalization of education and the growth of the tourist link. From the professional point of view, however, what has also changed over the intervening years has been the sophistication of the financial system, and the way that it is now integrated within the global financial system, while retaining its own distinctive features. I am often asked, for instance, whether it is sensible for such a small country to retain its own currency, especially one with so much instability. There is indeed much economic logic to a currency union with Australia or even with the United States. There is probably equal logic for a merger of the respective stock markets. Yet in many ways that would be a pity. Wellington enjoys the attention that derives from being an international centre, and not just the small regional one that it would otherwise become.

Notes

The author would like to thank Dawn Lorimer for many conversation on the topics herein; Gary Hawke for the stimulus to write such a chapter; staff of the Reserve Bank of New Zealand for some useful data; and conference participants for some useful comments.

1. Thus it was claimed that the QWERTY keyboard arose because it was the configuration that prevented jamming of the mechanical arms of early typewriters, and that the configuration continued into the electronic era simply because everyone had become accustomed to it. The classic reference to path dependence in economics is Arthur, W. Brian, *Increasing Returns and Path Dependence in the Economy*, Ann Arbor, Michigan: University of Michigan Press, 1994. There has been much debate and discussion in the economic literature since that time, including whether QWERTY was really an example.
2. The only cloud on the horizon might be carbon-driven trade protectionism. The tyranny of distance applies to the carbon footprint of tourism; and yes, cows are flatulent, though we're working on it.
3. Roger Bowden and Jennifer Zhu, *Kiwicap: An Introduction to NZ Capital Markets*, 2nd ed. (Wellington: Kiwicap Education, 2000).
4. This model may change following a more recent deregulation of the dairy industry which has seen foreign entry into processing plants. There is an accompanying trend towards large-scale production, with farms now milking thousands of cows as distinct from the old norm of one or two hundred, for which the capital requirements are considerable more onerous. More demanding capital requirements could lead to corporate structures.
5. See, for example, R.J. Bowden, "The Ordered Mean Difference as a Portfolio

Performance Measure", *Journal of Empirical Finance* 7 (2000): 195–233, which contains some N.Z. examples.

6. Roger. J. Bowden, "Lifecycle Derivatives and Retirement Income Assurance using Long-term Debt", *Journal of Pension Economics and Finance*, published online by Cambridge University Press, 6 December 2007, doi:10.1017/S1474747207003332.
7. R.J. Bowden and J. Zhu, "Which are the World's Wobblier Currencies? Reference Exchange Rates and Their Variation", *BE Studies in Nonlinear Dynamics and Econometrics* 11, no. 3, Article 5 (2007) <http://www.bepress.com/snde/vol11/iss3/art5>.
8. The Kraken was a mythical giant octopus appearing in a poem by Alfred Tennyson, and echoed in Jules Verne's classic, *Twenty Thousand Leagues under the Sea*, where it tried to snaffle the Nautilus. It was also a star of horror movies of the 1930s to 1950s. The general idea was that mariners should at all costs avoid stirring up the Kraken.
9. Foreign exchange swaps have two legs, namely an initial spot sale and purchase, followed by a reversing forward purchase and sale at the designated future date. They can be used to fund short-term currency borrowings or roll existing positions forward. A currency swap is where the initial and terminal exchanges are made at the same rate, with the difference picked up by differential interest payments between the parties. Note that currency swaps are sometimes confused with the technically more correct cross-currency interest rates swaps.
10. The graph was constructed using data from RBNZ and Thompson Financial Datastream, and appears in R.J. Bowden, "Instrument Insufficiency and Economic Stabilisation", *Australian Economic Review* 39 (2006): 257–72.
11. The apocryphal "Belgian dentists" appeared fairly early on in the Eurodollar literature, though I do not know who originated the saying. Belgian dentists were supposed to like bearer bonds for tax avoidance reasons, cashing the coupons on their periodic ski trips to Switzerland. The "Japanese housewives" are a recent invention to correspond.
12. Though note also the earlier comments that straight FX swaps are now used by the banks in the monetary clearing process to secure end-of-day accommodation by the central bank. Disaggregated figures as to the precise type of swap are not published by the RBNZ.
13. I believe the first place to see the new day is in fact the far eastern tip of Siberia, but the Tongans have the more exclusive time zone.

9

SEOUL AS AN INTERNATIONAL FINANCIAL CENTRE
Roadmap, Progress and Challenges

Hansoo Kim

1. INTRODUCTION

The proposal to develop Seoul as an international financial centre was introduced as early as January 2002. In his New Year's message, then President Kim Dae-jung, shared the vision of becoming an international hub for business. The following government, headed by President Roh Moo-hyun, inherited the vision and developed the idea further. President Roh launched the Northeast Asian business hub project as one of his administration's main agenda. The vision of the government was to strengthen Korea's economic competitiveness with the internalization of the business environment.

One of the areas of focus of the project was building a Northeast Asian financial hub. At a presidential committee in December 2003, the Korean national administration resolved to construct a Northeast Asian financial centre in Korea. The initiative elaborated the vision by proposing a three-step strategy and seven major tasks. The basic idea was to create a favourable condition for foreign financial companies to start business in Korea.

Korea's financial market is a rapidly growing sector. Its growth rate is higher than most sectors, and its market size is also growing rapidly. The fast globalization of the sector in the 1990s highlighted its importance. As a result, foreign presence expanded and thus employment and market size grew very rapidly, while growth in other sectors was moderate.

Korea's economic policy shifted with the increasing importance of the financial market in the Korean economy. The contribution of the financial sector to GDP reached more than double the proportion in the 1980s. At the same time, Korea's manufacturing began to stagnate, indicating that it had reached a threshold and could grow no further. Naturally, the government shifted its attention away from manufacturing to the financial sector.

In the beginning, the government's strategies were designed to strengthen domestic financial institutions. However, as Korea faced the lessons of the financial crisis in 1997, it recognized the weakness of the financial sector and the need for globalization. Korea's strategy for building an international hub was established to strengthen the financial market and globalize it. Furthermore, the Korean government recognized that this sector's advancement would be a new growth engine for the overall economy.

This chapter examines the strategies taken by the Korean government to build an international financial centre. In particular, this study evaluates the strategies with which Korea approached the seven tasks it identified. However, since many of the achievements were made very recently to be effective in the near future, it is not yet possible to fully measure the consequences. Instead, the prospects of the policies taken are evaluated and some necessary conditions for an international financial centre that have not yet been addressed by the government are suggested. This chaper is organized as follows. First, the financial markets in Korea are examined, with a focus on the capital market. Second, government policies with specific achievements will be examined. Lastly, the difficulties and implications from our evaluation of Korea's strategy are discussed.

2. KOREA'S CAPITAL MARKET

2.1. Overall Situation

Korea's capital market is growing at a very fast pace. Capitalization of the stock market more than doubled since 2003. As of December 2006, the total capitalization of Korea's stock market was US$834 billion — Asia's sixth largest in size. The asset management sector has also grown rapidly, reaching US$230 billion by September 2007.

The financial sector of Korea is already a major part of the Korean economy. Growth of this sector averaged an annual rate of 5.3 per cent for the last decade while GDP has grown a mere 3.8 per cent during the same period. The growth accelerated with Korea's active capital market opening, beginning in the early 1990s. The speed of market opening was accelerated further resulting from Korea's reaction to the 1997 Asian financial crisis. Finally in 1998, the Korean capital market reached full liberalization of foreign investment. As a result, currently the financial services sector contributes 8.5 per cent to Korea's GDP, while the contribution was only 3.8 per cent in 1985.

The capital market opened up quickly since the early 1990s. Before 1992, foreigners could only invest in the Korean stock market by using indirect methods — through the "Korea Fund" listed on the NYSE. In 1991, the Korean government announced the initial plan to open the capital market. Foreign direct investment in Korea's stock market was first permitted in 1992, but the government put a limit on foreign ownership of domestic equities. The opening of the stock market was to take place gradually, permitting more and more foreign ownership until the ceiling was completely abolished by 2002. This initial schedule for complete market opening was shortened, when the Korean economy entered and needed to overcome the financial crisis. By December 1998, the Korean government abolished the ceiling on foreign ownership in both the stock and bond markets.

Figure 9.1
Contribution of Financial Sector to GDP
(Percentage)

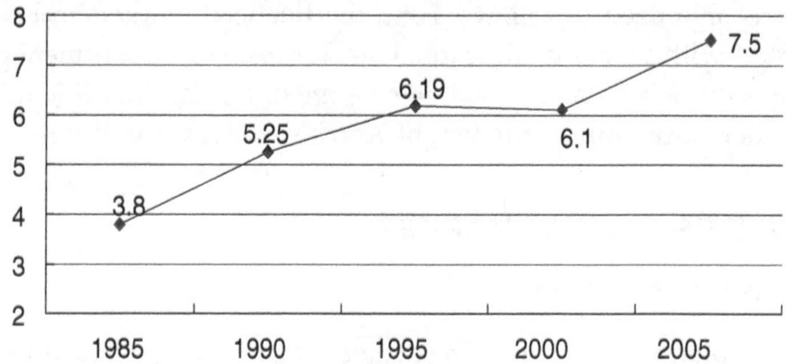

Source: Financial Statistics Information System, Financial Supervisory Service.

Figure 9.2
Increase in Foreign Shares in Korea's Stock Market, 1997–2004

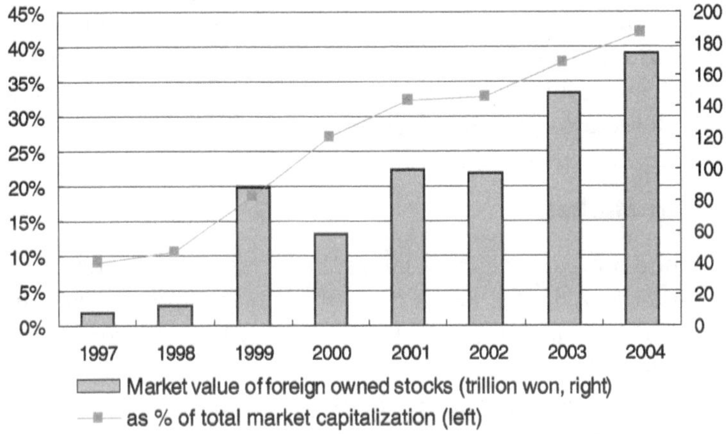

Source: Financial Statistics Information System, Financial Supervisory Service.

Now, Korea's capital market is a widely globalized market in terms of foreign participation in owning Korea's financial assets. Foreign ownership of Korea's stock market is over 30 per cent this year (it was more than 40 per cent in 2005). There are ninety-five foreign financial institutions doing business in Korea, 45 per cent of the total number of financial institutions.[1]

2.2. Equity Market

Korea's stock market is sixth in size in the Asia-Pacific region. Korea's market is comparable to that of Australia and China (excluding Hong Kong) in size already and still has potential for growth for a number of reasons:

— Its size relative to GDP is still low compared to financially advanced countries such as Hong Kong and Singapore.[2]
— The price earning ratio (PER) is very low at around 14. It is low not only in comparison to Asian markets (16.5), but also in comparison to the world average (15.7) and the advanced economies' average (15.8).
— The proportion of Collective Investment Schemes (CIS) portfolio distribution on equity investment is still very low at around 20 per cent.[3]

Foreign participation in Korea's stock market is significant. Foreigners own more than 30 per cent of listed stocks (reached over 40 per cent in 2005). There are fifteen branches of foreign securities companies operating in Korea, four local subsidiaries, and the largest shareholders of seven domestic firms are foreign entities (2005). Fifteen foreign branches account for 7.7 per cent of all stock market transactions and 8 per cent of the total assets of all securities firms in Korea.

2.3. Bond Market

Korea's bond market is the third largest in the region. Japan has the largest bond market in Asia. Its size is more than three times Korea's market.[4] Bonds in Korea are mostly issued by domestic entities. Government bonds accounted for 57 per cent of the total trade volume in 2006.

In terms of globalization, Korea's bond market is mostly a domestically oriented market thus far. Foreign bonds issuance (denominated both in Korean currency and foreign currency) is very minimal. Also, foreign investment in the bond market is less than 1 per

Figure 9.3
Market Capitalization of Regional Stock Markets, 2006

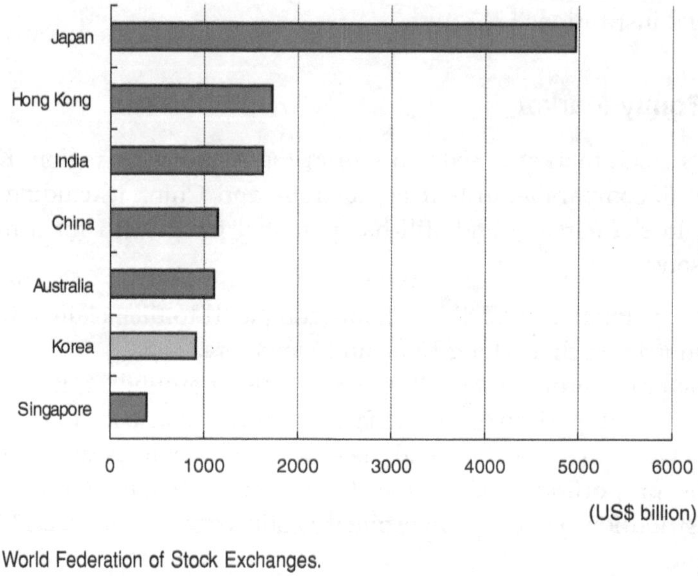

Source: World Federation of Stock Exchanges.

Figure 9.4
Trade Volume
(Domestic and Foreign Institutions)

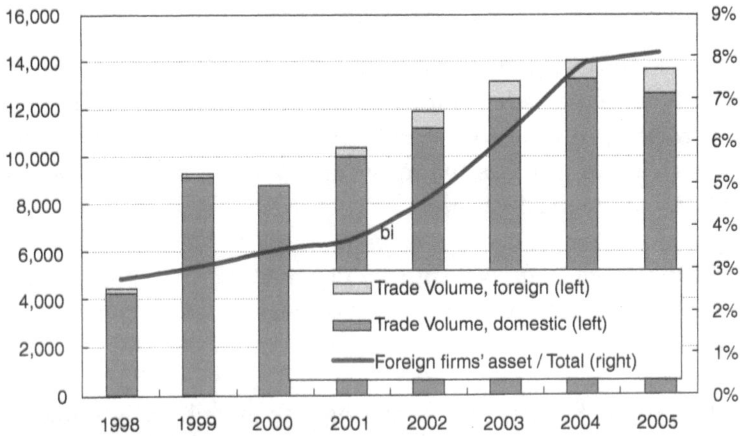

Source: Financial Statistics Information System, Financial Supervisory Service.

Figure 9.5
International and Domestic Bonds, 2006
(Amounts Outstanding)

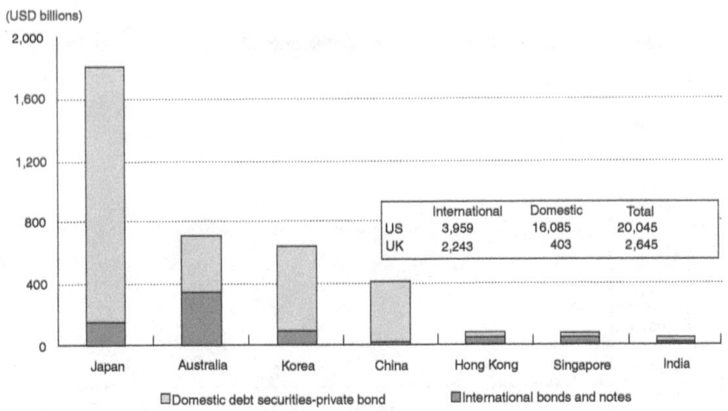

Source: Bank for International Settlements.

cent, which is a very low rate of foreign participation when compared to the activity in the stock market.

2.4. Derivatives

The derivatives market is one area in which Korea has had great success recently. In terms of trade volume, the Korea Exchange (KRX) is the largest in the world according to the Futures Industry Association. The stock index derivatives leads as the most traded in the market. Korea's most traded derivative products are:

— KOSPI (Korea Composite Stock Price Index) 200 has the world's most heavily traded derivative contracts. The number of traded contracts is sixteen times larger than the second largest, Eurex DJ EURO Stoxx 50, in 2006.

— Also, the KOSPI 200 futures are the fifth most heavily traded.

On the other hand, the OTC derivatives market is relatively less developed. According to the Bank for International Settlements (BIS),

Figure 9.6
Stock Index Derivatives
(Trade volume, US$ million)

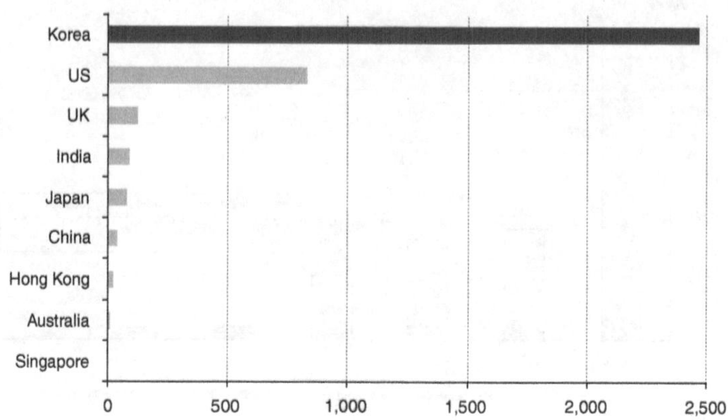

Source: Futures Industry Association.

Korea's OTC derivatives accounts only for 0.3 per cent of the world market and is the nineteenth largest in the world. However, the OTC market is rapidly growing. Compared to 2004, the market size increased 354 per cent, according to a BIS survey.

2.5. Asset Management

Although Korea's asset management sector has grown rapidly in recent years, its share of the world market is only 1.2 per cent. It is a very disappointing figure even with the 12 per cent increase during 2005–06. Total market share in the world market was even higher in 1998 with 1.3 per cent of the world's total assets under management.

In the Asia-Pacific region, Korea's asset management market is the fifth largest following Australia, Japan, Hong Kong and Singapore. However, the gap between Korea and the top four countries is very large. Korea's asset management sector accounts for 9.4 per cent of the total assets under management in the region in 2006 while the top four countries account for 86 per cent of the total assets under management.

Figure 9.7
Assets under Management, 2006

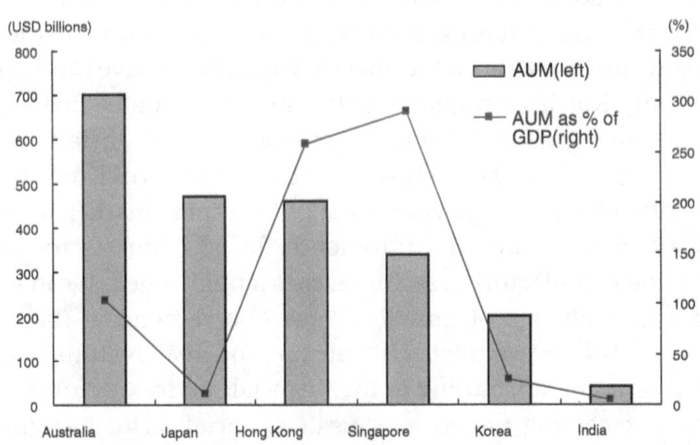

Source: Worldwide Mutual Fund Assets and Flows.

Korea's asset management sector possesses great potential for growth for a number of reasons. They are:

- Korea's household financial wealth is increasing rapidly. For the last decade, it grew at annual rate of more than 10 per cent.
- Although most wealth is held in bank deposits and currencies (60 per cent) and only 8 per cent is invested in stocks, more funds are expected to move into the asset management sector.
- Importance of the real estate market is losing momentum as government takes very serious measures to stabilize the real estate market. The funds are expected to eventually flow into the asset management sector.
- The Korean government is targeting the asset management sector as a key area to build an international financial centre.[5]

3. KOREA'S STRATEGY

3.1. Policy Shift

Until 1997, Korea's financial sector was not given high priority in the government's economic policies. Throughout the country's economic development in the 1970s and 1980s, Korea focused on achieving high growth through fostering its manufacturing sector. Financing was mostly done via traditional bank loans. Even in the early 1990s, the government focused on strengthening its manufacturing sector further while recognizing that the financial sector acted as an alternative funding source.

Ironically, Korea's recognition of the importance of the financial sector as an important growth factor of the economy was instigated by the 1997 Asian financial crisis. The crisis showed the weakness of Korea's financial sector. Without balanced development of the capital market, an economy cannot avoid such financial turbulence. In addition, as the economy matures, the manufacturing sector reaches a point where it can no longer maintain its high rate of growth. Korea also recognized that financial services had still not yet realized their full potential. Naturally, attention migrated from manufacturing to the financial services sector.

Since overcoming the crisis, Korea's financial sector has grown at a very fast pace. With the full liberalization of foreign investment in Korea's capital market in 1998, a number of foreign financial companies have

Figure 9.8
Policy Paradigm Shifts

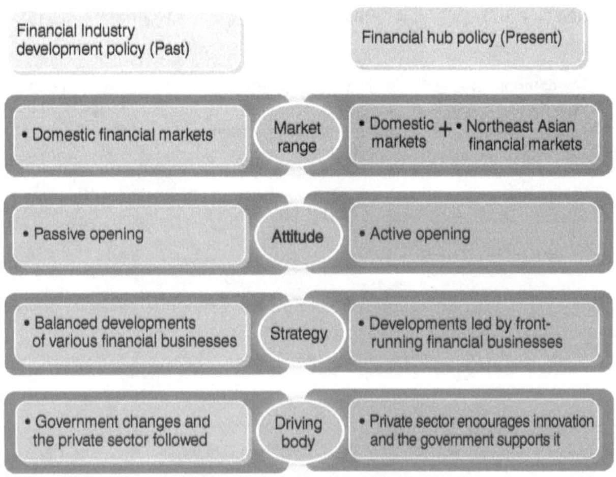

Source: Ministry of Finance and Economy.

opened branches in Korea and the capital market rallied as the foreign share of Korean markets increased. In fact, the fast opening of the market boosted the growth of the financial sector and the Korean government believes that the opportunities there are a new growth engine.

In the earlier stages when fostering the capital market was given high priority in Korea's economic policies, the main focus was limited to domestic institutions and the market. However, Korea's rapid market opening reveals the opportunities in a more global capital market. As the number of foreign institutions increases in the market, more domestic employment is created and the growth of the market contributes to the gross output. Also, the knowledge that Korea built up through overcoming the financial crisis in 1997 became an asset to Korea's financial sector supporting further growth in the global market. The focus of economic policy shifted from domestic markets to the international market; from financial industry development policies to a financial hub policy.

3.2. Strategy and Achievements

At the presidential committee meeting in December 2003, the Korean government resolved to create a Northeast Asian financial hub. Korea

Figure 9.9
Three-stage "Northeast Asian Financial Hub Promotion Strategy"

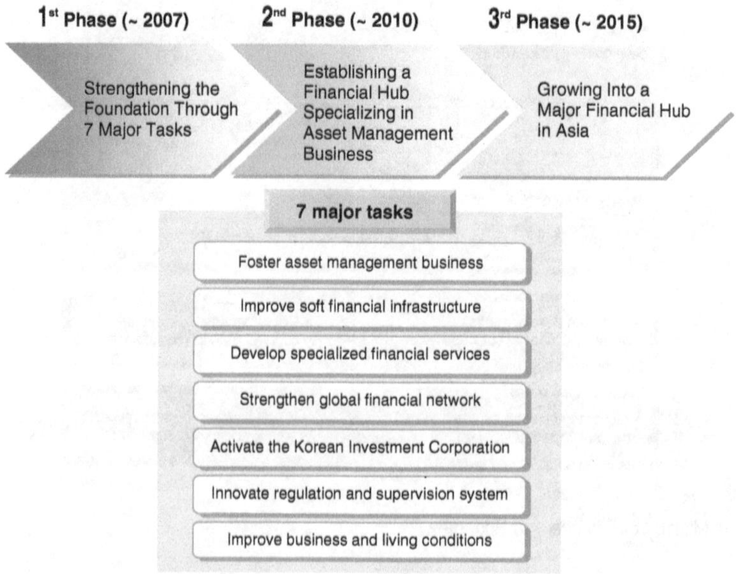

Source: "Strategies to Build Northeast Financial Hub", Ministry of Finance and Economy, 2003.

established its goal to be a major financial hub in Asia by 2015. This vision is to fashion Korea into a major financial hub through three phases. In the first phase, Korea will strengthen the foundation of its financial industry and the target date for completion is 2007. Second, Korea will also create a niche financial centre by specializing in the asset management sector by 2010. Lastly, Korea will develop into a major advanced financial centre by 2015. The following seven tasks are focus areas in the first phase of this strategy.

3.2.1. Foster the Asset Management Business

The first task of the Korean government is to develop the asset management sector. Specifically, the government will increase the demand for long-term asset management through a public-sector initiative. To this end, Korea took the following measures:

- Introduction of the corporate pension system in 2005 (Employment Retirement Securities Act (ERSA).
  This replaces the existing retirement allowance system. The biggest changes expected with the new system are the increase in outsourced management of pension funds. Under the previous system, most corporate funds were internally managed.
- National pension funds are permitted to invest in equities.
  Investment proportion in equities is very low, especially compared to other major funds. The National Pension Service announced its plans to increase its proportion of equity investment to 40 per cent by 2012 from the current level of 18 per cent.

Figure 9.10
Proportion of Equity Investment of Major Pension Funds

	CalPERS (2006.6)**	CPPIB (2006.3)	ABP (2006.9)
Proportion on equity investments	67%	63%	53.2%

CalPERS: California Public Employee Pension Funds, Operations Summary 2006
CPPIB: Canada Pension Plan Investment Board, Annual Report 2006
ABP: Dutch Public Pension Funds, ABP Annual Report 2006
**Measured dates differ as noted in the parenthesis

The Korean government also legislated the establishment of high risk/return funds. The government recently allowed the establishment of private equity funds (PEF) by a special law passed in 2004.[6] In addition, some limitations were relaxed further in 2006 with the special law. Now the minimum private investment requirement is 2 billion won, which is a significant reduction from the previous requirement of 5 billion won. These types of funds are also permitted to invest in non-performing loans (NPL).

The government has also taken steps to foster a market for the management of household financial assets. High government officials reiterate the government's intention to increase the fund inflow from the real estate sector to the financial sector. Currently, it is estimated that 80 per cent of Korea's household assets are invested in the real estate sector. Of the remaining 20 per cent of assets, investment in the capital market is less than 40 per cent.

3.2.2. Improve Soft Financial Infrastructure

Soft financial infrastructure was improved in many ways. First, Korea has reformed its financial regulation. The Financial Investment Services and Capital Market Act (commonly referred to as the Capital Market Consolidation Act) was ratified in 2007 by the parliament. This new regulation consolidates many finance related regulations into a single framework. The burden of multiple licensing requirements for varying products is expected to be significantly lifted with enactment of the new law in 2009. Also, the new regulation will change the current positive-list

Figure 9.11
Changes in Financial Regulation with the Capital Market Consolidation Act

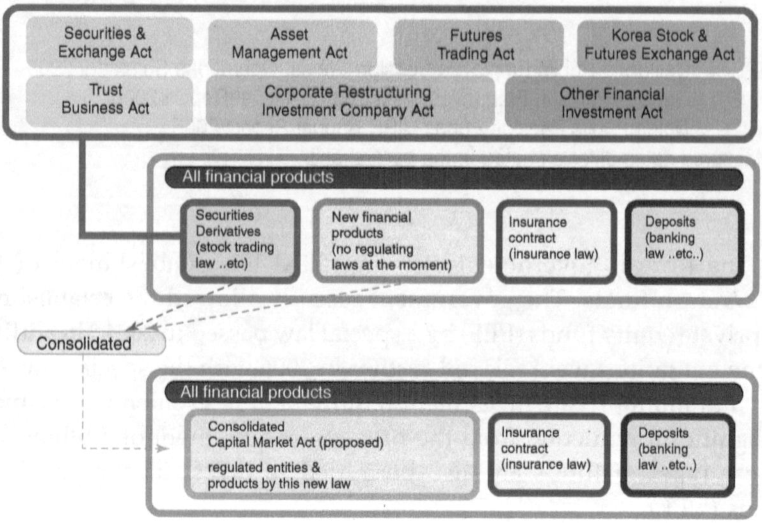

Source: Financial Hub Initiative in Korea, Ministry of Finance and Economy.

system (listing the allowed actions) to a negative-list system (listing the prohibited actions) so that coverage of the allowed actions or products will be broadened with the new system.

Another big achievement in regulation concerns foreign exchange control. Foreign financial companies often complain about difficulties arising from Korea's rather strict control of international capital movements. The Korean government announced its plan to fully liberalize the foreign exchange by 2009. Some restrictions already relaxed in 2006 are:

— Abolish the existing licence requirement for international capital transactions; now only a "report" *ex post* is required.
— Eliminate the limit on foreign residential housing investment (for residential purposes only. There was a limit of $1 million until 2006).

In the bond market, there were several achievements, such as:

— Separate Trading of Registered Interest and Principal of Securities (STRIPS) was introduced.
— Treasury inflation protected securities were introduced.
— Longer term government bonds (twenty-year) were issued.
— Simplified the issue process of foreign currency denominated bonds.

3.2.3. Engage in Regional Financial Projects to Develop Specialized Financial Services

Government-sponsored banks engaged in many Asian development projects such as:

- Korea Development Bank (KDB), which cooperated with regional financial firms such as the China Development Bank and Mizuho Bank on the Northeast Asia Development Financial Council (NADFC 2004) to research and investigate development infrastructure needs.
- The Export-Import Bank of Korea (EXIM), Export-Import Bank of China and the Japan Bank for International Cooperation, which cooperated on the Northeast Asia Export Credit Agency Summit to jointly finance development projects in Northeast Asia.
- KDB and EXIM, which financed shipbuilding and other marine transport projects.

3.2.4. Strengthen the Global Financial Network

In January 2006, the Ministry of Finance and Economy launched "FN hub Korea", which is a government sponsored organization that identifies and tries to handle difficulties that foreign financial institutions may face in their business operations in the Korean market. FN hub Korea plans to perform web-based surveys and have in-depth interviews with foreign and domestic financial firms in Korea.

3.2.5. Activate the Korea Investment Corporation

The government established the Korea Investment Corporation (KIC) in 2005 with the Ministry of Finance and Economy's (MOFE) initial investment of US$100 million. It was launched with a view of stimulating the development of a stronger asset management industry. KIC is mandated to manage part of Korea's foreign exchange reserves and other public funds by investing in a variety of financial assets in the international financial market. Now it is estimated that total assets are more than US$20 billion, 85 per cent of which are Bank of Korea's foreign reserves. According to a newspaper report in November 2006, KIC had invested US$12 billion, 38 per cent of which were invested in foreign stocks.

3.2.6. Innovate Regulation and the Supervision System

The Korean government is promoting a zero-base deregulation process among financial authorities. It is a process that helps government officials considering the demander's point of view in finding the areas for deregulation. Through the first and second stage of the zero-based deregulation process, 203 tasks were identified, 154 reviewed, and fifty-two tasks were deregulated. Deregulations include, for example, permitting insurance companies to own PEFs or shipbuilding investment companies as their subsidiaries. For more effective deregulation, four taskforce teams with different functions (Business operation, Corporate Finance, Consumer Protection, Finance Sanction) were established and have been actively involved in identifying reform tasks.

The FSS has also implemented market-friendly policies to provide a reasonable supervision system. This includes:

- Launching a no-action letter system, which will enhance the legal certainty for financial firms in a course of action.
- Disclosing the supervisory manual through its homepage.
- Introducing relationship managers (RM) who can consult and provide information to financial firms when it is requested.
- Launching a taskforce for supporting foreign financial institutions that will support them with business licensing, etc.

3.2.7. Improve Business and Living Conditions

To provide much demanded international schools, Yongsan International School of Seoul was opened last year. The project was the first joint project between the central and local governments to create better living conditions for foreign nationals living in Korea. Seoul leased the land for free, and the Ministry of Commerce and Industry provided about one third of the construction costs.

In an effort to raise financial experts, KAIST, a government sponsored university, opened a graduate school of finance. Also, the government launched the financial skills network centre in 2006. Its tasks include the creation and maintenance of a database of financial experts; the creation of a network among financial institutions, universities, financial experts; performing and publishing surveys of available financial skills; and developing the financial education system.

4. IMPLICATIONS

Korea's achievements were significant especially in its regulation changes. Most of all, Korea transformed its financial regulation framework to a single consolidated regulation framework. The new set-up will eliminate the difficulties arising from possible conflicts in many different laws in the existing system. And, more importantly, Korea's regulations are in line with the global standard. Also, the government is promoting its zero-based deregulation to continuously update its regulation to reflect the needs of the market participants.

There, however, there still exist areas for improvement. One of the areas will be the transparent and fair implementation of the regulations. Many surveys indicate that foreign firms still perceive that Korea's regulations are unfairly implemented. Also they complain about inefficient practices that may arise from customs. It is critically important to promote fair competition to establish an environment for a financial hub. Fair competition standards need to be strictly enforced especially in the implementation of financial regulation. Facilitating communication via publishing regulations would be a good way to promote transparency of Korea's regulation system. Also, existing self-regulatory organizations (SRO) can contribute to fair practice. Self-regulation is effective when the franchise values of individual businesses in a community stand to receive a considerable boost from cooperation to reduce the costs of dealing with limited trust and asymmetric information. Thus, strengthening the SRO's role would be an effective way to minimize costs associated with the inefficiencies in implementation.

Korea will focus on the asset management sector in its second phase of the financial hub strategy. This sector can grow very quickly when it is led by the government initiative. The sector can expand through an increase in outsourced management of public funds (the Korean national pension fund is the world's fifth largest pension fund). To promote this sector further, further allowances of various investment schemes is suggested. For example, hedge funds are one of the fastest growing investment schemes with total assets reaching US$1.2 trillion in 2006. In London, more than 20 per cent of total funds are managed by hedge funds. Currently, Korea is permitting the establishment of PEFs which specialize in buy-outs. However, having a broader legal background to include various investment schemes should also be considered.

In the second phase, Korea should consider promoting outward portfolio investment to globalize the domestic financial market. It is a given fact that effective foreign investment can increase risk-adjusted returns. This is another positive externality arising from building an international financial hub. The Korean government is making efforts to make effective outward portfolio investments through the establishment of the Korea Investment Corporation (KIC). It is noted by many financial experts that there are still too many restrictions for KIC to use the best strategies to manage its foreign investment funds. The success of KIC is critical in establishing an international financial hub. As KIC allocates more funds more effectively, top-class asset management companies will start doing business in Korea. Korea's asset management sector will benefit from hosting these institutions with high technology.

In addition, the construction of a cohesive leadership team that includes central and local governments, financial regulatory authorities, universities and leading financial institutions is suggested. Government leadership in building a financial hub is important and necessary but not sufficient. To be successful in building a financial hub, the availability of many high-skilled financial experts, office space, foreigner-friendly facilities, and more requires cooperation from government, and financial firms, etc. A high-level leadership team built from the top that could be co-chaired by the minister of the MOFE, the SMG chairman, chairmen of financial institutions and presidents of universities, would be desirable. The committee can then utilize sub-committees to focus on specific areas.

Korea has the framework for building a financial hub in place. The government has created an environment that is supportive of a financial centre. Now, the framework must be fleshed out. NGOs, private firms and the society as a whole must follow the government's leadership to change cultural attitudes, habits and education.

Notes

1. Financial institutions included are: banks, merchant banking corporations, life insurance companies, non-life insurance companies, securities companies, futures companies, and asset management companies.
2. This is low even comparing to some countries with small stock market size. For example, Taiwan's stock market is relatively small in size but the size relative to GDP exceeds 150 per cent.
3. One may note that CIS investment in stocks is growing. One of the contributing factors to this trend is that some of the restrictions on public funds are relaxed to include more stocks in their portfolio.
4. Japan's bond market is dominated by government bonds (more than 90 per cent).
5. This factor will be elaborated upon in the next section.
6. For now, only a special type of PEF (buy-out funds) is allowed with this enactment.

References

Asset Management Association of Korea. *Asset Management Industry in China* (in Korean), 2006.

American Chamber of Commerce in Korea. *Dynamic Korea Hub of Asia*, 2002.

California Public Employee Pension Funds. *Operations Summary, 2006.*

Canada Pension Plan Investment Board. *Annual Report, 2006.*

Corporate Restructuring Market Enhancement Task Force Report. *Corporate Restructuring Market in East Asia* (in Korean), 2006.

Dutch Public Pension Funds. *ABP Annual Report, 2006.*

Financial Supervisory Service. *Monthly Financial Statistics Bulletin,* 2007.

Fn Hub Korea. *Financial Hub Initiative in Korea,* 2007.

H. Kim, et al. *Seoul's International Finance Environment: A Comparative Study.* Korea Securities Research Institute, 2007.

Invest Korea. *Comparative Study of Investment Environment in Korea, Singapore and Taiwan: Comparison of Investment Promotion Agency, Incentive Programs and Investment Environment in Each Country,* 2006.

Korea Institute for International Economic Policy. *Development of a Northeast Asian Financial Hub in Korea: Case Studies and Their Implications* (in Korean), 2003.

Korea Investment Corporation Research Project Report. *Development of the Asset Management Market for a Financial Hub in Korea* (in Korean), 2007.

Ministry of Finance and Economy. *Building a Northeast Financial Hub via Strengthening Financial Industry* (in Korean), 2007.

So Cho, et al. *KRX Market Confidence Index* (in Korean). Korea Securities Research Institute, 2005.

The World Federation of Exchanges. *Annual Report, 2006.*

10

COMMENTS ON CASE STUDIES BY DISCUSSANTS

1. SESSION I: HONG KONG AND SINGAPORE

Comments by Sang Kee Min

Let me begin my comments by asking what has been and will be the role of a financial centre in Asia.

Before the Asian financial crisis, the answer was rather straightforward: Its aim was to work as a distribution centre of international funds to Asian countries that pursued rapid economic growth without sufficient domestic savings and well developed financial sector. After the Asian financial crisis, there was a huge and sudden reversal of capital flows from Asian countries. The rates of investment and growth of most Asian countries fell. These countries began to record current account surpluses and thus did not need to borrow from the international market. China was probably the only country that recorded a sustained, high growth rate. China's high growth, however, was not funded by foreign borrowing but rather, by foreign direct investments.

Unlike the situation before the crisis, Asian countries are now saddled with huge foreign exchange reserves. These countries are now more concerned with returns on these foreign exchange reserves than ways to borrow from the international market. Thus distribution of international funds has become less important for the Asian financial centre. The volume has been falling even in absolute amount. Businesses are commoditized and thus margins are not very attractive. Cross-border capital flows continued to grow even in Asia. But instead of straight bank borrowing, they are now taking the forms of equity, debt and derivative products. Singapore and Hong Kong have adjusted to the changes by adding new lines of businesses after the crisis. Dominic Barton described extensively the efforts made by Singapore to promote cross-border investment activities with special emphasis on the promotion of asset management business. Jesús Seade examined the role of Hong Kong in the traditional lines of financial activities in banking, foreign exchange and bond. The paper would have shed more light on Hong Kong's effort to adjust to the changing role of a financial sector, had it extended its analysis to the equity, derivative and asset management businesses.

I want to also comment on the newly emerging role of an Asian financial centre. In the years to come, the centre will be asked to assume an important role of promoting an Asian financial community. Intra-regional trade and investment are becoming more important. So far, however, capital flows to and from Asian countries have been with countries out of the region. Intra-regional capital flows have not been big in volume due to the under-development of national financial markets and prevalent capital controls over cross-border financial trade. One may argue that with the rapidly developing globalization of the financial markets, the discussion of an Asian financial community would be meaningless. The claim is that there will be only one global market and one global governing standard. But just as countries have preferred the regional Free Trade Area agreements to global free trade agreements, the development of an Asian financial market will help supplement rather than supplant a global financial market. As Tan Khee Giap discusses, Asian countries have a twin (maturity and foreign exchange) mismatch problem. An Asian financial centre would do a great service of promoting an Asian financial community if it can help resolve these mismatch problems.

Let me now move onto the lessons learned from Hong Kong and Singapore's effort to become and remain as an international financial centre. Benefits of becoming a leading financial centre are very well documented in Tan's chapter for the case of Singapore, so they will not be repeated here. But I find a grave lack of discussion on the demerits or cost of being a financial centre, especially with respect to exposing a country to the threat of foreign dominance. A country wanting to become an international financial centre will inevitably face the following questions:

- Is the country willing to accept the Wimbledon Phenomenon and see foreign capital and foreign financial companies dominating in its backyard?
- Is the country willing to accept a global standard in regulating financial businesses?
- Is the country willing to accept foreign nationals to run financial companies and/or to assume important positions at regulatory agencies?
- Is the country willing to accept English as the governing language in financial law and daily financial transactions?
- Is the country willing to accept a huge disparity in salary in its financial sector and do away with progressivity in the personal income tax system?
- Is the country willing to accept one of its cities to become over-developed compared to its other cities to become an international financial centre?
- Is the country willing to exempt tax withholding for international financial transactions?

For small city-states like Hong Kong and Singapore, it may not have been too difficult to say "yes" to all the questions above. But for countries with a larger population and a greater geography, domestic politics will not allow easy answers to the questions. Thus for those countries, temptation is high to fall back on nationalism to run the international finance in their own ways. Everybody must be familiar with the famous quote from President Abraham Lincoln's Gettysburg Address: "the government of the people, by the people and for the people shall not perish from the earth." The phrase is known to have expressed most succinctly the principle of a democratic government. But a similar phrase can have a totally different connotation in the field of international finance. "A financial centre of a nation, by a nation and for a nation shall never become an international financial centre." Japan, China and Korea should not substitute their names for "a nation" if they want to promote an international financial centre. Nationalism is the Number One enemy of an international financial centre. Nationalism remains very popular and makes it very difficult for a country with a large population and a diverse economy to build political consensus to say "yes" to all of the above questions. The presence of a big domestic market therefore can be a curse rather than a blessing.

Before I close, let me ask both Singapore and Hong Kong on their assessment of contrasting approaches they have taken in the order and speed of opening up their onshore businesses and in the internationalization of currency. Singapore adopted a "dichotomized approach" in that it allowed foreign banks to conduct only the offshore financial business. In contrast, Hong Kong adopted a "uniform approach" and allowed foreign banks to conduct both on- and offshore businesses. In hindsight, what are the assessments of each country on the contrasting approaches? Now that the Organization for Economic Cooperation and Development (OECD) has banned harmful tax competition and prohibited offering tax breaks exclusively for offshore transactions, the adoption of a dichotomized financial system is no longer feasible for OECD member countries. This raises the question of how long Singapore can maintain its dichotomized financial system. The two countries also differed in the strategy of currency internationalization. Singapore was very cautious and restricted the use of local currency for non-residents while Hong Kong allowed free convertibility and flow. Perfect freedom in cross-border capital flow undoubtedly gave Hong Kong a competitive edge over Singapore as a financial centre. The perfect convertibility together with a pegged-to-the-dollar exchange rate system in Hong Kong, however, at times, posed very serious adjustment problems to its economy. Korea and China would have to allow full convertibility of their currencies to make Seoul and Shanghai serious international financial centres. Challenges lie before them in deciding whether they should take the Hong Kong or Singapore model.

1.2. Comments by David Hong

Unless a particular location has a big lead over its other rivals, it may be difficult for one city to be a dominant financial centre in Asia, given that due to modern technology, people can work from almost anywhere. Even New York and London, the two most dominant global financial centres, have not been able to increase their lead over other cities. In fact, the opposite has happened, with the number of financial centres growing over the past few years, with some — such as Dubai's and Singapore's financial centres — practically being built from scratch within a short period of time.

There are different types of financial centres. Some are global centres (London and New York), financial capitals serving large national markets (Tokyo, Sydney, Frankfurt, Paris), financial centres serving as a gateway to fast-growing regions (Hong Kong, Singapore, Dubai), and financial centres that have specialized in particular niches (Geneva for private banking, Zurich and Bermuda for insurance, Chicago for futures and options, Qatar for infrastructure finance, Bahrain for Islamic finance, Houston for energy trading and energy-specialized hedge funds, and Boston for asset management and private equity). Given this situation, there are many ways by which Asian cities may aspire to become financial centres. A more realistic objective for Asian economies would be to try to find a niche where they can excel.

Demutualization of exchanges (going public), which increases efficiency and enhances competitiveness, is gaining ground in America and Europe, but not in Asia. Unless Asian exchanges become more efficient and competitive, they will lag behind their counterparts in these developed markets.

There has been a recent trend toward cross-border consolidation of exchanges. Big exchanges are merging (for example, New York Stock Exchange with Euronext, London Stock Exchange with Borsa Italiana, and the International Securities Exchange of New York with the German Stock Exchange). As financial exchanges are now also increasingly demutualizing and becoming publicly traded firms, private entities are likely to gain ownership of exchanges (Macquarie Bank attempted to acquire the London Stock Exchange, though this did not push through). Unless Asia's exchanges grow through consolidation, for example, through the merger of several Asian exchanges, they are likely to remain small in comparison to the large American and European exchanges and will be vulnerable to being taken over (if they become publicly traded firms).

Because of globalization, deregulation and liberalization, Asia's exchanges face very strong competition from established financial centres like New York and London, which are attracting an increasing number of Asian companies to go to their capital markets. For Asian financial markets to become more efficient and to be encouraged to find their own niches, they must be exposed to competition. Competition among Asian markets would be beneficial, but this would require cross-border financial integration, which in turn would necessitate capital account liberalization and deregulation, which involve political challenges.

There is no single route to success in becoming an important financial centre. Different factors have been dominant contributors to the success of different financial centres. However, the credibility of markets appear to depend a lot on the quality of regulation, legal systems and corporate governance, an open financial sector and political stability. Other factors include:

— Infrastructure (international air links, efficient telecommunications systems, etc.)
— Openness and attractiveness to talent (quality of life, taxes, immigration policies)
— Location (proximity to large, fast-growing or affluent market for financial services)
— Low levels of corruption
— Wide use of English (the language of global finance)
— Presence of high-quality support services (international law firms, accounting firms, public relations firms, consultants) and institutional investors (which give the market depth and maturity, in contrast to retail investors which dominate less developed markets)
— Financial incentives.

2. SESSION II: TOKYO AND SYDNEY

2.1. Comments by Simon Cooper

"Why is an international financial centre so important? It's certainly not a new trend that many countries and cities in Asia are trying to become financial services hubs."

Why? A financial services hub, a world class financial centre, creates a large pull of technological know how, a range of products within the country's economy that both improves efficiency and size of the market, benefit for both the producer and the consumer. International competition is what forces financial companies to be efficient. And the end result is higher GDP. The volume of additional business and GDP creates employment opportunities, and a financial services centre connects a country to the global world economy.

So what makes a financial services centre? There are many components and I would like to synthesize those themes into two main areas: Innovation and globalization.

Innovation is largely encouraged and stimulated by advantageous tax systems, educated financiers, or at least, access to well educated human capital, by free competition between domestic and foreign participants, and finally by regulatory liberalization.

Take tax for example. In order to attract international financial companies and global financial talent, an economy needs to offers attractive tax benefits or tax system. If you look at Hong Kong, which is arguably one of the best financial centres not just in Asia but in the world, they have already had low tax rates: 16 per cent and 17.5 per cent for individuals and corporates respectively. But even they are looking to lower their tax rates further. It has just announced that they will lower it to 15 per cent for personal tax, and 16.5 per cent for corporate. I do not believe in special treatment but it is true that lower tax leads to higher investment. Governments have a budget to balance but to promote the financial services sector, the more they can do to reduce taxes the better. It has been argued that Tokyo and Sydney could both benefit from a reform of their tax structures.

Next is education. This could be the single most important ingredient to innovation. Simply put, international financial companies need access to a large pool of highly trained financial professionals. Sydney scores highly on this and Sydney's financial workforce is something like 375,000 as of May 2005. That is nearly half the size of London's and more than a third of the size of New York's. If you look at the IMD's 2006 survey, Australia ranked fifth and seventh, in the categories of education and finance and economic literacy respectively. This is in part attributable to the Australian government and its efforts to cultivate a skilled financial workforce. Axiss Australia created the financial services training alliance which works with key organizations involved in the provision of financial services training and education in Australia.

AFSTA has provided a forum for promoting Australia's expertise in the industry. Australia's expertise in the delivery of financial services, education and training and also its role in joint marketing around the world, means that it attracts people to come to Australia — non-Australians to come for training.

If you contrast that with Japan, many talented people in Japan join the government or they tend to join the large Japanese banks. We are starting to see signs of change in that with college graduates increasingly choosing to work in international financial service companies. There is clearly some way to go. If one is giving advice to governments, I think ultimately every dollar that is spent on improving the quality of higher education for domestic and foreign students will bring significant rewards in terms of enhancing the capability of an international financial centre.

To be successful requires a mix of foreign and local human capital. To be an international financial centre, you need to provide an environment where foreigners are welcomed. To my mind London remains a best example of that. One of London's key success factors has been the level playing field, and commitment to bring the best talent from around the world to work in the London market. In the bank industry alone, there are 255 foreign banks. More than 50 per cent of the total assets of the total U.K. banking industry are held by foreign banks.

London gives a valuable lesson to Tokyo and Australia, especially Tokyo. As a result of the financial "Big Bang" in 1996, foreign investment in the Japanese stock market has increased but the fact that only four foreign companies have listed since 2004 suggests that there is still tremendous work to be done in terms of globalization. One has to ask how much stronger the Japanese market could have been if they allowed foreign investors sooner and with more open arms.

Australia's model is clearly viewed as successful by simplifying and unifying the financial regulations and the financial services reform act in

2002. Australia successfully reformed the financial regulatory system in an efficient way. This allowed the Australian capital market to grow and Australian is the fourth largest asset management market in the world and Asia is the largest.

Looking at Japan, the bank agency system, provisionary corporation law allowing a foreign firm to merge with or acquire a Japanese firm through its subsidiary, are all part of the "Big Bang" in 1996, as were the plans to further re-arrange the firewalls and encourage competition between banks and securities companies. Any form of competition ultimately benefits customers. The best thing a regulator can to do is to stimulate competition: bring down barriers between elements of a market, be that banks versus securities companies, or enabling foreign interests to compete on a level playing field. All of this will stimulate competition, which will lead to product and service innovation. Let the market do its job. That will force innovation and productivity.

My second strand of thought concerns globalization. Undoubtedly you need to attract as many global financial players into a city as possible in order to be a financial hub or centre. It is important to attract inward as well as outward investment. One of London's high advantages has been its high proficiency of English. After all, English is the global language of finance. If a city wants to become or improve its positioning as a financial centre, then English has to be encouraged as a common language. Global financial institutions need a city to provide a large pool with good English communication skills. That language skill affects daily life as well. Foreign workers find it difficult to live in a city if English is not really used. Road signs, restaurant menus, government manuals, they should all be able to be read in English anywhere they feel comfortable.

If we come back to Sydney versus Tokyo, and compare them to other hubs in Asia, clearly hubs like Hong Kong, Singapore, and Sydney have a comparative advantage over Tokyo and Seoul in this regard. But this is changing rapidly and living here in Seoul, we are seeing a prevalence of the English language.

Also, global expansion of domestic businesses is also important. If you look at manufacturing, Japan has Sony, Australia has Fosters. These are global brands we are familiar with. Korea has its Samsung. Why can't there be an equivalent of a Sony or a Fosters in the financial services sector? One has started to see many Australian banks begin their expansion into Asia. Increasing competition amongst the Australian banks has resulted in decreasing trust margins and started to push them offshore. They are looking at China and other Asian countries for new sources of revenue. The Macquarie Group, for example, has successfully positioned itself in Asia as a global investment bank. It already operates in twenty-four countries, has fifty offices, and is a bank that earns 55 per cent of revenues outside of Australia. Looking at Korea, some of the Korean financial institutions are benchmarks themselves against Macquarie in terms of asset management.

To conclude, the fact that major Asian cities are competing to be a regional financial services centre is a good thing. Competition by definition is a good thing and will drive all of them forward. As a banker, I also think that such competition will bring tremendous synergistic benefits. The international financial services organizations will benefit from it and will enjoy a better business environment. It does not mean that competition has to be a zero-sum game. I think Asia can support a number of financial services centres and we have started to see already that different financial services centres, like Tokyo and Sydney, can develop on their own characteristics and their own strengths. There can be different sub-regional strengths as the market's development. For lack of a better cliché, it should really be a win-win game for all involved.

2.2. Comments by Hugh Patrick

The authors of these two chapters have in common their emphasis on policies whereby the financial systems in Australia and Japan can become more financially competitive internationally and more rapidly, focusing particularly on their respective regulatory and tax policies. However these two papers, both good, are fundamentally different in approach, focus, and style. Sayuri Shirai excellently and comprehensively discusses, with a great deal of detail, the evolutionary development of Japan's financial system, from being banking based to capital market oriented. She ends with a series of proposals as to what should be done further to make Japan an international financial centre.

Nicholas Gruen's paper is not specifically on Sydney; rather, it addresses a set of important regulatory issues, and proposes policies by which Australia can become an exporter of financial services. He draws a nice analogy for financial services with manufacturing, shifting from import-competing to export-oriented. One of the important parts of his paper is his focus on the requirements both of regulatory regimes and of tax regimes so as to make Australian asset management funds attractive to foreigners.

Gruen focuses on how a financial regulatory system has to balance domestic needs and international needs. It has to be prudential, and be concerned about tax avoidance issues. But basically it must create conditions that make it attractive for foreign funds to be allocated to Australian management. His particularly important themes are that the regulatory system must be both responsive and adaptive to rapidly advancing financial technologies and market conditions. He argues that effectively this can be achieved through feedback mechanisms involving co-evolutionary adjustments between the regulators and the market players. That is a nice contribution.

So why is Sydney not an even greater international financial markets player? After all, it has the fourth largest asset management industry in the world. Gruen has two answers. The main answer is that the shift to its required pension system has forced Australians to decide how their pension funds are to be allocated. This has created a huge pool of domestic financial assets that have to be managed by someone. That policy has been the foundation of the very successful development of the Australian asset management industry. Because these have been domestic in origin and are so large and presumably so profitable, that they have reduced incentives of Australian asset managers to think in international terms for sources of funds. Only 3 per cent of Australian assets under management have originated from foreign sources.

Interestingly, Gruen's paper takes a global, not an Asian regional approach. His national models are Dublin and Luxembourg. He appropriately stresses the importance of niche markets, and of creating a highly competitive environment globally, not just regionally.

In a comparative context, Australia has some interesting similarities to as well as many differences from Japan. Both had protectionist real economies and financial systems, and both then moved increasingly to being open. Both countries implemented financial "Big Bang" policies. Australia's, about two decades ago, was big and sudden, whereas Japan's financial liberalization has been much more gradual and is still ongoing. Both Australia and Japan have, relative to their economies, very large domestic financial markets. This is indicated by asset management in the case of Australia; since Japan is the world's second largest economy it has a huge domestic financial market. Importantly, that generates a domestic rather than an international focus in both market players and policymakers.

Another similarity, somewhat surprisingly, is that Sydney and Tokyo rank about equal in the most recent global market centres index. Sydney ranks as number 7 and Tokyo ranks as number 9. Since the differences between numbers six, seven, eight, nine and ten, are small, they are roughly equivalent, albeit for very different reasons. According to the index study and Gruen's paper, Sydney is strong in the quality of life and has good regulation, but somehow it is losing quality human resources to foreign markets. Tokyo has good physical infrastructure but is weak in human resources and its regulatory environment.

Shirai's paper fits well into the purposes of this volume. She nicely explains the evolution of the Japanese financial system, particularly in the most recent fifteen years or so, as it makes efforts to become more international. A major goal of the Japanese Big Bang of 1996, in addition to creating a free and fair financial system, was to make Japanese financial markets global in orientation and competitiveness. Since the mid-1990s Japan has been moving away from its previous anti-competitive, convoy regulatory system and towards a prudential system. Nonetheless, it still has a considerable way to go. While the Big Bang aimed to free up capital markets, it was subsequently overwhelmed by the non-performing loan problems of Japanese banks. That became the first priority to solve, and was accomplished by 2005. Now the regulatory authorities are turning to financial market reforms.

Shirai discusses four reasons why Japanese policymakers want to make Tokyo a top international financial centre. Two are essentially domestic in nature. One is to utilize Japanese financial wealth more efficiently, thereby raising yields; the other is to enhance Japanese financial sector productivity and thereby GDP growth. The other two reasons are more international. Japan has a potential comparative advantage in finance. Its wealth makes a good platform for Asian finance; exploiting its comparative advantage will benefit Japan in terms of high quality jobs and tax revenues. Second, Japanese financial institutions, after having withdrawn internationally since the urban real estate and stock market burst bubbles in the early 1990s, have completed their restructuring and are once again prepared to expand international business. To a large extent their focus is on Asia, where Japanese production and assembly activities create demand for financial services. Japanese foreign subsidiaries and partners consider Japanese banks a preferred source of finance.

There are two further benefits. Strengthening international competitiveness of Japanese financial markets is an important way to strengthen other Japanese domestic markets. To improve its international competitiveness, an industry first must improve domestic competitiveness. This is crucial in the case of Japanese international financial market competitiveness.

A second, perhaps even more important, reason for Japan's financial internationalization effort is to alter the mindset of Japanese financial institutions, regulators, and other players, from domestic and parochial to international and competitive. This mindset is not unique to Japan of course. Moreover, as Shirai points out, despite its huge size, even the Japanese domestic market remains under-developed in important areas. Most notably are the lack of a developed corporate bond market; the lack of a middle level, relatively high yield loan or bond market; and the lack of securitization and the use of derivatives.

Japanese accounting standards are gradually approaching international standards but have not yet reached them. The Financial Services Agency (FSA) is a relatively new organization which initially had to overcome the reputation of its predecessor, the Ministry of Finance, as being excessively close to and indeed cozy with private sector financial players. So it initially had to take a hands off, distant attitude. That meant that good communication and cooperation, co-evolution with private sector players, have not yet been developed in Japan. The FSA has now established sufficient credibility and independence that the time has come to initiate adequate communications with the private-sector players, learning from the Australian model.

Some factors are beyond the ability of government or markets to control. One is distance. Why are Japanese hedge funds moving to Singapore and not to Sydney, given the high quality of life in Sydney? Sydney is just too far away; it takes somewhat more time to travel there from Tokyo. Cultural differences probably are a factor as well. One of the biggest obstacles for Japan to become an international financial centre is that the language of Japan, and indeed its domestic markets, is Japanese and language of international finance and business is English. In contrast, that English is its language is a great economic and financial benefit to Australia.

2.3. Comments by Tan Teck Meng[1]

1. What Makes a "Financial Centre?"

While a myriad of definitions exist for the term "financial centre", a common theme underscored by them is that a "financial centre" is a city which acts as a clearing house for international financial transactions that are both voluminous and varied. The efficiencies arising from a centralized position are thought to stem from the economies of scale of such functions as (1) quick and easy access to the knowledge and services of complementary and competitive institutions; (2) clearing and exchange process for checks, drafts, and stock certificates; (3) availability of larger and cheaper amounts of capital for borrowers and greater liquidity for lenders; and (4) the personal expertise of those experienced in international management matters.[2]

Kindleberger summarized the attributes of financial centres by the functions they perform:

> Financial centres are needed not only to balance through time the savings and investments of individual entrepreneurs and to transfer financial capital from savers to investors, but to also effect payment and to transfer savings between places. Banking and financial centres perform a medium of exchange function and an inter-spatial store-of-value function. Single payments between separate points in a country are made more efficiently though a centre, and both seasonal and long-run surpluses and deficits are best matched in a centre. Furthermore, the specialized functions of international payments and foreign lending or borrowing are typically best performed at one central place that is also [in most instances] the specialized centre for domestic interregional payments.[3]

2. Background

Financial services is an attractive business sector for cities seeking to develop because it has been a successful, high-growth sector for the past quarter of the century and also because it is a highly mobile sector, which can be influenced by policy and planning.

Financial sector foreign direct investment (FDI) results in:[4]

- Higher technology transfer rates;
- Higher wages;

- Strengthened institutional development through improved regulation and supervision;
- Acceleration of a country's integration with world business cycles (through heightened allocative efficiency); and
- A multiplier effect to the economy.

In recent years, the financial industry has seen more offshoring of analytics from more developed financial centres in the United States and Europe to the Asia-Pacific region. This makes it an even more lucrative sector as financial centres in the Asia-Pacific region rush to attract these opportunities. In September 2005, PricewaterhouseCoopers found that the scale of offshoring in the financial services sector is set virtually to double by 2008.[5] Additional benefits are seen in the potential technology transfer and training from these offshoring opportunities. These may expand the human capital of the employees of the foreign firms within these host countries. The expansion of human capital may manifest itself in greater worker productivity.

3. Sydney and Tokyo: In Retrospect

Previous research has indicated that there are many factors of competitiveness. A study conducted by Z/Yen for the City of London has grouped these factors into five key areas — people, business environment, market access, infrastructure and lastly, critical mass arising from the synergistic interplay of the first four factors. Four of these factors will be discussed by reference to their current state, namely, people, business environment and market access, and infrastructure. The interplay of these factors will be covered later as we bring into view what both cities have done so far to attain critical mass.

3.1. People

A high percentage of individuals in both countries complete upper secondary education before moving onto tertiary education. However, tertiary education in Japan does not meet the standards of excellence set at the primary and secondary level. A lower share of GDP is assigned to education, with results manifesting in the poor state of academic facilities.[6] A recent report published by the OECD in 2007 has also shown similar failures of the Howard government in Australia to invest in higher education.

Where tertiary and higher education is concerned, the Educational Policy Institute has ranked Australia sixth and twelfth in accessibility and affordability respectively; Tokyo was not ranked on accessibility, but was ranked sixteenth in terms of affordability. But even so, both Japan and Australia boast a highly skilled and educated workforce.

3.2. Business Environment and Market Access

3.2.1. *Overview*

While Japan's equity market[7] is among the world's largest, its growth has largely been checked due to onerous listing procedures and heightened competition from its other Southeast Asian neighbours. The Japanese version of Sarbanes-Oxley (J-Sox), expected to come into effect in 2008, will result in even more stringent accounting oversight and detailed screening of listings. On August 2007, the credit contagion from the United States' subprime and asset-backed markets spilled over into Japan's markets, far more than any other country's;[8] at the height of the panic, the Nikkei 225 fell by 9 per cent in a single week.

While the size of the Australian equity market is only about a quarter of that of Japan, there has been substantial financial deepening in Australia since the 1980s as real incomes of households have increased. This has sparked an increasing demand for a greater variety of sophisticated financial products. This is coupled with a growing realization amongst individuals of the need to self-fund their retirement, rather than rely entirely on the public provision of pensions.[9] Together with deregulation, these factors provide the market with various opportunities that can be tapped.

3.2.2. *Regulation*

The key difference between the Australian and Japanese business environment seems to lie in the level of regulation. Australia's already deregulated financial sector may provide it with the edge over Japan, which is in the midst of remodelling its financial sector.

With the bursting of the asset bubble in the earlier part of the 1990s, Japan was for many years saddled with bad debt. The "Big Bang" initiative was introduced in the mid-1990s to revitalize the financial sector. These reforms to the financial infrastructure were aimed at the insurance, securities and banking sectors; other key elements included the creation of an efficient and fair market, as well as improving the overall stability of the financial system.[10]

However, bankers in Japan still bemoan existing regulative barriers which reduce efficiency, increase risk for everybody and weaken the country's reputation as a financial centre. As a result of the use of firewalls between banks and their brokerage units, the different businesses are regarded as different legal entities, with rules in place limiting how they are run. This in turn requires that these business units be represented by separate managers, which is both costly and inefficient. Foreign financial institutions, faced with intense scrutiny from regulators and tax authorities and a 40 per cent-plus corporate and personal income tax rate, are starting to decamp to regional competitors such as Singapore and Hong Kong.[11]

Despite the gloom, the Financial Services Agency (FSA) has taken important regulatory and legal steps to address the anemic financial sector in recent years. In June 2007, it unveiled plans to revamp the existing financial framework.[12] Some of the proposed initiatives are a re-look at the existing tax regime as well as the firewall systems that compartmentalize banks and their brokers; overall, these plans aim to further develop the country's financial markets.

Australia, on the other hand, had begun its reforms in the financial sector much earlier than Japan by implementing a number of new policies progressively after the 1980s. Policies implemented based on the suggestions of two inquiries into the financial sector — the Campbell Committee in 1979 and the Wallis Committee in 1996 — brought significant changes to the financial landscape in Australia. Key changes include the creation of the Australian Competition and Consumer Commission, responsible for competition, the Australian Securities and Investment Commission, responsible for market conduct and consumer protection, and the establishment of a new institution called the Australian Prudential Regulation Authority (APRA) in July 1998. APRA serves as the prudential regulator of the entire Australian financial services industry. Deregulation in the banking sector was argued to have brought greater competition and efficiency as shown in studies by Avkiran (2000) and Strum and William (2002).

However, the Business Council of Australia, in a 2007 report[13] on Australia's tax system, identified key problems in the Australian tax regime. A notable issue brought up was the divide between federal and state tax systems, which added to the complexity of the tax system, rendering it inefficient. It was argued that reform in business taxes is needed to sustain high levels of economic growth and maintain the global competitiveness of Australia.

3.3. *Infrastructure*

Growing affluence has resulted in increased car ownership, which has led to roads in both cities being strained despite being extended and improved in recent years. Fortunately, efficient and extensive subway and rail systems that connect to congested Tokyo business districts help reduce the traffic load. This is reflected in the 31.7 per cent increase in passengers carried on the country's public and private railways between 1970–71 and 2002–03.[14] Where the cost of office occupancy is concerned, Sydney has a relative advantage over Tokyo.[15]

Studies[16] have shown the use of IT in banking yields improvement in productivity in terms of quality and variety of banking services. Despite an embarrassing and abrupt closure of the Tokyo Stock Exchange (TSE) caused by Livedoor, Japan's technological sophistication is still rivalled only by the United States. In a BSA sponsored study conducted by the Economist Intelligence Unit (EIU), Japan was placed second and Australia fifth. The information technology (IT) industries in both countries act as "competitiveness enablers" in their financial sector, especially in banking, where IT is heavily relied upon by its large scale "back-office" operations.

Living standards in Japan are among the highest in the world, but still lag behind Australia's, according to a study conducted by Mercer earlier this year.[17]

4. Vision

4.1. *Tokyo*

Two government agencies, FSA and the Council of Economic and Fiscal Policy (CEFP), are responsible for economic development and revival in Japan. Regarding the development of Tokyo into a Global Financial Centre, the two organizations offered no explicit vision. However, the International Banker's Association (IBA), which works closely with the FSA, has recommended the following vision in its paper dated 16 March 2007:

- The largest, most dynamic financial market in Asia;
- "Made in Japan" financial innovation to set the standard for the world;
- A highly competitive and open financial sector serving both institutional and individual clients;
- Capital markets to be the critical source of financing for Japanese corporations to carry out their operations, hence reducing the risk of an over-reliance on bank financing;
- Play a leadership role in innovative regulatory and supervisory practices;
- Financial services industry is seen as a viable and rewarding career option.

We believe it serves as a good proxy for the Japanese government's vision for Tokyo.

To sum up, IBA's vision sees Tokyo as "a marketplace that is both truly international yet unmistakably built on the key strengths of Japan" by 2015.

4.2. Sydney

In 1999, the Australian government established Axiss Australia to aid financial institutions in setting up or expanding their operations within Australia. This is done through providing legal advice and facilitating communication between the private and public sectors. The vision of Axiss is to position Sydney as a global financial services centre in the Asian time zone. In 2003, it merged with Invest Australia. Some of the strengths the agency identified to promote globally include the following:

- Economic strength and sophisticated market;
- Skilled, multilingual workforce;
- Low-cost business environment;
- World-class information, communications and technology infrastructure;
- Best practice regulatory framework;
- Favourable time zone;
- High quality of life;
- Ideal gateway into the Asia-Pacific region.

5. Strategies and Roadmap

5.1. People

Tokyo

There are no strategies in place specifically to improve the quality of the workforce in the financial industry.

Sydney

In Sydney, through Axiss Australia, two initiatives are in place to improve the quality of labour in the financial industry. Axiss Australia continues to work closely with Australian university and training institutions to ensure that the quality of financial graduates is maintained. Besides working with its education partners, Axiss Australia also offers scholarships through its Axiss Scholars Programme to groom outstanding individuals for a career in the finance industry.

5.2. Business Environment

Tokyo

In 2005, Tokyo took steps to bring its accounting practices into conformity to those set by the International Accounting Standards Board (IASB) with a goal of ultimately attaining full convergence.[18] This move is geared towards improving the recognition of Japanese accounting standards globally and aid the development of Japanese capital markets into a global institution.

A series of scandals involving firms such as Livedoor, Murakami Fund and Kanebo have prompted the Japanese government to amend their Securities and Exchange Law. In June 2006, the Financial Instruments and Exchange Law, an equivalent of the Sarbanes-Oxley Act, or "J-Sox" for short, was passed by the Diet. The government felt that it was important to increase the transparency of Japanese capital markets as a necessary condition to restore investors' confidence. At the same time, by adopting the best practices adopted by other financial centres, the Japanese government believes Japan's attractiveness as a global financial hub will improve.

Discussions are also ongoing to debate the merits of restoring taxes on capital gains and dividends to their 2001 levels.[19] Currently, the FSA is a staunch supporter of maintaining the status quo of the tax arrangements, even though the exemptions had drawn dissension for causing an increase in the income gap. The FSA feels that the exemptions play an important role in diverting funds away from saving and towards equity investment, which is an essential ingredient in establishing a global capital market.

Sydney

In June 2007, the Australian Parliament passed a law exempting both local and foreign partners of venture capital firms from paying income and capital gain taxes.[20] Additionally, a US$80 million is allocated to four venture capital funds through the Innovation Investment Fund to explore the potential of a wide spectrum of opportunities available in Australia. The intention behind these developments was to provide a further boost to the strong venture capital market that Australia currently enjoys. Currently, Australia is the venture capital hub of the Asia-Pacific, with a market share of 32 per cent of all funds invested in the region.

5.3. Market Access

Tokyo

In April 2007, four members of CEFP recommended that the TSE and its commodities counterparts merge[21] to strengthen Tokyo's image and competitiveness as an investment centre. The rationale behind the proposed merger is to facilitate cross-selling and maintain its global standing amid the wave of consolidation throughout global financial markets. More details will be available when CEFP publishes "The Plan for Enhancing Competitiveness of Financial and Capital Markets" at the end of 2007.

The FSA also wants to evolve the financial system into one that attracts international investors and talent to Japan. An example of its strategy to do so is the raising of the international standing of Japanese financial markets. This could be done by decreasing the duration required between settlement and payment dates.[22]

Sydney

In June, the Australian prime minister proposed the establishment of a carbon-trading exchange by 2012.[23] Besides the environmental benefits, the exchange would also facilitate the further development of the derivatives market in Australia with the availability of a wider range of instruments. Presently, European Climate Exchange, the top carbon exchange in the world, resides in London with an annual turnover of €10 billion (US$12.8 billion) annually.

5.4. Infrastructure

Tokyo

The FSA plans to strengthen financial institutions and develop financial infrastructure using information technology.[24] Currently, Japanese financial institutions have lagged behind its regional rivals in terms of information technology investment and this has resulted in poor cost competitiveness. With the proposed increase in IT capabilities, cheaper and superior dissemination of information in an accurate and timely fashion will be available to meet market demand.

Plans to bolster the market functions are also in place to raise the confidence level within the markets. Some of the measures proposed include improving the companies' disclosure system as well as reforming existing tax laws.

Besides the plans drawn up by the FSA, plans are also in place to develop a specialized financial district[25] in Tokyo. Spearheaded by the Urban Renaissance Headquarters, a district in central Tokyo will be devoted to the development of Tokyo's version of Canary Wharf, which will cater specially to financial services firms and their supporting institutions. Under the proposed plan, firms operating within the zone will enjoy preferential treatment such as tax incentives and expedited construction permits. Amenities such as English-speaking schools and hospitals will also be provided within the zone.

Sydney

There are no strategies in place specifically to improve the infrastructure in the financial industry. Most of the infrastructure reform within Sydney is focused on improving the transportation system,[26] which has been a major source of unhappiness in recent times due to the heavy congestion experienced in key areas such as the Central Business District.

5.5. Other Strategies

Sydney

According to its official website, Axiss Australia employs four primary strategies to further its cause, namely, promotion, attraction, facilitation and aftercare.

As part of its promotion efforts, Axiss provides useful information to its business contacts through frequent updates. Information provided by Axiss includes statistical data, industry newsletters, and minutes of executive briefings. These sources are also made easily available on its website, which also provides links to related government and industry sites. Advertising campaigns have also been launched, and speakers have been sent to industry conferences to promote Sydney as a financial centre.

In order to effectively promote Sydney as a financial centre, Axiss has assembled a team of researchers to identify and collate information on the attractions of Sydney as a financial centre. Currently, Axiss Australia is basing its promotional efforts on the following competitive advantages: educated and skilled workforce, low-cost business infrastructure, favourable time zone, stable regulatory and political environment, advanced IT and support services and a high quality of life.

In order to ensure the seamless transition of international financial services firms into Sydney, Axiss Australia assists these firms by providing advice on issues such as regulation, taxation and immigration. Furthermore, Axiss will provide opportunities for leaders of incoming firms to meet up with the relevant government agencies and industry associations, hence helping to forge strong ties between all parties involved. Relevant data on the sectors these firms are operating in will also be made available.

Axiss Australia does not stop at smoothing the entry process for financial institutions, as it will introduce initiatives to ensure that the environment in Sydney remains conducive to the development of financial institutions. According to a publication detailing its achievements, Axiss has provided a forum for regular dialogue between the financial sector and the government on issues regarding Sydney's competitiveness as a financial centre and played a part in facilitating regulatory changes, for example, amendments to interest-withholding tax.

6. Progress

6.1. Tokyo

With respect to the business environment strategies, headway is made on all three fronts. On 8 August 2007, Accounting Standards Board of Japan (ASBJ) and International Accounting Standards Board (IASB) came to a consensus, through the Tokyo Agreement, to expedite the process of bringing Japan's GAAP into conformity to the International Financial Reporting Standards (IFRS) by mid-2011.[27] The major discrepancies identified within the 2005 agreement will also be eliminated by 2008. The Financial Instruments and Exchange Law has also been progressively implemented even though it is not expected to come into force in its entirety until 1 April 2008.[28] For example, the legislation governing market manipulation stipulated higher penalties was in place on 4 July 2006 while other legislation governing transactions of large shareholdings came into force on 13 June 2007. Finally, negotiations are still ongoing to determine the status of capital gains and dividend taxes. A decision will be made by the end of the year when the annual tax reform is announced.[29]

As for market access strategies, progress was made on the possibility of a merger of four of Tokyo's exchanges. Following the recommendation by the CEFP, Tokyo Commodities Exchange (TOCOM) swiftly announced that it will be revamping its seven-year-old trading system by March 2009 and create a twenty-four-hour exchange by March 2010 to make it more accessible and attractive to hedge funds.[30] A successful implementation could possibly propel TOCOM back into the lead globally. More importantly, it provides TOCOM with the flexibility needed to stave off the threat of a potential merger.

Although there are intensive business environment strategies to increase transparency via the implementation of J-Sox from 2008 onwards as well as greater compliance and conversion towards IFRS, some view this as an additional cost to doing business in Japan. Already, Japan has highly restrictive rules governing the financial services industry, such as the separation of banking and securities.

The European Business Council in Japan noted that, despite regulatory reforms that have partially reduced firewalls, financial companies are still not permitted to operate in Japan on a group basis, although they can do so in every other advanced market. In line with the International Monetary Fund's view that Japan could benefit from universal banking, the Japanese government has finally started to seriously contemplate measures to bring down the firewalls between banking and brokering as part of its efforts to improve the country's competitiveness as a global financial centre.

6.2. Sydney

Through the educational strategies of agencies like Axiss, the educational level of the workforce within the financial services industries has improved. This is indicated by an increase in the industry proportion of people with post-school qualifications, from 42 per cent in 2001[31] to 60 per cent in 2006. An increasingly well-educated workforce will greatly improve Sydney's chances of being a financial centre.

However, despite the higher qualifications of the workforce, remuneration of finance professionals in Sydney has not kept pace and it is generally at a lower level compared to other financial centres.[32] Australia has been promoting this as "low-cost" in order to attract financial institutions but this is actually a double-edged sword. The lower compensation packages for finance professionals will mean that top minds in the industry will be less inclined to relocate to Sydney.[33] The attractiveness of a financial centre is heavily dependent on the people in it so the lack of a competitive compensation structure may hinder Sydney's attempt to be a global financial centre.

The efforts of the Australian government in trying to make regulations more business-friendly has paid off. According to an OECD survey, Australia scores well on economic and administrative regulation, outperforming even the United States and United Kingdom.[34] With less red tape than other financial centres, Sydney can present itself as an attractive location for financial institutions looking to expand into the Asia-Pacific region.

Despite having favourable laws, tax rates in Australia are not as competitive when stacked up against its rivals. According to a competitiveness study conducted by Z/Yen on financial centres, Sydney's total corporate tax rate (52 per cent) and employee tax rate (36 per cent) for 2006 are higher than the tax rates in most major financial centres such as New York and London. This will deter financial institutions from relocating their operations to Sydney.

7. Conclusion

Despite Australia's much-lauded steps to transform itself into a global financial centre, it still falls short in a few key areas. The country is less accessible geographically than regional rivals such as Hong Kong and Singapore. Tax rates and compensation packages, as mentioned earlier, are not conducive to the attraction of top financial talent to Sydney. This problem is exacerbated by the flight of human capital towards larger English-speaking centres in pursuit of better opportunities.

Furthermore, it seems that Australia's promotional efforts have not managed to garner the sort of reactions from financial institutions for which it was hoping. To attain the status of a global financial centre, Sydney would have to pull in "front line", revenue-generating operations such as investment banking units of these institutions and get them to relocate to its shores. Instead, the "success stories" provided by Axiss tell a different story: The institutions (JPMorgan, UBS and Morgan Stanley) have made Sydney a hub for their various back-office support functions. One possible reason for this could be the low cost of labour which has led the banks to view it as an ideal location for situating non-core, non-revenue generative support activities.

Tokyo, on the other hand is bogged by issues centring on its people and regulatory and tax environments. However, the recent reviews of the financial industry carried out by the FSA has shown that it is determined to set things right. Proposed initiatives to enhance business collaboration as well as improvements to the existing regulatory framework may just give the country's flagging financial sector its much-needed boost to pick up from where it left off. Unlike Sydney, Tokyo has nearly all that it takes to come out ahead – remuneration rates are above average, a good number of financial institutions have decided to make Tokyo their home in Asia, and the Japanese are very patriotic.

With all these in place, Japan seems well placed to be a successful global financial centre. Expectations are indeed rising in the land of the rising sun.

Notes

1. This section was submitted by Tan Teck Meng after the conference and elaborates the comments he made as one of the panelists in the Concluding Session. It is inserted here, however, in view of the fact that this section compares Tokyo and Sydney as financial centres.
2. Howard Curtis Reed, "The Ascent of Tokyo as An International Financial Centre". *Journal of International Business Studies* (pre-1986); Winter 1980.
3. Charles P. Kindleberger, "The Formation of Financial Centres: A Study in Comparative Economic History". *Princeton Studies in International Finance*, no. 36 (Princeton: Princeton University, November 1974). BIS Review 34/2004.
4. Linda S. Goldberg, "Financial Sector FDI and Host Countries: New and Old Lessons". <http://www.newyorkfed.org/research/epr/07v13n1/0703gold.pdf>.
5. PricewaterhouseCoopers, "Offshoring in the Financial Services Industry: Risks and Rewards", 2005.
6. Education at a Glance, "OECD Briefing Note for Japan" <http://www.oecd.org/dataoecd/41/12/35341224.pdf>; Economist Intelligence Unit, "Country Reports: Japan 2006".
7. Japan has an equity market capitalization of US$4,674,472 million as of July 2007. <http://www.world-exchanges.org>.

8. *The Economist*, "So Unfair", 6 Sept 2007. <http://economist.com/displayStory.cfm?story_id=9769389>.
9. Reserve Bank of Australia, "Trends in the Australian Banking System: Implications for Financial System Stability and Monetary Policy", March 1999.
10. Financial Services Agency, "Schedule for Financial Reform" <http://fsa.go.jp/p_mof/English/big-bang/ebb33.pdf>.
11. *Financial Times*, "The Truth about Tokyo — The Financial Sector has been 'Hollowed out' ". <http://ftalphaville.ft.com/blog/2007/06/25/5389/the-truth-about-tokyo-the-financial-sector-has-been-hollowed-out/>.
12. Financial Services Agency, "Interim Summary of The Study Group on the Internationalization of Japanese Financial and Capital Markets". <http://www.fsa.go.jp/singi/singi_kinyu/tosin/20070613/03.pdf>.
13. Tax Nation: Business Taxes and the Federal State Divide, 9 April 2007, <http://www.bca.com.au/content/101017.aspx>.
14. Economist Intelligence Unit, "Country Profile 2007: Japan".
15. Global Market Rents, CB Richard Ellis, August 2005.
16. Allen N. Berger, "The Economic Effects of Technological Progress: Evidence from the Banking Industry", *Journal of Money, Credit and Banking* 35, no. 2 (April 2003): 141–76.
17. Mercer, "Highlights from the 2007 Quality of Living Survey" <http://www.mercer.com/referencecontent.jhtml?idContent=1128060#top50all>.
18. IASB, "IASB and Accounting Standards Board of Japan", 21 January 2005. <http://www.iasb.org/News/Press+Releases/IASB+and+Accounting+Standards+Board+of+Japan.htm>.
19. Ministry of Finance, "Recent Development: Proposed Reform to the Taxation of Capital Gain of Stocks", 30 October 2001. <http://www.mof.go.jp/english/tax/011030a.htm>.
20. Invest Australia, "More Incentive for Venture Capital", 2007. <http://www.austrade.com/>.
21. Reuters, "Japan Mulls Merger of Tokyo Bourse, Commodities", 17 April 2007. <http://www.cnbc.com/id/18146052>.
22. Financial Supervisory Agency, Official Strategy of FSA.
23. Bloomberg, "Australia's Carbon Trading Proposal Isn't Enough, Group Says", 31 August 2007. <http://www.bloomberg.com/apps/news?pid=20601081&sid=a_EXvvsR8ZHM&refer=australia>.
24. Financial Supervisory Agency, Official Strategy of FSA.
25. *Kyodo News*, "Gov't Crafts Plan to Develop Int'l Financial Hub in Tokyo", 19 June 2007. <http://asia.news.yahoo.com/070619/kyodo/d8prm5v80.html>. *The Times*, "Canary Wharf II could provide key to Tokyo's Survival", 22 May 2007. <http://business.timesonline.co.uk/tol/business/markets/japan/article1821018.ece>.

26. *The Sydney Morning Herald*, "New East-West Line may Cut Congestion", 14 September 2007. <http://www.smh.com.au/articles/2007/09/13/1189276899575.html?page=2>.
27. Accounting Standards Board of Japan (ASBJ), "Press Release: The ASBJ and The IASB Announce Tokyo Agreement on Achieving Convergence of Accounting Standards by 2011", 8 August 2007. <http://www.asb.or.jp/html_e/asbj/pressrelease/pressrelease_20070808_e.pdf>.
28. Financial Services Agency, "New Legislative Framework for Investor Protection". <http://www.fsa.go.jp/en/policy/fiel/20061010.pdf>.
29. Japan's Corporate News, "Tokyo Report: FSA shifts strategy for Stock Tax Breaks", 18 September 2007. <http://www.japancorp.net/Article.Asp?Art_ID=15455>.
30. David Turner, *Financial Times*, "Tokyo Commodity Exchange Plots Comeback", 28 May 2007. <http://www.ft.com/cms/s/0/db49a950-0d5f-11dc-937a-000b5df10621.html>; Chikafumi Hodo, *Reuters Africa*, "Standard Bank Eyes more Physical Gold Trade in Japan", 20 September 2007. <http://africa.reuters.com/business/news/usnBAN045610.html>.
31. AXISS Australia, "Australia's Skilled Workforce for Financial Services". <http://www.austrade.com/>.
32. Australian Government — Invest Australia, "Australia — A Global Financial Services Centre". <http://www.investaustralia.gov.au/NR/rdonlyres/6C28D71A-EA6F-459C-8807-07E0FA088E1A/0/goldbook_2007.pdf>.
33. eFinancialCareers.com.au, "London, New York, Tokyo – and Sydney?", 18 July 2007. <http://news.efinancialcareers.com.au/NEWS_ITEM/newsItemId-10763>.
34. City of London, "The Global Financial Centres Index (GFCI)", 1 March 2007. <http://server-uk.imrworldwide.com/cgi-bin/b?cg=downloadsedo&ci=cityoflondon&tu=http://213.86.34.248/NR/rdonlyres/0C0332C0-4CE5-4012-9AF7-2CF98A32E618/0/BC_RS_GFCI07_FR.pdf>.

3. SESSION III: SHANGHAI, WELLINGTON AND SEOUL

3.1. Comments by James Rooney

We have heard a lot of excellent presentations, all of them stimulating and some of them perhaps rather depressing. I will talk about the ones from this session first.

So Wellington is a "cow economy"? Because cows are very valuable, even milk powder has become a derivative. The New Zealand people love to buy land, the land that the cows and sheep roam on, but what is most interesting about New Zealand people buying land is that they are funding it using Japanese housewives' money and apparently arbitraging it with the Japanese grandmothers! That shows you who the real "hedge fund managers" are in Japan today!

The second subject that we heard about is Shanghai. And the story is that Shanghai is going to become an international financial centre by 2020. Well, I am not sure that I am going to be so active in my business by then so perhaps it is not an immediate threat to my life. But more important is the subtlety that is hidden in the details. Xu Mingqui was kind enough to tell us Shanghai has difficulties even being a domestic financial centre because the real power is in Beijing, and Shanghai is not in Beijing. So actually Shanghai is rather challenged.

It reminds me China is not one single economy — it is really about six different regional economies that are each gradually emerging and competing with each other. You can see how twenty years ago it was the decade of the Pearl River Delta area, with Guangzhou and Guangdong becoming economic centres.

And ten years ago it was the decade of Shanghai and the Yangtze River Delta cities to bask in the glory of hyperactive development. But last year Shanghai found itself politically compromised and was challenged by the Chinese leadership. Perhaps it has taken some steps back in terms of autonomy and local power.

Now we are seeing the decade of the Yellow River Delta, or the Bohai Sea, where Shandong Province, Tianjin, and Beijing become the economic development engines and take on a new significance in balancing up China's economy.

I do not think that you want to bet on any one financial centre location yet in a huge country like China, where the population is huge and the land mass is vast, where financial assets are widely distributed and financial needs are widely distributed. It is not even clear that one centre will be really enough. There will probably be more than one important financial centre in China. That will be a good thing. It is also true in America, where you have New York, Chicago, San Francisco, Atlanta, Boston, and the most surprising of them all, Charlotte, North Carolina.

China is still struggling to develop a market-driven domestic financial system and is probably still a long way away from releasing the financial forces within the country in the form of an international financial centre. Even with New York, we can see the compromises that occur with trying to balance domestic financial system needs and regulatory structures with a role in the international arena — many international activities prefer to be conducted out of London than New York. So the international role still falls primarily to Hong Kong, which sits on the far southern edge of the country rather like a tiny limpet. Hong Kong benefits greatly from being a gateway to China, for money moving in and out of the country, and for the provision of advanced professional services reaching the global standard. It does this without requiring China's domestic environment to match the global standard at this time, and so provides a controllable bridge or a halfway house for the global financial system to meet the local financial system.

As Hansoo Kim has shared with us, Seoul and Korea have made great progress mentally in thinking about the need to become an international financial centre. But the most disappointing thing was right there on the front page of his presentation. If you read the fine print, it said "Government-led" ... No, I am sorry, if we are going to have an international financial centre anywhere in the world, it is not going to be government-led because this is not the nature of finance.

And so perhaps before I spend too much time critiquing the individual papers and even more, appreciating the subtle messages that they deliver to us about cows and milk derivatives, or about the challenges of China, or even about the excitement of Seoul, let me try to share with you something a little different that I think has not yet come out in today's forum, but actually is there hiding underneath the surface, and is more important perhaps than anything I have heard so far today.

What I want to tell you about is what I call "String Theory".

To show you what I mean, let me share with you this piece of string. At one end of this piece of string is an economic project — let me use a real life example of a project that I am currently working on. There is a technology that came to us from Ireland. That technology is able to build power plants in China that consume their municipal waste. So here at one end of the piece of string is the technology, and a little bit along the string is the project that needs investing. That project came to be here in Korea which is a third location on the piece of string, and we went hunting for capital for this project and started to discover that there was interested capital in Australia. And as we kept pulling on the piece of string, it got longer and longer. And we discovered that that Australian capital was actually being raised in London, and I have not looked beyond that but some part of it probably came from the United States, some part of it from the Middle East, some part of it from Europe, and maybe in the future even some part of that interested capital will come from here in Asia.

So this brings us to the "String Theory of Financial Centres". There are projects at one end of the piece of string that need capital, and there is capital at the other end that needs projects in which to invest. And the interesting opportunity for financial centres has nothing to do with how big their local stock market is or what happens in their domestic bond market. It has a lot to do with whether or not they can get on this piece of string. Who did I name? I named Ireland — the technology is from Ireland. I named China — it is a project in China. To get to that project the money will go through Hong Kong. The money will come out of Australia but was originated in London and perhaps some of it came from the United States. And we are sitting here in Korea working to help make it all happen. So there is room for a lot of people on this peace of string. And I am not just talking about geography.

For example, we can talk about the service providers that must add value along this piece of string. The financial intermediaries, the legal advisers, the tax specialists and the accounting firms, let alone the business consultants and technical experts, or the administrators. There is value creation all along this piece of string, and the key is whether or not you are on the string. There is room for you to get on the string. What am I doing in Seoul, sitting here promoting a project in China that is being sourced out of Ireland by capital that is coming through intermediation in Australia?

That is the global economy, that is the global financial economy and that is what I think the real opportunity is when you become a global financial centre. The goal is to be sitting somewhere on this piece of string. There is lots of money in Seoul, which needs to be mobilized to projects that are elsewhere. Because as long as the piece of string stays inside the country, it is just a domestic financial market. The real issue and the real opportunity is learning how to play anywhere along this whole piece of string regardless of where the project or the capital is based.

Now let me use the analogy of the Internet. The Internet opened up a whole new world of activity when we started to connect computers to each other without borders. These pieces of string that go all over the world are rather like the Internet that we use. They represent opportunities to do something you could never do before. But to get there, we have to do some connecting.

We have to network. We have to have knowledge of other counterparts in other countries. I have travelled to London to meet investment bankers there, met the people from Australia, as well as visited the plant in China. You have to get out there and network and know how to connect with those people and speak the same language. Not just the human language but also the "Internet Protocols" of finance in the world today.

You have to know how to innovate because many of these things need innovation to be realized. And that is where Australia was actually the most interesting. Because after their Big Bang in the 1980s, there was innovation in the financing of infrastructure. This infrastructure financing needed innovation and that needed deregulation.

Innovation needs freedom. But creating freedom is worth nothing without action. So I call it "Climbing The Mountains": Climbing those mountains of freedom because somebody has taken away the fences and the gates. And I do not care if you get to the top of the mountain or just part way up, because climbing the mountain itself is good for your health. But you had better hurry up. Because whether Shanghai gets there in 2020 or not, there is somebody else who is moving faster than you are. So hurry up. Let us not talk too much now but focus more on taking action.

3.2. Comments by Sang Yong Park

I decided not to make comments on each specific paper but hit this session with a few points about problems that I have been struggling to grasp whenever I think about building an international financial centre initiative.

To me a financial hub requires both financial deepening and financial opening. Since financial deepening and financial opening are obvious concepts, I am not going to define them in the interest of time. To achieve these objectives, legal and regulatory systems are needed that are conducive to achieving them and to building an international financial centre. But for those countries which do not have a financial hub yet, someone has to build them and someone has to take action. The question is who should push for this? So I am going to talk about some political dimensions of building an international financial centre and also about why the political systems of countries like Korea and France are such that it is very difficult to build a necessary legal and regulatory system that can support well-functioning capital markets and financial industry in general.

My first question is this: Are there domestic interest groups that have natural incentives to push for building an international financial centre? Who would they be? Would it be industrial companies? Probably not. In the case of Korea, large industrial companies are very cash rich and they do not have strong external funding needs and they are not quite interested in deepening the financial industry. And some large Korean corporations have a fairly good access to the international financial market. These large companies may not want financial markets to be developed very aggressively because well-developed financial markets will help the emergence of new industrial players that come and compete with established financial companies. So the push would not come from the industrial sector. The established financial companies may not like financial opening either because it enhances competition in the domestic market. Many large financial companies are enjoying very good profitability with a 20 per cent return on equity.

If building a financial hub involves more players, more foreign players in particular, established companies may not welcome it. So the push does not seem to be coming from financial companies in Korea. Labour unions do not like financial development because competition induced by financial development will involve restructuring of companies. So the labour unions do not want to see very active development of a financial centre. Government agencies may not welcome this either because, in a country like Korea, government agencies are very much accustomed to administrative guidance and moral suasion. If foreign players are actively participating in the domestic financial market, such traditional tools of regulation may not be very effective. So the government agencies may not push this initiative very aggressively. And political parties are not very active either. The question is then who should push for this? The supposedly neutral groups like the media and academia may advocate building an international finance centre, but in the case of Korea, the media and academia are not very aggressive in this regard.

So what is the case in China or New Zealand? Who is pushing this initiative to build legal and regulatory systems that are more conducive to building and sustaining international financial centres? So this is my first point.

My second point is about the political system. We talked about the legal system, civil law origin versus common law origin. The legal system affects the flexibility of laws and regulations. The British system is common law, therefore laws and regulations are more flexible. The French system is more rigid and less flexible. But what about the difference between the United States and the United Kingdom? Both are Anglo-Saxon countries. Both countries have legal regimes that weigh heavily on case laws, so their legal system is more flexible. But why are U.S. regulators less flexible and more rigid than the U.K. regulators?

We often forget that it is not just the legal system that brings about this difference. The political scientists and researchers in public administration have been aware of the possibility that the differences between political systems could affect the flexibility of bureaucracies in general and regulators in particular. There are two types of systems. One is the parliamentary system like the United Kingdom's, where the prime minister belongs to the majority party. In a country with a parliamentary political system, regulators face rather friendly relations with the legislative branch that monitors and oversees the executive branch. So regulators in those countries can be more market-friendly and flexible. But in a country with a presidential system, the United States being a good example, the president can belong to a party that is not the majority in the Congress. The executive branch or regulators could face an adversarial relationship with the legislative branch. And the regulators and bureaucrats in general in the United States are more rigid relative to those in the United Kingdom where the parliamentary system is the norm.

Let us look at this two-by-two matrix. A good example is the United States with a common law and a presidential system. The United Kingdom has a common law and a parliamentary system. Japan is a civil law country with a parliamentary system and France is a country with a civil law and a presidential system. So, which country is the most disadvantaged? It is the country that has the civil law system and the presidential system, which is France. I have never heard of Paris striving

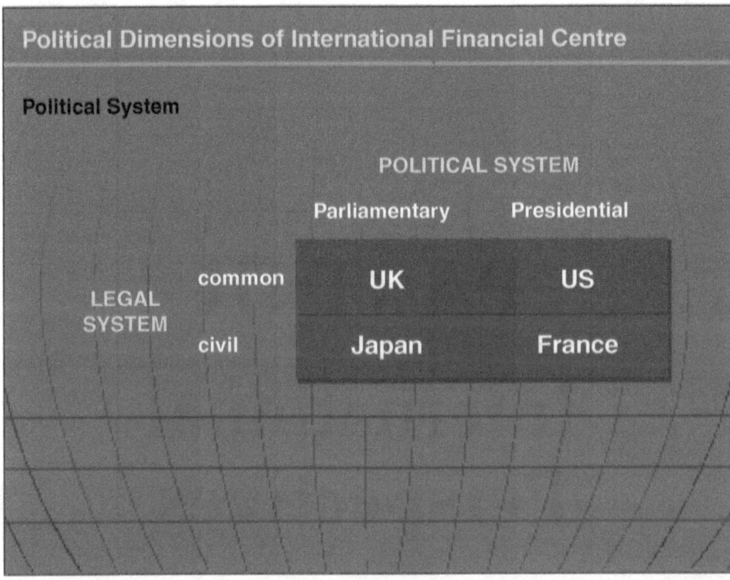

to become an international financial centre. I guess it will be very difficult for France to build an international financial centre given a disadvantageous legal and political system.

Unfortunately, Korea is like France in that Korea has a civil law system and a presidential system. Laws and regulations are thus very rigid. Regulators tend to be very rigid. So how can it overcome the difficulties arising from the fact that its system is like the French system? Hopefully we can discuss this issue further along the lines of the problems I just summarized.

PART III
International Perspectives

11

FINANCIAL CENTRES IN THE ASIA-PACIFIC REGION
Recent Trends and Developments

David Cowen[1]

1. INTRODUCTION

This chapter provides an overview of macroeconomic and structural trends in East Asia that are conducive to financial centre growth. It also examines the link between the quality of domestic financial markets and level of foreign capital flows. The chapter concludes by highlighting a few key reforms needed for Asian financial centres (AFCs) to play a bigger role in the regional and global economy.

2. ASIAN FINANCIAL CENTRES

The rapid growth and development of AFCs has been attributable to a number of factors, which are covered in other parts of this volume. However, the changes experienced over the past two decades have not come without concerns about their impact on market stability and integration. As it relates to this conference, the main concerns can be summarized at follows:

- First, growth in AFCs is sometimes attributed to significant regulatory forbearance and/or unhealthful tax competition. Evidence of these practices is limited in the region, and thus they have not likely played a major role in AFC growth or exposed economies to heightened risks. Rather, AFCs appear to be moving from rules to principles-based regulation and to strengthened risk management controls at a time when we have witnessed significant growth in their trading activities.
- Second, development of AFCs is said to expose the region's economies to excessive volatility. As discussed later, the opposite seems likely to occur. That is, as financial centres develop and capital inflows increase, markets become more liquid and volatility may actually fall.
- Finally, concern has been expressed that competition among AFCs may come at the expense of greater regional financial integration. This, too, is not likely to be the case. That is, to the extent that competition between financial markets results in a more level playing field for all types of investors and acts to reduce barriers imposed by capital and exchange controls, it should lead to greater integration.

3. MACROECONOMIC TRENDS

Recent macroeconomic trends have generally been supportive of financial centre growth in the Asia-Pacific region. The main factors are large, under-utilized private savings; increased capital flows and more intra-regional investment; rapid accumulation of foreign reserves and emergence of sovereign wealth funds (SWFs); rising hedge fund and private equity activity; and underweighted institutional investors in emerging Asia.

Focusing on a few of these factors, it has been noted that emerging Asia has experienced a sharp surge in capital flows in the past four or five years — both inflows and outflows (see Figure 11.1). Each is now approaching 4–5 per cent of emerging Asia GDP.[2] Based on data from the IMF's annual *Coordinated Portfolio Investment Survey*, intra-regional flows are increasing, but from a very low base (see Figure 11.2). This holds — at least through 2005 (the latest available data) — whether we look at portfolio investment from — the Asia-Pacific region back into the region as a share of total inflows into the region, or as a share of the region's output.[3] It suggests that if we are indeed observing competition among AFCs, it does

Figure 11.1
Emerging Asia Capital Flows — Recent Surge

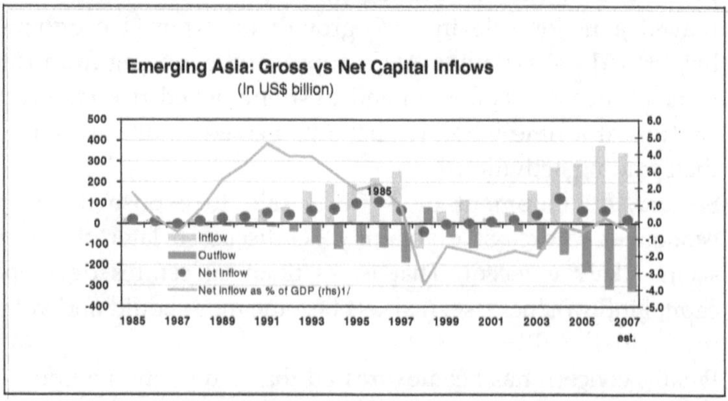

Note: 1. Simple average
Source: IMF, WEO database, April 2007.

Figure 11.2
Asia-Pacific Intra-Regional Portfolio Investment

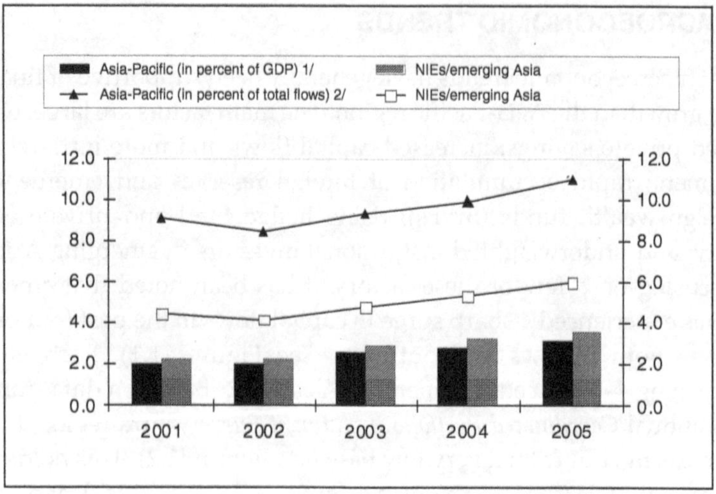

Notes: 1. Asia-Pacific portfolio outflows to region as a share of regional GDP.
2. Asia-Pacific portfolio outflows to region as a share of total portfolio.
Source: IMF, Coordinated Portfolio Investment Survey.

not appear to be having an adverse impact on intra-regional portfolio investment flows.

Turning to the influence of SWFs, they are only likely to become an increasingly important factor in the growth and development of AFCs. No precise forecasts exist on how much these funds are expected to grow over the medium term and to invest in the Asia-Pacific region (see Table 11.1). However, recent IMF estimates suggest their impact will only increase with time, when one considers that foreign assets held by sovereigns (Asia and elsewhere) currently include more than US$5.5 trillion in international reserves and US$2–3 trillion in SWF-related assets.[4] According to the IMF, expectations are that sovereigns will continue to accumulate international assets at a rate of US$800–900 billion annually over the next five years, with aggregate foreign assets under sovereign management reaching about US$12 trillion by 2012.[5]

The direct impact of SWFs on AFC development is difficult to assess, given the lack of published information on their activities. These funds also have different investment objectives, institutional structure, and management styles, suggesting they will not affect markets uniformly. However, the conventional view is that portfolio management by SWFs

Table 11.1
Sovereign Wealth Funds in the Asia-Pacific Region

Sovereign Wealth Funds in Asia
(In US$ billion)

Country/economy	Assets	Amount	Source of Funds
Australia	Future fund	0.049	Fiscal surplus
China	China Investment Corporation	up to 200	Current accounts surplus
Hong Kong SAR	Exchange Fund (Investment Portfolio)	120	Fiscal surplus
Korea	Korea Investment Corporation	20	Current accounts surplus
Singapore	General Investment Corporation	100	Multiple[a]
Singapore	Temasek	100	Multiple[b]

Notes: a. Fiscal and current account surplus and proceeds from the sale of government bonds to the Central Provident Fund.
b. Initial transfer of holdings, retained earnings, and borrowing.

Sources: Country authorities; IMF staff estimates.

will be relatively passive, suggesting they may punch below their weight in terms of market activity (for example, market turnover). At the same time, as SWFs grow and diversify, they may take a larger stake in alternative investments or go farther down the credit curve. This could mean increased activity in some more thinly traded markets in the region. While their impact remains to be seen, SWF growth on the whole will likely be a net positive for AFC development.

Lastly, regarding hedge funds, we have witnessed dramatic growth of Asian-focused hedge funds over the past five years, but also from a small base (see Figure 11.3).[6] This is particularly true for those managed in Hong Kong Special Administrative Region (SAR) and Singapore. Traditionally, the investment strategy of Asian-focused funds has been concentrated in the area of long-short Asian equities, but more and more we are seeing moves toward multi-strategy approaches, which should have some impact on the breadth and scope of financial products and trading opportunities

Figure 11.3
Asia-focused Hedge Funds

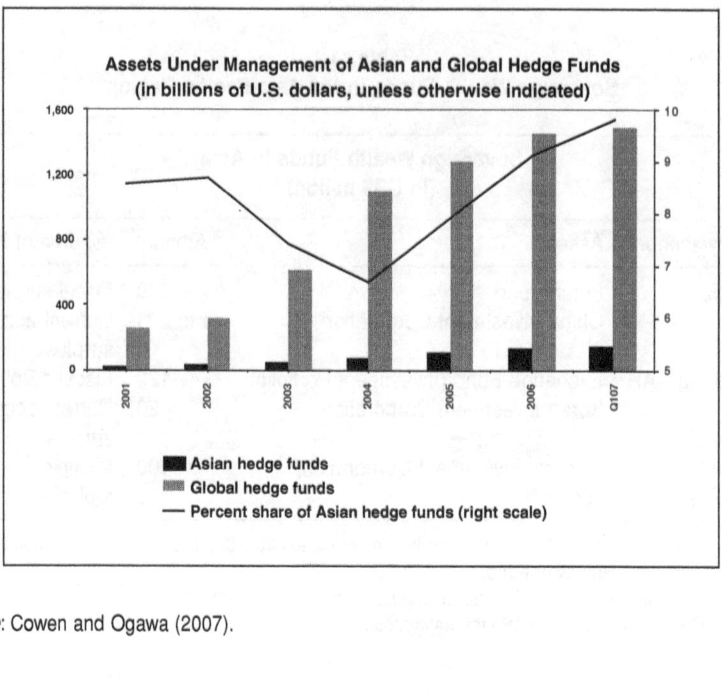

Source: Cowen and Ogawa (2007).

offered by AFCs. As AFCs become more receptive to hedge fund activity, regulators will have to decide the degree to which they attempt to control the funds' activities. Here, indirect regulation has been viewed by most experts as a more effective approach rather than direct regulation, focusing on strengthening counterparty risk management, concentrating on large and systemically important banks, prime brokers, and other dealers who provide leverage, settle trades, and undertake back office activities for hedge funds. On the other hand, direct regulation could raise moral hazard concerns if the additional information gathered from hedge fund positions is perceived from investors and counterparties as providing implicit safeguards, possibly leading them to take on excessive risk and undermining market discipline.

4. STRUCTURAL TRENDS

Structural trends observed in the region are also affecting growth in AFCs. Significant factors include strengthened domestic financial systems, deeper domestic financial markets, improvements in market governance and infrastructure (clearing and payments systems, credit rating agencies, etc.), and further liberalization of the capital account and trade in services and the removal of exchange controls. New financial products are also changing the structure of AFCs, which should aid their growth. Recently, these include increased securitization of domestic assets and the rapid growth in Islamic finance.

4.1. Financial Market Development and Capital Flows

Deeper, more open and better governed financial markets are generally viewed as key factors influencing financial centre growth and associated inflows, with emerging Asia appearing to be no exception.[7] A recent IMF study takes on this issue by examining whether domestic financial market development affects the level as well as the volatility of capital flows.[8] The study considers fifty-six developed and emerging economies over the period of 1998–2006. Together, this group comprised an estimated 81 per cent of world capital inflows in 2005.[9]

Among the findings in the study most relevant to AFCs is that equity market turnover and financial openness (but not equity market capitalization) are statistically significant factors in explaining capital inflows into emerging markets.[10] See Tables 11.2 and 11.3. These results suggest that smaller AFCs may be able to develop certain niche activities in order to attract considerable inflows. The study also finds that financial openness tends to reduce the volatility of capital flows — another incentive for — AFC development. Finally, broad set of institutional quality variables is found to have a negative relationship with capital inflow volatility. That is, with improvements in such factors as regulatory quality, rule of law, the control of corruption, level of political stability, and government effectiveness in policy implementation, less volatility is observed in capital inflows.

4.2. Capital Account Liberalization, Outflows, and AFCs

Recent measures have been taken in emerging Asia to further open the external capital account and encourage greater outflows, which over time should engender further growth in AFCs. Among the more significant ones are:

- In China, mainland retail investors were recently granted unlimited convertibility of the renminbi into Hong Kong dollars for the

Table 11.2
Panel Least-Squares Estimate of Determinants of Capital Inflows, 1998–2006[a]

	All Countries	Emerging Markets
Financial Development Indicators		
Equity market turnover	√	√
Equity market capitalization	?	?
Financial openness	√	√
Corporate governance quality	√	?
Accounting standards	?	?
Macroeconomic Factors		
Growth expectation	√	√
Interest rate differential	√	√
Global liquidity	?	?

Note: a. Total capita inflows/GDP. √ = statistically significant.
Source: IMF, *Global Financial Stability Report* (Chapter 3), October 2007.

Table 11.3
Panel GMM Estimation of the Determinants of the Volatility of Capital Inflows, 1998–2006[a]

	All Countries	Emerging Markets
Financial Development Indicators		
Equity market turnover	?	?
Equity market capitalization	?	?
Financial openness	√	√
Corporate governance quality	?	?
Accounting standards	?	?
Macroeconomic Factors		
Growth expectation	?	?
Interest rate differential	?	?
Global liquidity	√	√

Note: a. Standard deviation of total capital inflows/GDP. √ = statistically significant.
Source: IMF, *Global Financial Stability Report* (Chapter 3), October 2007.

purpose of investing in Hong Kong H-shares. This change represents yet another very significant measure adopted since early 2006, aimed at giving individual Chinese savers greater access to non-mainland assets.

- In Malaysia, the limit on holdings of foreign assets by some institutional investors and investment trusts was raised from 10 to 30 per cent in early 2005, and again, to 50 per cent in early 2007. Investors are reported to have responded to these measures as portfolio outflows have increased from around US$700 million in 2005 to US$2.2 billion in 2006.
- In Korea, successful measures have been taken in recent years to liberalize outflows, with equity outflows rising from less than US$4 billion a year in 2004 and 2005 to more than US$15 billion in 2006, due in part to more intensive marketing efforts of mutual funds investing in foreign equities, often in emerging markets. Bond outflows have also accelerated, but this has been primarily due to purchases by institutional investors including life insurers. Although changes here and in Malaysia are no guarantee that outflows have aided AFC growth, local investor interest in regional markets is seen as strong.

- Governments have also moved to encourage capital outflows through institutions under their control, notably national pension funds. Although outside emerging Asia, the experience of Japan's Government Pension Investment Fund (GPIF) is instructive. The GPIF has increased the share of foreign stocks and bonds in its JP¥70 trillion (US$600 billion) portfolio to about 25 per cent in 2005, from an initial level near zero in 2001. Korea's Pension Fund Association raised its allocation to foreign assets to about 8 per cent of its 156 trillion won (US$170 billion) in 2005. More than nine-tenths of the allocation is in foreign fixed income, almost all of which is currency hedged. National pension funds elsewhere, including Thailand, have also raised targets for holdings of foreign assets.

4.3. New Products and Markets

A recent study by the Bank for International Settlements indicates a rapid increase in the Asian securitization, providing new opportunity for broadening and deepening AFC activity.[11] Initially limited to Australia, Japan, and Korea, asset-backed securities (ABS) have taken off in Hong Kong SAR and Singapore, and to a lesser degree in the Philippines and Indonesia. As a result, the domestic issuance of ABS doubled on a U.S. dollar basis between 2000 and 2005, albeit from a low base. Regarding Islamic finance in the region, most activity is currently concentrated in Malaysia (and to a lesser extent in Singapore and Indonesia). Given much discussion in recent years about the growth of "East-East flows", the region's presence in this market is only likely to grow. Malaysia, in fact, established the International Islamic Financial Centre in 2006, an initiative that covers institutional development, market infrastructure, the regulatory and supervisory framework, human capital development, and tax incentives related to Islamic finance. As of June 2006, 11 per cent of Malaysia's banking system assets were Shariah-compliant (equivalent to about US$32 billion).[12]

5. ADDITIONAL REFORMS

Within the region, growth in AFCs is also likely to depend on such factors as developing a local institutional investor base and taking further steps to enhance market depth and liquidity. Regarding institutional investors, relevant factors for broadening this base are the appropriate tax treatment of and adequate transparency in long-term savings products, the ease of entry of domestic institutions into foreign markets, and ensuring a level playing field between banks and non-banks competing for household savings. In addition, pension reforms aimed at moving away from state-sponsored plans, providing greater choice between pension types, and improving risk management could increase institutional investor activity. As for enhancing market depth and liquidity, the experience over the past decade with the development of Asian bond markets suggests more effort is necessary. Foremost, additional transparency in these markets would likely increase market activity. At the micro level, the absence of full disclosure on general issuance strategies and lack of secondary market trading activity are among the frequently cited factors constraining market development. On the macro front, more predictable information (including timely data) and policies, in particular on taxation, regulation, and accounting standards, are seen as important. In addition, market depth and liquidity are linked to the aforementioned development of an institutional investor base, as well as the provision of more traded instruments for managing risk (futures, swaps, repos, securities lending, etc.).

6. CONCLUDING REMARKS

This brief chapter is intended to be indicative rather than exhaustive of the factors that are influencing AFC development. Future prospects appear strong for growth in a number of centres and activities in the Asia-Pacific region, notwithstanding concerns about the impact competition among centres may have on the pace of expansion.

Notes

1. The views in this chapter are those of the author and do not necessarily represent those of the International Monetary Fund.
2. Gross inflows (outflows) as defined here are not fully gross and may be negative, reflecting either non-resident accumulation of domestic assets or reduction in domestic liabilities (increase in residents' foreign assets or decline in foreign liabilities). Data on true gross flows are not readily available.
3. The Asia-Pacific region comprises industrialized economies (Japan, Australia, and New Zealand) and newly industrialized and emerging economies in East Asia as well as India. However, for Emerging Asia, investment from the

Asia-Pacific region does not include investment from either China or Vietnam, but does include investment into these countries.

4. See the IMF's *Global Financial Stability Report*, Annex 1.2: Sovereign Wealth Funds, October 2007.
5. See the IMF's *Asia-Pacific Regional Economic Outlook*, Box 1.3. Sovereign Wealth Funds, October 2007.
6. Asian-focused hedge funds are considered those with an Asian mandate managed both inside and outside the region.
7. This chapter does not cover in-depth the role of market infrastructure. See Cowen, Salgado, Shah, Teo, and Zanello (2006) for a recent discussion of developments in this area.
8. See IMF's *Global Financial Stability Report*, "The Quality of Domestic Financial Markets and Capital Inflows" (Chapter 3), October 2007. (Prepared by Shinobu Nakagawa and L. Effie Psalida).
9. Included within the study are Japan, Australia, and New Zealand as mature markets in the region, as well as most South and East Asian emerging markets.
10. In the study, financial openness is measured by a composite index that draws upon the IMF's *Annual Report on Exchange Arrangements and Exchange Restrictions*.
11. See Gyntelberg and Remolona (2006).
12. See the IMF's *Asia-Pacific Regional Economic Outlook*, Box 15. Islamic Finance in Malaysia, April 2007.

References

Cowen, David, and Sumiko Ogawa. *Hedge Fund Activities: Implications for Financial Market Development and Stability in East Asia*. Unpublished mimeograph. Presented at ASEAN Working Committee Seminar on Capital Account Liberalization, 2007.

Cowen, David, et al. *Financial Integration in Asia: Recent Developments and Next Steps*. IMF Working Paper (WP/06/196), Washington, D.C., August 2006.

IMF. *Asia and Pacific Regional Economic Outlook*. Washington, D.C., April and October 2007.

———. *Coordinated Portfolio Investment Survey*. Washington, D.C.

———. *Global Financial Stability Report*. Washington, D.C., October 2007.

———. *World Economic Outlook*. Washington, D.C., April 2007.

Gyntelberg, Jacob and Eli M. Remolona. "Securitisation in Asia and the Pacific: Implications for Liquidity and Credit Risks". *BIS Quarterly Review* (June 2006).

12

COMPETITION AND INTEGRATION Financial Centres and Financial Market Integration in Asia

Jong-Wha Lee[1]

From the excellent case study reports presented in this volume, it is clear that many cities are vying to become financial centres, and that there will be fierce competition over the next decades. One fundamental question is the relationship between competition and integration: Whether competition will contribute to the integration of financial markets in the region or not. The risk of excessive competition is a major theme of the conference, as it may lead to segmentation of financial markets, and has the potential of creating financial instability in the region. So what are the implications of competition over international financial centres among the cities in the region for financial integration? This is one of the topics that will be covered here.

This chapter will focus on the relationship between competition among the financial centres in the region and financial market integration. There are several fundamental questions: Why is financial integration important — especially at the regional level; why not just integrate into global markets; what is the current status of financial integration; and what is the relationship between financial centres and regional financial development and integration?

Let me mention briefly about the major trends in Asia and focus on issues related to financial market integration. We are all well aware of the very dynamic changes going on in the region. Asia continues to emerge as a major trade and economic power. Because of strong economic growth, high savings and wealth accumulation — and, needless to say, the emergence of the two giants of the region, China and India — the region is expected to eventually emerge as a global financial power. Usually trade is followed by finance. The region's increased strong trade links have led to market-driven integration of the goods market. This will create demand for financial market integration. Over the past ten years, there has been continuous financial liberalization, innovation, and globalization across the region. And this will contribute to financial market integration in the region later on.

The question is, what is the current status of Asian financial market integration? Especially over the past decade, there has been significant progress in financial market integration through financial liberalization and financial market opening. Empirical evidence, however, shows that the extent of regional financial integration remains weak. Current literature examines three measures of integration in the region: asset price co-movements, quantitative measures, and institutional and regulatory changes.

Quantitative measures compare the portion of investment made by Asian investors within the region with investments made outside the region. 2006 data — based on the IMF's Coordinated Portfolio Investment Survey (CPIS) — shows that only 8.4 per cent of total investment made by East Asian investors was within Asia, with more than 90 per cent invested outside the region. Thus, in terms of quantitative measures, Asian financial integration remains very low.

Then the next question is: Why is regional integration weak? From the investors side it is most important to minimize risk and maximize returns. Incentives for portfolio diversification within Asia must be low because the local risk is high compared with that in global markets. And from the perspective of global investors, global diversification is much better than regional diversification. That's also true with regional investors. For example, Japanese investors tend to move toward global markets rather than East Asia.

With regard to financial infrastructure, however, the supply side is also important. In most Asian countries, financial market development is still weak, and issues of excessive regulation still exists. How to improve legal and regulatory frameworks has been a key issue. Comparing Asia with Europe, one important thing is the fundamental instability of exchange rates. And these diverse regimes in monetary and exchange rate policy frameworks have also created some hindrances to capital flows within the region.

In trade integration, distance matters. Countries would like to trade more with their neighbours. Distance is fundamentally related to costs. But in finance, geographical distance does not matter much. Global players even dominate regional financial markets.

Another important question is why financial markets should integrate. If this were not really important for Asia, then we would not think too much about the implications of financial centre competition. But this is as important as the goods market integration because financial integration will lower capital costs, especially for long-term investment. The region still needs major investment in infrastructure. That is why we need to attract more investment from global markets, especially on a long-term basis.

Financial market integration will help allocate financial resources more efficiently. Competition and peer pressure will help policymakers as well as private firms contribute more to the development of domestic financial infrastructure. Fundamentally, financial market integration will help investors diversify risk and help smooth consumption, which helps increase welfare.

Questions still remain: Does Asian financial integration hold any special advantage? If one emphasizes low capital cost and risk diversification, then go to global markets. Global markets will provide more advantages. Why should one integrate the rest of Asia? This has an important historical root. After the Asian financial crisis, the region realized that it could not rely on the global financial architecture. It needed a more regional mechanism to provide liquidity when it liquidity problems appeared. And having Asia's own mechanisms in place could help avoid the next financial crisis. Double mismatches — a maturity mismatch and a currency mismatch — contributed to the significant negative impact of the financial crisis. Borrowing in U.S. dollars short term, while investing in local currency long term, creates the fundamental "original sin", as several people have pointed out. How to build an integrated regional financial market in Asia has been an important issue over the past ten years.

There are huge savings in Asia, but many countries still lack investment, in particular for infrastructure. Most economies boast current account surpluses. But that does not necessarily imply oversaving — even if often emphasized as a saving "glut". Fundamentally, many countries, especially the low-income ASEAN countries (Cambodia, Lao PDR, and Vietnam) and large economies like India lack investment. The investment rate in Indonesia and Thailand, for example, declined by more than 10 per cent of GDP after the 1997/98 Asian financial crisis and still has not recovered. So while many Asian countries may save a lot, many others still lack investment. Why do so many Asian countries lend money to global markets, especially to low-yielding treasuries in the United States? How should Asian savings be re-channelled into Asian economies? This also relates to how excessive international reserves may be reduced.

For Asian countries, regional financial integration is coming together with cooperation among policymakers, who meet quite often and discuss how to contribute to regional financial stability. Regional financial integration is not a substitute for global financial stability or global financial architecture. Basically, they complement each other. So the region should build more toward regional financial stability and integration. That will then contribute to maintaining global financial stability. The Asia-Pacific region has become important to global markets. There are links between the financial market integration and the trade and monetary integration. So if one has a vision for economic integration for Asia, financial integration will become an important part of the agenda. There are some fundamental differences between Asian integration and European integration. In European integration, financial market integration came even after monetary integration. But with financial market liberalization and opening over the past ten years, Asia will be dealing with financial integration sooner.

There has been much progress in regional financial integration. There are several ASEAN and ASEAN+3 initiatives. There are bond market initiatives designed to avoid the double mismatch problems, the original sin. Building up local currency bond market has been very important. For the last five years, the Asian Bond Markets Initiative (ABMI) under ASEAN+3 — ASEAN plus People's Republic of China, Japan, and Republic of Korea — helped the development of the Asian bond markets. Local currency markets attract long-term investors to the region to invest in local currency. This has been very important. Also, the Asian Bond

Fund (ABF) is of the result of work done by eleven of the region's central banks via the Executives' Meeting of East Asia and Pacific Central Banks (EMEAP). The ABF is currently in its second phase — it has raised US$1 billion to purchase local currency bonds.

The crucial question is: What is the role of financial centres in financial market integration? If financial market integration and financial market development are important for the region, then there will be an influx of financial centres. We need to acknowledge the positive role competition plays developing financial centres, which can provide a full range of financial services to the economies in the region. Diversification and globalization will help achieve more efficient and more liquid financial markets in the region. As emphasized, the region is exhibiting real dynamism. So how should regional financial centres effectively support the fast growing economic dynamism in this region?

Where financial centres are located is often important, because in the region, financial markets and financial service industries have the fundamental characteristic of scale economies, so they will help create more efficiency. Having a financial centre close to your country will definitely create positive spillovers. Proximity to a major regional financial centre could become important enough to warrant the existence of more than one.

Competition has its risks, but like the example mentioned by James Rooney (see Chapter 10, Session III in this volume), that mountain climbing is good for your health even if you fail to reach the summit. I think a healthy competition for a financial centre contributes to the development of the domestic financial market, which is one pre-condition of becoming a financial centre.

We have learned that many countries that are trying to become financial centres are first trying to improve the local financial market. These are very positive signs. This is what happened in Europe. In the free market, competition will make the cities think about specializing in the financial sectors where each country has a comparative advantage. Therefore it will certainly help financial market development and integration. Of course, there are issues and challenges for Asian financial centres. There is the risk of excessive competition; lack of discipline and regulation; duplicating will waste resources in some sense; financial interdependence also increases risk of great volatility. As can be seen from the way that the U.S. subprime fallout moved from the local loan market to the global market, financial globalization and financial innovation spread risk across borders and across many investors. This is a very important phenomenon.

Building a conducive regulatory environment is also important. There is the risk of too much deregulation. And countries need to avoid becoming copycats. Asian markets are not homogeneous, as they are in North America and Europe. Asia is very diverse, so countries should not emulate New York; London; Hong Kong, China; or Singapore. Each centre should try to be specialized.

Major financial cities have a first-mover advantage and generally become dominant players. They are natural monopolies. There is the issue of how regional financial centres compete with global financial centres. Eventually, this will be an important topic as Asian countries aspire to became major financial capitals over the next several decades. We have heard that Shanghai will become a financial centre in 2020, and Seoul in 2015. But Asian countries should focus first on national markets: As mentioned, bond markets compared with equity markets or the banking sectors are still quite weak. Financial sector diversification is important. Human resources and regulatory frameworks are key factors, not just for national financial market development, but for success of the financial centres.

Asian countries remain dominated by banking sectors and the corporation debt market is very weak (Figure 12.1). In size, bond markets are very weak (Table 12.1).

Figure 12.1
Financial Assets
(Percentage of GDP)

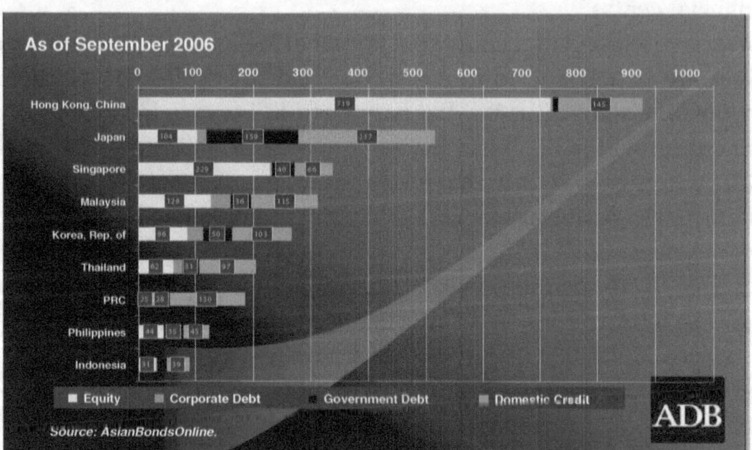

Table 12.1
Bond and Equity Markets
(June 2007, US$ billion)

	Bonds	Equity	GDP
Australia	729.91	1,355.56	888.1
China, People's Rep. of	1,368.41	2,183.48	2,971.1
Hong Kong, China	99.20	2,028.00	194.9
Japan	6,843.13	4,681.05	4,163.4
Korea, Rep. of	1,035.84	1,042.16	943.9
Malaysia	139.13	306.96	172.5
New Zealand	37.53	51.99	128.8
Singapore	60.90	505.59	144.7
United States	28,725.40	20,785.76	13,768.8

Source: AsianBondsOnline.

Compared with GDP, Hong Kong and Singapore have bigger equity markets than the United States, but bond markets, compared with GDP size, show that many countries in Asia are still weak (Figure 12.2).

In cross-border financial activity, Asia still has big gaps compared with Europe and the United States (see Table 12.2).

Figure 12.2
Bond and Equity Market Size
(June 2007, Percentage of GDP)

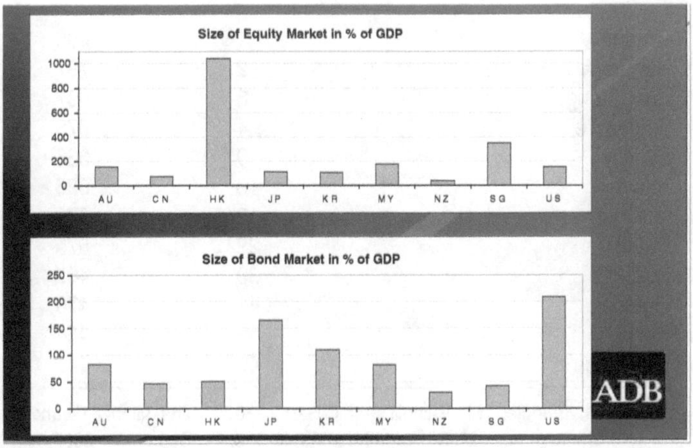

Asian economies host eight of the world's fifty most important financial centres, according to City of London Corporation's Index in 2007. Hong Kong, China and Singapore rank third and fourth respectively, but they are far behind first- and second-placed London and New York (see Table 12.3).

Table 12.2
Cross-border Financial Activity, 2003

Economies	Net exports of financial services to GDP ratio (%)	Portfolio assets to GDP ratio (%)*	International Investment Position Asset (US$ million)
Australia	0.052	25.30	380,848
Hong Kong, China	1.860	215.90	1,185,407
Japan	0.030	40.09	3,599,804
Korea	0.098	2.85	256,643
New Zealand	–0.034	27.00	53,274
Singapore	1.481	155.76	450,587
United Kingdom	0.900	95.78	6,394,917
United States	0.135	28.57	7,863,967

Source: A. Zarome 2007. "Concept of Offshore Financial Centres: In Search of an Operational Definition". IMF Working Paper, Tables 8.

Table 12.3
Global Financial Centres Index (GFCI):
Ranks and Ratings of Selected Financial Centres

Financial Centre	GFCI Rank	GFCI Rating
London	1	806
New York	2	787
Hong Kong	3	697
Singapore	4	673
Sydney	9	636
Tokyo	10	625
Melbourne	19	588
Dubai	22	575
Beijing	39	482
Mumbai	41	470
Seoul	42	464
Wellington	46	447

Source: M. Yeandle, M. Mainelli and I. Harris, 2007. "The Global Financial Centres Index 2". City of London. Table 2, p. 11. September 2007.

To summarize the key messages: The trend continues that Asia will emerge, or is emerging, as a major global financial player. To do this, Asia will develop large dynamic, and competing financial centres. Competition will contribute to financial market development and financial market integration. Of course, there are some conditions. Countries need to work on domestic financial market development. But competition has its risks. It should develop in tandem with cooperation and integration, where there are many initiatives in the region. This competition can be aligned with these initiatives. A vision for the region is a stable, efficient, and fully integrated regional financial community. Financial centres will eventually emerge in the region in a bigger and on a more dynamic scale. And they will help promote that vision.

Note

1. The views expressed here are the author's own and not officially those of ADB.

13

FINANCIAL CENTRES IN THE ASIA-PACIFIC REGION

John Walker

Five years ago under the administration of President Roh, there was a strong push by the Korean government to make Korea a regional and financial hub for Asia. The Korean government and other agencies have sought to deliver that vision but questions remain on whether Korea has become a financial hub for the North Asian region only, or for the whole of Asia. There is evidence that achieving that goal may be possible for Korea by 2015, though competition is intensifying with Shanghai also targeting financial hub status by 2020.

Whilst this volume may focus on competition among financial centres, Macquarie regards the issue differently. The focus should not be on competition among the centres, but competition within domestic financial sectors as a lever to drive the growth of financial institutions within those financial centres.

The stakes are high for both financial institutions, governments and the community. And with this in mind, and the objective of enhancing competition within the domestic financial environment, the focus should be not on the financial centre itself, but on the development of quality financial institutions. As Jong-Wha Lee and David Cowen have said elsewhere in this volume, the integration or cooperation of financial centres is valuable, but that integration process has been slowed as a result of the focus of global financial groups on the Asian financial markets. For Asian financial centres to achieve increased growth, competition, cooperation and integration, they need the emergence of Asian-based financial institutions that can compete with these global financial institutions in key financial sectors including trading banks, private equity funds, investment banking and securities.

Taking a bottom-up approach to this issue instead of the top-down approach typically taken, can be more useful. A financial centre is a largely conceptual goal, and if Korea wants to become a financial centre, it must foster and support the growth of a new generation of Asia-Pacific based global financial institutions which will compete in size and scope with the Morgan Stanleys, Goldman Sachs and KKRs of the current financial world. Only then can it become a true financial centre.

Given the unique characteristics of the Asian region, the importance of having strong financial sector is growing as economies develop and become wealthier and as a result a number of financial regions can be seen developing (see Figure 13.1).

Figure 13.1
What Are the Key Financial Regions?

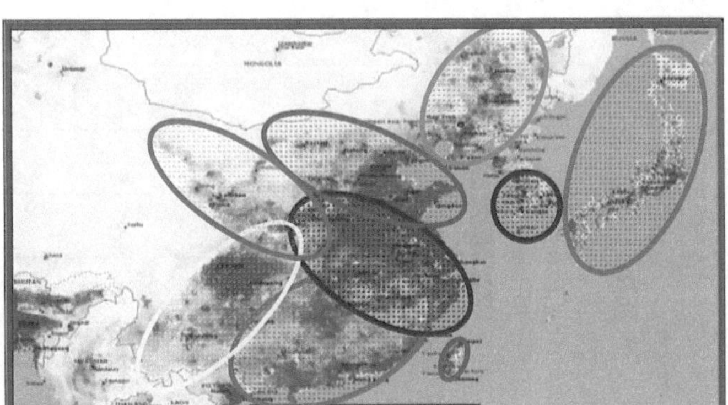

Source: Macquarie.

According to 2004 data, North America and Europe each account for around 33 per cent of the world economy, with North Asia at 18 per cent. In the recent years, however, the strong growth in North Asia has resulted in a significant change. The 2040 figures may be contentious, but according to the World Bank and Market Force predictions, China has overtaken the United States to become the world's largest economy. Figure 13.2 shows how key North Asian economies of China, Japan and South Korea are expected to rank highly within the top twenty world economies by 2040. Figure 13.3 shows that the North Asian region is growing significantly faster than the rest of the world and therefore growing in its share of the world economy.

The focus should be on supporting those financial institutions that can grow and develop into new Asia-Pacific based global financial institutions, as the growth of these companies will foster growth of the financial centre itself.

From Macquarie's experience, the global and local institutions must cooperate, especially in Korea. Cooperation and integration are both important, but competition must not be overlooked as a key factor necessary in order to create a strong financial community.

Figure 13.2
Top Twenty World Economies, 2040

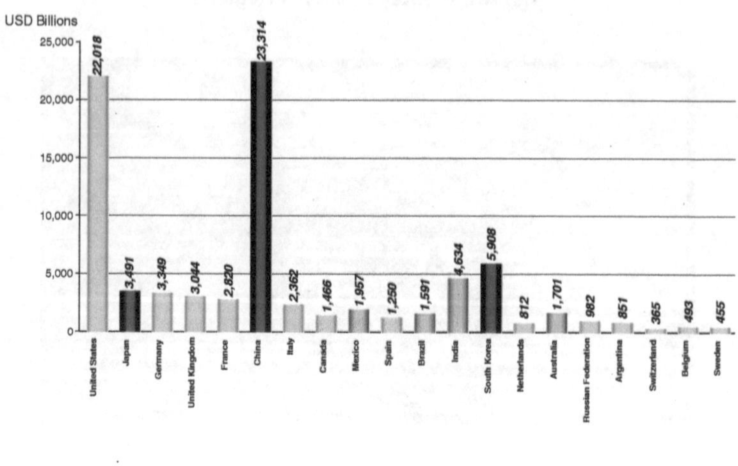

Source: World Bank Market Force Projection before inflation at constant FX rates, Macquarie.

Figure 13.3
Share of World GDP, 2002–2040

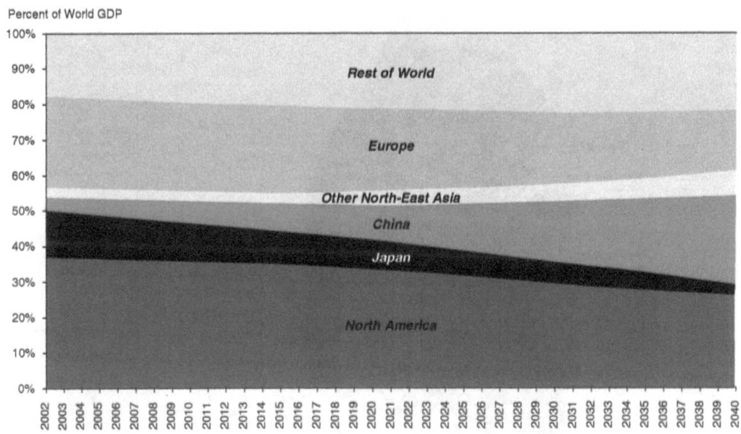

Source: World Bank Market Force Projection before inflation at constant FX rates, Macquarie.

Macquarie itself is an interesting institution. The head office is in Australia. However, more than 50 per cent of Macquarie's revenues come from outside Australia. In fact, Korea has become one of the focal points of Macquarie globally with Seoul growing to be one of the largest offices outside Australia and the largest single office in Asia. Macquarie has achieved this growth through cooperation and partnership with local institutions. At one stage, Macquarie boasted a true business partnership with each of the five largest Korean financial institutions. These partnerships, joint ventures and cooperation have also allowed Macquarie's expertise in its relevant business to be shared with the five institutions.

Macquarie's business in Korea goes beyond financial services to also encompass management of a range of private equity funds which have invested both in Korean and international assets with a particular focus on transportation infrastructure and media assets (Figure 13.4). In many cases, these assets are managed jointly with local institutions. Macquarie's approach to business in Korea can be characterized as a business in partnership with Korean companies, managing Korean and international assets purchased with Korean money. In fact, Macquarie has fostered competition in its particular niche market of infrastructure management

Figure 13.4
Partnerships Create Value: Macquarie Korea's Assets in Korea and Abroad

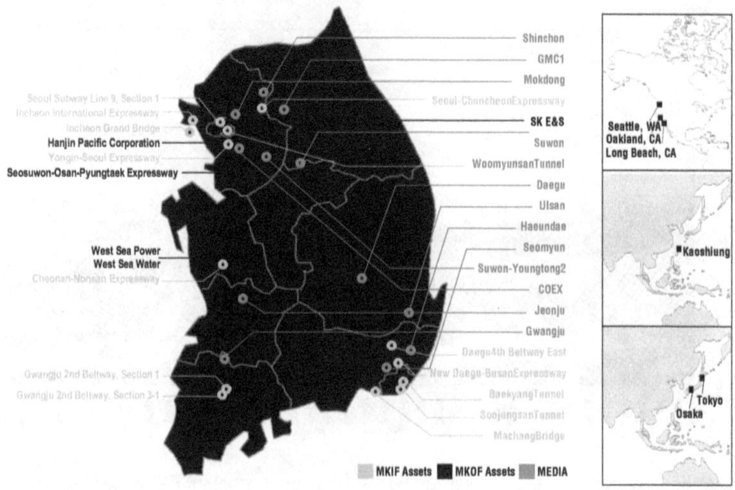

Source: Macquarie.

to such an extent that it now has two of the four largest Korean institutions competing with its funds. This competition is strengthening the skills of each entity and allowed them to go out of Korea, to China and other parts of Asia and apply the skills and fund management expertise they developed in Korea and thereby promote Korea as a regional financial centre.

It is this bottom-up development approach of building a financial centre through local competition that Macquarie supports: growing domestic financial institutions which then develop into regional and global financial groups and foster the development of a financial centre in their home countries. Competition is therefore essential at every level of the financial hierarchy to develop better financial model that will support the financial centre status of a city.

This competition causes the development of better institutions for a number of reasons: it promotes creativity within firms, it provides incentives for firms to be efficient and this therefore prompts regulators to focus on quality rather than protectionism. In Korea, like other Asian countries, traditionally competition has been sector-specific, but as markets develop, there will be competition among financial institutions in different key sectors including for deposits, equity for managed funds, asset management services and securities services. (See Figure 13.5a for the current competitive environment, and 13.5b for the likely competitive environment as the market develops.)

The regulatory environment obviously plays a key role in allowing the development of a new generation of Asia-Pacific based global financial institutions. In Macquarie's case, it was the opening of the Australian market to this kind of competition that allowed for the formation of Macquarie in 1985 as a small merchant bank owned by Hill Samuel of the United Kingdom. Macquarie is now a remarkable enterprise with many of its senior executives and board members having stayed with the bank for more than twenty years. The reforms, deregulation and competition introduced by the Australian government during the 1980s and 1990s have pushed Macquarie to improve its business and focus on niche markets where it can lead the market globally. Once it had established itself with market leading expertise, Macquarie commenced its global expansion including Asia where, while not the largest financial institution, it has still played a leading role in development of Asian financial centres (see Figure 13.6).

Macquarie's stable management team has maintained a consistent organization culture over time despite its rapid overseas expansion with six key points as summarized in Figure 13.7. The focus on people has been critical in maintaining Macquarie's growth and competitive edge. Macquarie is proud about its senior management's long tenor which also applies to its business here in Korea where this author started the Korean business and has remained here ever since.

In terms of competition in Korea, traditionally competition has been between banks (both domestic and foreign); between securities companies; between investment companies and between private equity funds (Figure 13.5a). This paradigm is shifting very rapidly, however, and Korean regulators need to move swiftly and decisively to capitalize on these changes and develop its financial sector.

A number of recommendations can be made to achieve this:

- Presidential office should give full backing and support for Korea's development as a financial hub;
- Regulations should shift from "rules-based" approach to "principles based" determinations;

Figure 13.5a
Korea as an Example of Competition

→ **RECENT COMPETITION VERY STRONG ...**

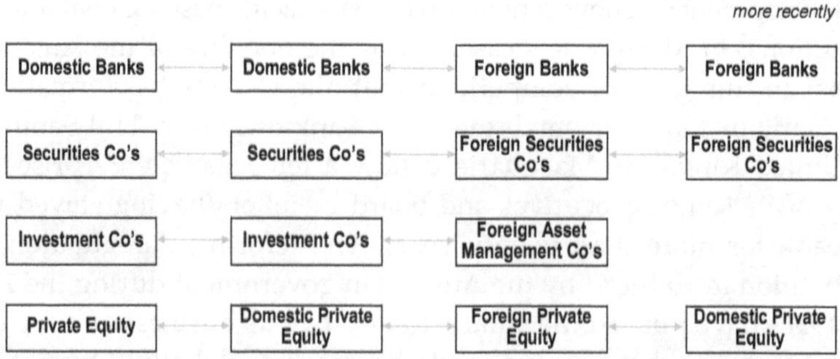

BUT...

Figure 13.5b
The New World of Competition

→ **BUT THE PARADIGM IS CHANGING.**

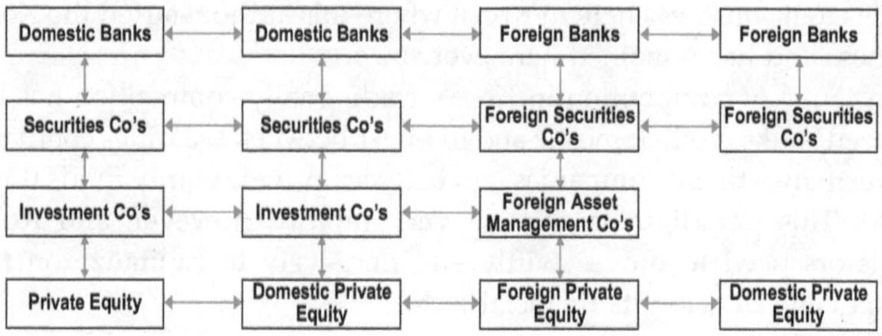

"People don't seem to understand that it's a war out there"
Jimmy Connors, tennis player

Figure 13.6
Competition-spurred Growth

- Big commercial banks and global investment banks were all competing in Australia when Macquarie was established
- Deregulation of the 1980s and 1990s spurred competition and forced Macquarie to focus on new markets

1983	AUSTRALIAN DOLLAR FLOATED
1984	HILL SAMUEL AUSTRALIA AUTHORISED AS FOREIGN EXCHANGE DEALER
1984	14 NEW FOREIGN EXCHANGE LICENSES GRANTED
1985	16 FOREIGN BANKS GET BANKING LICENCES
1985	HILL SAMUEL'S NAME CHANGED TO MACQUARIE BANK
1988	REFORMS OVERHAUL AUSTRALIA'S REGULATORY AGENCIES
1989	MACQUARIE BEGINS GLOBAL EXPANSION INTO EUROPE, US AND ASIA. STILL CONTINUING
1990s	MACQUARIE BECOMES GLOBAL LEADER IN INFRASTRUCTURE ASSET MANAGEMENT

Figure 13.7
Macquarie's Organizational Culture

- It is not all about external regulation — the organizational culture within financial institutions plays a key role
- Macquarie's culture emphasizes desperation, prudential systems, the right people, and initiative

- Communications channels between different regulatory agencies improved;
- Government should take a more "hands-off" approach towards business;
- Application process for new business licences should be streamlined and shortened; and
- All remaining restrictions on capital account transactions should be removed.

The new paradigm involves competition between different sectors (Figure 13.5b). Examples include, banks competing against private equity funds in relation to available investment assets, securities companies competing with private equity funds for equity investments and banks competing with securities companies for deposits. Macquarie believes supporting and encouraging this competition will develop stronger financial institutions in Korea and thereby strengthen Korea's credentials as a financial hub.

Suggestions for Korean financial institutions to gain a competitive advantage:

- Develop skills to design products, effectively manage risk and efficiently manage corporate assets to drive value;
- Replace top-down management style with bottom-up approach;
- Improve and develop partnerships with experienced foreign global financial institutions;
- Utilize Korea's significant cash pool and inefficient corporate balance sheets;
- Increase offshore investment;
- Selectively acquire visionary companies; and
- Identify unique niches where a strong position can be developed.

In summary, Korean financial institutions must win for Korea to achieve its goals of becoming a global financial hub. Competition breeds desperation, and desperation breeds success, and success breeds world-class financial institutions. And only through having locally based world class financial institutions can Korea or any other Asian country genuinely claim to have become a global financial centre.

PART IV
Observations

14

ISSUES AND FINDINGS

1. COMMENTS BY KIHWAN KIM

For all of us who share a strong commitment to promoting a well-functioning, first-class international financial centre in Asia, what are the kinds of questions we ought to ask to realize that goal? I have come up with four sets of questions. I am not sure if you will agree with them, but here they are.

The first set has to do with the impact of the last financial crisis. This year marks the tenth anniversary of the Asian financial crisis. To many, the last crisis is already a receding memory. Asia overcame the crisis, and today its economies are doing fine. So, what is the problem? But has Asia really overcome the last crisis in a fundamental sense? I think the answer is not as unequivocal as one might think. Lee Jong-Wha observed that the crisis was due to the "original sin", meaning three mismatches: (1) currency mismatch, (2) maturity mismatch, and (3) capital structure mismatch. Has this region overcome these mismatches? I believe these mismatches are still with us. Why? Basically, this region has not yet developed a well-functioning, cross-border, long-term capital market. If you do not have such a long-term capital market in the region, what would you do if you were a businessperson wanting to undertake a large investment? Of course, you would have no choice but to go outside the region to get the capital you need. As you go outside, you automatically incur a currency mismatch. When you go outside the region, your firm is not as well known to potential investors or lenders. Hence, you are not likely to get your financing at the maturity you like. So you are set for a maturity mismatch. And since the equity market is not very well developed in this region, you are more likely to finance your investment through debt financing than equity financing. That of course entails a capital structure mismatch. In short, as long as the region fails to have a well-developed and well-functioning, cross-border, long-term capital market, it cannot be free of the three mismatches and will continue to suffer from the "original sin".

The second set of questions relates to the fact that while Asia has already achieved an economic community of a sort in the area of trade, it has not done so in the area of finance. In recent years there has been a tremendous rise in intra-regional trade, but this has not happened in finance. To increase intra-regional flows in finance, we should ask ourselves at least two questions: First, how should cross-border competition be promoted among financial firms in the region? Second, what will be the basic rules under which cross-border competition is promoted? The answers to these questions are not as straightforward as you might think. Nowadays, it is fashionable to talk about following global standards. But before talking about global standards, those in this region should realize that so-called "global standards" are not ordained by God. Hence, this region should participate more actively in international discussions setting "global standards". In addition, financial institutions in this region should get together and agree on what "global standards" should be in light of the practices followed in the region and its interests.

The third set of questions relates to the question raised by Jesús Seade. If I understood him correctly, he said maybe it is a little misguided for Asia to try to develop another London in its midst, especially in this global age when communication is not only easy but instant. It may be enough for the world now to have only one or two global centres like London. But is this really so? Are one or two global centres going to provide services in such a way that the Asia-Pacific region will no longer have to suffer the three mismatches? Asking this question will force us to be clear about the kinds of efforts we should make to accelerate the development of the financial centre in this region. If you do not want to become like London, then what kind of a financial centre do you want to be? How differentiated is it going to be, that is, what areas is it going to specialize in? Or, put still differently, what niche do you want your financial centre to serve? And so on. Unless we keep asking these questions, we may end up building a financial centre or centres that are totally irrelevant.

The fourth set of questions has to do with the very useful point made by Dominic Barton. Barton noted that one of the most important and exciting developments taking place in the world of finance today is the re-emergence of the Silk Road. I agree with this observation. But there are a number of questions that should be raised if we are to make good use of the financial Silk Road. The financial Silk Road to me is synonymous with the exploitation of the opportunities Islamic finance provides. Is Islamic finance very different from, say, what one might call orthodox Western finance for the lack of a better description? I personally think Islamic finance is not very different from Western orthodox finance, except maybe in some areas of consumer finance. But to make use of Islamic financing, we should know clearly what differentiates Islamic finance from others. There is another issue to raise in this regard. Both the Middle East and East Asia today are saving-surplus regions. The question is, is East Asian economic dynamism so great as to require capital imports from the Middle East? If so, in what particular areas is Asian dynamism so great as to justify capital imports from the Middle East? The re-emergence of the Silk Road should also mean that capital imports from the Middle East are no longer to be channelled through Europe or America. But a question you would ask is, have Asia and the Middle East developed enough financial infrastructure to make direct capital imports from Middle East feasible? In short, there are many questions we have yet to ask before we can make full use of the opportunities implied by the re-emergence of the Silk Road in finance.

2. COMMENTS BY YUNG-CHUL PARK

Financial centres are places where all sorts of financial services and legal services like underwriting, trading, dealing and brokerage of services are produced, sold and exported. In terms of such services, one might wonder if New Zealand can be a global or, for that matter, a regional financial centre. Roger Bowden in his chapter contribution has suggested that it has become, and it will continue to be, a respectable regional financial centre. I know very little about New Zealand. I thought all along that a kiwi is a fruit, but then learned that it is also a bird that can fly. You see how ignorant I am. Please excuse me for my ignorance. Surprisingly, it is becoming a financial centre by carving out a niche market for medium-term bonds, which are taken up by Japanese grandmothers and possibly housewives. New Zealand has been a chronic borrower. Its current account deficit amounts to 10 per cent of GDP, which is the highest, higher than the U.S. current account deficit. I am not sure if they might be able to develop an expertise in selling New Zealand bonds to Japanese, Koreans and Chinese. I am not sure if their expertise is enough to sell services related to marketing and underwriting these bonds in the global or regional marketplace. But I wish New Zealand the best of everything.

Another interesting thing is that New Zealand is trying to securitize everything: land, sheep, cows, milk, what have you. Again, they may be able to develop a market for these securitized products in Asia or in the global financial markets. The question is no matter how many real and financial assets are produced by New Zealand, how many securitized products can New Zealand produce and sell? I do not think they can be a major player in the financial securitized product market.

But then we come to currency trading. Apparently, New Zealand has acquired a tremendous amount of experience in managing currency trading, simply because the New Zealand currency has been flexible for a long time. But when it comes to trading, location matters a lot. I do not know if Auckland would be an ideal place for currency trading. Currency trading seems to be taking place mostly in New York, London and Tokyo and other major financial centres. It is interesting that New Zealand is trying to invest and acquire advantages in selling and exporting financial services.

The next country to be discussed is China. It is a growing economic power and no matter where you go these days, without Chinese participants, it will be very hard to gather any kind of audience. This conference was very lucky to have an excellent speaker from the Shanghai Academy of Social Sciences. The question is: China has the potential of developing an onshore international financial centre like the one in New York. Most international finance centres are offshore. For instance, the London market: You think it is onshore; it is an offshore market. Singapore is offshore, and Hong Kong is offshore. Most of these international financial centres are offshore. In fact, offshore markets can be developed overnight like the one in Dubai if you spend a lot of money. But China, because of its sheer size of economy and the availability to export so many manufactured products, has the potential to develop an onshore international financial centre. But in order to do that, as Xu Mingqi (in Chapter 7 of this volume) suggested, it has lots of things to do: First, China has to deregulate and open its financial markets and financial institutions; second, it will have to build the market infrastructure — better governance, legal system, accounting system, and prudential regulatory structure. All these things will take lots of time to develop and become effective in providing these services.

Xu suggested that it would take another ten years. The target date is 2020. I do not know if the outside world will be patient enough to wait that long, but what can you do? You cannot force the Chinese to do something they do not want to do. In the case of China, they are in no hurry for two reasons: One, they have access to excellent financial services supplied by Hong Kong, which has the largest regional market. They can go to Hong Kong to buy financial services and through Hong Kong sell financial services too. Another reason is that Chinese leaders, apparently, have shifted the strategy of economic development to be more inward looking, emphasizing equity, regional balance, environment and so on, which would make it harder, based on the experiences of other countries, for China to deregulate its financial institutions. It might have to rely on more state-owned institutions to achieve these internal economic policy objectives. But then how is China going to continue to be the major supplier of global savings, the largest holder of global savings? There must be many kinds of services that China will have to import to remain a major supplier of savings. In this respect, smaller regional centres in East Asia have opportunities to acquire a lot of China-related business along with Hong Kong. Their competitors will be Hong Kong and Singapore. And now that China is going to spend another ten years putting its financial house in order, other countries can have time to develop their financial centres before China catches up with them.

Then we come to Korea. It has never been clear to me what the motives are for creating a financial centre in Korea or what kind of financial centre Korea would be — whether Korea has any advantages in producing and exporting any type of financial services. As Sang Yong Park has suggested in this volume, the lack of consensus has a lot to do with the confusion on what a financial centre is. What is a financial centre? If you build large buildings that can house many international investment banks or commercial banks, does that create a financial centre? Or if you can bring in top talents in the financial services industry, does that create a financial centre? It is not clear.

Then which market is Korea going to provide services to? China? North Korea? Because of these unanswered questions, I do not think Korea will have an easier time achieving consensus on the type of financial centre it wants to develop. To what extent, how much will they invest in developing a financial centre? What will be the role of the government? In fact, when Korea says it has to develop this and that, the government will invariably step in and take the lead. It has been remarked that that is not a good way of doing things. Where is Korea now? It has been thinking and talking about developing a financial centre for the last ten years and have not come very close to setting up a respectable regional centre for niche markets. For instance, many planners believe that Korea may have advantages in asset management. But asset management is one type of service that can be provided anywhere in the world. Asset managers can live anywhere. Location does not matter very much unlike other kinds of financial services. What does matter is a sense of understanding market development and the ability to predict what will happen to major international financial markets, including exchange rates and interest rates. That is all you need. Additionally, asset management is one industry where you need to have a large number of clients from oil-producing countries and Chinese or Japanese savers. Again, one has to consider whether Korea has the ability to attract these customers and manage their money.

I was really surprised to read the report on Harvard endowment fund and Yale endowment fund managers — how well they have done. Harvard has earned 14 per cent on their portfolio, Yale more than 20 per cent. Do you think Korea can match their ability to produce such high rates of return? It is something to think about. I am not saying we should not work on it, but it will take lots of time. As long as there are these unanswered questions, it is not going to be easy.

Nowadays, wherever I go, I hear lots of grumbling about financial globalization and the problems with capital account liberalization. Capital account liberalization has done very little in terms of promoting growth or financial stability. A couple of studies have suggested that financial market opening has caused substantial disparity in global income distribution and distribution of wealth. Given this anti-globalization movement seeping into international finance, the countries aspiring to develop financial centres will have to think about their strategy. What are they trying to do by developing financial centres? What is the purpose? Is it simply to export more? The mindset in East Asia is that, now that they have exhausted exporting manufactured products, they are moving into exporting financial services. If that is the strategy, I think they must think over whether it is the right kind of strategy.

3. COMMENTS BY JOHN BURTON

There are three general conclusions that I have reached after listening to the discussions.

The first is that history is important. If you were a trading post that was started by the British in the nineteenth century, you had a head start. It is like being born with a silver spoon in your mouth. These trading ports were automatically plugged into the globalized economy. They were exposed early to open flows of capital and investment. One example is Singapore, which was started by Stamford Raffles from the East India Company, who was a great believer in the ideas of Adam Smith. That meant that from the beginning, Singapore was a free-trade port. As a result, it was able to create a financial services industry because of its role as a centre for shipping since trade is based on the supply of credit. For a long time Singapore has served as the New York of Southeast Asia. A similar story can be made for Hong Kong as well. Being a British colony offered other advantages. Most of the population learned English, which is the global language of business. They adopted the Anglo-Saxon legal system, which is preferred by the global financial industry because it is dominated by U.S. and British banks.

Contrast these historical advantages with the background of Korea and its reputation as the Hermit Kingdom. Korea has only been plugged into the global economy since the 1950s, which is why there remains a strong sense of nationalism. But Korea has made great strides in the last ten years. It has recognized the obstacles that have prevented it from becoming a regional financial centre and has adopted measures that have put it ahead of Singapore in some areas. For example, the Singapore government is still opposed to a foreign takeover of a Singapore bank, while Korea has allowed private equity funds or other foreign investors to buy KEB and other Korean banks.

My second general observation is that we are seeing the emergence of complementary, instead of competing, financial centres in Asia. This is something akin to the United States, where you have New York, Chicago and other cities all playing different roles in providing financial services. The financial markets in Tokyo, Shanghai, and Seoul are mainly geared to serving their large domestic economies and they will continue to grow because of the economic growth in Asia. Then there are more specialized international financial centres like Singapore and Hong Kong. But even these centres are concentrating on developing different niches amongst themselves. There has been a great rivalry between Hong Kong and Singapore. But over the last ten years, we have seen investment banks drifting more towards Hong Kong. The reason is obvious. Hong Kong is on the geographical doorstep of China. There are a lot more M&A deals coming out of China as well as Northeast Asia, which benefits Hong Kong. Most big Chinese companies are choosing Hong Kong to make many of their overseas listings. In contrast, Singapore has focused on becoming a centre for foreign exchange trading because of time zone advantages with New York and London. In addition, Singapore wants medium-sized companies to list in Singapore, claiming they will get more attention being listed there while the big Chinese companies go to Hong Kong or New York. Another initiative is that Singapore wants to become the Zurich of Asia by becoming one of the world's leading private banking and global management centres. More big Swiss private banks are setting up operations in Singapore because of its favourable tax and bank secrecy laws. Singapore is now the world's fastest growing offshore banking centre. We are starting to see specialization in other Asian financial centres. Malaysia, for example, is becoming a regional centre for Islamic finance. This is an example of a nation using its comparative advantage to develop a niche in financial services since Malaysia has a majority Muslim population that dominates the government. Malaysia is attracting attention from Middle East financial institutions. Kuwait Finance House, for example, is setting up Islamic banking operations in Malaysia. So we are starting to see a network of complementary financial hubs in Asia. There are signs of growing links among the various financial centres to improve cooperation, such as among stock exchanges. Recently the Tokyo Stock Exchange bought a small stake in the Singapore Exchange and the Singapore Exchange bought a stake in the Bombay Stock Exchange, which lays the foundation for a possible regional alliance. So we are starting to see these interconnections in some aspects of the financial industry. That is healthy in the sense that it develops financial services across the region. One reason why Singapore is investing in the Indian Stock Exchange is because Singapore wants to be a provider of services in terms of derivatives trading. It also sees an investment in India as a way to attract secondary listings from Indian companies. But there are challenges at the same time in developing financial services, particularly in terms of regulation. Singapore's ambitions to become a private banking centre is one example. Singapore now has some of the toughest bank secrecy laws in the world. And it is starting to come under international scrutiny because of that. The European Union (EU), for example, wants more financial transparency in Singapore because they want to apply the EU Savings Directive to Asia. They want to catch European tax evaders who are moving their money to Singapore and Hong Kong, where bank secrecy laws are also tough. So this is going to be a challenge in maintaining momentum as demands for regulatory supervision increase.

A third point is the important role of sovereign wealth funds in developing financial centres. This goes into the whole debate about whether bottom-up financial reform or state-led financial reform is best in developing regional financial centres. In the case of Singapore, there is a very clear argument that the state plays a crucial role in developing the city-state as a financial centre, including the participation of the two main Singapore sovereign wealth funds. One example is the Government of Singapore Investment Corporation (GIC), which invests Singapore's foreign exchange reserves. It now outsources 20–25 per cent of its funds to external fund managers, which thus attracts asset management funds into Singapore. We are also starting to see now the growth of hedge funds in Singapore. So Singapore is trying to carve out a specialty niche in competition with Hong Kong. Then there is the case of Temasek Holdings which is the Singapore state investment company. Temasek is making massive investments in the financial sector. It has about US$130 billion in assets, with 40 per cent in financial services. It is interesting to see what Temasek is doing. It has bought stakes in two big Chinese banks and others in Indonesia and India. More importantly, it has bought stakes in such Western financial groups as Merrill Lynch, Standard Chartered and Barclays. What Temasek is trying to do is erect a network of pan-Asian banks that will challenge Western banks down the road. We should keep our eyes on this.

Appendix

I. KOREA'S FINANCIAL GLOBALIZATION AND CHALLENGES AHEAD*

Yong-Ro Yun
Vice-Chairman,
Financial Supervisory Commission,
Republic of Korea

I am pleased to join you this evening for the 2007 PECC International Conference, a unique occasion to discuss the drive for financial centres in the Asia-Pacific region and [to] explore opportunities as well as challenges we all face.

Developing a financial centre is a goal shared by Korea and others in the region. And it is certainly a topic that comes up increasingly frequently as Asian economies continue to expand at a robust pace. Just last month, *The Economist* ran a special report on the prospect for Asia's financial centres and some of the key issues Asian markets and policymakers will need to grapple with to realize their goals.

The drive for financial centres is more or less fuelled by the recognition that financial markets nowadays are indispensable to wealth creation and economic growth. With China and India vying for an ever-large share of global output and creating new competitive dynamics in Asia, developing a financial centre is viewed by many in Korea as both urgent and crucial if the economy is to move to the next level.

* This is the text of the dinner speech delivered by Vice-Chairman Yun at the conference.

As you all know, Korea achieved enormous economic success from the ruins of a war more than a half century ago. A significant part of Korea's real economy is now driven by top-notch, globally recognized high-tech manufacturing companies, and there is now a clear recognition that the real economy must be paired with an equally sophisticated, world-class financial centre.

FINANCIAL GLOBALIZATION

Financial globalization began to take shape in the 1980s. In the United States, the second oil shock in late 1970s unleashed immense inflationary pressures on the economy, and as interest-rate sensitive bank depositors shifted their savings elsewhere, bank disintermediation accelerated. This phenomenon coincided with significant banking deregulation and advances in information technology that further magnified the wave of liberalization sweeping across the financial sector.

Financial liberalization heralded a new era of competition, which drove financial institutions across borders to new markets in search of ever-higher return on capital and fuelled financial globalization. For financial institutions, this meant mergers and acquisitions with each other as well as an incessant drive for innovation to gain an upper hand in the global competition.

For the latecomers to the global competition, the reality now is that there are formidable challenges to overcome in levelling the competitive field.

KOREA'S FINANCIAL GLOBALIZATION

For Korea's financial globalization, the crisis in late 1997 proved a pivotal turning point. Market liberalization and overseas expansion, though limited in scale and gradual in pace, have been going on for some time.

Following favourable current account balances in the late 1980s and membership in OECD in 1996, Korea began to take a more aggressive stance on financial market liberalization. By this time, domestic banks had also established fairly active overseas banking operations, numbering at one point about 200 worldwide, though many were scaled back following the 1997 financial crisis.

The financial crisis was a watershed event that ushered in a new era of fast-paced market liberalization and financial globalization, including lifting of capital controls and restrictions on market activities that were previously closed to foreign investors, such as investment cap on listed companies at home.

Now, after a decade since the crisis, Korea stands out as one of the most open, globalized economies in the Asia-Pacific region.

Just to cite a few examples, foreign equity ownership in Korea's seven commercial banks is about 64 per cent, and more than 50 per cent in at least twenty insurance companies. A total of nineteen securities companies are wholly-owned by foreign investors.

In the stock market, the share of foreign equity stands at about a-third of the total market capitalization, the ninth highest from the world's top thirty-three stock markets. With the Korea-U.S. Free Trade Agreement (FTA) and the government's commitment to the financial hub initiative, Korea's financial globalization is set to continue even more vigorously going forward.

To be sure, there are challenges ahead. One is the relatively small presence of domestic financial institutions in overseas markets, which generated about 3 per cent of total revenue last year, well below 71 per cent for UBS, 48 per cent for HSBC, and 33 per cent for Citibank.

There are other shortcomings as well in terms of financing, business management, and localization in overseas markets. Excessive competition in a limited number of markets is another concern.

It is true that domestic financial institutions scaled back their overseas operations sharply in the wake of the financial crisis as the focus shifted to restructuring and business turnaround at home.

But as domestic financial institutions continue to generate record earnings, and growth momentum at home slows, a consensus is emerging that the time may have come for more aggressive business expansion in overseas markets. Indeed, we see domestic banks stepping up their business in China, Vietnam, and other emerging markets in Asia and seeking out takeover and joint investment opportunities.

The same is true for securities companies, which have been most aggressive in overseas expansion since 2005 and are diversifying their business into East Asia, Australia, and South America, albeit at a small scale. We also see insurance companies taking an active interest in China, a market with huge potentials, and mutual savings banks seeking project financing opportunities in East Asia.

CHALLENGES FOR KOREA'S FINANCIAL GLOBALIZATION

Looking ahead, I see several tasks that regulators and the financial services industry must work on in order to move Korea's financial market development to the next level.

First, I would stress that Korea's market liberalization is very much on track and will continue.

Insofar as foreign capital is concerned, our stance remains the same: We stand for a level playing field for all, equal treatment for all, and fair and consistent enforcement for all.

We also recognize that financial supervision and regulation must be responsive to the market and encourage a positive and effective regulatory environment for investors.

In tandem with changes expected from the Capital Market Consolidation Act, we will continue to improve our regulatory framework comparable to that of developed markets. Deregulation, coupled with transparent and consistent financial supervision, will also continue so as to facilitate market liquidity and raise market efficiency.

CLOSING REMARKS

China's CCTV recently ran a documentary that looked at the rise and fall of great powers. There are several common attributes the documentary finds in great powers — openness, willingness to embrace ideas from outside, an ability to seize opportunities, and a drive for more and better.

So it may be said that these are the very attributes that propelled Korea's real economy to what it is today. The challenge now is to move to the next level with a world-class financial centre. And with a bold vision for the future, I believe Korea can achieve one of Asia's most dynamic financial centres and contribute toward a regional financial community that all of us would like to see.

It is an important debate, and I thank all of you for taking part in the conference and sharing your ideas.

Thank you.

PECC INTERNATIONAL CONFERENCE

Competition among Financial Centres in the Asia-Pacific: Prospects, Benefits, and Costs — Stumbling Blocks or Building Blocks towards a Regional Financial Community?

Organized by the
Korea National Committee for Pacific Economic Cooperation (KOPEC)
in collaboration with the **Korea Securities Research Institute (KSRI)**

With the support of *The Financial Times* as Media Partner

Westin Chosun Hotel, Seoul, Korea
15–16 October 2007

PROGRAMME

Synopsis of the Theme

The conference will bring together distinguished experts on the subject and many leading finance professionals and businessmen from around the Asia-Pacific region, up to 150 in number, to share their views and insights on the following and related issues:

Many cities in the Asia-Pacific region each have claimed their intention to become an international financial centre. The national and metropolitan authorities for those cities have launched ambitious programmes to develop or enhance their respective financial centres as international financial centres (IFCs). What will those ambitions and programmes in the end add up to? Which ones among them are likely to be the winners? Would the competition among these financial centres facilitate the emergence of a regional financial community by helping financial institutions to become more competitive and financial markets more integrated? Or would it thwart financial integration, regional or global, due to cross-purpose competition? Would it result in excessive competitive deregulation and thus undermine the financial stability in the region? What are the policy implications for regional governments and financial institutions? How can we all win?

PROGRAMME

SUNDAY, 14 OCTOBER

17:00 Participants arrive and register.

18:30 **Welcoming reception and dinner** hosted by Dr Soogil Young, Chair, Korea National Committee for Pacific Economic Cooperation (KOPEC)

MONDAY, 15 OCTOBER

08:30–09:00 Registration

09:00–10:20 Opening Session

09:00–09:15 Opening Remarks
- Dr Soogil Young, Chair, KOPEC
- Dr Dosoung Choi, President, Korea Securities Research Institute (KSRI)

09:15–09:55 Keynote Address by Mr Dominic Barton, Chairman, Asia, McKinsey & Company, on "International Financial Centres — the Terms of Competition and Prospects for the Asia-Pacific Region"

09:55–10:20 Q&A

10:20–10:40 ***Coffee Break***

Case Study Reports: Vision, Strategies, Roadmaps, and Progress
Why do the cities want to become IFCs? What are the visions, strategies, and the roadmaps that individual cities have set out to pursue? What has been the progress thus far in the respective cities? What are the difficulties and prospects? What would be the benefits and costs of the competition to those cities?

10:40–12:10 Session I: Hong Kong and Singapore
Chair: Dr Kihwan Kim, Chairman, Seoul Financial Forum; International Advisor, Goldman Sachs Asia

10:40–11:20 Presentations
- Hong Kong: Prof Jesús Seade, Lingnan University, Hong Kong
- Singapore: Prof Tan Khee Giap, Nanyang Technological University

11:20–11:40 Comments
- Prof Sang Kee Min, Seoul National University
- Dr David Hong, President, Taiwan Institute for Economic Research

11:40–12:10 Discussion

12:10–14:00 **Luncheon** hosted by Mr Andreas Neuber, Chairman and CEO, UBS Hana Asset Management
- Guest Speech by Mayor Se-hoon Oh, Seoul Metropolitan Government, on "Seoul Metropolitan Government's Vision of Seoul"

14:00–15:30 **Session II: Tokyo and Sydney**
Chair: Prof Tan Teck Meng, Singapore Management University

14:00–14:40 Presentations
- Tokyo: Prof Sayuri Shirai, Keio University
- Sydney and Melbourne: Mr Nicholas Gruen, CEO, Lateral Economics

14:40–15:00 Comments
- Mr Simon Cooper, President and CEO, HSBC Korea
- Prof Hugh Patrick, R.D. Calkins Professor of International Business Emeritus, and Director of the Centre on Japanese Economy and Business, Columbia University Graduate School of Business

15:00–15:30 Discussion

15:30–15:50 ***Coffee Break***

15:50–17:50 **Session III: Shanghai, Wellington and Seoul**
Chair: Prof Yung-Chul Park, Seoul National University

15:50–16:50 Presentations
- Shanghai and Beijing: Dr Xu Mingqi, Professor and Deputy Director, Institute of World Economy, Shanghai Academy of Social Sciences
- Wellington: Prof Roger Bowden, Victoria University of Wellington; Director, Kiwicap Research Ltd.
- Seoul: Dr Hansoo Kim, Research Fellow, Korea Securities Research Institute

16:50–17:10 Comments
- Mr James Rooney, President and CEO, Market Force Company, Seoul
- Dr Sang Yong Park, Professor of Finance, Yonsei University

17:20–17:40 Discussion

18:30–21:00 **Welcoming Dinner** hosted by Mr Chung Won Kang, President and CEO, Kookmin Bank
- Dinner speech by Mr Yong-Ro Yun, Vice-Chairman, Financial Supervisory Commission, Korea, on "Korea's Financial Internationalization: Progress and Prospects"

TUESDAY, 16 OCTOBER

International Perspectives: Issues and Implications for the Asia-Pacific Region

What will be the impact on commercial banks, investment banks, securities companies, etc., in the region? What will be the role of global financial institutions in this competition? What are the stakes involved in the competition among the financial centres for the region as a whole and the global financial markets? Will this competition be conducive to the emergence of a regional financial community? Or will it create stumbling blocks in building such a community? How serious is the risk of over-deregulation in the region as a result of the competition? Are there ways of harnessing this competition to better promote financial development and integration in the region?

09:00–10:20 **Session IV: Financial Centre Competition among Asia-Pacific Cities — Benefits and Costs to the Region and Implications for Financial Development and Integration in the Region**
Chair: Dr Masahiro Kawai, Dean, Asian Development Bank Institute (ADBI)

09:00–10:00 Presentations:
- Mr David Cowen, Senior Economist, Regional Office for Asia and the Pacific, IMF
- Dr Jong-Wha Lee, Head of Regional Economic Integration, ADB
- Mr Kyu Bang, Division Director, Macquarie Securities Korea

10:00–10:20 Discussion

10:20–10:40 ***Coffee break***

10:40–12:00 **Panel Discussion — Issues and Findings**
Chair: Prof Hugh Patrick, R.D. Calkins Professor of International Business Emeritus, and Director of the Centre on Japanese Economy and Business, Columbia University Graduate School of Business

Comments by Session Chairs:
- Dr Kihwan Kim, Chair of Session I
- Prof Tan Teck Meng, Chair of Session II
- Prof Yung-Chul Park, Chair of Session III
- Dr Masahiro Kawai, Chair of Session IV
- Mr John Burton, Singapore Bureau Chief, *The Financial Times*

Discussion

12:00–12:30 **Closing Session: Concluding Observations**
Chair: Dr Soogil Young, Chair,
KOPEC and Project Coordinator
- Prof Hugh Patrick, Chair, Panel Discussion Session
- Prof Dosoung Choi, Lead Author of the Project Report
- Prof Sayuri Shirai, Co-author of the Project Report

12:40–14:00 **Farewell Luncheon** hosted by Dr Dosoung Choi, President, Korea Securities Research Institute (KSRI)

Index

A
Abe, Shinzo, 131
ABF (Asian Bond Fund), xxxv, 50, 52, 94, 348
ABMI (Asian Bond Market Initiative), xxxv, 50, 52, 54, 94, 347
ABN Amro, 75
ABS (asset-backed securities), 341
Abu Dhabi Securities Exchange, 12
accounting standards, xxxviii
Accounting Standards Board of Japan, *see* ASBJ
ACU (Asian Currency Unit), 106–08, 112–13, 115
ADR (American Depository Receipts), 248
AFC (Asian financial centre), 333–34, 336, 338–39, 341–42
  criteria for, lix, lxi, lxii, lxiii, lxiv
  historical perspective, 62–64
  macroeconomic trends, 334–38
  structural trends, 338–41
AIG, lii
AIM (Alternative Investment Market), 173
Air New Zealand, 248
algorithmic investments, 92
American Depository Receipts, *see* ADR
American Express Bank, 75
APEC (Asia-Pacific Economic Cooperation), 273
Apple Computer, 151
APRA (Australian Prudential Regulation Authority), 312
APT (ASEAN+3) Finance Minister's Meeting, xxxv, xxxvi, 50–51, 54, 347
arbitration, 53
Asahi Bank, 140
ASBJ (Accounting Standards Board of Japan), 318
ASEAN-5, 125
ASEAN+6, xxxv, 53
ASEAN 10+5 Economies, 101
Asia, as global economic power, xl, xli, xlii
"Asia", as Western invention, xliii, xliv
Asiadollar market, 82
Asian Bond Fund, *see* ABF
Asian Bond Market Initiative, *see* ABMI
Asian central banks, xlix
Asian consumer class, xl, xlii, xliii
Asian Currency Unit, *see* ACU
Asian Development Bank, 159, 190
Asian family-owned business, xlvi
Asian financial centre, *see* AFC
Asian financial crisis, xxx, xxxi, xxxiii, xxxv, xxxvi, xlvi, 18, 30, 39, 41–42, 47, 54, 61, 66, 74, 77, 83, 87,

100–05, 117, 119, 124–25, 127, 183, 273, 278, 285–86, 296, 346–47, 365, 376–77
Asian Gateway Initiative, 33
Asian merger-acquisition boom, xli
Asian Research Centre, 103
Asian Tigers, 28
Asia-Pacific Economic Cooperation, *see* APEC
Asia-Pacific financial community, 5
Asia-Pacific IFC Network, xxxiv, xxxvi, 50–55
Asia-Pacific markets, xxxiii,
ASIC (Australian Securities and Investments Commission), 199, 207, 312, 315
asset-backed securities, 341
ASX (Australian Stock Exchange), 27, 248
AUD (Australian dollar), 86, 253
AUM (assets under management), 8, 124, 306
Australia
  as financial centre, 198–200, 224–25
  costs of exporting fund management, 211–13
  export orientation, 220–21
  fund management industry, 194–98, 201, 216–17
  government IFC efforts, 12–13
  reform efforts, 24
  regulation measures, 204–06
  venture capital hub, 316
  see also Sydney
Australian Competition and Consumer Commission, 312
Australian dollar, *see* AUD
Australian Prudential Regulation Authority, *see* APRA
Australian retirement (superannuation) scheme, 11
Australian Securities and Investments Commission, *see* ASIC
Australian Stock Exchange, 27, 248
Axiss Australia, 21, 223, 303, 314, 317–19, 321

B

Bangkok International Financial Facilities, *see* BIBF
Banker, The, 80
Bank for International Settlements, *see* BIS
Bank Holding Company Act, 119
Bank of England, lvi
Bank of Japan, 142, 153, 177
Bank of Korea, 291
Bank of Tokyo, 139
Bank of Tokyo-Mitsubishi, 139
Bank of Tokyo-Mitsubishi UFJ Bank, 139
bank secrecy laws, 373
banks, fifteen largest in the world, 73–74
Barclays, 373
Barings Bank, 100
Barton, Dominic, 20, 297, 367
Basle Capital Accord, 107
Basle Initiatives, 126
BCCS (Board of Commissioners of Currency, Singapore), 112
Beijing Olympics, 29
Beirut, as financial centre, 62
"Belgian dentists", 270, 276
Berlin Wall, xxxviii
"Better Regulations" Initiatives, 185–88
BHQ (Business Headquarters) status, 100
BIBF (Bangkok International Financial Facilities), 107
"Big Bang", l, 109, 216
  see also Japanese Big Bang

BIS (Bank for International Settlements), 64–65, 69, 82–83, 96, 259, 283–84, 341, 368
BNP Paribas, 96
Board of Commissioners of Currency, Singapore, *see* BCCS
BOJ (Bank of Japan), 142, 153, 177
Bombay Stock Exchange, 372
bond markets, 27, 28, 86–91, 96, 116–19, 143, 148–52, 281–83, 308, 342, 347, 349–50
  trends, 152–55
  yen-denominated, 159–60
Bowden, Roger, 367
Brunei dollar, 112
Bursas Italiana, 27, 300
Business Council of Australia, 312
Business Headquarters status, *see* BHQ

C
California State Teachers' Retirement System, 150
CalPERS (California Public Employees' Retirement System), 150, 176, 288
capital account globalization, 371
Capital Market Consolidation Act, 289, 378
capital markets, xlv, 49–50
Cayman Islands taxation, 214
CBRC (China Banking Regulatory Commission), 239
CCF (Common Contractual Funds), 196, 216, 219, 223
CDO (collateralized debt obligations), 156
CEFP (Council on Economic and Fiscal Policy), 166–68, 177, 313, 316, 319
Central Provident Fund, 114, 117–18, 124
Chiang Mai Initiative, xxxv, 54
Chicago Mercantile Exchange, 19, 116
China
  as supplier of global savings, 16
  companies in Hong Kong securities market, 6
  developing IFC in Shanghai, 14–15, 231–32, 235
  influence on Hong Kong, 29
  rise of consumer class, xlii
  see also Shanghai; Shenzhen
China Banking Regulatory Commission, 239
China Development Bank, 290
China Securities Regulatory Commission, 236, 239
CIC (China Investment Corporation), xlix, l
CIRC (China Insurance Regulatory Commission), 239
CIRS (cross-currency interest rate swap), 260, 262, 270, 276
CIS (Collective Investment Schemes), 280, 294
Citibank, 377
Citigroup, 73, 172
City of London Corporation, liv, 6, 35, 56, 63, 91, 144, 180, 351
civil law tradition, 23
CME (Chicago Mercantile Exchange), 19, 116
Collective Investment Schemes, 280, 294
Commodity Exchange Law, 169
Communist Party of China, 231
Company Law, 169, 177
competition, financial, 93
  rewards of, 41–42
  risks, 43–44, 51
"Controlled Foreign Corporations" regulation, 195

Coordinated Portfolio Investment Survey, 334, 345
corporate governance, xxxii, xxxviii, 103, 208, 301
Corporation Law, 172
Council of Economic and Fiscal Policy, 27
Cowen, David, 38–39, 354
CPC (Communist Party of China), 231
CPF (Central Provident Fund), 114, 117–18, 124
CPIS (Coordinated Portfolio Investment Survey), 334, 345
cross-currency interest rate swap, 260, 262, 270, 276
cross-border banking, 64–72
cross-border capital flows, xxxix, xl, xlv, 103, 134, 157–66, 237, 297, 299, 366
cross-border claims, 65–66, 68
cross-border liabilities, 65–67
cross-listings, 53
CSRC (China Securities Regulatory Commission), 236, 239
currency distribution of foreign exchange, 86
currency speculation, 108–09, 115, 122
currency swaps, 114, 260, 270–71, 274, 276
currency trading, 17
current account deficit, 16
cyber-banking, *see* Internet banking

D

Dai-Ichi Kangyo Bank, 139
Daimler Chrysler, 151
Daiwa Bank Holdings, 140
DBU (Domestic Banking Unit), 106–07, 110–11, 113, 115, 122
debt market, lviii, 28
Delaware, corporate law and regulation in, 208
Deng Xiaoping, xli, 29, 231, 233
derivatives, 64
Deutsche Bank, 151
dichotomized financial system, 106–08, 113, 115, 121–23, 125, 299
DI (direct investment), 125
disaggregation of financial system, l
disclosure systems, xxxiv, xxxv
Domestic Banking Unit, *see* DBU
domestic market capitalization, 64
domestic market concentration, 75–80
double listings, 53, 151
Dow Jones Thailand Stock Index futures, 116
Dubai, as financial centre, l

E

East Asia FTA, 53
East Asian Financial Area, 94
East Asian Stock Exchanges, 64
eBank, 140
economies of scale, 48
Economist Intelligence Unit, 32, 313
Economist, The, 193, 375
ECU (European Currency Unit), 106
EDI (Electronic Data Interchange), 169
Eichengreen, Barry, 96
Eleventh Five-Year Plan, 14
EMEAP (Emerging Market Economies of Asia-Pacific Central Bankers), xxxv, 51, 348
equity markets, 247–50, 349–50
ERSA (Employment Retirement Securities Act), 288
ETF (exchange traded funds), 26, 138, 155–56, 168–69, 172
  trends, 155–57
EU (European Union), 373
euro, 135, 164
Eurobonds, 250
Euronext, 27, 94, 300
European banks, 69, 70–71

European Business Council, 319
European Central Bank, 84
European Climate Exchange, 316
European Commission, 217
European Currency Unit, 106
European Investment Bank, 159
European Union, 373
Euroyen LIBOR futures, 116
eurokiwi, 260, 262, 266–70
euro-yen market, 159–60
exchange traded funds, 26, 138, 155–56, 168–69, 172
  trends, 155–57
EXIM (Export-Import Bank of Korea), 290
Export-Import Bank of China, 290

F

FCP (*Fonds Commun de Placement*), 219
FDI (foreign direct investment), 39, 100, 135, 309
Federal Old-Age, Survivors, and Disability Insurance, *see* OASDI
financial centre strategic map, li, lii
financial centres, in Asia Pacific, 353–61
financial deregulation, 119–20, 133, 136, 159, 291, 349, 369
"financial industry districts", 31
Financial Instruments and Exchange Law, *see under* Japan
financial integration, xxxi, xxxiv, 50–52
financial market integration, 344–52
Financial Reconstruction Commission, 140, 191
Financial Service Modernization Act, 119
Financial Services Agency, *see* FSA
Financial Services Authority, 79–80
Financial Supervisory Agency, 136
financial volatility, 43–44
fiscal incentives, 107
"FN hub Korea", 291
Fonds Commun de Placement, 219
Fonterra, 251
foreign direct investment, *see* FDI
Foreign Exchange, *see* Forex
Foreign Exchange and Foreign Trade Control Law, 175
foreign exchange currency markets, xxxiv
Foreign Exchange Law, 136, 141
foreign exchange reserves, 296
foreign reserve currency, xxxiv
Forex (Foreign Exchange), 82–86
  currency distribution, 86
  geographical distribution, 84
  market, 63
  trading, 48–49, 92
  traditional markets, 161–66
Fortune Global 1000, xliii
FRA (forward rate agreement), 252
framework for monetary policy, 113–15
FRC (Financial Reconstruction Commission), 140, 191
Free Trade Agreements, 95
FSA (Financial Services Agency), 11, 21, 23, 140, 166–67, 171, 173, 184–88, 191, 308, 312–13, 315–17
FTA (Free Trade Area), xxxv, 9, 53, 297, 377
Fuji Bank, 139
fund managers, 120

G

German Stock Exchange, 300
GFCI (Global Financial Centres Index), liv, 6–7, 9, 20, 30, 35, 39, 56, 144
  definition of market accessibility, 25
GIC (Government Investment Corporation of Singapore), lviii, 25, 114, 117, 373

Glass-Steagal Act, 119, 175
GLC (government-linked companies), 116, 123
Global 500 companies, 28
global banking, 72–75
"global business zones", 33
"global cultural exchange zones", 33
Global Financial Centres Index, *see* GFCI
global financial stock, xxxviii
global fund management, 194–95, 197, 225
"global standards", 366
global stock crash, 100
"global villages", 33
Globex, 19
Goh Keng Swee, 99
Goldman Sachs, 159, 354
Goods and Services Tax, 195, 256
Government Investment Corporation of Singapore, *see* GIC
government-linked companies, *see* GLC
GPIF (Government Pension Investment Fund), 150, 154, 170, 176, 341
Gramm-Leach-Bliley Act, 175
Gruen, Nicholas, 305–06
GST (Goods and Services Tax), 195, 256

H

Hashimoto, Ryutaro, 132, 135, 183
hedge funds, 92, 139, 143, 157, 174, 177, 224, 227, 293, 308, 319, 334, 337–38
Heritage Foundation, 103
Hermit Kingdom, 371
Hokkaido Takushoku Bank, 175
home mortgage debt, 260–62
Hong Kong
  as financial centre, 6–7, 25, 63, 91, 181, 325
  bond market, 87–90
  Chinese companies in securities market, 6
  cross-border banking, 65
  influence of Chinese government, 29
  SWOTs, 7
Hong Kong H-shares, 340
Hong Kong Securities and Futures Commission, 20
Hong Kong Stock Exchange, 144
Howard, John, 311
HSBC (Hongkong and Shanghai Banking Corporation), lii, 73, 75, 96, 377
human capital, 273–75

I

IASB (International Accounting Standards Board), 315, 318
IBA (International Bankers Association), 174, 177, 179, 313–14
IBF (International Banking Facility), 161
ICBC (Industrial and Commercial Bank of China), xlvii
ICT (information and communications technology), 180, 183
IFC, *see* International Financial Centre
IFI (investment fund industry), 207
IFRSs (International Financial Reporting Standards), 169, 318, 319
IFSB (Islamic Financial Services Board), 8
IFSL (International Finances Services), 69, 96
IMD World Competitiveness Handbook, 103
IMD (International Institute for Management Development), 32

IMF (International Monetary Fund), 38, 54, 125, 145, 183, 319, 334, 336, 338, 342, 345
information and communications technology, 180, 183
India, rise of consumer class, xlii
Indian Stock Exchange, 373
Individual Retirement Account, 167
Individual Savings Account, 167, 168
Industrial and Commercial Bank of China, xlvii
Industrial Bank of Japan, 139
"infrastructure bonds", 250
initial public offerings, 6, 64
Institute of Southeast Asian Studies, 101
International Accounting Standards Board, 315, 318
International Bankers Association, 174, 177, 179, 313–14
International Banking Facility, 161
International Finances Services, 69, 96
International Financial Centre
  assessment of, 20, 33–34, 301
  business environment, 23–24
  case study, 215–16
  competition, xxx, xxxi, xxxiv, 33–46
  countries competing for, 4, 5, 124
  definition, 100, 309, 369–70
  development, 182–83
  efficiency gains and regional integration, 40–42
  features, 180–81
  human resources, 21, 22, 302–03
  in Asia-Pacific, xxxvi, 5
  infrastructure, 28–31
  landscape, 34–37
  market accessibility, 25–26
  prospects for financial business, 38–40
  quality of life, 32
  regional integration, 46–55
  risks, 43–50
  strategies and SWOTs, 5–6
  world's top ten, lv, 35–37, 180
International Financial Corporation, 116
International Financial Reporting Standards, 169, 318, 319
International Institute for Management Development, 32
International Islamic Financial Centre, 341
international monetary crisis, 100
International Monetary Fund, *see* IMF
International Securities Exchange of New York, 300
International Swaps and Derivatives Association, 157
International Tax Review, 202, 210
Internationalization of Japanese Financial and Capital Markets, 166
Internet banking, 81–82, 92
intra-Asian trade and integration, xl, xliii, xliv
Invest Australia, 21
investment fund industry, *see* IFI
Investment Manager Exemption, 174
invoice currency, xxxiv
IPO (initial public offerings), 6, 64
IRA (Individual Retirement Account), 167
Ireland
  as financial centre, 196, 199, 211, 227
  tax and regulatory structure, 210
Irish Unit Trust, *see* IUT
ISA (Individual Savings Account), 167, 168
ISDA (International Swaps and Derivatives Association), 157
ISEAS (Institute of Southeast Asian Studies), 101
ISEAS-NTU Index, 101–02
Islamic banking, 8

Islamic finance, xxx, 39, 338, 341, 367, 372
Islamic Financial Services Board, 8
Ito Yokado Group, 140
IUT (Irish Unit Trust), 218–19
IY Bank, 140

J
JACD (Japan Association of Corporate Directors), 177
Japan
  assets held by foreign investors, 147
  bond market 87, 143, 148–53, 308
  cross-border banking, 68–71
  cross border capital flows, 157–66
  financial background, 131–35
  Financial Instrument and Exchange Law, 10–11, 23, 169, 171, 173–74, 177, 318
  GDP (Gross Domestic Product), 130–31, 134
  government initiatives for Tokyo, 171–73
  government vision for Tokyo, 166–70, 180, 313–14
  incentives for foreign entities, 174–75
  market performance, 144–66
  see also Tokyo
Japan as Number One, 131
Japan Association of Corporate Directors, 177
Japan Bank for International Cooperation, 290
Japan Depository Receipt, 167, 169
Japanese Big Bang, 10, 77, 132–33, 148, 175, 303–04, 306–07, 311
  effect on Tokyo, 183–84
  impact, 138–41
  overview, 135–38
  perspectives, 141–43
  see also "Big Bang"
Japanese government bonds, 149, 152–53, 155
Japanese postal savings bank, xliii
Japanese Sarbanes-Oxley, 311, 315, 319
Japan Net Bank, 140
Japan real estate investment trusts, 138–39, 156, 168–69
Japan Research Institute, 140
Japan Securities Dealers Association, 170
JDR (Japan Depository Receipt), 167, 169
JGB (Japanese government bonds), 149, 152–53, 155
JP Morgan, 14, 140, 321
J-REITs (Japan real estate investment trusts), 138–39, 156, 168–69
J-Sox (Japanese Sarbanes-Oxley), 311, 315, 319
JTC (Jurong Town Corporation), 118
"*Junsen*", 132
Jurong Industrial Park, 100

K
KAIST (Korea Advanced Institute of Science and Technology), 19, 22, 292
Kanebo, 315
KDB (Korea Development Bank), 290
Keating, Paul, 221
KIC (Korean Investment Corporation), 18–19, 26, 291, 293
Kim Dae-jung, 277
Kindleberger, Charles P., 309, 321
Kinki Osaka Bank, 140
Koizumi, Junichiro, 23
Kokusai Securities, 139
KOPEC (Korea National Committee for Pacific Economic Cooperation), 379

Korea
  asset management, 284–85, 287, 288–89, 371
  bond market, 281–83
  capital market, 278–79, 280
  Capital Market Consolidation Act, 18, 24
  challenges, 375–78
  derivatives market, 283–84
  equity market, 280–81
  government IFC initiatives, 18–20
  government strategy, 285–94
  liberalization of outflows, 340
  see also Seoul
Korea Advanced Institute of Science and Technology, 19, 22, 292
Korea Composite Stock Price Index, 283
Korea Development Bank, 290
Korea Exchange, 12, 24, 283
"Korea Fund", 279
Korea National Committee for Pacific Economic Cooperation, 379
Korean Investment Corporation, 18–19, 26, 291, 293
Korean Stock Exchange, 26, 155, 172
Korea Securities Research Institute, 28, 30, 379
KOSPI (Korea Composite Stock Price Index), 283
KRX (Korea Exchange), 12, 24, 283
KSRI (Korea Securities Research Institute), 28, 30, 379
Kuwait Finance House, 372

L

laissez faire market-driven system, 126
Lee Hsien Loong, 122
Lee Jong-Wha, 38, 46, 354, 365
Lee Myung Bak, 24
Lincoln, Abraham, quote, 298
Lingnan University, 75, 80, 95
Livedoor, 313, 315
locational statistics, 65
"local knowledge" factor, 93
London, as financial centre, xxxiv, xxxvi, xxxviii, xliv, li, liii, liv, lvi, lvii, 5, 25, 62, 80, 181, 299
London Stock Exchange, *see* LSE
Long-term Credit Bank of Japan, 141
"lost decade", 132, 142
LSE (London Stock Exchange), 11, 27, 144–45, 151–52, 173, 300
Luxembourg
  as global financial centre, 207
  wealth management, 217

M

M&As (mergers and acquisition), xlvi, 6, 75, 119–20, 141, 372
Macquarie Bank, 199, 300
Macquarie Group, 305, 356–61
MAFF (Ministry of Agriculture, Forestry, and Fisheries), 173
Malaysia, limit on foreign assets, 340
Malaysian ringgit, 112
market accessibility, definition of, 25
market capitalization, xlvii
Market Force, 355
market fragmentation, xxxi, 45–46, 53
market integration, xxxi, xxxiii, 42, 45–46
MAS (Monetary Authority of Singapore), 8, 106–09, 111–15, 117–19, 121–24
Mastercard Worldwide Centres of Commerce Index, 30
McKinsey & Company, xlix
mergers and acquisition, xlvi, 6, 75, 119–20, 141, 372
Merrill Lynch, 159, 373
METI (Ministry of Economy, Trade and Industry), 172

Ministry of Agriculture, Forestry, and Fisheries, 173
Mitsubishi Securities, 139
Mitsubishi Tokyo Financial Group, 139
Mitsubishi Trust & Banking, 139
Mitsubishi UFJ Financial Group, 139
Mitsubishi UFJ Securities, 139
Mizuho Bank, 139, 290
Mizuho Corporate Bank, 139
Mizuho Financial Group, 139
Mizuho Holdings, 139
Mizuho Security, 139
MNCs (multinational corporations), 100
Monetary Authority of Singapore, *see* MAS
monetary policy and foreign exchange, 252–55
Morgan Stanley, 14, 321, 354
MSCI Singapore stock index futures, 116
MTI (Ministry of Trade and Industry), 112
multinational corporations, 100
Mumbai, as financial centre, 62–63
Murakami Fund, 315

N
NADFC (Northeast Asia Development Financial Council), 290
Nanyang Technological University, 101, 103
Nara Bank
Nasdaq, 144–45
National Superannuation Fund, 256
National Wages Council, 115
negative-list regulation rules, 23
  see also positive-list regulation rules
NETs (Network for Electronic Transfers, Singapore), 110
New York, as financial centre, xxxiv, xxxvi, xxxviii, xliv, li, liii, liv, lvi, lvii, 5, 25, 62, 181, 299
New York Securities Exchange, 27
New York Stock Exchange, *see* NYSE
New Zealand
  current account deficit, 16
  debt market, 28, 250–52, 368
  equity market, 247–50
  exchange rates, 257, 259
  home mortgage debt, 260–62
  human capital, 273–75
  monetary policy and foreign exchange, 252–55
  savings habits, 255–56
  securitizations, 17
  SWOTs, 17
  see also Wellington
New Zealand dollar, *see* NZD
New Zealand Stock Exchange, *see* NZX
Nikkei Index, 132, 311
Nikko Cordial Corporation, 172
Nippon Trust Bank, 139
Nomura Securities, 171
Nomura Trust Bank, 171
non-performing loans, 184, 288
Northeast Asia Development Financial Council, 290
Northeast Asia Export Credit Agency Summit, 290
Northeast Asian financial centre, 277, 286
Northeast Asian Financial Hub, 18
Northern Trust, 218–20
NPLs (non-performing loans), 184, 288
NSF (National Superannuation Fund), 256
NTT DoCoMo, 140
NTU (Nanyang Technological University), 101, 103
NYSE (New York Stock Exchange), 10, 94, 144–45, 151–52, 155, 279, 300
NZD (New Zealand dollar), 16, 253, 257, 259–60, 262, 270–74

NZX (New Zealand Stock Exchange), 247, 259, 271

O

OASDI (Federal Old-Age, Survivors, and Disability Insurance), 176
OBUs (Offshore Banking Units), 222–23
OCR (Official Cash Rate), 252, 261
OECD (Organization for Economic Cooperation and Development), xxxiii, 45, 225, 299, 310, 320, 376
offshore financial centre, 100, 368
OFS (online financial services), 121
OHQ (Operational Headquarters), 100
OI (other net investment), 125
Olympics, Beijing, 29
Omnibus Act, 120, 127
online banking, 81–82, 92
onshore financial centre, 100, 368, 369
Operational Headquarters, 100
Organization for Economic Cooperation and Development, *see* OECD
Osaka Securities Exchange, 172
OTC (over-the-counter) derivatives, 25, 63, 161–66, 234, 251–53, 274, 283
other net investment, *see* OI
"out-in" transactions, 107
"out-out" transactions, 107
Overseas Investment Commission, 248
Overseas Investment Office, 248

P

Panama, as financial centre, li
Pan-El incident, 100
payment systems, 49
PBOC (People's Bank of China), 233
PECC (Pacific Economic Cooperation Council) International Conference, 375, 379
PEF (private equity funds), 288, 293–94, 334
Pension Fund Association, 150
PER (price earning ratio), 280
"petrodollars", xliv, 82
PI (Pioneer Industry) status, 100
PI (portfolio investment), 125
policy competition, xxix
policy coordination, 50
Political and Economic Risk Consultancy, 103
positive-list regulation rules, 23
see also negative-list regulation rules
pound sterling, 164
"power brokers", xlix
POWL (public offering without listing), 151–52
preferential tax treatments, 143
price earning ratio, 280
PricewaterhouseCoopers, 310
principles-based supervision, 24
private banking, 120
private equity funds, 288, 293–94, 334
protectionism, 40
PSM (Professional Securities Market), 168
Public Company Law, 169, 177
public offering without listing, 151–52
Public Pension Reserve Funds, 150

Q

QFII (Qualified Foreign Institutional Investor), 241
"quantitative easing" monetary policy, 142

R

RBNZ (Reserve Bank of New Zealand), 252, 257, 259, 261–62, 275–76
RCC (Resolution and Collection Corporation), 175
regional cooperation, 52–53

regional integration, xxxiii, 46–50
"regulatory dovetailing", 209, 214–15
"regulatory environment", 23
regulatory framework, 75–80, 94, 111–13, 115, 121, 136, 183, 188, 314, 349
regulatory laxity, 43–44
regulatory oversight, xxxviii
REIT index, 156
"relationship banking", 158
renminbi, 14, 237, 242–44, 339
Reserve Bank of New Zealand, *see* RBNZ
Resolution and Collection Corporation, 175
Resona Holdings, 140
Ripplewood, 141
risk perceptions, 47
RMB (renminbi), 14, 237, 242–44, 339
Roh Moo-Hyun, 18, 277, 353
Rooney, James, 348
rules-based supervision, 24

S
Sakura Bank, 139
"Samurai bonds", 10, 159
Sang Yong Park, 369
Sanwa Bank, 176
SARS (Severe Acute Respiratory Syndrome), 102
savings habits, 255–56
Seade, Jesús, 297, 366
Securities and Exchange Surveillance Commission, 136, 170
securitizations, 17
self-regulatory organizations, 293
Seoul
  as financial centre, 62–63, 190
  government IFC initiatives, 18–20
  infrastructure, 31
  progress, 33
  SWOTs, 19
  see also Korea
Separate Trading of Registered Interest and Principal of Securities, 290
SES (Stock Exchange of Singapore), 116, 144, 155
SESC (Securities and Exchange Surveillance Commission), 136, 170
Severe Acute Respiratory Syndrome, 102
SGX (Singapore Exchange), 119, 372
Shanghai
  as financial centre, li, lii, 14, 29, 62, 179, 190
  challenges, 235–39, 324
  China developing an onshore IFC, 14–15
  Eleventh Five-Year Plan, 14
  government measures, 239–44
  progress, 32–33
  strategic targets, 231–35
  SWOTs, 15
  see also China; Shenzhen
Shanghai Expo, 29
Shanghai Foreign Exchange Trading Centre, 243
Shanghai Securities Exchange, 237, 240, 242
Shanghai Stock Exchange, 26
Shenzhen, xli, xlii, 235, *see also* China; Shanghai
Shenzhen Securities Exchange, 242
Shinsei Bank, 141
Shirai, Sayuri, 305, 307
Silk Road, xli, xliv, 367
SIMEX (Singapore Exchange), 108, 116
Singapore
  as financial centre, lvi, lviii, lix, lx,

6, 8, 25, 62–63, 91, 99, 102, 121, 181
as Zurich of Asia, 372
bond market, 116–19
consumer price index, 103
cross-border banking, 65
debt market, lviii
fiscal incentives, 107
framework for monetary policy, 113–15
GDP (Gross Domestic Product), 99, 102
government IFC strategy, 8, 99, 100–05, 272
liberalizing pricing mechanism, 112–13, 117
regional expansion, 110–11
SWOTs, 9
two-tier financial entity, 106–07
Singapore dollar, 106, 108–10, 112, 114–18, 122–23
Singapore Exchange, 119, 372
see also SIMEX
single market regions, 94
small- and medium-sized enterprises, 235
SMBC Friend Securities, 140
SMBC Leasing Company, 140
SMBC (Sumitomo Mitsui Banking Corporation), 140
SMEs (small- and medium-sized enterprises), 235
SMFG (Sumitomo Mitsui Financial Group), 139, 140
Smith Glaxo Kline, 249
Societe des Bourses Francaises, 116
Société de Gestion de Patrimoine Familial, 196, 217
Society for Worldwide Interbank Financial Telecommunication, 169
soft infrastructure, 29
Sony Bank, 140
sovereign wealth fund, xliii, xlvii, xlix, 38, 256, 334, 336–37, 373
special economic zone, 31
SPF (*Société de Gestion de Patrimoine Familial*), 196, 217
spot currency trading, 259
SRO (self-regulatory organizations), 293
stagflation, 100
Standard Chartered, 373
standards, of financial centre, li
Stock Exchange of Singapore, 116, 144, 155
"stock swap", 172
strengths, weaknesses, opportunities, and threats, *see* SWOTs
"String Theory", 325–26
STRIPS (Separate Trading of Registered Interest and Principal of Securities), 290
subprime mortgage crisis, xxxii, 55, 43–44, 120, 348
Sumitomo Bank, 139
Sumitomo Mitsui Banking Corporation, *see* SMBC
Sumitomo
Mitsui Card Company, 140
Sumitomo Mitsui Financial Group, *see* SMFG
Sunguard Treasury Systems, 253
SWF, *see* sovereign wealth fund
SWIFT (Society for Worldwide Interbank Financial Telecommunication), 169
Switzerland, foreign exchange transactions, 84–85
SWOTs (strengths, weaknesses, opportunities, and threats), xxix, 5, 37

Sydney, 11
  as financial centre, 62–63, 306, 318
  infrastructure, 30–31, 307
  SWOTs, 13
  tax rate, 320
  see also Australia
Sydney Futures Exchange, 27, 248, 251, 272

T

Tan Khee Giap, 297
Tax Laws Amendment (Loss Recoupment Rules and Other Measures) Act, 227
Telecom NZ, 251
Temasek Holdings, 373
TFP (total factor productivity), 131, 134
"time difference" factor, 93
TOCOM (Tokyo Commodities Exchange), 319
Tokai Bank, 176
Tokyo
  as financial centre, 25–26, 62, 131–35, 181, 188
  challenges and opportunities, 187–90
  effect of Japanese Big Bang, 183–84
  government initiatives, 171–73
  government vision, 166–70
  infrastructure, 30
  offshore market, 161
  stock market collapse, 10
  SWOTs, 11, 12
  weakness, 179–80, 189, 307
  see also Japan
Tokyo Commodities Exchange, 319
Tokyo Stock Exchange, 10, 12, 26–27, 131, 138, 143–45, 151–52, 155–56, 172–73, 188, 313, 372
total factor productivity, 131, 134
Toyo Trust & Banking, 176
Trade Me, 249
"traditional foreign exchange markets", 83
"transport costs", 48
Treaty of Rome, 196
"triad of incompatibilities", 123
Triangular Mergers, 172
TSE, *see* Tokyo Stock Exchange
Tsubasa Securities, 176
two-tier financial entity, 106–07

U

UBS, 14, 321, 377
UFJ Bank, 176
UFJ Holdings, 139, 176
UFJ Tsubasa Securities, 176
UFS Capital Market Securities, 176
"uniform approach", 299
uridashis, 250, 260, 262–65, 269–70, 273
U.S. banks, 69–72
USD (U.S. dollar), 42, 47, 85–86, 114, 116, 161, 164–66, 176, 270–71, 346
U.S. Federal Reserve, lvi

V

Vogel, Ezra, 131

W

Wall Street, 54
Wall Street Journal, 103
Wellington
  as financial centre, 16, 324
  see also New Zealand
Wen Jiabao, 240
"Wimbledon effect", 181
Wimbledon Phenomenon, 298
World Bank, 159, 355
World Economic Forum, 32

World Federation of Exchanges, 96
world's fifteen largest banks, 73–74
world's top 10 IFC, lv, 35–37, 180
world's top 20 economies, projected 2040, 355
WTO (World Trade Organization), xxxii, xxxv, xxxv, 45, 53, 95, 125

X

Xu Mingqi, 369

Y

Yahoo Japan Corp, 140
Yamaichi Securities, 175
Yasuda Trust Bank, 139
yen, 164
"yen carry trade", 142
Yongsan International School, 292

Z

Z/Yen Limited, 179–80, 310, 320

www.ingramcontent.com/pod-product-compliance
Lightning Source LLC
LaVergne TN
LVHW090105250926
848814LV00044B/11
* 9 7 8 9 8 1 2 3 0 9 3 0 3 *